A · POLITICAL · SOCIAL · AND · ECONOMI

HISTORY OF BRITAIN

1760-1914: THE CHALLENGE OF GREATNESS

A · POLITICAL · SOCIAL · AND · ECONOMIC
HISTORY OF BRITAIN

1760-1914: THE CHALLENGE OF GREATNESS

R. BEN JONES

HODDER AND STOUGHTON
LONDON SYDNEY AUCKLAND TORONTO

British Library Cataloguing in Publication Data

Jones, R. Ben
  A political, social and economic
  history of Britain 1760–1914:
  the challenge of greatness
  1. Great Britain—History—George III,
  1760–1820 2. Great Britain—History—
  19th century 3. Great Britain—History—
  20th century
  I. Title
  941.07   DA470

ISBN 0 340 27896 X

First printed 1987

Typeset in Times and Univers by Macmillan India Ltd, Bangalore 25
Printed in Great Britain for
Hodder and Stoughton Educational, a division of
Hodder and Stoughton Ltd, Mill Road, Dunton Green,
Sevenoaks, Kent by The Eastern Press Ltd, Reading

Preface

This volume covers the period from the mid-eighteenth century to the beginning of the First World War. It was a period full of change, during which the nature of British society and the basis of the British economy was transformed. It was also a time during which immense strain was placed upon the institutions and traditions of the country. To the credit of the generations of men and women whose history is told in these pages, Britain, in many ways, became a better, more prosperous, more caring place, as well as a more powerful force in the world. This book tells the story of these changes and helps to explain how and why they happened and what resulted from them. Much of the story is concerned with political history, but the social and economic perspective is also presented and cultural history (so often neglected) earns a place in the pages.

The volume is intended not merely to explain the history of this immense series of changes, but also to help candidates preparing for the GCSE and similar examinations, both at sixteen and beyond, to come to terms with the new and different types of question, and the handling of documentary and other sources that now feature as an essential part of public examinations. Whilst it is primarily intended for those at sixteen, its methods and its investigation of examination techniques will benefit those beyond sixteen, particularly those who have not studied modern British history before. It presents a familiar period in the form of what has come to be called the 'New History'.

R. Ben Jones
1987

Note

All good history books contain references to people and events that are not immediately explained in the text. This may be simply because there is not space to explain everything, or it may be that the name is introduced early so that when it is later explained more fully it is already familiar. Whatever the reason, readers of this book are encouraged to do their own research and to discover for themselves the importance of a particular name or event.

Some of the historical and technical words used in the text are explained in the glossary on page 222. They are printed in bold letters like this: **enclosure**.

Acknowledgements

The author and publishers wish to thank the following examining bodies for allowing the reproduction of questions from their past papers. In brackets after each is the abbreviation used after the questions in the text to refer to their source:

Associated Examining Board (AEB)
Oxford and Cambridge Schools Examination Board (O&C)
Southern Regional Examinations Board (SREB)
University of Cambridge Local Examinations Syndicate (UCLES)

The author and publishers wish to thank the following for permission to reproduce photographs, portraits and prints (page numbers in brackets):

(15, 214 below) Aerofilms Ltd; (27, 74, 75, 85, 99, 161, 175, 176, 189, 201 below, 205, 210) BBC Hulton Picture Library; (4 right) The British Library; (219 left) Glasgow School of Art Collection; (141, 151, 152, 153, 155, 196 above, 200, 207) The Illustrated London News Picture Library; (29 below) Ironbridge Gorge Museum Trust; (16) Leicestershire Museums, Art Galleries and Records Service; (98) Lincolnshire County Council Recreational Services; (4 left, 6, 42, 60, 64, 89, 116, 138, 142 left, 144) The Mansell Collection; (2, 11, 13, 23 above, 33, 35, 37, 68, 80, 124, 132, 142 right, 159, 178, 182, 193 below, 196 below, 201 above, 208, 211 below right, 215, 217) Mary Evans Picture Library; (211 above) The National Motor Museum at Beaulieu; (214 above) The National Trust; (147, 162, 164, 171, 174, 193 above, 204) Reproduced by permission of Punch; (186 below) Raymonds (Midlands) Photographic Agency Ltd; (216, 219 above) Royal Commission on the Historical Monuments of England; (29 above) The Royal Pavilion Art Gallery and Museums, Brighton; (21, 28, 30, 190, 191, 192, 197, 211 below left) the Science Museum; (105) Students of the Publishing Studies postgraduate course, Centre for Bibliographic Studies, University of Stirling; (168) This work is in the collection of the Towns Docks Museum, Hull City Museums and Art Galleries; (54, 65, 87, 88, 90, 97) Reproduced by courtesy of the Trustees of the British Museum; (5, 50, 219 right, 220) the Victoria and Albert Museum.

The photographs on pages 20, 23 below and 186 above were taken by the author.

The photograph on the cover shows *The Iron Forge* by Joseph Wright, painted in 1772. Reproduced from the Broadlands collection by permission of Lord Romsey.

The publishers have made every effort to trace copyright holders, but if they have inadvertently overlooked any, they will be pleased to make the necessary arrangement at the first opportunity.

Contents

1 Changing Britain

The dawn of the modern era

To study history, you must use your imagination. To understand what was happening over two hundred years ago, you have to collect as many facts as you can and try to explain what the facts mean. But you must also try to appreciate how people felt and thought at the time. In this way you can come to understand the period, and this is as important as learning lots of facts about it. We call this effort to understand *empathy*: without it we could easily make judgements about the past based only on our knowledge and experience of today, a quite different age from the one we are studying.

Looking back, we can see that what we think of as the modern world was just dawning during the eighteenth century. A person living at the time could not see this. It is hard to try to understand the ideas of a past age, but it is harder still to recognise those forces that are actually changing our own world. Try it. Ask around the class for suggestions of the things that are changing our society into that of the twenty-first century. Is there much agreement? In the eighteenth century it was no easier to identify those forces of change. The remarkable thing is that British society then so quickly came to terms with conditions that were totally new in the whole experience of humankind.

What were these new conditions? If someone from Shakespeare's England had been able to visit the England of 1760, he would have found much that was familiar. Of course, the buildings and clothes would be different and people would be better fed, but the countryside would look pretty much the same and there would be the familiar differences between the few wealthy land-owning families and the many poor (though he would find far fewer wretchedly poor). The towns would not be much bigger, and even London would have fields and farms in St Marylebone. The smell and 'general nastiness' would still be there, even in the new fashionable streets and squares. The workers would still be 'pallid, undersized and wretchedly clad, perpetually suffering from ill health'. It would still be as dangerous to walk the streets (Leon Garfield

gives us good reasons why in his novel, *Smith*). He would see the pickpockets, beggars and starved children (some were scarred and crippled by their parents in the hope of inspiring pity in the wealthy; some of the girls sent out as prostitutes would be no more than twelve). Most of these wretches went in fear of the gallows, or at best **transportation** for trivial offences. Cruel sports were still popular: bull-baiting, cat-dropping and cock-fighting were to be common sights for another hundred years, supported by rich and poor alike. Our Shakespearean visitor might have met gangs of young gentlemen in the streets, like the Mohocks, dedicated to 'all possible hurt to their fellow creatures', who would roam the streets after drunken orgies, slashing faces and even gouging out eyes, believing (usually rightly) that their wealth and social position would be sufficient security against punishment. Drunkenness was very common, especially in London, where gin drinking among the populace eventually led an unwilling government to enforce new licensing laws in an effort to curb the social evil.

Our visitor might have thought that England had not changed all that much: he would have been wrong. A new age was dawning. Tremendous social and economic changes were already transforming the life of the country. Within a couple of generations, people would complain (as they never had before) that they were dominated by the clock.

There were big changes in social attitudes, too. The eighteenth century saw the rise of **humanitarianism**, and movements were launched that would make Britain a pleasanter place to live in. The Fieldings, for example, brought a quite different atmosphere into their magistrates' court at Bow Street – they would not be bribed; their sentences also took account of the needs of the prisoner and were often remarkably light. Their Bow Street Runners began a tradition that would lead to our modern police force. A new opinion was that the wealthy would give more to relieve the poor if they were aware of the conditions in which some had to live, and in 1796 the Society for Bettering the Condition of the Poor was founded. Many hospitals, dispensaries, and a host of societies to help the poor were founded. One of these was the Anti-Slavery Society, whose careful work to inform the public of the harsh conditions of the slave trade was to triumph in the abolition of the trade in 1807. Even prize-fighting, where the tradition was for two men to punch each other until one dropped dead or unconscious, was made respectable by the Queensberry Rules.

Eighteenth-century aristocratic society has a well-founded reputation for loose living, self-indulgence and lechery, but it also showed much concern for others.

Hogarth's Gin Lane contrasted with Beer Street
Hogarth was a well known artist of the time, whose cartoons were popular. They present scenes that are reasonably accurate. The buildings, streets, tools and dresses are what you would have seen then. The cartoons clearly tell a 'moral' tale: Hogarth was on the side of beer – pure water was rare in large towns until the mid-nineteenth century.

A good way to find out just how great was this concern is to organise a class project on charities and humanitarian movements during the eighteenth century. You could divide into groups, each dealing with particular humanitarians, such as Thomas Coram, Jonas Hanway or William Wilberforce, and begin by making a simple list of the societies with which they were associated. Then go on to find out about their activities (avoiding the trap of merely writing a biography of the person you have chosen). There may be local charities dating from this time in your own town: ask at your local Records Office and see if there are any surviving documents. Ask your teacher to arrange for a book-box loan from the local library to help. Contemporary writings will prove useful and there are many *secondary* sources: for example, Dorothy George's *London Life in the Eighteenth Century* and *England in Transition*. You might find useful T. H. White's *The Age of Scandal*, E. S. Turner's *Roads to Ruin*, Christopher Hibbert's *The Roots of Evil* and Elizabeth Jaggar's *Before Victoria*. After your research is written up, each group could share its findings, and in this way the form would cover a very great deal – for there is much to discover.

The surprisingly large number of societies formed to help the poor suggests that 'social conscience', which is often associated with the mid-Victorians, was already alive a whole century before. However, it was not only attitudes that were changing. The whole nature of traditional society was being altered by economic and social developments. These are often called 'revolutions', not because they were sudden and violent, but because they changed society completely over the next hundred years or so. These revolutions are usually divided into convenient topics such as population changes (demography), developments in trade and wealth, agriculture, transport and industry. We will examine each in turn, but remember that they were happening at much the same time and that each revolution was influencing the others. Remember also that we are really studying the emergence of the modern world. Britain was changing from a traditional agricultural country to the world's first industrial nation.

Population changes

The most fundamental of the revolutions was what has been called the population 'explosion' (see Fig. 1). This sudden growth of population was happening in Europe as well as in Britain. It took everyone by surprise and helped to produce a society quite different from what had been known before. Britain's population had been growing slowly since Tudor times: in the 1770s it was about 8.9 million. Then the pace changed. By 1801 it was 10.5 million and by 1871 about 26 million – nearly three times what it had been a century before. Never

Make a list of consequences that would follow this dramatic increase after the 1770s. Discuss it in class and you will see how many things are affected. Remember that an increasing population will act as a spur to greater wealth, if a country's wealth is already increasing.

had such a change been experienced. Today, we are used to the idea of a rapidly increasing population on a world scale. Then, it was unknown.

With more people earning more money, more goods would be bought: this would stimulate farmers and manufacturers to *supply* the increasing *demand* for goods. In its turn, this would create more work for more people, and more money would be invested in production (economists call this effect a *multiplier*). We understand this today, but it was not understood two hundred years ago.

Indeed, there was much concern that the population might increase too rapidly. In 1798 the Reverend Dr Thomas Malthus published a very influential book, *Essay on the Principle of Population as it Affects the Future Improvement of Society*. He argued that it was natural for population to increase, but that it was held in check by natural forces such as disease, plague, famine, even war. He observed that population grew much more rapidly than food supply: if it were not checked it would rapidly outstrip available food supplies, and

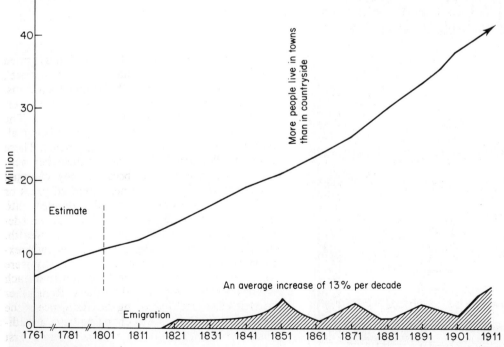

Fig. 1 Population growth

famine and destitution would result. He was right: where an increasing population is not sustained by increasing wealth and resources, disaster threatens. This 'Malthusian trap', as it is called, is recognised today as a danger for the developing countries of the world. It was not a danger for eighteenth-century Britain because of her increasing wealth and the expansion of her trade and natural resources. As the population increased, the standard of living rose for almost everyone. Of course, there were plenty of poor people about, but they did not suffer that grinding poverty that had been common earlier in the century. Instead, they were more conscious of how much better off others were than themselves. Here was a social change: a new age had dawned.

Finding the statistics

During the century there was much discussion about population, but there were no accurate statistics. Parish registers were not always properly kept, and bills of mortality may have been a guide to what was happening in particular towns, but they were not helpful for the country as a whole. Several surveys had been made by Treasury officials anxious to assess taxes properly. The most accurate seems to have been made by Gregory King in 1696, whose estimate of Britain's population was 5.5 million. Life assurance firms were becoming important during the eighteenth century and they were keen to have accurate figures on which to base their policies: Dr Price undertook research on their behalf in Norwich later in the century and came to the conclusion that the population was declining! It was not until 1801 that the government, following the advice of John Rickman, held a *census* (a count of the population), which established the amazing increase. A census was held every ten years thereafter (except in 1941), and at last an accurate picture of population changes began to emerge.

Bills of Mortality
   These notices gave a list of deaths in a parish or ward of a town, sometimes showing the cause of death. They were not very accurate and the cause of death was often a guess rather than a doctor's opinion. But they are often the only evidence we have, since parish registers were frequently not kept.

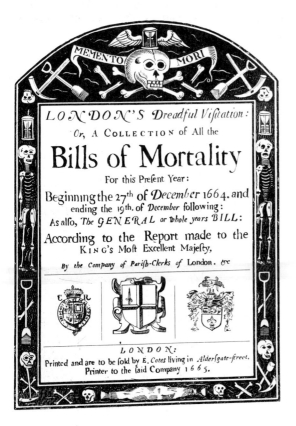

Life Assurance: table of premiums prepared by James Dodson FRS in 1756
   Calculating the premium for life assurance is a skilled job which today is done by actuaries. In 1756 a mathematician, Fellow of the Royal Society, produced this table of figures: it was a sign of developing skill among businessmen. Dr Price also prepared tables of figures to help with life assurance.

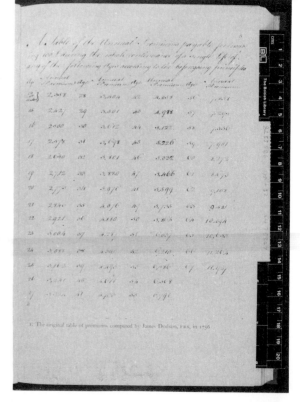

Analysing the causes

Why did the population explosion take place? There have been many attempts to explain it, but, on examination, most turn out to be merely descriptions of what had taken place. For example, people argued that the explosion was caused by an increase in the *birth rate* (the total births per 1000 of the population in a year). The birth rate was indeed increasing, but after 1871 it decreased, yet the population continued to grow! The *fertility rate* (total live births per 1000 women of child-bearing age in a year) is a better guide to population growth. Do you see why? Again, it was argued that the *death rate* (total deaths per 1000) was falling: it was, but it rose significantly in the 1820s when the population was increasing rapidly! In any case, the death rate is not particularly useful as a guide – the age of death would be much more useful (why?).

birthplace to their present residence). You could produce some useful maps and charts to illustrate this. Seek out the Secretary of the local Historical Association, and the County or Borough Archivist, and discuss your project with them. You might eventually stage an exhibition of your findings for the general public.

Social factors

Population growth is a complex thing and no single explanation will be satisfactory. Instead we have to build up an acceptable argument from a number of ideas. Obviously food supply is important (in bad harvest years infants died, which meant they could not become parents in their turn): after the 1750s, harvests seem to have been generally good and the climate drier. The standard of living of two hundred years ago is a very difficult thing to measure, but there are indications of an improvement – by 1800 bread, the staple diet of labourers, was mainly made from wheat flour instead of the cheaper rye; local improvements in transport meant a more abundant food and fuel supply over a wider area. Increasing imports changed drinking habits: in 1700 tea, cocoa, coffee and sugar were such luxuries that they were kept from servants (early tea-caddies were fitted with locks), but by 1800 they had become common items:

Imports	1700	1800
tea	£14 000	£2 980 000
sugar	£668 000	£5 436 000

An eighteenth-century tea caddy (note the lock)

Fig. 2 Birth and death rates
  Accurate figures for births and deaths are available only from the late 1830s, for compulsory registration began in 1836. Compare this graph with Fig. 1. You will see that the population continues to grow at much the same rate after 1801 despite the up-swing in the death rate between 1810 and 1850 and the down-swing in the birth rate after 1870. Can you explain why this should be so?

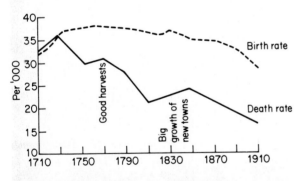

A useful way of studying the social history of your own town is to obtain census returns over a period and try to explain why an increase, or a decrease, in population occurred at particular times. Your survey could be enlarged into a *demographic* study. You might be lucky enough to see an *enumerator's book*, showing details of each family living in each house of a street, their occupation and where they were born. From this you might be able to judge the class of person living in certain streets, and also to reveal their *geographical mobility* (tracing their movement from their

Other social points helpful for our explanation concern the way the young labourers and craftsmen lived. During the eighteenth century, there was a steady decline in the numbers of *apprentices* and **journeymen** who 'lived in' with their master craftsmen. This meant they were freer to marry, and a young marriage is likely to result in more children than one where the couple are in their late twenties before they marry. Farm labourers were often no longer lodged in the farmer's house, and this meant they too might marry earlier. Better wages could be earned in the towns (especially in the North) and this also encouraged early marriage. In the Midlands and the North, the *urban* (town) birth rate was much higher than the (*rural*) agricultural one. All these points suggest that society was changing and help explain the population explosion.

Improvements in health care

There were great advances in medicine in the eighteenth century, but arguments drawn from medical practice are less satisfactory explanations. There were no plagues or serious epidemics in the later part of the century. Smallpox, for example, a killer among children, seems to have become less dangerous, perhaps because of *inoculation*. Lady Mary Wortley Montagu seems to have introduced inoculation from Turkey in about 1721. (Find out more about this remarkable lady). It consisted of confining children in an overheated room with a smallpox victim in the hope that they would catch a mild infection from which they would quickly recover and so gain an *immunity*. It was not very successful: a safer method was developed by Robert Sutton in 1765. Later still (1798), Dr Edward Jenner introduced the technique of *vaccination* – inserting serum from cowpox sufferers into a tiny cut. This proved effective and many villagers, and especially soldiers, were obliged to be vaccinated (it was made compulsory in 1853). The method was very unpopular at first. Think of it – introducing a *cattle* disease to prevent a human disease! Doctors themselves had little understanding of the causes of

Gillray's cartoon of Dr Jenner vaccinating

The Cow Pock – or – the Wonderful Effects of the New Inoculation! – Vide the Publications of ŷ Ann Vaccine Society

disease; the idea must have seemed preposterous to uneducated labourers and soldiers!

In the eighteenth century, doctors were being better trained, especially at Edinburgh and Glasgow. (One of the reasons why the British navy was better than the French was because so many Scottish-trained doctors became naval surgeons in order to earn enough money to buy themselves a partnership or even a practice.) Even at Oxford and Cambridge, where gentlemen physicians took their degree, training was much improved. There was more understanding of drugs (doctors had to make up their own medicines), but an incredible number of patent medicines and pills were also sold by 'quacks' – the columns of newspapers carried many advertisements for them. Perhaps the biggest improvement was in the knowledge of surgery and the training of surgeons. At the beginning of the century, surgeons were linked with barbers as a professional body, but in 1745 they were formally divided from that trade, and many advances in the knowledge of anatomy were made. It was not always easy; it was hard for surgeons to obtain a body for scientific dissection – they often had to rely on grave-robbers. Dr John Hunter, 'founder of modern surgery', made many anatomical discoveries that helped doctors to diagnose diseases accurately. One of his pupils was Dr Jenner.

> You might like to visit the Hunterian Museum in London, or the medical section of the Science Museum, and make a particular study of developments in surgery and medicine at this time. A useful book is D. Sylvester's *The Story of Medicine*.

Surgeons had to work quickly because pain, shock and the loss of blood could kill a patient: surgery was 'the last resort'. Dr Simpson's use of chloroform in Edinburgh (1847) and Dr Lister's use of an antiseptic spray (1865) did not arrive until the nineteenth century, too late to help explain the population explosion. Furthermore, better-trained doctors would mainly help the wealthy in prosperous parts of town, but they would not have much effect in the poorer parts, where people could not afford a doctor. However, the population growth occurred as much among the poor as among the rich. Of course, people helped the poor in the towns: Dr Armstrong founded the first 'Dispensary for the Relief of the Infant Poor' at Red Lion Square,

Holborn, in 1769. Later there were other dispensaries where the poor could seek advice and obtain cheap and effective medicines. Similarly, there were improvements in midwifery and the training of midwives by Sir Richard Manningham (1739) and Dr Smellie (1741), and lying-in hospitals were opened. A large number of general hospitals were also opened. The small ones in market towns such as York had a good reputation, but larger ones in big towns, especially London, had a high death rate. A century later Florence Nightingale wrote in a nursing manual: 'The first requirement of a hospital is that it should do the sick no harm.'

(Note two possible difficulties about these medical explanations: first, they do not necessarily affect the poor at all; and, secondly, their impact in any case would be too late to have much effect on the *start* of the population explosion.)

Developments in the chemical industry during the eighteenth century made the manufacture of soap cheaper, so that more people used it more frequently. Also the growing cotton industry made it possible even for the poor to have cheap garments that could easily be washed. Francis Place remembered when

> the wives of journeymen, tradesmen and shopkeepers either wore leather stays, or what were called full-boned stays . . . These were never washed, although worn day by day for years. The wives and grown daughters of tradesmen, even, wore petticoats of camblet, lined with dyed linen, stuffed with wool and horsehair and quilted; these were also worn day by day until they were rotten.

By the end of the century, he noted that soap and cotton goods had changed this – even the poor were hygienic, 'particularly the women, partly from the success of the cotton manufacture . . . partly from increased knowledge of domestic concerns and general management of children.'

> But how extensive was this wearing of cotton underclothing? Ask your grandfather or other elderly person whether young boys in the 1930s wore underpants, or whether such things were regarded as 'sissy' or 'what girls wear'. The idea of better hygiene as a cause of better health is a good one, but will it do for the eighteenth century? You should always check from as many angles as you can any argument that is put forward.

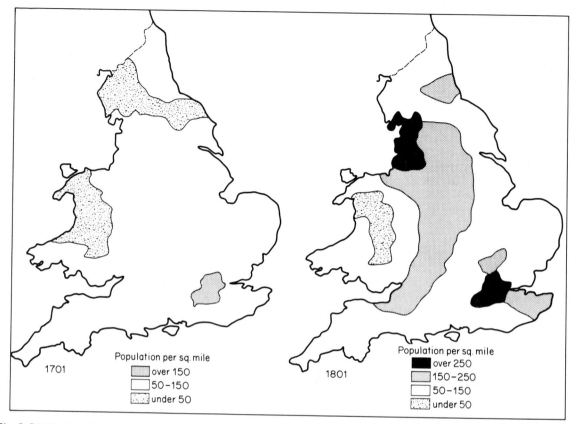

Fig. 3 Distribution of population, 1701 and 1801

The growth of towns

The *distribution* of the population was changing. Towns were growing, but not always at the same rate, nor at the expense of the rural areas – it was 1851 before more people lived in towns than in the countryside. The old wool areas of East Anglia and the Cotswolds had given way by 1801 to the West Midlands and the North as the principal areas of population concentration. This was not because of a huge movement of people from the South in search of work in the industrial North – indeed, there seems to have been more movement in the other direction. The North grew more rapidly because of its higher birth rate – higher wages, early marriage and ample opportunity for child labour provide the reasons.

But people did move into the towns, sometimes from a considerable distance. More often it was from the villages around the towns. What seems to have happened was that people moved relatively short distances from the countryside into the villages round the towns, where there were houses left by those who had moved into the towns. It was like a series of waves. Some towns grew quickly, like

Liverpool and Manchester, or Oldham, a village of 400 in 1760 and a growing town of 20 000 in 1801; others grew more slowly. Only by studying each local area can a general picture be built up.

Some problems in history have a simple and direct answer; others have no simple answer and can only be explained by indicating different influences affecting them. History is not an exact science, and so it is quite acceptable to have different explanations, or no very clear explanation if the evidence is not available. Where there is no direct answer, the historian has to make a number of suggestions and point out their limitations. There is no simple explanation for the population explosion, but it was a major influence upon the social and economic changes that followed it.

Increasing wealth

Where population growth and increasing wealth go together, prosperity is likely to result. Wealth was increasing in the eighteenth century. You can still see the obvious signs today in the streets, squares and substantial houses of older towns (see page 207). In the countryside, many great houses were completely rebuilt, and a host of large farm houses date from this time.

The wealth came from good farming practice, and also from increasing trade. India supplied much of it. Merchants (called *nabobs*) returning with huge fortunes purchased an estate 'to keep up with the Joneses' (the local gentry) and to qualify for a seat in the House of Commons (a seat could, in effect, be purchased, see page 102) so that no one would enquire into how their wealth was made.

Trade with the colonies

Trade with India came under special regulation and was jealously guarded. But trade with the rest of the colonies was also very important. It was closely controlled by what has been called the **Mercantile System** which sought to protect trade against competition from other countries. To achieve this, all the trade of the Empire was confined as far as possible to British possessions, with (at least in theory) the colonies supplying raw materials and Britain supplying them with manufactured goods.

Since the seventeenth century, the Navigation Acts required British trade to be carried in British ships (on 'British bottoms', as they put it), or in ships with British sailors and captain. This was very profitable and ensured that Britain's merchant fleet was huge. If a colony was in the tropics, it had a ready market for its agricultural products. What Britain did not consume was re-exported to Europe. The colony was not allowed to trade with a foreign country nor trade in any of a whole series of goods, called *enumerated articles*. The system of trade was made tight in order to exclude foreign competitors, and regulated solely in Britain's interests. Some colonies did not object, especially as Britain looked after their defence and administration. A good example of the mutually advantageous arrangements possible is provided by what has been called the 'triangular system of trade' (see Fig. 4): Britain supplied trinkets and manufactured goods for exchange in Africa for slaves, who were transported (by the infamous 'middle passage') to Jamaica or other slave markets to be sold, and sugar was then carried back to Liverpool or Bristol. The system worked well (though it was never quite so simple as the map suggests); it was said that the bricks of Bristol and of Liverpool were cemented by the blood of the slaves.

Fig. 4 18th century 'triangular system' of trade
This 'triangular system' of trade across the Atlantic was never quite as simple as the diagram suggests.

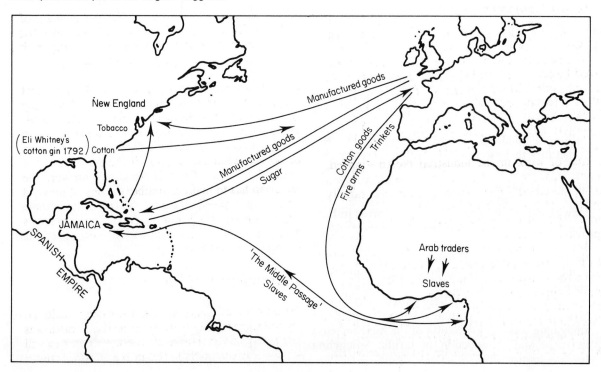

Much has been written about the slave trade; it provides an excellent research project. You could study the organisation of the slave trade. Look at some of the logs that have survived among the papers of captains of slave ships (not all were brutal men – after all, they got no cash for a dead slave!). The Anti-Slavery Society was very active – you could visit Wilberforce House, Hull, and study some of the *archives* available there. But because so much money was made from the trade, Liverpool merchants were particularly keen to maintain it. Their archives are worth consulting and the Liverpool Records Office might supply photocopies of letters to Members of Parliament defending the trade.

Trade with the empire encouraged British manufacture and *diversified* her exports – axes, nails, firearms, clocks, for example. But the Navigation Acts prevented colonies manufacturing and trading in goods that would compete with Britain's exports, and if the colony was in the same latitude as Europe (such as New England), its trade would certainly suffer. New England merchants were more or less obliged to become smugglers, trading illegally with other trading systems such as the French or Spanish. They were successful traders, but when Britain tried to tighten up her regulations, the New England colonies objected. This was a principal cause of the American Revolution (see page 39).

It was not only the New England Merchants who were smugglers. The *tariff* (customs duty) imposed on imports was often so high that it was very profitable to smuggle spirits, tea and even sugar. Smuggling was widespread in eighteenth-century Britain, and all classes indulged in it. The revenue men were too few to control all the coast and ports – and many were making a good living by turning a blind eye to what was going on! But sometimes there were bloody encounters between the revenue men and organised smuggling gangs. Smuggling was highly organised – for example, the established centre for tea smuggling was Hawkhurst, Kent, where tea was imported in bulk and divided into small lots that found their way to London to be sold for five shillings a pound (when the tax itself was four shillings and nine pence!). It would have cost too much to have suppressed smuggling by force, and the savage punishments meted out to those who were caught clearly had little effect. What eventually stopped organised smuggling was a combination of the huge increase in trade and a reduction in tariffs. Smuggling became unprofitable.

In 1776, Adam Smith published a very influential book, *An Inquiry into the Nature and Causes of the Wealth of Nations*. He argued that people tend to pursue their own advantage, but in doing so they promote the advantage of society as a whole. Government regulation tended to stifle enterprise; left to themselves, traders would supply goods at the lowest effective price and all would benefit. If as many regulations as possible were removed, then free competition would ensure that producer and consumer gained the maximum advantage. In particular, if tariffs were removed, allowing **free trade** (trade between nations with no artificial barriers), then goods would be cheaper and competition would ensure that international trade brought prosperity to all countries. Adam Smith's ideas were not accepted there and then, but during the next century the demand for free trade was to dominate political life and help to build Victorian prosperity. His wish for as little government interference as possible was

Fig. 5 Growth of foreign trade, 1760–1800
After 1780 foreign trade leapt forward: exports were affected by the Napoleonic War, particularly when the Continental System was developed (see page 76).

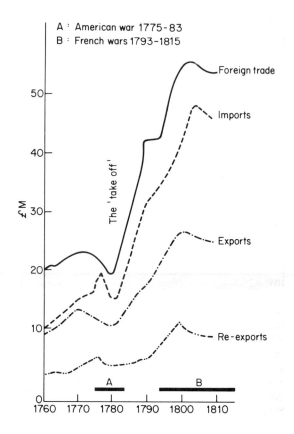

taken up by reformers, who used the French phrase **laissez-faire** to sum up their demand for the ending of such interference.

However, long before Adam Smith's ideas were adopted, Britain's trade had increased phenomenally. By the 1780s there was a significant change; growth in trade was so great that it seemed Britain had entered a period of continuous expansion. An American historian, W. W. Rostow, called it 'the take-off into self-sustained economic growth'.

Financial institutions

This expansion was helped by Britain's well-developed financial institutions. The Bank of England had been founded in 1694, but it dealt mainly with merchants and the wealthy. There were private banks in London, but during the century many 'country banks' were established by local business people – there were nearly four hundred such banks by 1790. These provided funds for local merchants and farmers, and sometimes industrialists. They produced their own banknotes because there were not sufficient coins in circulation; indeed, banks and some merchants took to issuing tokens to be exchanged for goods. The country banks were family concerns, often begun by corn merchants or wool merchants (such as the Gurneys of Norwich), or goldsmiths (such as the Vaughans of Gloucester). Sometimes they failed and dragged local business people down with them. But the country banks helped the flow of money, and after 1826 corporate banks (*joint stock* banks commanding greater funds) did much to help industrial expansion.

The Stock Exchange also helped to provide **capital**: it had its own premises by 1773, and thirty years later had issued its own List of Companies in whose shares it was prepared to deal. Companies raised money by offering shares which people would buy in the hope of getting a *dividend* if the company's profits were good enough; they also offered *debentures* (a long-term loan with a fixed rate of interest). Already, a *rentier* class of people (whose income came from investments and who provided more funds for expansion through further investments), had appeared. Money was invested abroad, and foreigners were happy to invest in Britain because of the evident safety of her money market. By the 1790s, London had overtaken Amsterdam as the world's banking centre. Insurance companies providing cover for risks such as fire, theft and losses, were becoming important. The early fire service was begun by insurance companies anxious to save their clients' property. Such properties had the company's sign on the wall

Fire office mark
These metal signs were fixed to the houses of subscribers to tell which company's fire engine should put out the fire! Sometimes the policy number was included in the sign, as in this case.

to inform the firemen. You can still see these on eighteenth-century buildings today, and a collection of them can be seen at the Chartered Insurance Hall, London. There is also an excellent collection of items about early fire-fighting at the Braidwood and Rushbrook Museum in Edinburgh.

Agricultural improvements

In 1760 agriculture was Britain's prime industry. It provided food and was also the basis of many of the trades and manufactures: brewing (already developing into a 'scientific' industry), flour-milling, millwrights, wheelwrights, cart-building, coopering, leather-working, smithies and much of the iron industry. Already big changes were taking place in farming, and the pace of those changes was to increase in the next eighty years, so much so that it used to be popular to talk of the 'agricultural revolution'. However, more recent research has led us to alter our interpretation of what was happening in farming. It is well to remember three things about farming, so that our ideas remain realistic: firstly, farming is dependent on the weather and the soil (it is not the same all over the country, and changes in one area will not necessarily appear in another); secondly, two hundred years ago it was not possible to develop new types of grain or strains of beast very rapidly (it was much more a matter of letting nature take its course); and, thirdly, farmers then, as now, generally knew what they were doing, so that it was unlikely that any of them would need to change their methods overnight.

The changes in farming that were so widely discussed in the late eighteenth century were the result of several generations of careful farming, and it is important to remember that the people whose names are always quoted were building on the sound practice of many farmers during the previous hundred years. Already a good deal of investment in improvements had taken place – farmers were beginning to specialise and develop their farms on **capitalist** lines. They did not have to wait for the agricultural improvers to tell them how. Increased areas of land were coming into cultivation, for at the beginning of the century there were extensive areas uncultivated which were known as 'wastes'.

Who were the 'agricultural improvers'? They were a host of successful farmers all over the country, often local squires intent on increasing the value of their property, who learnt of new methods from friends and acquaintances (sometimes from different countries) and from travelling either to Parliament or to the new spa towns that were now becoming popular for family visits – Bath and Tunbridge Wells are examples. Some improvers were great lords with extensive lands in different parts of the country, such as the Bedfords, the Earls of Egremont, the Marquis of Rockingham at Wentworth Woodhouse, Lord Braybrook (stock-breeding at Audley End), Sir John Sinclair on his Scottish estates and Viscount 'Turnip' Townshend, a leading politician who retired to his Norfolk estates in the 1730s. Naturally enough, it is the great lords who are remembered, but the local squires deserve a mention, too. The very small farmer may well have lacked the money and the inclination to try out new methods.

New methods of farming

There were three broad categories of new methods: better husbandry with fertilisers and crop rotation, better breeding methods, better machines. In each case certain farmers are particularly remembered, more because they were effective popularisers than innovators. Many of the new methods were adapted from Dutch experience (especially in East Anglia). 'Turnip' Townshend has sometimes been credited with introducing the *Norfolk four-course rotation* (turnips, barley, clover, wheat, grown in successive seasons and, with additional fertilisers, avoiding the need for a *fallow* year which was customary in many

areas). But turnips were nothing new and had been used for winter cattle feed for years in light soil areas (they were less successful on heavy clay soils), and the Norfolk rotation was known in Charles II's day. But Townshend deserves to be remembered for popularising its use, just as George III does, who also encouraged new methods and lavished great care on his model farm at Windsor.

Thomas William Coke of Holkham, Norfolk (created Earl of Leicester towards the end of his long life), was much more of a farmer. His family were prosperous landowners with farms in several counties and were noted for the care they took of their farms, requiring tenants to follow particular methods of farming as a condition of holding their *long leases*. Coke continued this tradition, making his great country seat of Holkham a centre for advertising new methods, holding sheep-shearings and agricultural shows that attracted visits from prominent members of the aristocracy. His farming methods were fine examples of the best farming practices. He doubled his income from the Holkham estate from £12 332 in 1776 to £25 789 in 1816, but this was in a period of rapidly rising prices (some historians have quoted figures of his increased income that are patently absurd in agricultural terms).

Perhaps the best-known advocate of new farming methods was Arthur Young. He was not a successful farmer, but he was a very successful writer. His *Tours* were influential accounts of good farming practice in different parts of Britain and France. His *Annals of Agriculture* (1784–1809) were also influential; George III wrote for them under the pen-name of his shepherd, Ralph Robinson. But recent research has shown that Young exaggerated considerably in his accounts, and he may not be altogether reliable as a source. A more accurate writer, who deserves to be better remembered, was William Marshall. Another was Nathaniel Kent, whose book *Hints to Gentlemen of Landed Property* appeared in 1775. It is difficult to estimate the influence of the writers, since their books may have been read only by those already using the methods they advocated. But the government was on the side of the improvers and established the Board of Agriculture in 1793, with Sir John Sinclair as President and Arthur Young as Secretary. The Board did useful propaganda work, advising on many topics, from pig-feed to drainage, and it began a survey of the agricultural resources of each county (Young wrote six himself!). It was a pity the Board was dissolved in 1822 as an economy measure. The landed gentry were very interested in agricultural writers – have a look at the contents of the libraries of the country houses now open to the public – and they helped to found many local agricultural societies. Several of the famous societies date from this time: the Bath and West (1777), the Dishley Society (1783) and the Smithfield Club (1798), some of which held annual shows of considerable importance.

The great name in stock-breeding is Robert Bakewell, an ordinary tenant farmer who, after a long struggle, made Dishley Grange (Loughborough) the centre for outstanding breeds of sheep, cattle and horses – he was less successful with pigs. Bakewell was only the most successful of a long line of breeders; William Marshall noted that the Midlands 'abounds, and has for many years abounded, with intelligent and spirited breeders' (the Colling brothers of Ketton, Rutland, developed shorthorn cattle that soon superseded Bakewell's longhorn breed). But by 1786 Bakewell had earned such a name that he was able to choose his clients from among the aristocracy and to charge 400 guineas for the use of his prime rams for a third

of a season (in 1760 he had been happy to charge sixteen shillings for a whole season!). He was not scientific in his methods, but took pains to develop strains that sold well. The working class bought mutton and preferred it fat: 'You cannot eat bone, therefore give the public something to eat', said Bakewell. Pedigree stock-breeding became possible because of the work of these eighteenth-century farmers: the cow, for example, regarded as a useful draught animal in 1700, was by 1800 being bred for meat and increasingly for milk to supply the growing dairy industry.

Many agricultural machines were developed during the century, but none was widely used much before 1815. It needed larger farms and cheaper and better iron (see page 29) to make machinery in quantity to replace the wooden and wrought-iron tools that were traditionally used. Jethro Tull is often given pride of place for introducing new machinery, but, once again, he was not alone. His famous horse-hoe and seed-drill, which sowed in regular rows rather than the irregular, wasteful

Holkham Hall

pattern that resulted from broadcast sowing, were not commercially available for a hundred years after their invention (even his book, *Horse Hoeing Husbandry* (1731), failed to popularise them, and hand sowing remained common throughout the century, even on light soils). In 1780, Ransome of Ipswich produced his famous plough, which made his works the centre for agricultural machinery, but Andrew Meikle's thresher (1786) was not adopted for forty years, and then was a factor in causing the 'Swing Riots' of 1830 (see page 104), for corn was still being threshed by hand in 1850 – near Brighton, for example. You can see the barn that would have been used for hand-threshing if you visit old farm buildings. Several museums of agricultural machinery exist (Oakham, York, Hutton-le-Hole), but their exhibits are of models that date from the nineteenth century; mechanisation was a feature of 'high farming' (see page 197) in the mid-nineteenth century; the huge increase in crop yields achieved in the eighteenth century was harvested by a big labour force, not by a sudden switch to machinery.

Enclosure

The most obvious change in eighteenth-century farming affected only the Midlands, parts of East Anglia and the South: here the traditional medieval three-field or open field system existed, but in the hundred years after about 1730 it was swept aside to be replaced by the Midlands landscape we see today. The process by which the change was effected is known as **enclosure**, and it involved changes in the distribution and ownership of the land. Traditionally, each village was surrounded by huge fields without walls or fences, communally owned and divided into strips belonging to individual village farmers, each of whom owned strips in different parts of the fields to ensure that everyone got a share of the good and poor land. Traditionally, also, each field grew the same crop, varying according to a strict rotation that often involved one field lying fallow so that the soil did not become too impoverished. Village beasts grazed together on the fallow and on the meadows which also produced hay for winter fodder. Beyond the meadows lay the common, where villagers had a *common-law right* to graze their beasts free of charge; often, poor farmers would build a shack on the common, grow vegetables and graze beasts for a living. Such farmers were known as *squatters* and had no legal right to the land they occupied.

It is easy to think of the disadvantages of open-field farming. It had been devised for subsistence farming, and the sequence of crops and the times of

ploughing, sowing and harvesting were determined by a village meeting, or by custom, so that enterprising farmers had to abide by what was decided – they could not do whatever they wanted. The fallow year reduced productive land by perhaps a quarter. Much time was wasted moving between strips, and a bad farmer was a menace to his neighbours' strips because of weeds. Between the strips were *balks* left to divide holdings and to give access to the interior of the fields. The pattern of strips can easily be seen in the Midlands countryside today (but be careful to distinguish between later drainage work and the old strip survivals; the strips go in different directions and across the natural drainage pattern).

Fig. 6 Principal areas of 18th century enclosure
In Kent and the West Country the open field system was not normal: enclosure only affected the central areas. Agricultural wages were low by any standards, but they were much higher in the north where alternative employment was available in the growing industrial towns.

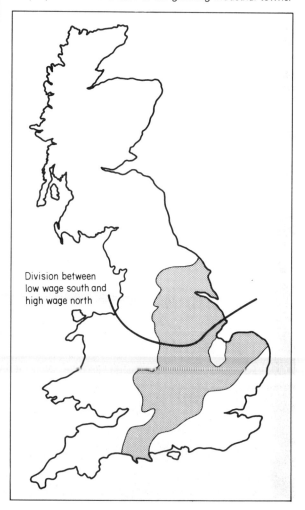

Division between low wage south and high wage north

Common pasturage of beasts meant that there was little opportunity for selective breeding, or confining outbreaks of disease, while the lack of winter fodder meant that many beasts had to be slaughtered and salted down (making a monotonous winter diet), and those surviving must have been wasted and undersized by the following spring. There was little incentive for bringing more land under cultivation – the wastes were extensive in the early part of the century. Agricultural improvers were very active in calling for enclosure in order to allow for better farming. Indeed, it is very easy to accept Arthur Young's view: 'The old open-field system must die off before new ideas can become generally rooted . . . Without enclosures there can be no good husbandry.' Enclosure of each person's legal holdings, consolidated into fields of reasonable size, was to be the answer.

It is easy to exaggerate the defects of open-field farming: heavy clay areas were backward in their methods, but there were already developments within the system. The Midlands was the great area for stock-breeding, after all, and as more local studies are completed we are learning that the open field system was altogether more flexible than the supporters of enclosure suggested. Within the great fields and on the commons, enclosure of a sort had begun to appear and in some ares (Oxfordshire is an example) enterprising farmers were introducing new crops into their strips. It was common for farmers to exchange strips in order to concentrate their holdings, and more of the wastes were being brought into cultivation, especially in fertile light-soil areas.

Enclosure, however, would simplify matters, and it became common practice in the open-field areas during the century. If the village agreed, the strips could be grouped into fields by general consent. Owners who refused would have to be bought out or persuaded, and this took time. A simpler method was to *petition* Parliament for the right to override common-law rights and enclose the land (a private Act of Parliament was necessary for each enclosure of a village's land until the General Enclosure Act 1845 when the process had almost ended). The whole process cost money – the legal costs of petitioning and preparing the enclosure act; paying the commissioners who made the Award after a

---

Medieval cultivation strips caught by the setting sun
Note the regular fields laid out by the Awarders, and the straight roads that replaced the old tracks that once led to the village (top right). Can you spot the canal that crosses the picture?

careful scrutiny of records and an examination of witnesses and anyone who could claim any legal right to ownership of land or grazing rights; fencing off new fields, building barns and digging ditches for drainage and making roads as the particular Acts required. But it was obviously profitable, for the expense was cheerfully borne by many farmers, even small farmers. Farming was profitable and prices were rising, especially during the French Wars between 1793 and 1815. At the same time, many wastes were brought into cultivation. Also, the opportunity was taken to *commute* (convert into money rents) the **tithe** (tax) that had to be paid to the Church of England clergy. This was traditionally paid in kind, and proved inconvenient and troublesome, especially in bad years; clergymen

were frequently happy to exchange it for a set rent from certain fields.

Years	Number of enclosure Acts	Years	Acres enclosed by Act of Parliament
1730–1759	212	1727–1760	74 518
1760–1789	1291	1761–1792	478 259
1790–1819	2169	1793–1815	1 013 634

The peak period was 1801–1811, when 1013 Acts were passed. The Acts continued into the nineteenth century, but were often more concerned with en-

Enclosure map, showing new landowner's plots on old fields

This is a section of a large-scale map in the Leicestershire Record Office. Every private enclosure Act of Parliament had a map presenting the details of the award. Ask to see some examples at your County Record Office. This example shows how the open fields were divided up into separate small fields belonging to individuals. You can just *make out the detail of the original strips shown around the village. Examine the roads. The commissioner ordered quite new roads to be cut – the village now lies across the road, not along it, as it originally did. Much of the East Midlands scenery was changed by the provisions of enclosure acts, and this map shows how the new scenery was devised.*

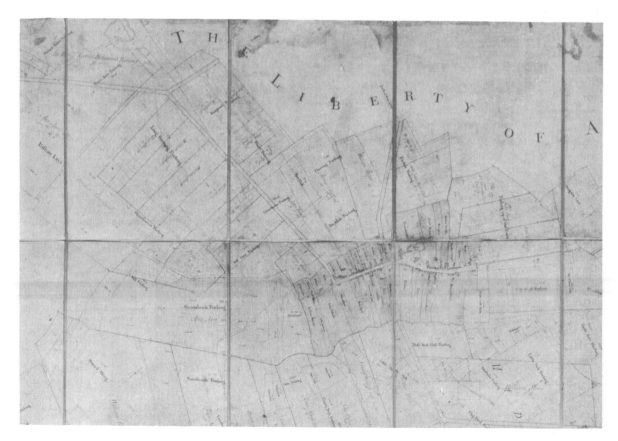

closing the remaining commons and wastes.

If Parliament accepted a petition, commissioners were appointed to make a careful survey and apportion land according to legal rights. The Award, accompanied by a detailed map, was incorporated into the private Act of Parliament (many survive and can be seen in the local Records Office – a study of the enclosure of a local village would make an excellent project). The commissioners were generally important local landowners. For this reason, and because many people lost what they supposed to be their common right to grazing and land, some historians have supported the tradition that the Award was made in the interests of the wealthy, against those of the poor. But research tends to support the view that the Commissioners were scrupulously fair, basing their award on legal rights: squatters had none and they suffered, and mere tenants did not own the land they occupied. Certainly, many very small farmers did lose the land they worked and had to become daylabourers; others sold their small allocation of land and joined them. Certainly, a great deal of common land was enclosed, and the opportunity of providing for the parish poor was usually not taken. However, the Commissioners seem to have done an honest job according to the law as it stood.

Another objection to enclosure was that it meant the end of the small farmer, because of the costs involved – the Board of Agriculture estimated that the average cost was twenty-eight shillings per acre in 1790 (eight and sixpence for the Act, ten shillings for the Commissioners and nine shillings and sixpence for fencing). Detailed studies, however, have shown that the many small farmers did survive, especially in prosperous areas, obtaining credit at low interest rates and spreading their payments over a number of years. The small farmer is with us still. Small and great farmers profited from enclosure which gave ample opportunity for new methods and helped to increase food production.

Rural poverty seemed to get very much worse at the time that the enclosure movement became more widespread, and the tradition soon arose that enclosure was responsible for it. But contemporaries were wrong. Enclosure did not *cause* poverty: areas unaffected by enclosure suffered just as badly. The real cause was linked with the population increase: there were more mouths to feed. It was linked also with rising prices. In fact, enclosure may have helped rural poverty initially by actually increasing employment: there were ditches to be dug, fences to be erected and roads to be made. New farming methods often meant more people employed per acre (until machinery began to make its

impact in the mid-nineteenth century). But in the South, poor agricultural labourers on extremely low wages tended to remain in the villages, where agriculture was the only real source of employment and where jobs became scarcer (except at harvest time). Such labourers had to wait for the coming of the railways before the opportunity arose for easy movement to new jobs elsewhere. In the North, there were growing industrial towns and villages where alternative employment could be found; agricultural wages were higher in such areas.

Rural poverty was not caused by enclosure, but as prices were rising steeply at this very time because of the French Wars (see page 64) contemporaries blamed enclosure. They can be forgiven for it, because they saw their traditional lifestyle being changed; they could not understand what we would call an *inflationary spiral*. So many contemporaries blamed the enclosure movement for its impact on the life of the poor. William Cobbett was especially eloquent in his defence of the rural poor. But we need to be careful not to be too easily swayed by popular writers: they may have misunderstood what was happening and may well have been biased, having 'an axe to grind'.

Examination questions

Examining Boards have introduced a new style of questions based on documentary material. They are called *stimulus questions*, and candidates are asked to explain points arising from the document or illustration used. The agricultural changes provide good stimulus material, for there are many particular points that can be asked. Here are two examples. The first is an extract from a well-known book on the period that presents a traditional interpretation from the evidence and leaves the impression that enclosure was to the benefit of the landowner and at the expense of the poor worker. The questions that follow are straightforward and can be answered from the passage, provided you know your work. But (*e*), (*f*) and (*g*) ask you to go further – and they carry more marks! The second example shows a map of a village before and after enclosure and asks similar questions based on it. (The large number of clerical gentlemen referred to on the map is because Lincoln Cathedral owned land in the village which it used to provide for its canons.)

Use the two examples to test how well you have understood the previous section. Then you could have a class discussion on whether enclosure was to the benefit of the country and whether the social changes that it brought could have been effected in a way that the ordinary worker might have found more acceptable. Remember, the people of the time would not have understood about price rises, as we understand today. Remember also that governments then did not have the huge civil service and vast technical skill that they have today – they simply could not have begun 'social security payments' even if the idea had occurred to them.

Impact on village life

The crops and cultivation of the late eighteenth century and early nineteenth differed but little from those of preceding centuries. Over vast areas of England wheat, rye and beans were sown in the autumn; barley, oats and peas or lentils in the spring; and roughly a third of the land left fallow every year.

The great mass of the farmers were slow to adopt new crops or new systems, if for no other reason
10 than that they were new. There was, however, another reason for the failure to change, namely that these new crops could not be cultivated on any worthwile scale so long as the 1 000-year-old system of open fields remained in operation.

15 What happened in Foxton is typical of what happened in a hundred other parishes. The chief instigators of the parliamentary bill for enclosure of the common fields were William Horrell and John Bendysh Esq., who between them owned
20 three-quarters of the land in the parish. On 23 June 1826 announcements were printed in the *Chronicle* and the campaign was launched. There was no opposition – there were none to oppose; few who would wish to and fewer still
25 with the vocal and financial resources needed. Exactly four years after the start of the campaign the award was proclaimed in the Parish Church.

It would be idle to deny that what facilitated the achievement more than anything else was the
30 general desire, on the part of those who had property, that it should be private property. The main objective was that henceforth a farmer should be free to cultivate own land in his own way, and it was hoped that he would at once put
35 into practice the improved farming techniques.

Twenty years after enclosure there were only eleven farmers left in Foxton. Ten years later there were only eight. The pattern of social stratifi-cation was set for the rest of the century and
40 beyond – fewer employers, more employed and the relationship between them was likewise firmly established for a long time.

R. Parker, *The common stream*

(a) What was most wasteful about the traditional system of farming described in the opening paragraph?   (1)
(b) (i) What were the main reasons which stopped the production of crops on a worthwhile scale?   (1)
(ii) Why would the small tenant farmer be unlikely to follow the new agricultural trends?   (1)
(c) Why is it not surprising that Messrs Horrell and Bendysh should be the instigators of enclosure?   (1)
(d) Why was it unlikely that any opposition to the Act would be successful?   (2)
(e) Who could suffer, and why, as a result of the desire to make property private? Give specific examples.   (4)
(f) What kind of improved farming techniques would be encouraged after enclosure?   (4)
(g) Explain why the number of farmers would decrease. What 'social stratification' would develop as a result of enclosure?   (6)

Total marks   (20)

UCLES

(a) Why would (i) Map I, and
(ii) Map II
have been drawn?   (4)
(b) Who received the largest amount of land in the enclosure award?   (2)
(c) What was the glebe?   (1)
(d) What had the Rector probably given up in return for his allocation?   (1)
(e) Give the names of two new enclosure roads.   (2)
(f) What distinctive difference is there between the enclosure roads and the old roads.   (1)
(g) Why were new roads made and whose responsibility was it to arrange where they went?   (2)
(h) What part was played by William Dixon of Holton-le-Moor in the enclosure of this village?   (1)
(i) Write a paragraph describing what the village of Waltham consisted of before it was enclosed. ('Ings' are water meadows.)   (6)

Total marks   (20)

O & C

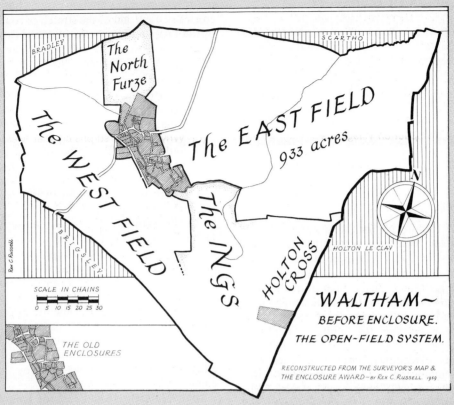

The North Furze

BRADLEY

SCARTHO

The EAST FIELD

933 acres

The WEST FIELD

BRIGSLEY

The N G S

HOLTON CROSS

HOLTON LE CLAY

N

SCALE IN CHAINS
0 5 10 15 20 25 30

THE OLD ENCLOSURES

WALTHAM~
BEFORE ENCLOSURE.
THE OPEN-FIELD SYSTEM.

RECONSTRUCTED FROM THE SURVEYOR'S MAP &
THE ENCLOSURE AWARD~ By Rex C. Russell 1959

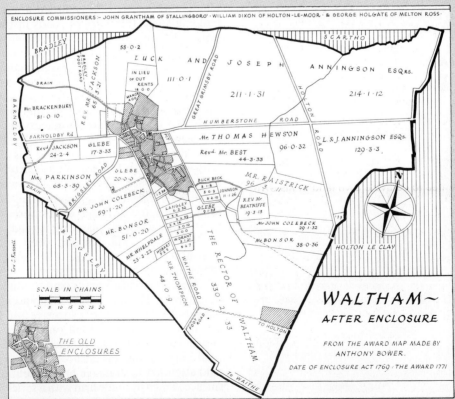

ENCLOSURE COMMISSIONERS ~ JOHN GRANTHAM OF STALLINGBORO' · WILLIAM DIXON OF HOLTON-LE-MOOR · & GEORGE HOLGATE OF MELTON ROSS.

BRADLEY

SCARTHO

58·0·2

LUCK AND JOSEPH ANNINGSON ESQRS.

BRADLEY FOOT ROAD

REV MR JACKSON 65·3·21

IN LIEU OF OUT RENTS 18·0·0

111·0·1

GREAT GRIMSBY ROAD

211·1·31

HOLTON ROAD

214·1·12

BARNOLDBY

DRAIN

Mr. BRACKENBURY 81·0·10

MANOR

HUMBERSTONE ROAD

BARNOLDBY Rd

Revd JACKSON 24·2·4

GLEBE 17·3·33

PIT

Mr. THOMAS HEWSON 96·0·32

L.S.J. ANNINGSON ESQs.

Revd. Mr BEST 44·3·33

129·3·3

Mr. PARKINSON 68·3·30

BRIGSLEY ROAD

GLEBE 20·0·0

BUCK BECK

MR. RAISTRICK 96·3·11

DRAIN

Mr. JOHN COLEBECK 59·1·20

LANGLEY

JOHNSON

REV Mr BEATNIFFE 19·3·13

MR. BONSOR 51·0·20

GLEBE

MR. WHELPDALE 25·3·22

HOBART

W DRANT

Mr.JOHN COLEBECK 29·1·32

BRIGSLEY

MR. THOMPSON 48·0·9

WAITHE ROAD

THE RECTOR OF WALTHAM 330·2·33

Mr. BONSOR 38·0·36

HOLTON LE CLAY

N

FOOT ROAD

TO HOLTON

TO WAITHE

Rex C. Russell

SCALE IN CHAINS
0 5 10 15 20 25 30

THE OLD ENCLOSURES

WALTHAM~
AFTER ENCLOSURE

FROM THE AWARD MAP MADE BY
ANTHONY BOWER.

DATE OF ENCLOSURE ACT 1769 : THE AWARD 1771

Improvements in transport

People did travel two hundred years ago: the idea that many people never left their village is no longer so easily accepted as it used to be. The wealthy travelled by horse or by carriage, merchants had pack horses, the poor walked. But everyone agreed that the roads were terrible, and since this made travel slow and cumbersome, it also made things easier for highwaymen! If prosperity were to increase and large quantitites of goods were to be transported around the country, big improvements were needed on the roads.

Road transport

Parishes were responsible for the upkeep of roads, but, since most road-users were travellers from other parishes, there was little incentive to keep the road surfaces in good condition: an unpaid 'surveyor of the highways' was elected annually, but little was done beyond filling pot-holes with rubble. Justices of the Peace at their Quarter Sessions quite frequently fined parishes for failing to maintain their roads.

In the late seventeenth century the idea had grown up of empowering a group of people to form a Trust for the purpose of improving a stretch of an important roadway, and to charge road-users a **toll** in order to pay for the work. This required an Act of Parliament for each Trust because the use of the

A toll house of the 1790s, built in 'gothick' style

roads was normally free. A gate or bar was usually erected at each end of the stretch of road supervised by the Trust, and everyone who used the road had to pay a toll. Some of the toll houses can still be seen today in country districts. The bar (pike) was made to turn easily and so the name Turnpike Trust became popular. Many were established during the eighteenth century and some were very efficient, producing road improvements that made possible the running of 'flying coaches' between London and important towns. The larger Trusts were able to employ specialist engineers (though not all Trusts were either efficient or successful – some were so bad that people merely had to pay for struggling along the same old ruts!).

As the century progressed, more roads came under Trusts. Better roads meant more traffic could move more quickly, and this greatly aided farming and industry, thus contributing to general prosperity. So great was the improvement on major routes that we can speak of a revolution in transport, but we must guard against exaggeration: in 1820 there were only 22 000 miles under the Trusts out of a total of at least 125 000 miles of roads! The larger Trusts tended to amalgamate for greater efficiency and so could employ outstanding engineers.

John Metcalfe, 'Blind Jack of Knaresborough', blind from the age of six, earned a reputation for building some 180 miles of roads in the Pennines across difficult country, always ensuring that the gradient was suited to horse-drawn traffic and the surface well drained. But the outstanding engineer was Thomas Telford, apprenticed as a stonemason, who journeyed to London and began a career that made him one of the foremost civil engineers of his generation (an excellent biography has been written by L. T. C. Rolt). He learnt much from the French engineers, and his designs for bridges (some still in use today carrying weights unheard of when they were built) owed much to them, but he had his own ideas on road-building: his foundations and drainage works were far superior to Metcalfe's, and he planned his roads so that the gradient was slight, making deep cuttings and embankments as required. The route he chose sometimes led him to by-pass towns (such as the London to Holyhead road), and to utilise the most direct route. His roads were magnificent constructions, but they were very expensive and because of this they could not be built on a large scale. The answer came from John Loudon Macadam, whose road-building was far cheaper and as effective: he paid attention to drainage but concentrated on the surface, which he made firm with a series of layers of finely graded stones well pressed down (tar-macadam came much later to keep down the dust raised by faster-moving motor cars!). In 1815 Macadam was Surveyor of the Bristol Roads and made possible the high coach speeds that Mr Pickwick so admired in Dickens' famous novel of the 1830s, *The Pickwick Papers*.

Turnpike Trusts made the coaching industry possible. Coach-building became a highly skilled business, with new developments allowing for better springing, heavier loads and faster speeds. Special teams of pairs of horses were needed: they had to be much the same size, but the pace-setter (the one on the first right-hand, called the 'parliamentary horse' because Parliament had made it illegal to gallop with a coach) had to be a *very* fast trotter; the second pair, the 'wheelers', had to be heavier and capable of sustained speed. The driver had to be very skilful (his brakes were rudimentary by our standards!), and since the different coach companies rivalled each other in the speed of travel, it was necessary to have frequent changes of teams. This meant a whole new industry of stables and studs, smiths and saddlers, and above all coaching inns at 'staging points' where the horses were changed and travellers could snatch a quick meal, warm themselves (especially if travelling 'outside'), or stay the night.

It was quicker, safer and more comfortable to travel by stage coach (the Royal Mail used them, for their speed was a guarantee against highwaymen),

but it was not cheap! The great coaching days were from 1820 to 1840, when some 150 000 horses were in use and about 30 000 people employed. Forty coaches a day went down the Brighton Road, and speeds of 10 mph were recorded (faster speeds would have killed the horses if maintained for any distance). In 1750 it took four days for a coach to reach London from York; in 1836 it took only twenty hours. But the heyday of the coach was short, for by 1840 the railway (see page 184) had destroyed the industry. (There are many books about coaching, but you might like to look at F. Knight's *Clemency Draper* and Leon Garfield's *Sound of Coaches*).

The canal age

Coaching was for people because it was fast; goods still took a long time. The need here was for an effective means of transporting heavy loads as cheaply (not necessarily as quickly) as possible. Then industry could really expand, coal could be easily transported and farmers at last get adequate supplies of manure and fertilisers such as lime and marl. The answer was canals. River transport had been improved during the century, but canals could be dug in whichever direction you wished, and they were not subject to flooding or changing depths, as rivers are.

Telford's design for London Bridge
This design shows Telford's vision as an engineer – ships could sail under the single span and the bridge would stand because it was made of iron (see p 27). It shows what might be done with this 'new' building material. The bridge was never built: John Rennie constructed a stone bridge, now preserved in the USA!

Make a list of the advantages offered by canal travel, remembering the additional employment it provided, both in building and maintaining the canal and in barge-building and repair work. The principal disadvantages were the limit on loads produced by the height of bridges and the size of locks and canals (British canals are small-scale), and the slow speed of transport – which matters less if the material is not in urgent demand. Then ask yourself why canals should have come so late, for there was nothing new about them and locks had been used for over a century.

The Duke of Bridgewater was the chief promoter of canals. His coal mines at Worsley frequently flooded. His estate manager, John Gilbert conceived the audacious plan of draining the mines through a canal – barges would load up actually *in* the mine – that would continue on to Manchester. He chose James Brindley to build the canal. Brindley was a millwright, so he understood a great deal about water power. He solved the problem of water draining away from the canal by using puddled clay as a lining, and was always careful to ensure an adequate flow of water to the topmost reach of the canal (incredibly enough, some canals failed because this elementary precaution had not been taken!). But the outstanding feature of the Bridgewater Canal was the Barton Aqueduct (1761), acknowledged a wonder of the age. Arthur Young recorded (1770):

> The effect of coming upon the Barton Bridge, and looking down upon a large river, with barges of great burthen sailing on it; and up to another river, hung in the air, with barges towing along it, form altogether a scenery somewhat like enchantment, and exhibit at once a view that must give you an idea of prodigious labour.

The canal almost ruined Bridgewater, but he was able to sell coal in Manchester at less than half the previous price and so he soon recouped his costs. The canal age was born. A host of canal companies were formed to increase the flow of goods (few ever contemplated canals for passengers). Brindley looked towards a time when Britain would be linked by canals between the principal rivers by what he called a 'grand cross', linking Thames, Severn, Mersey and Trent. This idea of a national system was eventually realised after his death, but most of the canals were local ones promoted by men of lesser vision.

Nevertheless, the canals began a 'canal mania' in the 1790s, when a tremendous number of companies were formed. This had its effect on the money market, for small investors were encouraged to risk their savings, and business people gained valuable experience in financial dealings. The idea of *limited liability companies* began to be talked about: they were to develop fully in the nineteenth century. Canals were expensive to maintain and involved much careful legal work. If the canal drew water from a mill (George Eliot's *The Mill on the Floss* deals with such a happening) or a canal reservoir burst its dam, serious legal problems ensued. In order to determine the route, canal companies needed a private Act of Parliament (sometimes involving compulsory purchase). Some of these Acts, together with surveyors' working papers and maps, are in County Record Offices. Some Offices have the minute books and accounts of actual companies.

Visit your local Record Office and seek permission to use the papers for researching into the problem of how canal companies administered their affairs.

Brindley's canals were undramatic and followed contours, so that they meandered a great deal (only occasionally did he dig a tunnel). But Telford built very different canals. His took a definite course, involving deep cuttings, aqueducts and tunnels. They were expensive. His most impressive aqueduct was Pont Cysyllte (1795–1805), where the canal is carried in a continuous iron trough over nineteen great arches. Such achievements were symbols of an age: yet, within a generation, the railway was to replace most of the canals as the more efficient and cheaper means of transport. But during its brief period of dominance, the canal had helped to expand British industry, increasing coal production, encouraging the iron industry (both ores and lime were heavy and costly to transport), and helping the pottery and china industry. Farmers were able to get large loads of lime, marl and manure and transport heavy grain loads to market or to mills.

Pont Cysyllte aqueduct [*opposite*]
This is one of Telford's most remarkable aqueducts, and is well worth a visit. It consists of a long iron trough set on huge stone pillars. The trough was prefabricated, much of the iron coming from local sources. Note the towpath as part of the iron construction. Note the size of the trough – this meant no barge larger than this could use the canal: do you see one of the limitations of constructing canals of this type?

Industrial changes

Just as there were changes in population and in agriculture, there were also changes in industry. Again, there is no simple explanation, but it seems likely that British society was able to respond more quickly than any other at the time to the conditions that prompted change. People were able to take advantage of opportunities and they did so. This is one major reason why England was the first country to *industrialise* in any modern sense of the word. There was prosperity, a growing population able to afford to buy new things, new means of transport to carry large quantities of merchandise, and also industrial changes that made it possible to produce vast quantities of goods. All these developments can be lumped together under the umbrella term **Industrial Revolution**. It took time – far longer than many books imply – and it changed Britain's traditional agricultural society into a modern industrial state.

Traditionally, industry provided for local needs – farming, building and clothing. It was generally on a small scale, in the hands of skilled workers (we would call them craftsmen, but they would not have regarded their skill as anything out of the ordinary). They used tools many of which had been known for thousands of years, and they used machines, some quite complicated, such as those for weaving. Improvements were always being made to these machines: what happened in the eighteenth century was a rapid succession of such improvements. It would be a mistake to think that suddenly a host of inventors with new ideas appeared: eighteenth-century developments were improvements on existing machines – but they made it possible to produce large quantities of goods of a consistent quality at a rate beyond the dreams of any craftsman.

Clever business people saw an opportunity: if such new machines were gathered in one place and driven by water power (later by steam power), vast quantities of goods could be produced quickly and cheaply – what we call *mass production*. The machines would only need unskilled hands to tend them – women and children would do, and cost less than craftsmen! This was the factory of the future, and if it were built by a canal, there would be no transport problem. It only needed one such business person to point the way. This is how the **factory system** develops. Business people can only succeed if conditions are right, but it is they who take the risk. They are the essential link in the Industrial Revolution. We call them by the French term *entrepreneurs*.

What about the industrial workers? Like the agricultural workers, they, too, had to adjust to changes – in their case, much bigger changes. They were to experience a quite different way of life. Skilled workers with control over their own work in a factory now had to take employment as unskilled 'hands' who had to turn up on time and work at the rate of the machine. They would be under severe discipline, for the business person had to train them quickly! Traditional ways disappeared in the new factories and towns. No wonder workers had difficulty getting used to such new conditions. Worse still, their low wages were not enough, for prices were rising steeply because of the war with France (see page 64). Workers' housing, which had never been good, was wretched and overcrowded as well as expensive. No wonder there were protests!

Looking back, we can understand why (we can use *empathy*). Wealthy contemporaries found it more difficult to understand, or even to know what was going on in those new factories and towns. Already, they were beginning to think of 'the workers' as a different class of people. But some thinkers and writers, distressed at what they saw as the passing of an old England, demanded reform. William Cobbett was one of them, and his vigorous writings did much to increase the *political consciousness* of workers in the first two decades of the nineteenth century. Determined to get some improvement in their conditions, the workers demanded the right to vote at Parliamentary elections (see page 90).

Cobbett was a remarkable man. A ploughman's son from Farnham in Hampshire, he had a colourful career as a soldier and journalist. The government soon feared the effect of his newspaper and he became a popular working-class hero, demanding fair play for the 'common Englishman'. It is worth reading his description of the England he loved in his *Rural Rides*. It was an England that was fast changing into what has been called 'the first industrial nation'.

Textile industries

Wool and cloth had been the basis of England's trade for centuries. Cloth was produced by a craft industry in which weavers and their families (including *very* small children) worked up the wool and wove cloth on looms in their houses (You can still see the cottages where the looms would be set by the window, and many local museums show rebuilt looms, some very specialised.) This style of industrial organisation is called the **domestic system**, and it was highly organised and very efficient.

There was no set pattern, for conditions varied in different localities, but in East Anglia and the West

Country, for example, merchants organised the supply of raw material, taking it to the weavers, who worked up an agreed set number of *pieces* according to the quantity of wool, which the merchants collected on their next visit. They then sold the cloth. The system gave the merchants considerable power and most of the profit. The looms were owned by the weavers: it was they who suffered if trade was poor – their looms were idle, and the merchants were cushioned against loss. In Yorkshire, weavers seem to have been better off than elsewhere, preserving a degree of independence, and some of them were part-time small farmers.

A weaver's hours were irregular. He could get through his wool quickly and have the rest of the week to himself – indeed, many worked hard so that they should have time for a drunken week end – this was the origin of *Saint Monday*, an enforced holiday because of the hangover! When weavers moved to a factory, they worked regular hours, but the risks of the business, and the machinery, belonged to the master – in a sense, factories were better for the workers! But they did not see it like this. They saw crowded, noisy, ill-paid and unskilled work under strict discipline replacing their old skills and independence. In a factory, the machine dictated the pace of work – the workers were fined if they were late, and Saint Monday was not allowed! Small wonder that skilled workers resented the new factories and began to unite against their conditions in a way that had simply not been possible under the domestic system: a factory brought together a large workforce and this helped form a political consciousness among the working class.

During the eighteenth century, a series of inventions allowed the textile industry to be transformed. It was the cotton industry that led the way; indeed, the wool industry was slow to take up the inventions and establish factories. But by the 1820s the growing towns of Lancashire (cotton) and West Yorkshire (wool) had become the centres of the textile industry, with factories driven by coal-fired steam engines. The other old centres of the textile trade declined rapidly. There had been a change in the *location* of the industry.

The textile industry was divided into spinning and weaving. Spinning was slow and used a lot of domestic labour; the weavers had to wait for the spinners. Many inventions had been tried, usually developing existing machines: some simply speeded up the work, but others were used by skilful entrepreneurs to establish the factory system.

It is usual to mention John Kay's *flying shuttle* (1733) as the development that began the great changes in the industry. His machine speeded up the weaving process and allowed broadcloth to be conveniently woven by one weaver. But it did not alter the domestic system. However, it did emphasise the need for a more rapid spinning process. Lewis Paul's *roller spinning* machine (1738) only quickened the laborious process of preparing cotton fibre for spinning. The big advance came with James Hargreaves' *spinning jenny* (1764) which allowed several threads to be spun at once. Soon the machine was improved to take sixteen spindles at the same time. The machine was *patented* (registered) in 1770. It cleared the bottle-neck in spinning – but it did not bring the factory system. Also the thread, although good enough for the cross-weave (weft), was too coarse for the length (warp) of the cloth.

It was Richard Arkwright who changed things. He was the *innovator*, an entrepreneur of genius, a man who rose from humble beginnings to be one of the first factory magnates, a model employer and wealthy enough to be welcomed into the traditional gentry class. His foresight and skill in adapting machinery, and his organising talents, made it possible for him to demonstrate the success of the new factory system. In 1769 he developed a *water frame*, a water-powered spinning machine producing thread fit for weft and warp alike. It made cotton goods into almost a new product. He opened a successful factory at Cromford (1771) and another nearby at Belper (1773) – both survive today. In 1780, he opened the biggest factory yet at Manchester, employing 600 workers.

The most important spinning machine was Samuel Crompton's *mule* (1779), a combination of Hargreaves' and Arkwright's machines. It produced thread as fine as any produced by hand, and in much greater quantity. (Soon one operator could handle 1000 spindles and by 1812 the mules had an output equivalent to four million spinning wheels.) British cotton goods could compete on the world market both as quality goods and also as cheap cottons. The mule remained *the* machine until the invention in the USA of the *ring spinning frame* in 1828.

The factory system had arrived and the great gaunt buildings began to dominate the new towns of Lancashire. In the USA Eli Whitney invented the *cotton gin* (1792), making it possible to export the huge quantities of pre-treated cotton that the Lancashire mills were now demanding.

In weaving, the breakthrough came with the Reverend Edmund Cartwright's *power loom* (1784), driven by water (later steam). But it was a crude machine, and it was not until after 1815 that it was improved sufficiently to be used on a large scale. Meanwhile, the huge increase in spinning meant the weavers were in great demand. Many young people trained as handloom weavers (there were some 200 000 in 1811). But, as power looms entered factories, these young, well-off weavers were often put out of a job. No wonder they became active recruits to Chartism (see page 123). But some craft weavers continued to exist as individual craftsmen working on their own account.

If the factory system meant a new machine-dominated world of work, loss of independence and of traditional skills, all of which the worker resented, it also meant the introduction of new skills and professions such as mechanical engineers, industrial chemists (chlorine was used in bleaching) and industrial managers. It meant the huge and continuing increase in production and wealth that helped to build Victorian prosperity. It also encouraged the movements for Parliamentary Reform (see page 90) and for Free Trade (see page 120).

Fig. 7 Increase in cotton production
Note that the huge increase begins in the 1820s, although the inventions had been patented in the previous generation. This shows how long new inventions and methods had to wait to achieve their full impact. ⊗marks the period of the American Civil War when imports from the USA were severely restricted. It was known in Lancashire as the 'cotton famine', and there was great distress and unemployment.

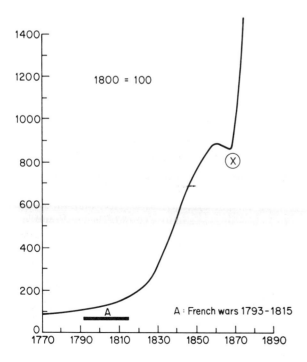

Fig. 8 (a) Employment in textiles
Spinners had been drawn into factories during the 1790s.
(b) Numbers of power looms

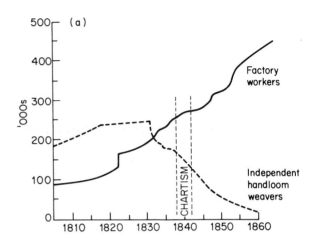

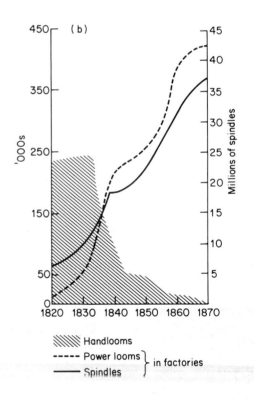

Handlooms
Power looms ⎫ in factories
Spindles ⎭

Look carefully at the information given in Figs 7 and 8. Reread the passage about new textile machinery. Now write a paragraph about what is meant by the industrial revolution in the textile industry, mentioning the timing of changes, the nature of the changes and their effect on the workforce. What do you think it would have been like to have been a highly-skilled handloom weaver in 1805? And in 1845?

Iron

The iron industry changed in the same way as the textile industry: in 1700 it was a craft industry incapable of supplying a large market, and by 1800 it had moved to new areas (locations) and developed quite new techniques that made mass production possible. Traditionally, iron was smelted with charcoal and the industry was centred in woodlands such as the Weald, the Forest of Dean, and Shropshire. It produced high-quality *wrought iron* that could be worked into beautiful shapes, or low-quality iron for nails and pieces of machinery. But the traditional areas were being worked out and costs were rising. If the industry was to expand, it needed a new source of fuel that could combine with lower quality ores. Coal supplied the need, improved transport helped, and the steam engine permitted larger *blast furnaces* to be constructed and power-driven machinery to be used in smelting and processing. Dutch experience helped in devising new methods, and although many iron masters were thinking along similar lines, the major develop-ments in the century were associated with only a few families.

Of these, the best-known is the Darby family of Coalbrookdale, where in 1709 Abraham Darby had used coal, converted into coke, for smelting. His iron was of low quality, but by 1749 his son, Abraham Darby II, was producing pig iron that could be forged into good bar iron. Their Coalbrookdale works has been made into an industrial museum (a visit there, and a research project which the museum organises, is the ideal way to learn about iron-making). Other areas took up coal for smelting – South Wales, Staffordshire, South Yorkshire and the Scottish Lowlands. Abraham Darby III demonstrated the many different uses of iron as a building material. He cast the first iron bridge, using prefabricated sections, and so spanned the Severn near his Coalbrookdale works (1779). Telford built several iron bridges and even projected a huge single-span bridge to replace London Bridge. Iron was now used in country houses, as at Eaton Hall and the Brighton Pavilion, and it was extensively used in large factories as a

Wrought iron gates, Trinity College, Oxford

The first iron bridge, Coalbrookdale, 1779

Fig. 9 Growth of iron, coal and steel production
Note how slow was the rate of increase for both coal and pig iron during and immediately after the Napoleonic Wars – another reason for saying the industrial revolution was not over in a few years. Clearly, it was the Railway Age that released productive capacity. By the end of the century, about 25% of coal, 40% of pig iron and 12% of steel was being exported. This helped to expand the market, so more goods could be produced and sold. Steel had to wait for technological developments before it could be produced on a mass scale and so replace iron (see page 194)

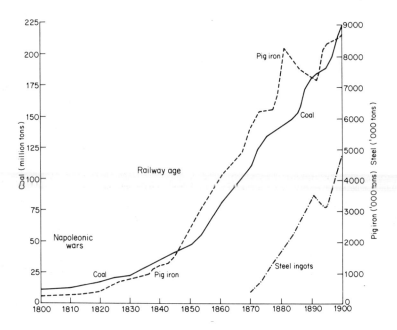

Brighton Pavilion–cast iron support for the kitchen roof
  Cast iron used as a building material is well illustrated
here. The pillar is actually a drainpipe running down the
centre of the kitchen. It is in the form of a palm tree with
the palm leaves in iron at the top.

main framework for carrying the weight of machines on several floors. (You can still see iron-framed Victorian factories today.) Good-quality iron could be used for machinery with moving parts, and by 1800 so many new uses were found for iron that there was an 'iron mania' – furniture and even coffins were made of iron.

John Wilkinson, iron-master of Bilston, Staffordshire, used a steam engine to improve the blast in his furnace and by 1760 he was the leading iron-master of the country (his machine for accurate boring made him particularly important). His son went to France to develop works there. But high-quality iron was only possible after the *puddling process* was developed in 1784 by Peter Onions at Merthyr Tydfil and Henry Cort at Fontley, near Farnham. Neilson's hot blast, economising on fuel in the furnace (1828), completed the major iron developments.

There were also developments in tin-plate, copper and zinc – many of the works are now derelict, but local surveys show how important they were, especially in South Wales. But steel was the great new development of the nineteenth century (see page 194).

Eighteenth-century iron-framed factory building
  This mill, built in 1796, shows how advanced were the designs of the early iron-framed buildings. Much the same technique was still in use in Victorian buildings a hundred years later. Note how much space and light there is.

Watt's steam engine, 1787

This engine was produced at the Boulton-Watt factory at Soho, Birmingham, and incorporated the improvements that made it so successful. The sun and planet gear (A), invented 1781, meant that the engine could be used to drive mill machinery; the centrifugal governor (C) of 1787 allowed it to run at a consistent speed – essential for textile machinery; the 'elegant device' of the parallel motion mechanism (B) which Watt developed in 1784 kept the piston perpendicular without the chains used by the clumsy early bar engines. But Watt did not believe the technology available to him could produce safe engines with pressure greater than air: his engines were all 'atmospheric' ones. The locomotive was a 'high pressure' engine and this is why Watt was not the 'father' of the railway engine.

The steam engine

The coal industry grew during the eighteenth century, but its problems increased as deeper pits were sunk. The steam engine solved many of these problems, and the invention of the safety lamp (in 1815 by Sir Humphrey Davy and also George Stephenson) reduced the danger of explosions. The coal industry made a huge contribution to Britain's prosperity, but it was the steam engine that was the vital link between all the industrial developments. The principle on which it worked had been known for centuries, but the difficulty was making an efficient machine. Thomas Savery managed this in 1698, and Newcomen developed an improved engine in 1711.

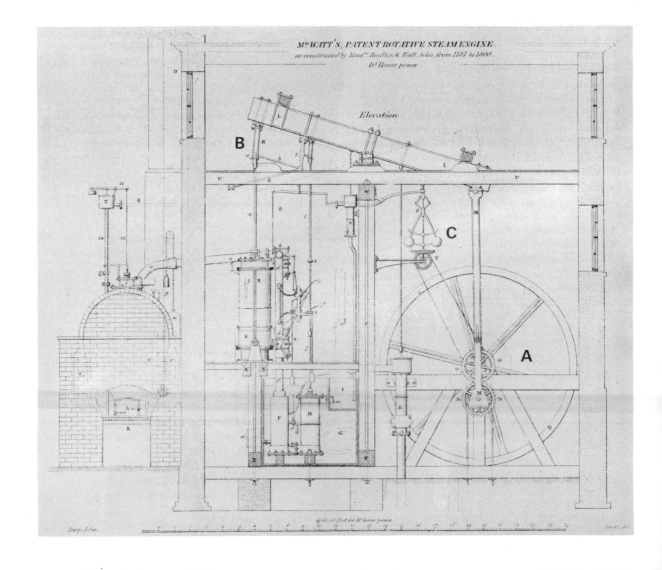

These engines were used for pumping in mines and for drainage. But it was James Watt who, by improving Newcomen's engine, effectively created a new machine. Again, Watt was not the only man working in this field, but his efforts are deservedly remembered.

His career makes a good project for study because it indicates how quite a number of the leading figures of the Industrial Revolution achieved their fame. There are many books available on James Watt. Find one or two in your library and trace Watt's career from his earliest inventions.

He came in contact with some leading scientists, including Dr Roebuck whose Carron works, near Edinburgh, was famous for the naval 'carronade' guns. It was Roebuck's failure in business (1773) that sent Watt to Soho, Birmingham, to begin a profitable partnership with Matthew Boulton, an iron-master and entrepreneur of genius who had made his money producing fire-backs and other items of domestic equipment in iron.

Watt's development of Newcomen's engine had by 1765 produced a machine which was twice as efficient, but the real step forward was the Boulton–Watt engine of 1775, with cylinders bored at John Wilkinson's works. It was confined to pumping, but the *sun and planet* gear (1781) and the *parallel motion* (1784) made it possible to transfer its action from the vertical to the horizontal plane and so to driving machinery by means of an 'endless' belt passing over a wheel. Machinery, especially textile machinery, requires a constant speed so that its action is entirely regular: this was achieved by the *centrifugal governor* (1787). The steam engine was now sufficiently developed for use in factories.

Watt's patent ended in 1800; there were then some 1200 steam engines (321 made at Soho). Thereafter many firms made steam engines and the number of factories grew – but it is easy to exaggerate the impact of steam power: by 1850 it is estimated that steam engines in factories were producing no more than 500 000 horsepower – the vast majority of firms were too small to install them, for they were very expensive to buy.

Summary

Recently there has been a great increase of interest in our industrial heritage and a whole new study of industrial archaeology has appeared. There are many collections of machines in important museums, such as the Science Museums in London and Birmingham, and a number of museums are now opened in old workings. Perhaps, the most well known is Coalbrookdale, or Beamish Open Air Museum, near Durham, but there are others.

If there is an industrial museum reasonably near you, go to visit it and make it the centre of a piece of work for the whole class. You might also arrange with your teacher to tour your local area in search of industrial buildings and machines that are now derelict or about to be taken away. Make a survey of them for posterity. Ask your local Historical Association to put you in touch with an organised industrial archaeological society to help you. There are many books produced on the developments in science and technology, and these, as well as the usual biographies, will make good topics for projects. The Newcomen Society might also help with suggestions, if you get in touch with their London office.

2 The political world in the mid-eighteenth century

How they governed Britain

The political world in 1760 was very different from our own. It was remarkably small, for only a few families, many of them linked by marriage, controlled the political life of the country. Much of the administration was in local hands (the civil service was particularly small) and the Justices of the Peace held considerable power and were expected to take an important part in running the affairs of their counties.

At Westminster were the Houses of Parliament, which did not meet as frequently as they do today. The House of Lords was very much more important then – perhaps as important as the House of Commons – and the titled men of the leading aristocratic families expected to be called upon to be important ministers. These men had great wealth, and greater influence, for very many families depended upon them for their livelihood: a great lord had considerable **patronage** – he was able to offer many 'offices of profit' (jobs) to his relations and to their relations and to a host of others. Sometimes these 'jobs' were important ones; more often they provided a useful addition to a family's income (and normally did not require much actual work). It would not do to offend a great lord – he might remove you and other members of your family from the office you occupied at his pleasure. So a great lord had his 'influence'. It extended to the House of Commons: you might owe your election to his 'influence', and if you hoped to get junior office (and the pay that went with it, for ordinary MPs were not paid until 1911), you would support 'your patron', vote for measures he approved, and vote against measures he disapproved.

If the great lords enjoyed considerable patronage in this way, the King enjoyed even more. Usually, it was not necessary for the King to use his patronage to support political aims he favoured – but he could do so, and he took a greater part in government than has since been the case. Ministers were simply his choice: offend the King and you might find yourself out of office, or unable to gain office. The King did not interfere actively in politics, but he took good care to see that the *ministry* (we would call it the government) was to his liking and followed a policy he approved – few ministries survived if they followed a policy against the King's wishes. The King had no direct influence in the House of Lords (though he had immense social influence) but, like the great lords, he had considerable influence in the House of Commons.

The House of Commons was elected every seven years. All members had to be land-owners – and male. But the *constituencies* for which the members sat differed greatly. There were the county seats, where the *electorate* was fairly large and spread over a wide area, and where it was too expensive to bribe voters on any scale. Then there were the borough constituencies: these varied greatly both in number of electors and in the qualification for the vote (*franchise*). It was in the boroughs that 'influence' was greatest. Some were actually owned by a great lord, or the Crown, in which case the seat would not normally be *contested* (and a remarkably large number of constituencies were uncontested throughout the century): such boroughs were useful in providing a parliamentary seat for younger son, or some other member of the family, or for someone who sought the lord's patronage – and who would support him in the House (or else he would lose the seat at the next election). The Crown controlled many such boroughs, but they were frequently left to be 'managed' by the Ministry (one minister, the Duke of Newcastle, was a master of this art). In other boroughs a great landlord, even if he did not own everything in the borough, might have considerable influence, especially through his tenants, whom he might evict from their house if they voted for the 'wrong' candidate. Bribery was openly resorted to – it was worth being an elector (if you could be, for usually there were not many) because, in a contested election, you would get open bribes, much drink and many dinners from both sides (and each constituency returned two members, which doubled the amount of bribes you might get).

Elections were noisy, disorderly, vigorous affairs; drunkenness was common, rioting not uncommon, and sometimes tricks were played – like getting the

Hogarth's election picture of polling day
This cartoon shows the platform, where one voted in public. You can see the cudgels of hired thugs beside the platform. Those voting are unlikely to be properly qualified to do so – one is an imbecile in a chair, the other, with a wooden leg, is clearly not taken seriously by the clerk, while the lawyer behind him holds up his hands at what he regards as impersonation (passing yourself off as someone else). This was a frequent happening.

other side's voters drunk and locking them in a cellar, or sailing them down the river or even out to sea until the election was over. (This could be costly, because elections did not take place on a single day, but over several days, and a general election might take up to three weeks from the first to the last constituency to vote.) 'Influence', not to say downright intimidation, was practised up to the moment of voting – and afterwards – for voting was in public: the voter mounted a platform, (the *hustings*) identified himself and in a clear voice – for all to hear – declared for whom he voted. A great crowd would be there, some with cudgels who supported one side, others with stout sticks who supported the other side: both sides knew how much the voter had been paid and both were anxious to get his vote. What if the people jostling at the foot of the platform were supporters of the other side? How would the voter get through them after he had voted? There would be no policeman to help him.

You might find it interesting to dramatise this situation in a story or a play about an eighteenth-century election. Remember that the candidates would be anxious to out-bid each other, and if you were the innkeeper you could expect to do a roaring trade; shopkeepers could expect quantities of unwanted goods to be bought – or promised – and individual voters could make quite a deal, if they were lucky. But remember the disorder, and the threats of violence, and the possibility of riots – and the lack of a police force. It was a picturesque world, but a rough one.

Bribery and corruption were normal at election time (the eighteenth century had different standards from our own) and the custom lasted well into the nineteenth century. But already in the eighteenth century the idea that the system of election should be made fairer was gathering support, and

Parliamentary Reform was to become a rallying cry of *reformers* and lead to a great crisis in 1830 (see page 102). Once elected, a member did not support a party – although the names *Whig* and *Tory* existed, political parties as we understand them today did not really begin until the 1860s – he supported the ministry. It was the usual thing to support the ministry, because it was responsible for carrying out the King's government.

Since the defeat of the **Jacobite** threats, there had been no great division of principle in British politics. Many of the members of Parliament were without political ambition – they became members of Parliament from family tradition, or to 'cut their teeth' before succeeding their father in the Lords, or because their wives persuaded them. These were known as the 'country gentlemen': they were unpredictable, for they did not always turn up to vote – but they would do so whenever they felt 'the national cause' was at stake. Usually they were not bribable – they were well off and their ambition was often achieved by merely becoming an MP. But there were others: those whose seats were at the disposal of great lords, or the Crown (the political manager *could* rely on them), and there were others anxious to gain an office of profit for themselves or a member of their family – perhaps nothing more than a commission or a place in the Excise – and these could be relied upon to support the Crown.

Divisions there were in politics, but they were between those fortunate enough to be in office, and the Opposition, who spent their time trying to get into office. If you were in opposition, you could try to make yourself such a nuisance that the ministry would offer you a place or a pension to 'keep you quiet' – and some did this. Otherwise, you hoped the ministry would put a foot wrong and that the King would call on you and your friends instead. Then you would be in office and able to offer patronage to all your supporters. Otherwise you stayed in Opposition.

Since there was no party system, once a stable 'pyramid' of political support had been built up, a ministry was safe. Walpole had managed to do this and since his time each leading politician had tried to recreate the stability he had achieved. The King was a vital force in politics, although he rarely intervened actively. However, with the Hanoverians (the Georges came from Hanover in Germany) it often happened that the King did not get on with his son and heir. Now, if you were in Opposition and the King was growing old, then you paid court to the heir, in the confident belief that on his succession he would dismiss his father's ministers and send for you. Your time would come. (This waiting for the heir to become King was known as the **reversionary interest**.)

When George II, a crotchety old man, died in his closet, Britain was engaged in an expensive, but victorious, Seven Years' War (1756–63). It was his grandson who succeeded him: George III (1760–1820). He was a charming, innocent and perhaps somewhat backward young man of 22. He was physically strong, very upright and moral, and seemed the opposite of everything that was associated with his grandfather. It seemed that a new age had dawned – the young King even issued a proclamation calling for reform of vice and ill-behaviour. He was very popular, for his bluff manner appealed to the people, and he had the highest sense of duty. Furthermore, unlike the previous two Georges, he had no intention of putting the interests of German Hanover above those of Britain. It looked as though Britain was about to enjoy a glorious period and a long reign: there were victories abroad, the young King was popular, and there would not be any reversionary interest for twenty years – until the Prince of Wales would come of age – so the Opposition had no one to form their natural focus. Yet within ten years George himself had become wildly unpopular, at least among the politicians, and had been accused of seeking to establish a **despotism** like that of the Stuarts in the previous century. How did this come about, and was it likely to be true?

When he succeeded to the throne, George III was terribly inexperienced. He put a touching faith in Lord Bute. Bute was a great friend of his mother, the Princess Augusta, whose life had not been happy and who had not been altogether well treated by George II. Bute was also a Scot. The Opposition made great play of Bute's relations with Augusta and of his being a Scotsman. Things might have been easier if Bute had been a capable politician: he was not, and he was easily outplayed by politicians who had learnt their craft under Walpole and knew what they were doing. As for George, the idea that he had a secret desire to establish a despotism was clearly the invention of politicians hoping to get office. He simply had not the ability to carry out such a scheme, even if he had thought of it. He had the greatest respect for the British Constitution, as he conceived of it, and he sought to do his duty. He considered that this involved playing a more active part in politics than the politicians expected, which meant his taking a part in forming ministries.

Certainly George III took an active part in parliamentary affairs, but the first changes of ministry were not due to George's interference. It was not until 1761 that he appointed Bute his minister, and when he proved a failure, it took George nearly ten years of trial and error to find a minister who could re-establish that solid basis of political power that had been typical of Walpole's day (for a Chief Minister had to have control over the Commons). The 1760s, then, seemed very turbulent, with frequent changes of ministry:

1760–61: Newcastle – Elder Pitt (the ministry already in office – Pitt resigned because the ministry would not extend the war to include Spain).
1761–63: Lord Bute
1763–65: Lord Greville
1765–66: Lord Rockingham
1766–68: Earl of Chatham (Elder Pitt)
1768–70: Lord Grafton
1770–82: Lord North

Lord North was the man who was able to establish that stable support necessary for a successful ministry.

Journalists at the time were more outspoken than today (even more outspoken than *Private Eye*, for example) and the journals were full of violent campaigns against the politicians in office, and sometimes, by implication, against the King. Reading the journals now, it is easy to mistake their tone for seething political discontent. But Britain was not in danger of revolution, and historians should be on their guard against highly-coloured writing. Many of the letters and private journals (that of Horace Walpole is especially worth looking at) are full of the political intrigues of the time and show how the campaigns were little more than fights for office between rival politicians. It is surprising that historians for nearly 150 years after 1770 repeated the stories that George was intent on overthrowing ministries in order to assert a new royal power to which he had no right. It is a good example of historians not checking their sources well enough, and not trying to understand how a previous age thought and worked.

'That Devil, Wilkes'

George III had problems trying to handle politicians, and he had particular trouble from John Wilkes, a wealthy and highly popular fellow who showed himself to be a journalist of genius. In 1762 Wilkes launched a journal, the *North Briton* (the name was a dig at Bute, the Scotsman, who got Tobias Smollett, a successful novelist, to run a rival

paper called the *True Briton*). The *North Briton* soon began attacking the government in terms that we would find shocking today, and George can be forgiven for speaking of 'That Devil, Wilkes'. (However, such was the power of Wilkes' personality that later the two men became friends.)

Wilkes was the son of a wealthy distiller who was fashionably educated at Leyden University in the Netherlands (some said he went there because he could indulge his taste for lechery with greater freedom). He was a brilliant conversationalist with a sharp wit that often caused offence, but he was also very good at making friends. His private life was dissolute even by the standards of the eighteenth century, and he became friendly with a group of wealthy lords who were as dissolute as he.

Among Wilkes' friends was Sir Francis Dashwood who formed the Brotherhood of Medmenham Abbey, a group who dressed as monks and held a black mass before resorting to drunken orgies with prostitutes specially sent down from London (and, it was rumoured, they were not always prostitutes). Wilkes joined the Brotherhood, but his sense of humour sometimes got the better of him – on one occasion he hid an ape in a chest during the black mass, releasing it at the moment when the Devil was supposed to appear and terrifying at least one of the Brothers. (If you visit West

John Wilkes, complete with squint

Wycombe, you can see the Hell Fire Club caves where Dashwood held further orgies.) The men who attended these sorts of parties were close relations of the leading politicians of the day, and Wilkes became ambitious for a political career (though some said he was only making a nuisance of himself so that the ministry would offer him a substantial pension, or a favoured post like that of ambassador to Constantinople where he hoped he would have ample opportunity to indulge his particular tastes). In 1757 Lord Temple, one of the powerful Grenville family, helped Wilkes to become MP for Aylesbury at a cost of £7000. Wilkes wrote to his agent, 'I will give two guineas per man, with the promise of whatever more offers. If you think two guineas not enough, I will offer three or even five.'

It was with the help of Charles Churchill that Wilkes launched the *North Briton*. Soon he was involved in a duel with Lord Talbot because of the way he had *lampooned* Talbot in the journal. (As Lord Steward at the Coronation, Talbot had trained his horse to back away from the King, but the horse got it wrong and entered backwards!) The journal was no more than a tiresomely successful Opposition paper at first, but in April 1763, Wilkes produced issue No. 45 of the *North Briton* in which he blamed the ministry for making the Peace of Paris to end the Seven Years' War. Although this Peace brought Britain great gains and was perhaps the apex of her fortunes during the century, it was condemned by some – including the great Elder Pitt – as betraying Britain's real interests. Wilkes was fortunate to find Pitt on his side. But No. 45 went further, for it imputed dishonourable conduct to the King in signing the Peace. George was furious and ordered his ministers to deal with Wilkes.

The row over *North Briton* No. 45 gave Wilkes his first great opportunity to be associated with a number of important causes. Some say he believed in the causes he took up; others say that he merely made use of them if they served his purpose. This first cause was that of the freedom of the individual from *arbitrary* arrest. Grenville ordered a *general warrant* to be issued. This warrant did not name a person but ordered the arrest and seizure of the papers of all concerned with publishing No. 45. Wilkes' house was searched, and in a blaze of publicity he was carried off to the Tower. He challenged the legality of the general warrant and was released by Chief Justice Pratt (later Lord Camden, a personal friend of the Elder Pitt). Later, after a series of important legal cases, general warrants were declared illegal and Wilkes recovered damages: he had scored a triumph for Englishmen against what was represented as an arbitrary mi-

nistry and a despotic King. The 'mob' worshipped him and raised a rallying cry of 'Wilkes and Liberty'.

However, the House of Commons had already declared No. 45 a 'false, scandalous and seditious libel'. To blacken Wilkes' character further, a poem 'Essay on Woman' was produced in the House. It may have been largely written by Charles Churchill, but Wilkes had been concerned with it, and so had a number of MPs. The poem proved to be so obscene, even for eighteenth-century tastes, that members felt justified in condemning Wilkes. They expelled him from the House, and when he failed to appear to answer the charge of issuing a seditious libel, he was declared an outlaw. In fact, Wilkes had escaped to Paris, where he recovered from a serious wound in the groin received in a further duel, thought by some to have been a plot upon his life. His expulsion from the House of Commons made him the defender of the private MP against ministerial despotism, the second of the great causes.

In 1768 Wilkes returned to fight the general election in the City of London (he would have returned earlier, but was disappointed when the Elder Pitt, now the Earl of Chatham, ignored him). He was defeated, but his popularity was very great, especially among the Spitalfields weavers. They were suffering unemployment at the time and took up the cries of 'Wilkes and Liberty', 'No. 45', 'Wilkes for ever'. There were riots – especially as the Irish chairmen were engaged to oppose the Wilkesite 'mob' – and disorders continued until May when the 'St George's Fields Massacre' occurred. In this incident an innocent youth was shot by soldiers who fired on the crowd and killed several others. Wilkes now had some 'martyrs' to give strength to his cause.

Meanwhile, amid scenes of great enthusiasm, Wilkes was elected MP for Middlesex in March 1768. (Middlesex was unusual in being one of the few constituencies with a low franchise of forty shillings, and so had many voters.) Wilkes then insisted on being arrested: he was acquitted on the charge of outlawry, but he had to serve a short sentence for the seditious libel. His time in prison was very comfortable, for he was allowed many visitors and received many gifts, including wines, oysters, swans, and also a special gift of tobacco and turtles from the American colonies – for the colonists, like the London mob, regarded him as a champion of liberty. Wilkes later defended the American colonies in their dispute with the ministry (see page 41) – a third cause with which he was associated.

The House of Commons decided that Wilkes had

to be crushed, and in February 1769 they expelled him from the House on the grounds that his election was technically invalid. This gave Wilkes his fourth great cause – the defence of the right of the electors of Middlesex to return their own choice of MP. He stood for re-election and was returned unopposed. He was promptly re-expelled and equally promptly returned once more. There had to be a fourth election, when he topped the poll with 800 votes more than Colonel Luttrell, who came second. The House insisted Wilkes was not eligible to stand and that Luttrell was therefore the rightful MP. The ministry at the time, under Lord Grafton, was made to appear dictatorial and became very unpopular (so much time was taken up by debates on the Wilkes issue that the Speaker, Sir John Cust, developed internal disorders and died suddenly). Wilkes was helped by the appearance in 1769 of the *Letters of Junius*, a piece of journalism that was very well informed and even more sharp in its criticism of the ministry than the *North Briton* (it remains a mystery who their author was).

Wilkes took up a fifth great cause – that of Parliamentary Reform. After he had become an MP and was allowed to take his seat (1773), he introduced a bill for Parliamentary Reform in 1776. He was less active in this cause (was it because he gained no especial advantage himself from it?), and much of the work was done by Horne Tooke, who formed the Society of the Bill of Rights, and Major Cartwright, who formed the Society for Constitutional Information (1770). (In 1776 Cartwright published *Take Your Choice*, advocating a programme of parliamentary reform that the Chartists (see page 123) were to take up sixty years later.) That Wilkes took little part in these suggests he was no revolutionary, or great reformer.

The sixth great cause with which Wilkes was associated was that of the publication of the debates in Parliament. It was illegal to publish any of the proceedings of Parliament, but the Wilkes debates had prompted many to ignore this and to print their own versions of the debates. In 1771 the House of Commons issued a summons which was intercepted by the Lord Mayor of London, Brass Crosby, and the two City Aldermen, Oliver and Wilkes himself. Lord North, now the King's minister, was wiser than Grafton had been: he proceeded against Brass

The Gordon Riots, 1780
Is the crowd a gang of ruffians? Does the artist support the rioters?

Crosby and Oliver only – they were sent to the Tower temporarily. The 'case of Brass Crosby' did not end the matter of publication of parliamentary debates – they were not published until the nineteenth century, when they appeared officially as 'Hansard' – but it was the end of prosecutions for publishing the proceedings of the House.

Wilkes was now getting older and becoming respectable. He had been made an Alderman of the City of London in 1770 and was made Lord Mayor in 1774. Allowed to take his seat in the Commons, he was no longer a thorn in the ministry's side – even with his support of the American colonists. Perhaps the best example of his change of heart is his action during the Gordon Riots, 1780, when London was in the grip of violent and drunken rioting (the guard that is mounted at the Bank of England every night dates from these riots). There was much disorder, looting, many fires and people feared a really serious outbreak: Wilkes sprang into action, ordering troops and shooting on the rioting mob. (There is a good description of the riots in Dickens' *Barnaby Rudge*.) By 1790 Wilkes had become a friend of the King himself. He died in 1797 and requested that the phrase 'a Friend to Liberty' be engraved on his coffin: was the phrase justified?

It is likely that Wilkes was cynical and used popular support for his own ends, but he represented several great causes. Historians differ in their judgement of him. Some think him a reformer who was sincere in defending the causes with which he was associated. Others think he was simply a typical eighteenth-century politician using these causes to get popularity in the hope of gaining some advantage. You can easily judge which of the two views has been presented here. But historians must be careful about their judgements and check the evidence, reading as much as they can about their subject to take account of all views.

If you have time to investigate the career of Wilkes, you can decide which of the two views you support. There are many books to use but you might like to start with R. Postgate, *That Devil Wilkes*, C. Hibbert, *King Mob* (on the Gordon Riots), P. Quennell, *Four Portraits* and look at some general books such as Steven Watson, *Reign of George III*. Decide which author gives the best picture of Wilkes and then write your own summary and judgement of his career.

3 The American Revolution

The causes of the Revolution

For citizens of the United States, the American Revolution is one of the most important events of all time. For this reason a great deal has been written about it, often from a prejudiced point of view – either the British are painted as brutal and stupid oppressors, or the Americans are presented as an unruly band of hooligans who did not know how to behave, even when the government was treating them well. There are many events in history that continue to be treated in this *partisan* way: if we wish to come to a fair judgement of them, we must consider both sides, look carefully at the evidence and use our own common sense in coming to our own opinion. Certainly, the American Revolution was an important event that sent 'tidal waves' across the Atlantic, but at the beginning, few Americans wanted to be free of Britain – war eventually came after a series of incidents that raised tensions and provoked ill-temper on both sides. It was not planned.

Firstly, one needs to get the Revolution into perspective. It arose because of the change that was overtaking the British Empire. During the eighteenth century the Empire had grown considerably – largely by the addition of territories won in wars with France, Britain's imperial rival. India was gained for Britain during the century and many islands were captured. In North America, not only was Georgia added to the British colonies along the Atlantic coastline, extending these as far as the

---

Fig. 10 The American Colonies, 1756–1763

The French controlled the hinterland westward of the Thirteen Colonies and the Ohio-Mississippi trade route. Both British and French made use of the Indians in their skirmishes and wars.

The Peace of Paris (1763) gave Britain control of the whole of North America east of the Mississippi. The American colonists now hoped to expand westwards beyond the Allegheny Mountains, but the Pontiac Rebellion (1763) caused Grenville to say 'No' and to ban settlement beyond the Proclamation Line. Can you say why the Americans in 1763 were confident and felt less need to look to Britain for their defence?

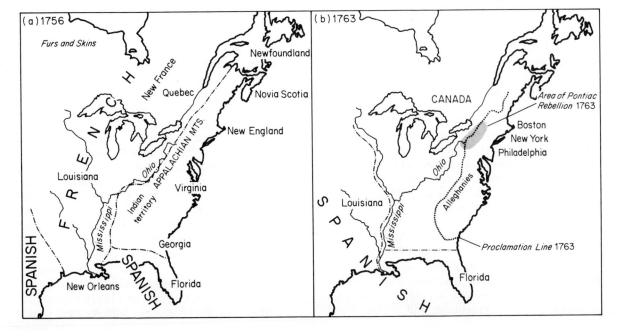

Spanish colony of Florida, but during the Seven Year's War Britain had defeated the French to gain Canada and control of the vast area of the Ohio. By the Peace of Paris, 1763, the apex of Britain's fortunes, she had become the leading imperial power, and France was defeated.

History books tell us a great deal about the battles – Clive at Plassey, Wolfe at Quebec – and make it appear that colonial history was a matter of wars. There were indeed wars, some important ones involving the major countries of Europe, as well as many minor ones, restricted to particular colonies – but the Empire was basically concerned with trade. Because the ministry wanted to safeguard and protect Britain's trade, successive governments were led into assuming control of territories, some of which they had never heard of before. By 1763 there was a growing need to exercise greater control from Westminster to bring some semblance of order to the huge areas across the globe that were now under British influence. The Navigation System (see page 10) kept the trade of the Empire firmly in the hands of British merchants, and in return for the wealth Britain received she was happy to undertake the defence of the colonies, and where necessary to look after their administration. But this system was only loosely applied. By 1763, however, the cost of administration and defence had become alarming and this, quite as much as the need to gain money to pay off the heavy **National Debt** resulting from the Seven Years' War, caused George III's ministries to begin to tighten up the whole system. It was out of this new situation that the American Revolution arose: there was understandable American resentment at increasing British control.

Secondly, we need to appreciate the American position. (Note that I have called them Americans; English people in 1763 would have called them 'colonials' and laughed at their provincial manners and generally scorned them – even such a remarkable man as Benjamin Franklin.)

The Thirteen Colonies were a mixed bunch. The New England group in the north were firmly Protestant, and had strong links with seventeenth-century Dissenters who had come to the Americas in search of freedom of religion – they had a proud tradition of liberty. They had made their colonies rich, and their merchants were highly skilled – it was no wonder that Boston was the centre of resistance to increasing British control. In the middle of this group of colonies was Virginia, a rich land of big plantations, where wealthy farmers, many with slaves, lived luxurious lives. Further south lay Georgia, founded in 1731 as a haven for reformed criminals, prostitutes and others. There

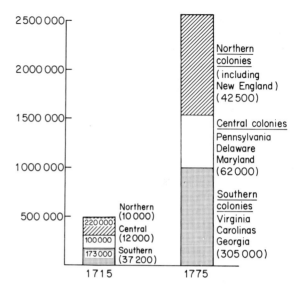

Fig. 11 Growth of the Thirteen colonies

Note the huge increase in population, and that the southern colonies and the New England colonies had roughly the same size population by 1775. Such numbers added to American confidence and their feeling of a sense of 'American identity'. The population of Britain in 1775 was about seven million. (All figures are approximate. Negro figures are in brackets; note the large number in the north.)

was little unity among the colonies in terms of their history, background or commercial interests, but what the British totally failed to understand was that a new consciousness of being 'American' had grown up – and this, quite as much as British mistakes, gave them a unity that took the British quite by surprise. We know already that the Navigation Acts worked to the disadvantage of New England merchants, and that many of them made their money by smuggling or trading illegally in enumerated articles or with different countries. The New England colonies did enjoy one major advantage, however – their prices for shipbuilding undercut British prices, and they were very important for naval stores without which no fleet could even put to sea: in 1760 a Massachusettes ship of 200 tonnes cost £2600, whilst in Britain it would be at least £3000. Virginia and Georgia produced cotton and tobacco, and suffered far less from the Navigation System – even so, as successive ministries restricted trade with the West Indies, these colonies also found their interests being hurt.

The whole situation was changed by the victories of the Seven Years' War and the Treaty of Paris, 1763. As a result, the colonists did not have to fear a French attack from Canada, or French control of the Ohio, or of the Mississippi with its great port, the 'French' city of New Orleans; nor did they have to fear the Spanish in the south. One of the reasons for accepting the Navigation System was removed, and this added to the Americans' sense of security and confidence. The Americans penetrated further into the Ohio – but this expansion was checked by a very serious Red Indian rising, called the Pontiac Rebellion. In panic, lest it be called upon to wage another large-scale war, Grenville's ministry limited the western expansion of the colonies to the Alleghenies. This caused immediate resentment and united New Englanders and Virginians in opposition to Britain – a development Britain quite failed to comprehend. (American Indians played a very important part in colonial history. If you read J. Fennimore Cooper's *The Last of the Mohicans* you will get an impression of this importance.)

Taxation from Westminster

Although the Seven Years' War had resulted in a massive victory for Britain, it had cost a fabulous amount: Grenville felt that the colonists might contribute towards paying off the war debt (since they had benefited from the war) and to the cost of maintaining a small garrison and fleet in American waters to put down piracy. It was quite a reasonable proposition. But he did not seek the advice and support of the assemblies in each of the colonies. Instead, in 1764 he announced stricter control of the trade laws and doubled the list of enumerated articles. There were objections, especially from Massachusetts. In 1764, Grenville also introduced the Sugar Act, reducing the duty on sugar imported into the colonies, but using the navy to ensure that the duty was collected. Boston merchants saw their profits from smuggling diminish, and protested, although they found it difficult to get support because the duty was reduced! This was not a new policy, only a more effective means of enforcing of the existing one.

A much more important development was the Stamp Act of March 1765. A year before, Grenville had announced the idea of a tax in the form of a stamp duty on legal documents and newspapers (a tax that raised no protest in Britain) and allowed a year for the colonies to discuss it and suggest an alternative method of raising the money to meet some of the cost of their defence. Taxes for regulating trade were nothing new, but stamp duty was – it was a tax for revenue, a quite new thing for the colonies, and it gave Boston a splendid rallying cry, 'No taxation without representation'. A constitutional issue had been raised – the Americans argued that the tax had not been voted by any of the assemblies of the colonies and that Westminster had no right to impose it without their consent. Riots broke out against the stamps, and agents dealing with them were ill-treated; some were tarred and feathered. In October a Stamp Congress was held in protest against the Act. The colonists had found a basis for unity, and the Act could not be enforced. Stamps were openly burnt. In the House of Commons itself some important members, such as the Elder Pitt and Edmund Burke, spoke in favour of the colonists. An issue of principle had arisen that was to divide politicians on both sides of the Atlantic.

In March, 1766, Rockingham, the next Chief Minister, repealed the Stamp Act, but passed the Declaratory Act, making it clear that Westminster had the right to tax the Americas directly. The opportunity to pacify the New England colonies had been lost. In 1767 Townshend introduced new duties on lead, glass, paper, tea etc., arguing that such duties were legal. They were met with resistance: Sam Adams of Boston drafted a Massachusetts Letter (1768) that was circulated throughout the colonies asserting the colonists' right to vote their own taxation. There was so much opposition and rioting that New York and Massachusetts had their assemblies suspended, but the disturbances continued. There were riots, but, more significantly, the colonies formed *non-importation agreements* to refuse to purchase any goods affected by the new duties – fashionable American women showed their support by dressing in homespun cloth and refusing to drink tea. Intimidation was widespread of those prepared to compromise themselves by buying the goods and paying the taxes. Indeed, throughout the dispute there was a significant group of people, especially in the southern colonies, who remained firmly against the protests: when the war began, they became known as the Loyalists and they suffered for their beliefs, both during and after the war.

In 1770, Lord North was made minister and he abolished the Townshend Duties, save that on tea. It was possible that this action might have divided the colonists and led to a settlement. But on the very day the duties were abolished in Boston, after considerable provocation, British troops fired on the crowd. There were some casualties and the 'Boston Massacre', as it was called, put fresh heart into opponents of Britain. In June 1772, the *Gaspée*, a naval ship chasing smugglers, ran aground off Rhode Island: after taking off the crew, some colonists burnt the ship. This raised very angry feelings in Britain – many people could not see why the Americans were being so troublesome; they could not appreciate that these 'colonists' were really demanding the right to run their own affairs. Already there were those who spoke of them as 'rebels' and who resented the efforts of men such as Burke to find a basis of compromise or conciliation. Lord North did not react to the insult to the navy over the *Gaspée*, but in May 1773, in order to help the East India Company which was in financial difficulties, he introduced his Tea Act, allowing the Company to import tea directly into the Americas, thus reducing the price by about 50 per cent. This caused consternation among the colonial opposition – could their unity hold against such a tempting price for tea? Smuggling tea would certainly now be unprofitable. The answer took Westminster by surprise. It was probably John Hancock who, on 16 December 1773, led a number of men dressed up as Red Indians to board the ships tied up in Boston harbour and to pitch the tea (to the value of over £10 000) into the sea before it could be unloaded. (There were similar, smaller 'tea parties' in Charleston, New York and Annapolis.)

The government reacted vigorously: the colonists had gone too far. It passed what the Americans immediately called the 'intolerable coercion Acts' of 1774. The Boston Harbour Act closed the port until compensation had been paid; the Massachusetts Government Act placed the colony directly under Whitehall (despite its Royal Charter of 1691) and put Boston under military control. But the colonists' unity had returned, and Sam Adams summoned a continental congress to meet at Philadelphia. All but Georgia sent representatives, where they reaffirmed their loyalty to King George (they did not wish to be called 'rebels') but supported Boston.

Meanwhile, the colonists had been deeply worried by Lord North's Quebec Act 1774. In fact this was not related to the disturbances at all, but was intended to end ten years of military rule in Canada by making arrangements for a new administration. However, it granted liberty of office to Roman Catholics (later this issue of Roman Catholic Emancipation, see page 99, was to become very important

America swallowing the bitter draught

   Published in 1774, the cartoon shows Lord North forcing America to drink from a tea pot. What is in his pocket? Lord Bute stands by with drawn sword labelled 'Military Law'. He is dressed like a Highlander. Lord

Sandwich peeps up her skirts whilst Britannia weeps, and France and Spain look on with interest. The cartoon was originally published by the Opposition in London, but copied and printed in America very quickly by Paul Revere.

to English politics), and the New England Puritans interpreted this as a threat to their religion. The Act also extended the boundary of Canada into the Ohio – the very area into which the New England colonists wished to expand. The Act was statesman-like, and helped to secure the loyalty even of the French in Canada during the ensuing war, but the colonists were convinced that Lord North threatened their interests. A policy of resistance was planned at the First Continental Congress at Philadelphia (to which all colonies except Georgia sent representatives), although the hope of negotiating a suitable settlement with the King was kept open. In February 1775, Lord North published his Conciliation Proposals, suggesting each colony raised its own taxes to pay Britain for its defence and recognised British sovereignty. In return, the Second Continental Congress (May 1775) offered an 'olive branch petition' to George III, suggesting a settlement. But George thought of them as rebels who should be punished.

The American War of Independence

However, in April 1775, the war in effect began at Lexington. Massachusetts had armed its **militia**, and, discovering that some arms were stored at Concord, General Gage sent a small force to seize them. Shots were exchanged along the road and a skirmish took place at Lexington. The arms at Concord were destroyed, but the troops returned to base under a humiliating fire in which British losses were 273 to 60 Americans. The war is usually dated from this skirmish, which features large in popular accounts (you might like to read *The Devil's Disciple*, a play by G. B. Shaw, for a clever portrayal of the attitudes on both sides – although the play is not intended as serious history). British reinforcements arrived at Boston under Generals Howe, Burgoyne and Clinton, and there was every confidence that the 'rebels' would be brought to justice very promptly.

But in May 1775, Benedict Arnold launched an

Fig. 12 The American War of Independence

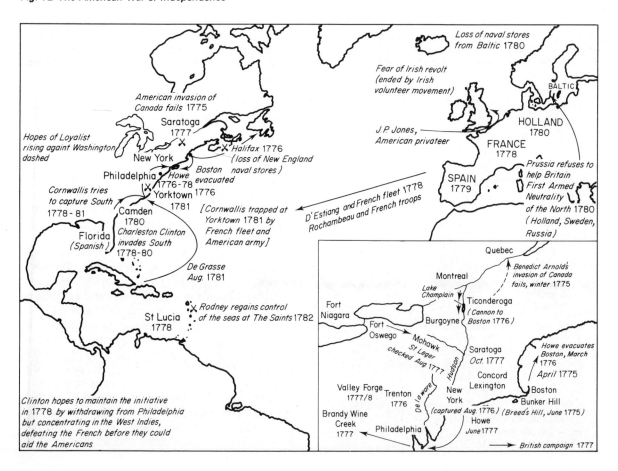

American attack on Canada, taking Fort Ticonderoga without firing a shot. Arnold went on to besiege Quebec, but the invasion failed. Meanwhile, the Americans besieged Boston and Howe decided to take Breed's Hill. The good discipline of the British troops enabled them to storm the American position and win the first real battle of the war – Bunker's Hill, June 1775 – but at the incredible loss of nearly half his army, some 1000 men to the American casualties of 400. The Continental Congress in July appointed George Washington as Commander-in-Chief: the war was in earnest now.

Lord North did not pursue the war with that vigour that had typified the Elder Pitt in the Seven Years' War. Also, Lord Germain, as American Secretary, and Lord Sandwich at the Admiralty were not effective ministers. Many believed the Americans would soon surrender, and expected their unity to break with a rising of the Loyalists.

However, in Britain an increasing number of people agreed with the Americans. In January 1776, Tom Paine produced his pamphlet *Common Sense*, arguing that the only sensible solution was to give the Americans their independence (he was later to be made an honorary American citizen). In February, Silas Deane sailed to France to seek aid for the Americans (France might have helped them against Britain, who had defeated her in 1763). On 4 July 1776, the Third Continental Congress agreed to sign the Declaration of Independence, which Thomas Jefferson had written: there was no going back now. As Benjamin Franklin put it, 'We must hang together, if we are not to hang separately.'

Meanwhile, with tremendous difficulty, fififty-nine guns had been dragged from Fort Ticonderoga and placed above Boston, threatening the harbour. Howe was not prepared now to repeat Bunker's Hill: he evacuated the port (March 1776) and went to Halifax in Nova Scotia. Were the Americans winning? In August Howe showed himself an effective general by launching an attack on New York; the city was his by September.

A tradition has grown up that the British generals were ineffective. You might like to read up about eighteenth century warfare. In Europe armies fought in well-drilled patterns; the British troops were not used to fighting untrained Americans who did not keep their formations. There were other problems, too. When you have read both sides, you will be able to judge whether the tradition of British incompetence – they lost, after all! – is a fair one.

Washington knew the quality of his troops: keen for a fight if the enemy were close to their home, but less keen if it meant travelling far, or being away from home for any length of time. He refused to give Howe a chance of fighting a full battle, which he might very well have lost. Instead he retired beyond the Delaware river, where his army melted away. To restore morale, he made a sudden attack across the Delaware on Christmas night 1776, and defeated the Hessian **mercenaries** encamped at Trenton. This restored American morale, but Washington was still wary of meeting the full British army.

In Britain, pressure was mounting for the war to be won quickly. Not only was it embarrassing that the war had not yet been won, but British efforts to use Indians against the Americans had alienated moderate opinion in the colonies, and the Loyalists had failed to support the British. Furthermore, there was increasing danger of France and other countries joining in on the American side. In 1777 Howe planned a complex campaign that would divide the American forces, weaken them and so lead to victory. Burgoyne would march south from Canada beside the Hudson river, St Leger would march from Fort Oswego beside the Mohawk river, and a force would march north from New York to join them. It was a good plan, but it needed careful coordination and good supplies; both were lacking. Furthermore, Burgoyne, known as 'Gentleman Johnny', although a very popular soldier, has often been portrayed as an ineffective commander (this could be correct, or it could be a means of shifting the blame for a British defeat – ask your teacher for books to read so that you can examine the evidence for the campaign and come to your own conclusion).

In the event, three things went wrong. St Leger was checked quite soon. Howe set off to defeat Washington at Philadelphia – he won the Battle of Brandywine Creek and captured the city, but did not return to New York, and the force that should have marched north along the Hudson to meet Burgoyne failed to do so. Meanwhile, Burgoyne advanced to Ticonderoga and beyond with considerable difficulty along bad roads and hindered by skirmishes. He won an engagement at Freeman's Farm, but had insufficient forces to press home his victory, and so decided to await the troops from New York. He waited three weeks, and by that time General Gates (that 'old midwife', Burgoyne called him) had superior forces. In Europe, where the rules of war were clear, the usual thing to do in such circumstances was *not* to seek a heroic death in a futile battle, but to arrange for suitable and honourable surrender terms and so get out of the danger. Burgoyne did just this: Gates agreed to allow him to return with his troops and weapons to England, on condition he did not fight again. This was what could well have happened in Europe without much comment – indeed, it was to happen again in 1808 (see page 78). But the American War was different: Congress refused to agree to the terms and made the British prisoners of war, and, in Britain and Europe, the surrender at Saratoga (October, 1777) was regarded as a tremendous American victory. It was, indeed, the turning point of the American War of Independence.

Europe enters the War

Europe realised that what had begun as a troublesome episode had now become a full-scale war which the British were in danger of losing. They came in on the American side: first the French in 1778, keen for revenge; then the Spanish in 1779. Prussia, Britain's former ally, refused to aid her – Frederick the Great remembered how Lord Bute had stopped paying him subsidies at a crucial moment in the Seven Years' War and now would not help 'Perfidious Albion', as he called her. In 1780 a further blow hurt Britain: the Dutch had been supplying the Americans, and British naval vessels had stopped Dutch merchantmen to search for *contraband*. The Dutch objected, but Britain refused to let neutral ships continue supplying the enemy. Holland declared war and formed the First Armed Neutrality of the North (1780) with Sweden and Russia, which closed the Baltic to British ships and caused serious shortages of naval stores. Indeed, the British navy was in serious difficulty at the time, and John Paul Jones, the American privateer, sailed at will in the Channel and the North Sea. There was even fear of a rebellion in Ireland, but this was checked by the formation of the Irish Volunteers (see page 52).

A French squadron under Admiral d'Estaing sailed for the Americas, and French troops under Rochambeau went to join Washington, now regarded as a hero in continental Europe (volunteers, including the famous Marquis de Lafayette, had already joined him). The war had changed in nature: it was now a 'world' (or at least European) war, and on her side Britain fought alone. Clinton, who had become commander in 1778, planned to defeat the French in the West Indies before they could invade the colonies (was he an ineffective commander?). He withdrew from Philadelphia, but gained St Lucia in the West Indies. However, the arrival of d'Estaing's squadron off New York seriously hampered his freedom of movement. The Spaniards laid siege to Gibraltar (1779), and there was even fear of invasion from France: the British navy was under very severe pressure. Britain had lost control of the seas. At home, Lord North, seeing how desperate things had become, begged to be allowed to resign, but George III stubbornly refused him. (Some historians have blamed George for this stubbornness, implying that an honourable settlement might have been achieved more quickly if he had been more flexible. But could that settlement have been anything other than the loss of the Americas? No one blamed Churchill in 1940 for refusing to surrender in a similarly desperate situation – has George been too harshly judged?)

Clinton refused to despair. Instead, taking advantage of disagreements among the Americans, he took Georgia in January 1780 and Charleston in May. Cornwallis moved north to attack General Gates, and defeated him at Camden (August 1780), going on to invade Virginia in 1781 (was he yet another ineffective British commander?). By this time Benedict Arnold had deserted to the British and joined Cornwallis. Together, they marched to Yorktown to await reinforcements from Clinton. There, he was besieged on land by French and American forces. A French fleet under de Grasse arrived. Cornwallis was trapped. On 17 October 1781, he asked for surrender terms.

With the surrender of Yorktown, the war was, in effect, won by the Americans. It continued elsewhere – Gibraltar survived the siege and in 1782 Rodney won a tremendous victory at The Saints, regaining for Britain control of the seas. But the American colonies were lost, and at the Treaty of Versailles, which ended the war in 1783 (see page 51), the new United States of America was granted all the land between the Atlantic coast of the former colonies and the Mississippi, and was recognised as a new and independent country. It was a great blow to British prestige – the nadir of Britain's diplomatic fortunes during the century – and George III commented, 'The die is now cast whether this country be a great empire or the least significant of European states'.

Why did Britain lose?

Britain was one of the most powerful states of the eighteenth century and only twelve years before this war had emerged victorious from the Seven Years' War. She was wealthy and had tremendous resources. It is incredible, at first sight, that she should have been defeated. No wonder the war features so much in United States' histories and tends to be passed over quickly in British books!

First, we must blame the leadership of the country. Lord North was a fine politician, but not a war leader like the Elder Pitt. He failed to give that direction the country needed – indeed, he probably hoped that a reasonable settlement, rather than an extended war, might result. Several historians blame George III for interfering and for refusing to replace North (he had to do so when North lost control of the House of Commons in 1782). The ministry itself has been blamed – especially Sandwich and Germain – but several of the junior ministers went on to become very effective under the Younger Pitt in the 1790s.

The commanders have been called ineffective: were they? It is said that the mercenaries, such as the Hessian troops, were ill-disciplined and poor fighters – but European armies were made up of mercenaries at that time. Certainly, there were great problems of supply over 3000 miles of ocean and then across country that was unknown to the soldiers and which was hostile to them. Again, the unconventional manner of fighting of the Americans made the concentrated training of the British army less effective than it might have been – and the Americans' use of rifles proved very effective. It is among these sorts of reasons that the causes of the British defeat are likely to be found. At the same time, Washington was outstanding as a leader (if not a great soldier) and he could inspire devotion and high morale. Even so, and remembering that the Americans were fighting for their lives, their country and their cause, Washington was often in difficulties over his men deserting. For instance, at Valley Forge in the hard winter months of 1777–8 (even despite the victory at Saratoga), he found it very difficult keeping an army together. So it is possible to exaggerate the quality of Washington's leadership and American morale. The Americans knew the countryside and were good at *guerrilla* fighting. (This type of combat, involving small, independent groups, is always difficult for a regular army to deal with – in the 1960s the US forces failed to defeat the communist guerrillas in Vietnam, although the USA was then the most powerful nation the world had ever seen.) Even so, in the War of Independence, American unity would have broken in the end, if the struggle had not changed in nature.

Here is the real cause of the British defeat; the war became a European war and Britain had to fight in different parts of the world as well as in the Americas. Her resources were suddenly over-stretched and there was a developing opinion in Britain that the war should end and the Americans be given their independence. Britain was not united in the war effort. And the European *coalition* that had developed by 1780 created a completely new situation. Britain's loss of control of the seas was a crucial factor, not only in the surrender at Yorktown, but also in the conduct of the war itself. Rodney's great victory at The Saints, by which Britain regained control of the seas, ensured that the Peace of Versailles was not more savage for her – and it is ironic that the French gained so little, in comparison to the help they had given the Americans.

There are very many books on the American War: you should read a good American history and compare it with the British view (a fine exercise in spotting just how biased historians can be!). When you come to make your own judgement, consider as much of the evidence as you can, and think hard about it from a direct and common-sense point of view – remember, for example, how long it took to travel by sailing ship across the Atlantic! You might also like to look at some historical novels that give impressions of the time – for example, Jean Fritz, *Early Thunder*, Esther Forbes, *Johnny Trumain* (on the Boston Tea Party), Ronald Syme, *The Forest Fighters*, Kenneth Roberts, *Rabble in Arms*, and on Burgoyne, Showell Styles, *Gentleman Johnny*. Robert Green, *Sergeant Lamb of the North* tells of the war from a soldier's point of view – quite different from that of the commanders. James Berbery's *Which side are you on?* is about John Paul Jones, and Orlo Miller's *Raiders of the Mohawk* is about that 'forgotten' group, who must have suffered badly, the Empire Loyalists who remained loyal to George III throughout.

The American Revolution had deep roots: it was not merely a dispute over a 'paltry revenue'. The Americans had staked their future on achieving political liberty and independence, and the powerful words of their Declaration of Independence (1776) were to ring out across the Atlantic and to inspire liberals everywhere:

We hold these things to be self-evident, that all men are created equal, that they are endowed by their Creator with certain inalienable Rights, that among these are Life, Liberty and the pursuit of Happiness.

But the division between Britain and the Americans was no simple one.

Consider the points raised by this question:

Contended colonists

It is easy to talk of penal laws, prohibitions and suchlike severities, to be executed by the force of power; but the most effectual and profitable way of restraining the subjects in the Plantations from
5 interfering with Great Britain in her home trade and manufactures will be to take due care that the colonies be always plentifully supplied with British cloths and other European commodities at a much cheaper rate than it is possible for them
10 to raise and manufacture such things within themselves; and likewise that the importation of all such product and manufacture from the colonies, as are fit to supply the wants of Great Britain and to assist the public in the balance of
15 national trade with other countries, be properly encouraged.
    We find by daily experience that men's minds are no other ways to be subdued under a just and free government than by making them feel that it
20 is their interest to submit themselves to, and cheerfully comply with, the laws and ordinances of the State; for as long as the generality of a people are truly sensible that their rulers and governors have nothing so much at heart as the
25 public good of the society, and the honour and prosperity of the Commonwealth, there will be no occasion to apprehend either discontent, insurrection or rebellion.

SIR WILLIAM KEITH, former Governor of Pennsylvania (1738).

(a) The writer expresses his confidence in the 'old colonial system'. What were the aims and principles of this policy? How was it applied?   (8)
(b) Explain 'the balance of national trade with other countries' (lines 14–15).   (2)
(c) The expectations of the second paragraph were soon to be disappointed. How far was Britain's policy of regulating colonial trade a cause of discontent and insurrection in America (lines 27–28)?

O & C

Although the date is 1738, the ideas were still true for 1768. The 'old colonial system' made all colonies part of the British trade system, and Britain administered them and defended them. Through the Navigation Acts she ensured that colonies would not compete with her industries, nor trade with a foreign power, but would provide a ready *market* for British goods – colonial products were absorbed by Britain, or re-exported to Europe and beyond. Note the extract comes from Pennsylvania, a colony producing goods that *competed* with British products; even so, the enumerated articles (see page 9) led New England merchants to become smugglers and increasingly to resent trade restrictions, especially when Grenville began to tighten and enforce them after 1763.

The 'balance of national trade with other countries' was the desire of governments to achieve as close a balance as possible between the value of exports and of imports – if these were balanced, the country 'lost' no gold; otherwise valuable wealth (it was supposed) would be drained away to the disadvantage of the home country. (This has been called the **mercantilist theory**.) Britain, possessing a large Empire, had less need to trade with other foreign countries and so did not fear such losses.

Problems arose when a colony felt its products were being discriminated against in order to *protect* British merchants. Again, colonists were angry at restrictions against trading with other countries and their empires. This was the case with Boston (see page 40). Their anger increased as the system was tightened and new regulations imposed after 1763. But there was more than trade involved. Britain failed to appreciate the force of American opinion, and did not make concessions early enough. A *constitutional* point was added with the Stamp and Declaratory Acts, and the succeeding disorder culminated in the 'Intolerable Acts' of 1774. What drove the two sides to war was Britain's determination to assert her right to control American affairs, and the equally strong determination of the Americans to resist. It was more than trade regulations that divided them.

Notice that I have given you the basis for an answer to the questions – a basis only, since there is not enough information included to support the answers with evidence. You can supply this by reading through the relevant parts of the book so far and filling in these facts (remember that the figures beside the questions denote the marks given and so indicate the amount you should write, since you cannot earn more than the maximum!). It is a skilful question, for it leads you on to reveal how well you know your facts, but also whether you can reveal their significance and *interpret* them in terms of the ideas of the time.

    Now try this second example. Here the questions are closely related to the passage and do not allow you to display so much background knowledge – but the last question asks for an *evaluation* to explain why so many politicians at first supported Lord North and George III. The passage gives an impression of the Elder Pitt's oratory, and shows his wisdom – remember to look at the date.

Chatham on the American Colonies

I contend not for indulgence, but justice to America; a brave, generous, and united people, with arms in their hands, and courage in their hearts; three millions of people, the genuine
5 descendants of a valiant and pious ancestry, driven to those deserts by the narrow maxims of a superstitious tyranny.

Their resistance to your arbitrary system of taxation might have been foreseen: it was ob-
10 vious from the nature of things, and of mankind; and above all, from the Whiggish spirit flourishing in that country.

This country superintends and controls their trade and navigation; but they tax themselves.
15 Trade is an extended and complicated consideration; it reaches as far as ships can sail or winds can blow; it is a great and various machine. To regulate the numberless movements of its several parts, and combine them with effect, for the good
20 of the whole, requires the superintending wisdom and energy of the supreme power in the Empire.

But this supreme power has no effect towards internal taxation, for it does not exist in that
25 relation; there is no such thing, no such idea in this constitution, as a supreme power operating upon property. Let this distinction remain for ever ascertained; taxation is theirs, commercial regulation is ours.
30 We shall be forced ultimately to retract; let us restrain while we can, not when we must. I say we must necessarily undo these violent oppressive Acts; they must be repealed—you will repeal them; I pledge myself for it, that you will in the
35 end repeal them. Avoid, then, this humiliating, disgraceful necessity.

House of Lords, 20 January 1775

(a) Explain 'the genuine descendants of a valiant and pious ancestry' (lines 4–5).   (2)
(b) What does Chatham mean by 'the Whiggish spirit' (lines 11–12)?   (2)
(c) In what ways had the British Government imposed 'internal taxation' on the colonies (line 24)?   (4)
(d) In what ways was 'commercial regulation' (lines 28–29) applied?   (4)
(e) What 'violent oppressive Acts' does Chatham refer to (lines 32–33)?   (4)
(f) Most politicians disagreed with Chatham. Why?   (4)

O & C

The rest of the Empire

The loss of the Thirteen Colonies was not a blow to Britain's trade and wealth, for these grew so rapidly at this very time that we have come to speak of a 'take-off into self-sustained economic growth' (see page 11). Does this suggest to you that the theory on which the old colonial system was based, namely that it was necessary to control one's trade and keep it within one's own system, was not sound? The new United States was left struggling. Britain retained effective control of the West Indies trade (sugar and slaves particularly) and tried to exclude United States ships. At last a commercial treaty, the Jay Treaty, 1794, was signed. It was so much to British advantage that there were riots in the States and Jay was burnt in *effigy*. In the 1790s no one would have imagined that within 150 years the USA would have become the most powerful nation the world had ever seen.

But the loss of the Thirteen Colonies was a tremendous blow to British prestige and seemed to mark the end of a chapter of imperial history. Indeed, some historians have spoken of it ending the 'first British Empire'. Some have suggested that the British turned away from the idea of Empire, disheartened at their defeat and at what they considered the ingratitude of the Americans; others have spoken of a rebuilding of the Empire on new lines, learning from the lessons of the American Revolution – 'The British must learn the lessons of their failure, building a wiser and wider Commonwealth on the wreckage of the Old Empire.'

But *did* the loss of the Americas mark a change in the history of the Empire? The evidence suggests exactly the opposite view. (In history, it is possible to come to different conclusions: you must look at the evidence, follow the arguments and then decide which interpretation is most convincing.) One of the causes of the American Revolution had been the tightening of the Navigation Acts and the strengthening of controls by Westminster. Britain's defeat in the war was not followed by any general relaxation of trade controls – indeed, the very policies that had provoked the Americans to rebel were continued elsewhere. Controls from Westminster were strengthened, not weakened.

Canada and Australia

Canada, for example, gained by Britain in 1763, had been allowed a good deal of local *self-government*, including Roman Catholic Emancipation (see page 42) by the Quebec Act 1774 – a statesmanlike measure by Lord North. Canada remained loyal during the American War, even when France joined on the American side. But the United Empire Loyalists left the new United States and settled in Upper Canada, the region of the Great Lakes' Peninsula. Soon there was active hostility between them and the French Canadians in Lower Canada. The Younger Pitt provided the solution in his Canada Act 1791 – he increased the power of Westminster. Canada was divided into two provinces, Upper and Lower Canada, each with its own assemblies, but the real power lay in the hands of the Governor-General, appointed and controlled from Westminster. The Act calmed the situation and removed any fear of the Americans seizing Canada (they tried, unsuccessfully during the 1812–1814 war), but there was no departure from existing policy.

The same was true of Eastern Australia, which Captain Cook had surveyed after mapping the New Zealand coastline. In 1788 the Younger Pitt began penal settlements in Australia (the many criminals convicted in Britain could no longer be sent to the Thirteen Colonies!). These penal settlements were closely controlled from Westminster, and the colonisation of Australia partly developed from them.

Life was hard in the early colonies and the penal settlements. You might like to read up about the early history of Australia and New Zealand. Three novels by Doris Chadwick give a picture of Botany Bay and the settlers; they are *John of the Sirius, John of Sydney Cove,* and *John and Nanbaree.*

India

There was no change in the developing policy towards India, the source of so much of Britain's eighteenth-century wealth. At the time of the Seven Years' War, Britain had defeated the French in India and gained control of Bengal and the Carnatic (see Fig. 13). The East India Company had the *monopoly* of the India trade and was responsible for maintaining British interests there – but British success had been such that the Company was now faced with something more than trading problems: it had to take charge of administering vast areas of India, and of defending them, too. Indian affairs took up a great deal of time in the House of Commons and became the concern of many import-

ant politicians. (You could make a project by studying the careers of Clive or Warren Hastings, whose **impeachment** lasted for so long, 1788–95.)

A major problem was the activity of Hyder Ali of Mysore, who gained the help of the French to attack the Carnatic several times. The Company had got into serious financial difficulties by 1772, as a result of dealing with these attacks. Lord North's solution was to increase Westminster's control. His Regulating Act 1773 transferred the Company's territory to the Crown (it was the financial arrangements of this Act that led to the Boston Tea Party, see page 42). A Governor-General (Warren Hastings) was appointed, aided by a Council of Four. North's Act went far to solve the immediate problem. Lord North, indeed, is often given too little credit for his achievements: it is true that he must bear part of the responsibility for the loss of the Americas, and he had certainly lost control of the House of Commons by 1780 – but he was a fine leading minister up to 1774, when most MPs looked to him to 'teach those damned colonials a lesson!'

Fig. 13 British India in the 18th Century

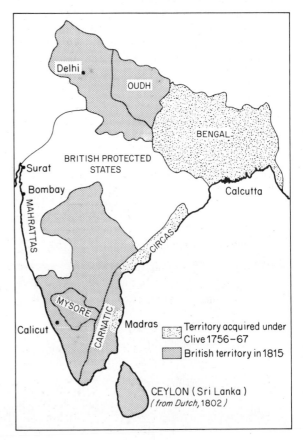

Find out about the career of Lord North. He had become a junior minister at the age of 26 in 1759 and was only 37 when the King chose him as leading minister. His position was unchallenged until after 1774, when he was ruined by the American War. He was skilled in finance, and a number of his reforms were later put into effect by the Younger Pitt. His handling of India, Canada, and Ireland (see below) deserve praise. But as the American War dragged on into defeat, he lost control and the Opposition made good use of their opportunities. Burke was able to carry through proposals to reform the way politicians ran the country, and in 1780 came Dunning's famous motion, 'that the influence of the Crown has increased, is increasing, and ought to be diminished'. At last George III agreed to let North resign (March 1782), but North's career was not by any means finished. Make a list of the reforms with which he is to be associated throughout his career and then decide whether he deserves to be so neglected by historians.

The Regulating Act did not stop Hyder Ali, and further wars began in the Carnatic in 1778 (note that this was at the height of the American War). Fighting lasted until 1784, by which time Hyder Ali had been succeeded by his remarkable son, Tipu Sahib, and the East India Company was again in serious financial difficulties. Charles James Fox tried to settle the matter with his India Bill 1783 (actually it was drafted by Burke), but it was defeated (see page 55) and in the following year the Younger Pitt passed his India Act 1784 which placed the administration of India firmly in the hands of the Governor-General and restricted the East India Company to trading only. There was no new development of policy here – Dundas, Pitt's friend, said that 'a direct interference by Government with affairs of India is necessary . . . I am more and more convinced.'

The new Governor-General was Cornwallis (1789–1793), – the man who had surrendered at Yorktown. (Does this support the view that he was an ineffective soldier?) There were further wars between 1790 and 1805, where Britain's enemies were again helped by the French. Tipu Sahib was killed and his capital looted – and the future Duke of Wellington gained good experience in the wars. By 1815, Britain controlled most of India.

Whatever lessons were to be learned from the loss of the Americas, there does not seem to have been any particular change of policy towards the Empire in the second half of the eighteenth century. Nor does there seem to have been any unwillingness for Britain to gain more territory. A comparison of the three major treaties between 1763 (Paris) and the Congress of Vienna, 1815 (see page 82) shows both what a close relationship there was among them, and how much territory had been added by 1815.

Tipu Sahib's musical box

The French gave Tipu Sahib this musical organ box (now in the Victoria and Albert Museum, and still in working order). It is in the form of a British East India servant being eaten by a tiger. Can you guess the meaning, and who is represented by the tiger? It is important to remember that French interest in India lasted until at least the end of the eighteenth century.

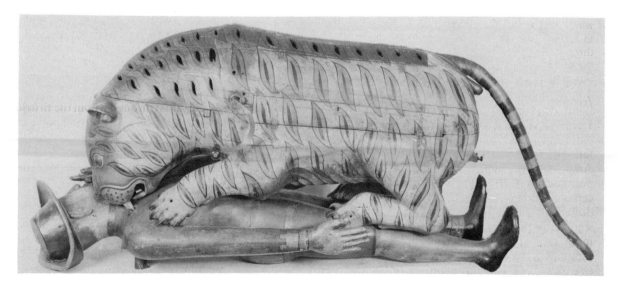

Growth of the British Empire

Treaty of Paris (1763) (the apex of Britain's fortunes in the eighteenth century)	Treaty of Versailles (1783) (the nadir of Britain's fortunes in the eighteenth century)	Congress of Vienna (1815) (Britain's fortunes restored)
America: Canada from France Ohio Valley from France Florida from Spain (The Thirteen Colonies held)	Ohio Valley to USA Florida to Spain (The Thirteen Colonies become USA)	
West Indies: Tobago, St Vincent, Dominica, Grenadines gained	Tobago and St Lucia to France	Tobago and St Lucia from France Trinidad and British Honduras from Spain British Guiana (£3 million paid to the Dutch)
Africa: Senegal from France	Senegal to France	Cape Colony (£6 million paid to the Dutch)
Indian Ocean: (British controls India after French defeated there)		Mauritius, Ceylon (Sri Lanka) (1802) Malacea (1824) Singapore (Raffles post 1822)
Europe: Minorca from Spain	Minorca to Spain	Malta and Ionian Islands, Heligoland from Denmark, Hanover restored

Throughout the period Britain extended her power in India. She also held Gibraltar, Jamaica, the Bermudas, Australia – and subsequently New Zealand, and other small islands.

There is a clear connecting link between the three treaties. After the Seven Years' War, Britain was moderate in her demands (1763), except in North America. Twenty years later she had lost everything except Canada in North America, but only a few minor colonies elsewhere; that Versailles was not a more unfavourable treaty to Britain was due to her regaining control of the seas through Rodney's great victory at the Saints. Control of the seas allowed Britain to blockade France and extend her Empire and trade during the wars with France between 1793 and 1815. As in 1763, her gains in 1815 were moderate – but she had established herself as the world's most important trading power.

In the difficult period after the Treaty of Versailles, the Younger Pitt's Imperial Policy did much to hold the Empire together (e.g. his India Act, 1784, and his Canada Act, 1791). In addition, the settlement of Australia (and subsequently of New Zealand, which Captain Cook had charted) was begun when Botany Bay was opened as a convict settlement in 1788. (This was an alternative to sending the convicts to North America, which had become the USA in 1783.)

Ireland

Ireland at this time was a colony, although, being so close to Britain, she was treated somewhat differently. Here again, despite all the troubles with America, there seems to have been no change in policy towards Ireland during the second half of the century. There were several important factors that dominated Irish conditions. Firstly, there were significant trade restrictions that protected British industry at the expense of the Irish, and tended to reduce Ireland to an agricultural country (and a poor one at that). Secondly, many of the land-owners were Protestants (through whom the British government controlled local affairs in Ireland), and they were often wealthy *absentee landlords* who left their estates in the hands of bailiffs, who could be very hard men and oppressive towards the poor Irish peasantry. Most of the Irish people were Roman Catholic, and the division between them and the Protestants was and remains one of the most important and disruptive elements in Irish life.

At the time, all the Acts of the English Parliament applied to Ireland, and the Irish Parliament at Dublin was corrupt and managed by 'undertakers', as they were called, in the interests of Britain. At Dublin Castle, the Lord Lieutenant was in charge of an administration that most Irish hated as an alien and exploiting force. At any time there could be serious disturbances, and the British army was employed to keep order, should there be a hint of rebellion, by shooting, burning cottages and flogging peasants. There was bitter hatred between peasant and landlord, Irish and British. Would Ireland rebel in the same way as the Americas? Irish trade was very badly affected by the American War, and the American privateer, John Paul Jones, cruised off the Irish coast.

In fact, the Irish did not take advantage of Britain's difficulties in order to rebel – this was probably due to the outstanding leadership of Irish politicians such as Flood and Grattan, who sought reform, not revolution. They were men of vision who saw the possibility of progress in cooperation with Britain – but they found it difficult to convince their own supporters. They had disappointments, too. For example, Lord North's attempts in 1778 to help Irish trade were checked by British merchants who did not want competition (the Younger Pitt was to have the same experience in the 1780s). The Irish replied with non-importation agreements, like those of the American colonies (see page 41), and the demand was raised for Irish independence. Would the French invade Ireland and lead a full-scale rebellion? (Do you see here another reason why North had so much difficulty during the American War, and why so many factors aided the Americans to victory? Not only had the war by 1778 become a European one, but North was faced with serious problems in different parts of the globe all at the same time.)

Henry Grattan helped to form a Volunteer Force (they were largely wealthy Protestants) who kept control of the country, and fears of a French invasion lessened. In 1778 North was able to induce a grateful English House of Commons to repeal some of the worst effects of the harsh penal code from which Irish peasants suffered. But agitation continued, with demands for free trade and concessions – concessions had been made with far less cause to the Americans, after all! In 1780 Lord North was able to allow freer trade for Ireland, but Grattan was not satisfied and a great meeting of Volunteers took place at Dungannon (February, 1782) demanding independence for the Irish Parliament. Fearing rebellion, the new government under Rockingham (who succeeded North in March, 1782) granted legislative independence for Ireland – but the administration remained as firmly as ever in the hands of English officials at Dublin Castle!

Demands for parliamentary reform soon followed, especially for the vote to be given to Roman Catholics. Grattan threw his weight behind the movement, but little progress was made. There was a demand, also, for Roman Catholic Emancipation in Ireland, and for a brief period in the 1780s and 1790s there was reasonably close cooperation between Irish Protestants and Roman Catholics to achieve further reform. In 1791, Wolfe Tone, one of Ireland's great leaders, formed the Society of United Irishmen demanding Roman Catholic Emancipation and reform. He was a Protestant and hoped to promote Irish unity, but his movement was soon dominated by Roman Catholics who sought to overthrow the Protestant domination, and to be separate from England. He was also greatly influenced by the French Revolution (see page 59) and was made an honorary French citizen. Fear of a French invasion, when war began again in 1793, led the Younger Pitt to grant Roman Catholics in Ireland the vote – but an attempt to grant Roman Catholic Emancipation in 1795 failed. Although there were a number of reforms for Ireland, they arose from Irish agitation and fear of the French, rather than from any wish to avoid the mistakes that had led to the American War.

4 Reform at home

Major political figures

In the eighteenth century, loyalty to particular leaders was very important in the House of Commons. Party names existed – Tories were generally on the side of the King's minister, Whigs frequently against him – but such names were of no great significance and even major politicians changed from one to the other without difficulty. The King's influence was important in politics (though not as great as some politicians at the time tried to make out), but just as important was the quality of political leaders in the Commons. There were some very great leaders whose power of oratory was such as to swing opinion in their favour when they spoke. The Elder Pitt was one; so was his son. So, also, were Henry Fox, Lord Holland, and his son Charles James Fox. Indeed, there was intense rivalry between the two fathers and the two sons. It was a rivalry based as much on differences of personality as on ambition for political power, for they were all passionately ambitious. The rivalry between Charles James Fox and the Younger William Pitt is the more famous, for it came at a time when England was threatened by great dangers.

The Younger Pitt

His father intended William to have a great political career – as a young boy he was brought downstairs late at night so that he might stand on the dinner table and address the Elder Pitt's guests (leading ministers of the day) as though he were speaking in the House of Commons. And he enjoyed it. Once, he said that he was glad that he was the *younger* son, for this meant his elder brother would succeed his father as Earl of Chatham and go to the Lords so that he could make his career in the Commons. He was single-minded in his pursuit of political power and more than fulfilled his father's hopes.

Born in 1759, a delicate child, he was returned in 1781 for the family *pocket borough* of Appleby and astounded the House of Commons with one of the greatest maiden speeches ever made. Here was a 'chip off the old block' indeed, a brilliant speaker with a powerful mind, capable of explaining in simple terms complicated financial matters that puzzled older members. He was not prepared to accept anything but the highest office, and was made Chancellor of the Exchequer in Shelburne's short-lived ministry of 1782. Within a couple of years he was to become unassailable as the King's personal choice of leading minister. (How old was William them?) For the next twenty years the Younger Pitt held this post, and his reputation in history is very great. He was responsible for many reforms and the country was prosperous under him (was this because of Pitt, or because of that 'take-off into self-sustained economic growth'? – see page 11). Then came the long war with France and Pitt struggled on, refusing to make an unfavourable peace.

In the end Pitt worked himself to death, for he would pore over documents and reports until the small hours so that he mastered every detail of the problems he had to deal with, and then he would be up early to see and examine experts, then to the House of Commons to defend his ministry's policies and so back to long hours of detailed work. Although he was so fine a financier, his own affairs were left to take care of themselves, and more than once he was in danger of being imprisoned for debt – his friends (and he had few friends) eventually persuaded him to let them look after his household affairs. Perhaps his only fault was drinking too much port, often alone. He was a great patriot, and a great *parliamentarian*, whose fame has lasted into our own century – yet he was not a likeable man.

When you have read about the Younger Pitt as a peace and a war minister, make a list of his achievements and try to decide whether he deserves the tremendous reputation he enjoys (see page 58).

Charles James Fox

Fox was Pitt's opposite in almost everything. He, too, was intended for a political career and was not even twenty-one when he was elected to the Commons (until the 1960s the age of majority was twenty-one). He had a very unconventional upbringing and turned out to be a warm, happy, outgoing man with lots of close friends: he was a rake, a gambler, a womaniser and has often been blamed for leading the Prince of Wales astray (certainly, he knew more than most about Mrs Fitzherbert – try to discover the story of the Prince of Wales and Mrs Fitzherbert and why his relations with her were so important). A brilliant speaker who could sway the Commons by his appeal to their emotions, he was older than his rival and much more likely to become leading minister. Why did he fail in this ambition? It was partly that his judgement was less cool and keen than Pitt's,

partly that he was too willing to change sides for personal advantage (even his contemporaries felt he went too far on occasions), but mostly it was because the King hated him. George III hated him because of his policies and his opposition to Lord North over the American War, but he hated him more for leading his son and heir into bad ways. Fox knew what he was doing: when the Prince of Wales came of age (actually when he was eighteen) the reversionary interest (see page 34) returned to English politics. The King was determined not to be saddled with Fox as minister.

When Fox was elected to the Commons he supported Lord North, but the latter broke with him over demands for parliamentary reform and over Fox's support for the Americans. Fox's attacks on North proved very damaging and brought the country gentlemen into the House to vote against the minister. Eventually, in March 1782, George III agreed to let North resign. Rockingham was im-

'The Fox and the Badger both in a Hole' – a contemporary cartoon of the Fox-North coalition
This coalition of two political enemies shocked contemporaries. A host of political cartoons was produced underlining how unlikely was the cooperation of Fox and North. This cartoon shows a badger and a fox sitting together. Which is meant to be North, and why? Beside them hides the devil, complete with horns and tail. Why do you think he is portrayed? Examine the title. What might lead you to say it has a double meaning?

posed on the King as his Chief Minister, with Fox as Secretary of State. When Rockingham died in July, Shelburne succeeded him – he appointed the Younger Pitt Chancellor of the Exchequer, so Pitt and Fox were together in the same ministry.

However, Shelburne proved a poor leader and Fox began scheming against him. (This is an example of how very personal politics were. If the King's choice of minister lost control, as North had done, then there was chaos and open squabbling.) The Younger Pitt played his cards well: he refused to join any scheme against Shelburne, and Fox was compelled to seek Lord North as his ally. Together, they defeated Shelburne and imposed themselves as the Fox–North coalition, in April 1783. The King was beside himself with rage, but he had to accept the ministry – for the moment. The coalition was thought an impossibility – the two leaders had become such bitter opponents that it seemed too much, even for eighteenth-century morals, that they should get together. This helped the King, for it was not a popular ministry: when it introduced Fox's India Bill, George let it be known in the Lords that anyone voting for the measure would be 'no friend of his'. On 17 December the Bill was rejected and the ministry contemptuously dismissed. There were howls from the Foxites that the King was behaving unconstitutionally. The howls became agonised when the King appointed the Younger Pitt as Chief Minister.

Pitt in office

George chose Pitt because he was not stained by the Fox–North coalition, because his ability was well recognised and because the country gentlemen would vote for him, because he was young (and George intended that Pitt should do as he was told) and, finally, because he had the magic name of William Pitt and had already shown himself a worthy son of his father. George was not disappointed, for Pitt had not only the King's support, he also had great personal courage. He needed it, for his ministry had no majority in the Commons and it was jeered at and subjected to ferocious opposition by the Foxites. That 'mince-pie' ministry, they called it. But, once again, Fox overplayed his hand. By March 1784, Pitt's courage in riding out the storm was rewarded, for the country gentlemen began to desert Fox. Then Pitt asked the King to *dissolve* the House. At the succeeding General Election of 1784, Fox's supporters suffered very badly indeed – Fox's Martyrs, they were called. Pitt won a safe majority.

Was it because of popular support, or was it the money spent by the Treasury to bribe voters? (Every effort was made to defeat Fox at Westminster, one of the most democratic constituencies, and even when Fox was returned, Pitt tried unsuccessfully to get his election declared invalid.) Write an account of the Westminster election (there are many sources) showing how Fox got important duchesses to support him, allowing voters to kiss them if they voted for Fox.

Pitt's majority was a safe one, but he knew well that he had to tread softly and not antagonise the King, or press his supporters too far. He was the King's minister and knew that his future lay in the King's hands. As to George, he had every reason to congratulate himself. Twenty years before he had dabbled in politics with Lord Bute, and the politicians had proved too clever and too strong for him (see page 35). He was young and innocent then, but now he had shown that he could manage politicians and overthrow a ministry that was distasteful to him. It is important to remember in any question on the power of the King that he was a force in politics: the Younger Pitt was well aware of it.

Fox in opposition

Fox remained in the House as leader of a strong group of politicians opposed to Pitt. He was still a powerful leader when the French Revolution happened – a revolution that was welcomed by very many in England. But, here again he 'backed the wrong horse'. As the Revolution developed and began to show violent tendencies, opinion changed. Pitt changed with public opinion, and when the war came in 1793, he put himself at the head of a patriotic struggle against the revolutionaries. Fox continued to support the principles of 'Liberty, Equality, Fraternity' which the revolutionaries proclaimed in 1789, but he became progressively unpopular as the war dragged on. By the end of the century he had even stopped attending the House of Commons. Fox had a brilliant career: was it, in the end, a failure? Unlike Pitt, he had a capacity for seeing what future generations would welcome as right, and many of his ideas were later to be accepted. He passed on to his supporters three great principles: the abolition of slavery, parliamentary reform, and Roman Catholic Emancipation – all achieved within thirty years of his death – and his defence of personal liberty has become part of the British tradition.

You have read a lot about Fox in this chapter. Find
library books on his career, or about the politics of
his day. You will see that a number of historians
have been fascinated by his career, and some of
the larger volumes will contain extracts from his
speeches and letters from his friends. He was a
warm and lovable character – was his career altogether a failure? Your task is to make an *assessment*
of Fox as a person and a politician. He died in
1807.

Pitt's reforms

When Pitt was appointed leading minister, the
country had just emerged from the disastrous
American War and had signed the Peace of
Versailles (1783). It was a moment of defeat, and
many must have felt that the country would take a
long time to recover. But, ten years later, Britain
stood unquestioned as the richest country in
Europe, powerful and respected. Was all this due to
the Younger Pitt? The prosperity was due to
economic changes beyond his control, but the
careful handling of government and the firm line
taken with foreign powers resulted from the sucess-
ful policies pursued by Pitt.

Finance

It was as well that Pitt was an outstanding finance
minister, for many believed the country was on the
verge of bankruptcy. In the eighteenth century the
money available for financing the governing of the
country was limited: governments regarded their
finances as though they were the accounts of a large
estate. Thus, if there was a big debt, bankruptcy was
feared. In 1783 the National Debt (the money
borrowed by the government to pay its bills) had
risen to what was believed to be the ruinous total of
£250 million. This had to be paid off – indeed, it
remained the principal idea of most Chancellors of
the Exchequer throughout the following century
that the National Debt should be reduced and
eventually paid off (we have different ideas today!).
The Budget did not balance, despite high taxation.
Trade was being damaged by high tariffs – which
made smuggling profitable. Pitt was determined to
end all this as soon as possible. He was a follower of
Adam Smith's views (see page 10) and hoped to
introduce some of his ideas on free trade to the
general benefit of the country.

However, Pitt was not *doctrinaire* and he began by
raising tariffs on luxury items but reducing indirect
taxes on goods in popular demand: this helped to
reduce the cost of living and benefited the poor. Next
he encouraged trade by simplifying customs and
excise duties (making smuggling less profitable) and
extending the system of *bonded warehouses*. These
were store-houses, generally at the ports, that accepted goods on which import duties were to be
paid, releasing them after payment of the duty: it
was a simple and cheap way of collecting the duty –
and it also helped to reduce smuggling. At the same
time Pitt passed the Hovering Act, allowing the
seizure of merchant ships that 'hovered' at anchor in
the roads outside ports or along the coast until the
customs men had gone elsewhere, so that they could
land their merchandise undisturbed. Pitt was no
friend to smugglers.

He was determined to have an efficient and cheap
administration and was at pains to have the
Treasury accounts properly kept by the Audit Office
(1785) – he would often examine the accounts personally. He hoped to pay off the National Debt by
reviving Walpole's Sinking Fund. (Lord North had
intended to do this, but it was Pitt who put it into
effect in 1786.) The Fund had a million pounds a
year provided for the purchase of government stock
in order to reduce the National Debt. Walpole used
to 'raid' his Fund when he needed money; Pitt
prevented this by placing the Fund in the hands of
Commissioners responsible directly to Parliament.
This was a sign of his efficiency and probity. He was
a finance minister looking to the future – he confidently predicted his Sinking Fund would pay off
the National Debt, but he reckoned without the
twenty years of war that began in 1793!

Another sign of his efficiency was his decision to
offer financiers the opportunity to compete to lend
the government the money it needed for its daily
business. This was called 'putting government loans
up for public tender' and it meant the government
got the best rates – much cheaper than the previous
system of working through only a few named
finance houses. His efficiency is best shown by his
most important reform, the *Consolidated Fund*
(1787). It was a simple device – government revenue
was paid into the Fund and all expenditure made
from it. Here was the beginning of the modern
budgetary techniques that Gladstone was to sys-
tematise (see page 139). It made government cheaper,
for departments no longer had to pay their way out
of the receipts from specific taxes, losing any moneys
they had not used during the year. Now, a closer
control could be exercised over expenditure, and
costs could be kept to a minimum.

Other reforms

A new efficiency was brought to government, but many of the measures were not Pitt's – he merely introduced what others had suggested. Even the Eden Treaty (1786) allowing extensive free trade with France was due to Sir William Eden, not Pitt. (It proved so advantageous to Britain and disadvantageous to France that the French Revolutionaries revoked it!) But Pitt *was* successful in his financial measures, and this helped Britain to bear the strain of the greatest war she had yet encountered, yet Pitt may have been given too much credit. He was a user of other men's ideas, and a very cautious reformer – he had no wish to push his supporters too far (remember that ideas of party loyalty were not then well developed).

Pitt was not prepared to put through measures that did not have considerable support. For example, a proposed Free Trade Treaty with Ireland (1785) was allowed to drop because of the active opposition of Liverpool merchants, and in the same year Pitt dropped a measure for parliamentary reform because of the opposition to it. It was the same with slavery, although one of his closest friends was William Wilberforce, who led the campaign against slavery. Wilberforce had had a somewhat riotous youth, but he experienced a religious conversion and his religious, moral and humanitarian ideals well fitted him for the moral campaign against the evil of slavery. Yet when there was vigorous opposition in the House to a measure against the slave trade, Pitt let the matter drop. He had had no riotous youth and no religious conversion. Some have even suggested that his motives over the abolition of slavery were purely commercial: as a supporter of Adam Smith's ideas, he believed the cheapest and most efficient course was the best – and Smith himself had written, 'It appears from the experience of ages and nations . . . that the work done by freemen comes cheaper in the end than that performed by slaves'.

Did Pitt seek abolition of slavery because it would improve Britain's competitive position against French merchants? You will find more about this in C. L. R. James's book, *Black Jacobins.*

Many historians have praised the work of the Younger Pitt as a peace minister and financier. Did his ministry seem so successful because it followed the disaster of the loss of the American colonies and came at the same time as national prosperity 'took off'? Pitt was a moderate reformer, certainly, and he established a strong and efficient administration on which others were later to build. His was a worthy achievement in the ten years of peace before the wars changed things; perhaps it was not as great an achievement as some historians have suggested.

Imperial policy

The loss of the American colonies might have led to a wish to give up the Empire – indeed, one school of historians has argued that the American Revolution resulted in the British losing interest in imperial affairs (see page 48). This was not true of Pitt. He strengthened government control of the existing colonies and made sure of their defence. In 1784 he passed his India Act (curiously similar to Fox's India Bill that had been defeated), separating the commercial affairs of the East India Company from political administration, which was placed under a Board of Control responsible to Westminster (see page 50). In 1788 he opened up Australia for convict settlements. From this small beginning a new country was to arise. In 1791 he resolved the problem of Canada with the Canada (Constitutional) Act (see page 49). The evidence here suggests a desire to achieve that efficiency and close control that is seen in the financial policies.

The Regency Crisis

But Pitt, despite his success, was not secure. He had to be careful to retain the support of the House and not to push reform too far. Above all, he remained the King's minister. Indeed, George III had created a large number of peers simply in order that Pitt should have adequate support in the Lords. However, in 1788, the King stopped his carriage in Windsor Great Park and got out in order to address an oak tree as though it were the King of Prussia. The King was mad. That was what people believed – he had shown signs of derangement on earlier occasions. For at least six months, Pitt's position was perilous. The Prince of Wales would, in the ordinary course of things, become Prince Regent on behalf of his father – and the Prince was a close friend of Fox. As soon as the Prince became Regent, Pitt would be out and Fox would be in! Naturally, Fox pressed forward a Regency Bill to give the Prince full powers during His Majesty's 'indisposition'.

It was a very serious crisis for Pitt, and, as the weeks passed, more and more of his supporters moved over to Fox – they calculated that Fox would be the minister of the future. Pitt tried hard to delay things, and at last the King began to show signs of recovery. The crisis passed, and Pitt was able, bleakly, to weed out from his ministry those who had been prepared to support Fox. The Regency Crisis showed clearly that Pitt was the King's minister, and that the King retained considerable political power. Pitt was lucky to survive the crisis. (In fact, the King was not mad, but suffering from porphyria – try to find out about the disease and about George III's personal life. In due course, the poor old man did go mad – from 1810, certainly. He had not always been a popular monarch, but the English people took him to their hearts during those last sad ten twilight years of his life from 1810 to 1820).

Foreign policy

At first, Pitt cared little about Europe, and until 1790 foreign policy was in the hands of Lord Carmarthen. British prestige was at its nadir in 1783, and Carmarthen did much to restore it. His opportunity came particularly in 1786 when Frederick the Great of Prussia died. Ever since Lord Bute had refused to renew subsidies to Prussia at a crucial moment in the Seven Years' War, Frederick had sworn never to come to the aid of 'perfidious Albion', as he called her (and he had demonstrated this during the American War – see page 45). With a new monarch, it was possible to have better relations, and these were achieved in 1788 by a *Triple Alliance* of Britain, Prussia and Holland, formed to resist French ambitions in what we now call Belgium. Britain was once more considered one of the Great Powers, and France suffered a severe diplomatic reverse.

In 1790 Spain, who claimed the whole Pacific coast of North America as far as Alaska (it had not yet been settled by Europeans, or even properly mapped), claimed Nootka Sound. This was part of a stretch of coast that Captain Cook and Captain Vancouver had surveyed in the 1770s. It was also directly west of the Great Lakes: should Canada ever expand westward, it would reach the Pacific coast at Vancouver Island and Nootka Sound. Pitt demanded that Spain withdraw. There was real danger of war – indeed, had not the French refused to help Spain (they were busy with their own Revolution at the time), war might have resulted.

But Spain found herself without allies and withdrew. Canada was now able, in the future, to expand from coast to coast.

Meanwhile, a war had been raging in Eastern Europe between Russia (under the Tsarina Catherine the Great) and Turkey. By 1790 Turkey was beginning to retreat, and Catherine seized the naval base of Ochakov on the Black Sea (see Fig. 14). This raised fears that Catherine intended to advance towards Constantinople, secure control of the whole of the Black Sea and also entry into the Mediterranean, where she might threaten British commercial interests. This was, for Britain, the beginning of the Eastern Question (see page 129). Pitt protested vigorously (1791), but Catherine ignored the protest and Pitt was not prepared to go to war about a port the other side of Europe. But it was a warning to Britain of a possible danger to her interests.

In 1792 Pitt proudly proclaimed that he foresaw fifteen years of peace for Britain; no one contradicted him. But in April 1792, France declared war on Austria, and so began the French Revolutionary and Napoleonic Wars that were to last twenty years and embroil Britain in a desperate struggle.

Pitt's period as a peace minister (1783–93) was marked by a great increase in prosperity and by the raising of British prestige from the nadir of 1783. Historians have called him a great peace minister – but he was not a great reformer, nor an original one. He did, however, bring a detailed and close control over administration, and in his command of the House of Commons he demonstrated his greatness as a parliamentarian. In 1793 France declared war on Britain, and this meant giving up reform and concentrating on a bitter war. Pitt was no more original as a war minister, and historians have judged him a failure here.

Your task is to make an assessment of Pitt as a peace minister – does he deserve his reputation? Was he a worthy son of his great father, the Elder Pitt? (Remember that the Elder Pitt had been a failure as a peace minister, although he had been so successful at war.)

5 War and reaction

The French Revolution

The French Revolution opened a new chapter in the history of Europe and the world. Compared to it, the American Revolution was like a local town football match as against a cup final. It was welcomed with enthusiasm throughout Europe as a people rising against their oppressors. When, amid the chaos of the summer of 1789, the Bastille (the royal fortress in Paris) surrendered, jubilation greeted the news. Fox wrote in a letter to a friend, 'How much the greatest event it is that ever happened in the world! and how much the best!' Pitt, too, joined the chorus of approval. There was a new burst of activity from those English **radicals** who favoured further reform, especially from the dissenters who hoped that the Test and Corporation Acts that restricted their rights as citizens might be replaced.

Then Edmund Burke produced his *Reflections on the Revolution in France* (1790), denouncing the Revolution as a destructive force seeking to wash away in a river of blood the long traditions of a people. The book achieved instant success throughout Europe and launched a great movement of *counter-revolution* that was to inspire many politicians for the next hundred years. In England, it marked a new rift in political life, for it divided those who continued to support the ideals of liberty and equality from those who rejected the Revolution as an evil force. It meant that for the first time for many years a genuine division of principle now distinguished the Whigs, who followed Fox, from the Tories, at whose head Pitt now placed himself. The rift went deep and changed the atmosphere of politics. Later in 1790, Fox burst into tears in the House of Commons as Burke publicly declared their long-standing friendship at an end (even when Burke was on his death-bed, and Fox sent a note asking permission to see him, the dying Burke refused). Sitting silent in the House, Pitt had witnessed that emotional scene: it was a moment for him to savour, for it marked the point at which Fox's support at last fell away. When war came, it was no longer fashionable to talk about reform.

Lord Torrington gives a good impression of the patronising welcome given to the Revolution: after the French King, Louis XVI, had tried in vain to escape in 1791, he wrote in his *Diary*,

> I read in the newspapers, with amazement, the accounts of the flight of the King of France; and of his capture, and being brought back: what a quick and wonderful retribution for his wanton assistance to our rebellious colonists, whose flame of liberty has now so scorched him! . . . My opinion of the French [is] allways, 'That they are 150 years behind this country in comforts, arts and science'; and now they are at our aera of 1640; wanting [only] men of abilities and a Cromwell.

But the French Revolution was very much more than the English Civil War, although quite soon it was to get a 'Cromwell' in the person of Napoleon Bonaparte.

Reform movements in Britain

However, Burke did not change everyone's opinion. There was a huge degree of support for radical reform, especially among the less wealthy professional classes and the artisans (skilled workers). Many replies to Burke were published, but the really important one was by Thomas Paine – his *Rights of Man* (1791). It was in two parts. The second part outlined a plan to change the present parliament altogether and bring greater liberty and equality to Britain. Its success was so worrying to the government that it published a Royal Proclamation (May 1792) against *sedition*. The news from France grew worse, and the French revolutionaries actually defeated both Austria and Prussia (who had begun a slow invasion of France when war was declared on them in 1792). The British government became increasingly alarmed. When the revolutionaries declared war on Britain (1793), Pitt felt obliged to adopt a *reactionary* and repressive policy and to restrict personal liberty in the interest of national security. In this, public opinion supported him: to suggest reform was now unpatriotic!

Nevertheless, this did not stop the demand for

reform. There was, indeed, something of a national movement supporting a programme of quite widespread reform. It was well organised and largely concentrated among shopkeepers and artisans – many of whom were better read than their social superiors. It followed the pattern of popular movements that had appeared in the Americas in the 1770s and took the form of local societies (usually in larger towns, London, Sheffield, Norwich, and also in Scotland) which corresponded with each other. The most important of them was the London Corresponding Society, whose secretary was a shoemaker, Thomas Hardy. This Society openly corresponded with the leaders of the French Revolution at the Jacobin Club in Paris (for this reason these English radicals were called 'English Jacobins'). The government feared a revolution was being organised under their very noses (their informers were spies and **agents provocateurs** whose reports were sometimes not even true!). They also feared that there was a connection between the Corresponding Societies and Wolfe Tone's United Irishmen (see p. 70).

Repressive measures

In response, the government adopted a repressive policy. First came the Aliens Act 1793, requiring all

---

Price surprised by Burke – 'Smelling a Rat'
  This famous cartoon by Gillray shows Dr Price at work on his Discourse on the Love of our Country, which favoured the French Revolution. It was this pamphlet that prompted Burke to write his Reflections and to head the anti-revolutionary forces. Note the picture of the beheading of Charles 1, and Burke holding the twin symbols of crown and cross—religion was to be enlisted by the counter-revolutionaries. Gillray catches the atmosphere of

witch-hunting that was present among the supporters of Burke—it was to dominate people's attitudes in the 1790s. Witch-hunting of political opponents in the hope of destroying them is a common thing in history—another reason to be cautious of what people wrote at the time. Ask your teacher about McCarthyism, which was another example of witch-hunting, inthe USA in the 1950s.

Smelling out a Rat; ___ or The Atheistical-Revolutionist disturbed in his Midnight Calculations.

aliens to register and permitting anyone to be imprisoned or deported as a suspected spy. The magistrates were encouraged to be severe against rioters and those of 'advanced' views (Lord Braxfield was especially savage in Scotland); Paine was declared an outlaw and his book a seditious libel. John Reeves, a government lawyer, organised a Loyalist Association that held patriotic 'Paine-burnings' and conducted a 'witch-hunt' against the English Jacobins. In 1794, the London Corresponding Society called for a British Convention (elected by working men who had no vote) in a direct challenge to Parliament. The government replied by suspending Habeas Corpus (the right of Englishmen to be free from arrest and imprisonment without cause), because, as they stated,

> A traitorous and detestable Conspiracy has been formed for subverting the existing laws and Constitution, and for introducing the System of Anarchy and Confusion which has so fatally prevailed in France.

In Scotland, the usual arrests were followed by a death sentence; in London, Pitt arrested the leading members of the Corresponding Society. They were put on trial, but their defence was handled by the great advocate Erskine, who managed to secure their acquittal. The trial, however, did much to break the back of the reform movement. Nevertheless, after the King had been attacked on his way to open Parliament in 1795, the Treasonable and Seditious Practices Act 1795 was passed, greatly extending the definition of treason – with its punishment of hanging, drawing and quartering. Next came the Seditious Meetings Act 1975, banning all meetings from being held without a licence from a local Justice of the Peace. The repressive policy was popular because England was at war and it was felt to be necessary – but it proved difficult to enforce the Acts, because juries would often not convict the accused, since the penalty would be so harsh. There was, however, something of a class division in the attack on the radicals – it reached a climax in the Combination Acts 1799 and 1800 (which were actually proposed by William Wilberforce). These forbade all combinations of workmen to put pressure on their employers for shorter hours and more pay (in effect, they made trade unions illegal).

The radical movement of the 1790s failed, and text books often concentrate on the war instead. However, it showed three important things. Firstly, it demonstrated that artisans were capable of political organisation rivalling that of national politicians – a fact that was not forgotten. Secondly,

it showed how seriously the government treated the movement – was it merely because of the war? And, thirdly, it clearly showed how leading politicians could stand up for the defence of English liberties, even in times of war: as the danger abroad passed (and the movement at home died down), the repressive measures were allowed to fall into disuse.

It would make a good piece of research to enquire further into Pitt's repression and how it worked, and into the 'English Jacobins'. Divide the class into groups, each researching a particular aspect: the movement in Scotland, in London, the leading radicals, the government attitude. (It would also be a good thing for two groups to examine the career and ideas of those two very remarkable men, Edmund Burke and Thomas Paine.) Your local Records Office might have some material to help, and your teacher might tell you about Home Office Reports in the Public Records Office. You will find a good deal in Cole and Postgate's *The Common People*, G. A. Williams, *Artisans and Sans-Culottes*, and there is much in a long but impressive volume by E. P. Thompson, *The Making of the English Working Class*.

The war was the real reason why Pitt turned against reform, for he was deeply conscious of the danger from France. Fox, of course, was not in office and could speak more freely. His defence of liberty in time of war, however, puts forward very clearly the British tradition.

Read the following extract and try your hand at the questions. Discuss in class what Fox's argument was and what he meant by mixed and balanced government'. The 'calamity in Ireland' was Wolfe Tone's rebellion (see page 70).

Liberty in time of war

In proportion as opinions are open, they are innocent and harmless. Opinions become dangerous to a state only when persecution makes it necessary for the people to communicate their
5 ideas under the bond of secrecy. Do you believe it possible that the calamity which now rages in Ireland would have come to its present height if the people had been allowed to meet and divulge their grievances? . . .
10 But it is said that these bills will expire in a few years; that they will expire when we shall have peace and tranquillity restored to us. What a sentiment to inculcate! You tell the people that when everything goes well, when they are happy
15 and comfortable, they may meet freely, to recognise their happiness and pass eulogiums on their government; but that in a moment of war and calamity, it is not permitted them to meet to-

gether because then, instead of eulogising, they
20 might think it proper to condemn ministers. What
a mockery is this! . . . If you mean that the mixed
and balanced government of England is good
only for holidays and sunshine, but that it is
inapplicable to a day of distress and difficulty, say
25 so; if you mean that freedom is not as conducive
to order and strength as it is to happiness, say so;
and I will enter the lists with you . . . Liberty is
order. Liberty is strength.
    Speech of CHARLES JAMES FOX *on a motion in*
30 1797 *to repeal the Treasonable and Seditious*
Practices Act and the Seditious Meetings Act.

(a) Who was Fox? Briefly explain and discuss
    his argument.   (8)
(b) What were the objects of these two acts?
    What other measures restricting personal
    liberty were passed in the 1790s, and for
    what reasons?   (6)
(c) What did Fox mean by 'the mixed and
    balanced government of England' (lines
    21–22?)   (2)
(d) What was 'the calamity which now rages in
    Ireland' (line 5)?   (4)

O & C

The war with France

War lasted for about twenty years: the French
Revolutionary War from 1793 to 1802, followed by
the Napoleonic War from 1803 to 1814 and again in
1815. It was the greatest struggle Britain had yet
undertaken; its heroes, such as Nelson and
Wellington, are household names today, and at the
time it was felt to be a great national struggle against
the 'tyrant Boney'. This struggle ended in complete
victory for the navy (at Trafalgar) and the army (at
Waterloo). English history books treat it as a story
showing how superior the British were in comparison to their enemies. Britain had tremendous
achievements – but do you see how these may be
presented to give a very biased picture? Were these
twenty years of war years during which the nation as
a whole put all its energy into the war effort, as it did
during the First and Second World Wars?

When we make judgements and present our
version of what happened, we must be careful not to
be over-persuaded by contemporary writers, or by
later writers. We must look carefully at our *primary*
sources – official documents, diaries, letters and any
artefacts surviving from the time – and compare

them with what our *secondary* sources tell us. For
example, if you dip into the pages of Jane Austen's
novels (they are also sometimes dramatised on
radio and television), you will find there is scarcely a
mention of this great national struggle against the
French. This illustrates how important it is to use
primary evidence with caution. Jane Austen was *not*
writing about the war, but about how people lived:
she had no *need* to mention the war if it made no
great difference to her characters. The war was
crucial to the development of Europe and of
Britain, but we must be careful to think about it in
terms of the early nineteenth century and the
people at the time – who did not know the outcome.

Britain, in fact, did not go to war willingly. The
war began in 1792 and was expected to be over very
quickly, but the French Revolutionaries proved too
much for the Austrians and Prussians, who were
defeated. Even so, it was France who declared war
on Britain – Pitt would have preferred to remain at
peace. We can list his reasons for going to war
against France. How convincing do they appear?

1. France was at war with Britain's ally, Prussia
(1788 Triple Alliance). Why, then, wait for the
French to declare war on Britain?
2. The Prussian offensive was defeated. This was a
reason to enter the war in 1792, not later.
3. The French offensive in Belgium threatened
Holland, also an ally under the Triple Alliance. Was
this a convincing reason for going to war?
4. The French declared the river Scheldt (closed by
the Treaty of Utrecht in 1713) open to navigation,
which meant that Antwerp could once more become
a rival port to London.
5. France, in effect, annexed Belgium.
6. In November 1792, France issued the Edict of
Fraternity, offering help to any 'nation struggling to
be free' – this was a direct threat to the crowned
heads of Europe.

These last three reasons are much more convincing. The French Revolution seemed now to promise
not peace, but aggression and war. On 31 December
1792, Lord Grenville wrote to the French, protest-
ing against the opening of the Scheldt as being
against international treaties (we would say against
international law), and, he went on,

This Government, adhering to the maxims which it
has followed for more than a century will also never
see with indifference that France shall make herself,
either directly or indirectly, sovereign of the Low
Countries, or general arbitress of the rights and
liberties of Europe.

Here was a warning, as clear as was possible in diplomatic language, that Britain would go to war if France did not retire. It was, in fact, the major principle upon which British foreign policy was based at the time.

7. In January, 1793, Louis XVI was executed, in effect for treason, having corresponded with foreign governments to try to defeat the French Revolution. Although Britain had executed Charles I (1649), this action of the French was regarded as unacceptable in Britain and outraged opinion throughout the country. But, even so, Pitt waited for France to declare war in February, 1793.

Everyone expected that the Revolution would be quickly defeated. This partly explains why Pitt took so few measures at first, expecting to be able to pay for the war simply by floating loans. Europe was united against France, and invaded her in 1793 on each of her frontiers. Pitt can be forgiven for expecting France to collapse – everyone's calculations were totally wrong, for the Revolution discovered a tremendous energy which enabled it to put all of France's resources into what had now become a national war of survival. It was, in fact, the first example of what we now call 'total war', and France won completely on land (she did not need Napoleon, for he first commanded an army in Italy in 1797, fully four years later). Few people at the time realised how important this quite new development in fighting a war would be. However, they did realise that what they had expected to be over in weeks would now become a very long war indeed. The twenty years of war changed Europe, and Britain, very quickly.

Pitt's war policy

The Elder Pitt had been an outstanding war minister – would his son prove equal to the challenge? It was natural that he should base his war policy on that of his father. We can analyse this and show it simply as a list of points. The Elder Pitt's policy had been:

1. To secure an ally on the continent, who might bear the brunt of the fighting on land. (Pitt formed the First Coalition (1793–1795) consisting of Prussia, Austria, Spain, Naples, Piedmont and Holland.)
2. To help the allies, Britain would supply subsidies, which she could well afford.
3. To encourage her allies and convince them she was in earnest, she would send an expeditionary force to fight on the Continent.
4. To control operations from the sea, using her

navy. This enabled her to blockade the French coast, to land and take off troops at any point, as well as keeping the French fleet bottled up in harbour and preventing a French invasion, especially of Ireland. It also allowed Britain to defend her trade, damage French trade and defend her colonies whilst attacking those of her enemy.

All this had proved highly successful under the Elder Pitt, and the policy was continued by his son – but he added two new items;

5. He printed a great many counterfeit *assignats* (paper currency) and tried to flood the French market with these worthless notes. He hoped this would bankrupt the French government.
6. He ran a highly efficient spy system. This was so successful that sometimes he knew what French commanders were to be told even before they knew themselves.

This war policy was well planned and in theory should have won quickly. It failed for three main reasons: namely, the French were rapidly victorious on land and destroyed the Coalition; the counterfeit assignats failed to bankrupt France (indeed, much of the gold paid as subsidies to the allies found its way to France); the allies were prepared to make peace if they could secure satisfactory terms. By 1797 Britain stood alone against France.

War on land and at sea

On land, British efforts were very poor. In 1793 the Duke of York laid siege to Dunkirk, but in 1794 the French success in Belgium obliged him to retreat rapidly under dreadful conditions into Germany (the nursery rhyme about the Grand Old Duke of York' dates from this time!). Much of the army was then sent off to the West Indies, where many died of fever. At sea there was greater success. There had been some reform of the Admiralty and a refitting of the fleets since 1783, and the British navy was worthy of its task. Admiral Hood actually seized the French naval base of Toulon (1793) – he was driven out by well-placed artillery, commanded by a young officer, Napoleon Bonaparte. However, Hood escaped, taking much of the Toulon fleet with him. This was a serious loss to the French that could not easily be remedied, since it took several years to build a battleship. Toulon remained blockaded. The other main French naval base was Brest, and it was also blockaded. This was not an easy task, not only because the Atlantic was liable to frequent storms, but also because of the need to keep up the blockade twenty-four hours of the day every day. The French fleet got out at least twice. In 1794 it emerged to escort a vital convoy of grain from the United States into harbour. Lord Howe engaged it and won the 'Glorious First of June' off Ushant, 1794 – but the grain convoy got through, so that starving Paris had food at last. In 1795 an attempt to help counter-revolutionaries in the Vendée proved a fiasco, but did result in a second defeat for the Brest fleet at Quiberon Bay.

However, in 1795 Holland and Prussia made peace, and in 1796 Spain joined France. There were now the remaining French fleets and also the Dutch and Spanish fleets to oppose Britain. In 1797 Napoleon Bonaparte was given command of the Army of Italy and swept Austria out of the area so effectively that Austria made peace at Campo Formio. Britain now stood alone. There were

attempts to find some basis for a peace, but these were unsuccessful. Pitt would not make a dishonourable peace.

1797 was, indeed, Britain's dangerous year. She stood alone. France with her two new allies, planned an invasion certainly of Ireland, and probably of Britain. At home conditions were bad because war had affected trade and the 1796 harvest had been very poor. Inflation had sent prices rocketing – they were to go higher – and there was widespread distress. (In Berkshire the magistrates, meeting at Speenhamland in 1795, had introduced a system of relief that became known as the Speenhamland System. See page 88. There was a very serious financial crisis. As a result Britain went off the gold standard for the rest of the war. Pitt had

---

Tables turned

Gillray is referring to the French landing in Pembrokeshire—their fleet can be seen in the background. Fox seizes Pitt, but when Jarvis defeated the Spanish fleet and the French withdrew, the tables are turned. Why is

Fox calling Pitt a traitor? Why is Fox represented as a devil? Look at the cartoon 'Smelling a Rat' (page 60): on whose side was Gillray in 1790? On whose side was he in 1797? Can you explain your answer?

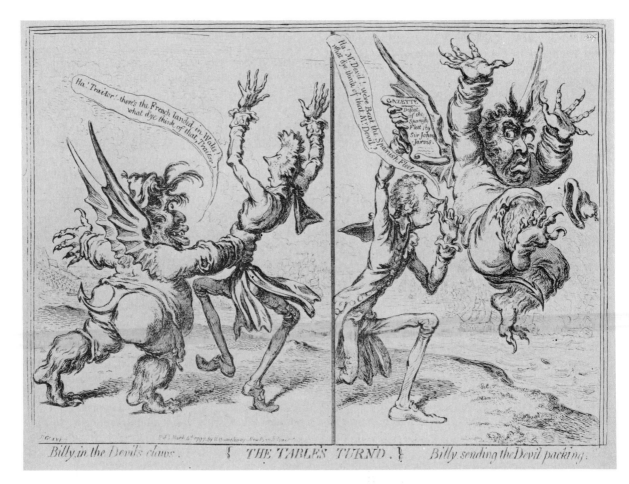

Billy in the Devil's claws.   { THE TABLES TURND. }   Billy sending the Devil packing.

introduced increased taxes, especially on luxuries (one of these luxuries was windows, and you can see bricked-up window spaces dating from this time). His major new tax was income tax, introduced as a war measure only, and aimed at the rich. Those with incomes below £60 paid nothing; incomes between £60 and £200 paid on an increasing scale to a maximum of 10p in the pound, which was the rate for all incomes over £200. It was a very unpopular tax, not because it was burdensome, but because it was regarded as an invasion of one's privacy to have to reveal the level of one's income. (In any case, Pitt's estimate of what it would yield proved wildly inaccurate, for it brought in little before 1806.)

However, there were more serious dangers. In Ireland, Wolfe Tone had provoked a rebellion (see page 70). The French were poised for invasion – there was a landing in Pembrokeshire. The Dutch and Spanish fleets were ready to sail. Then the British fleets at Spithead and the Nore mutinied

(see page 73). However, Britain quickly recovered. A French fleet did, after several attempts, land in Ireland, but it was too late, for the rebellion had been crushed and the invasion came to nothing. The mutinies were quickly dealt with and the fleets put to sea. Meanwhile, Admiral Duncan, an old sailor who had worked his way up to become an officer, had defeated the Dutch fleet at Camperdown. Aware of the mutinies, he had tricked the Dutch into supposing there was a full fleet awaiting them by maintaining a blockade of smaller ships right on the horizon, signalling to others. When the Dutch finally emerged, his fleet was strong enough to beat them. The Spanish Fleet was defeated by Jarvis, aided by Nelson, off Cape St Vincent. Britain was saved (see Fig. 14), but Pitt would not make peace. France was supreme on land; Britain now unchallenged on the sea.

Soon a new danger threatened. In 1798 Napoleon evaded the blockade at Toulon and took a huge

Income Tax 1798

   The little devils for 1798 depart, well content; then immediately John Bull is confronted by a greater monster for his 1799 taxes—the tax on income. 'Am I never to be at Peace?' he cries. Income tax was unpopular, but was this cartoon also intended to be anti-war? Remember the witch-hunt against any thought to want reform or be in favour of peace, and remember that England had successfully emerged from the dangers of 1797 by now.

invasion fleet eastward to Egypt. Was this in order to help Tipu Sahib in India (see page 50)? Nelson was in charge of the blockade and chased about the Mediterranean in search of the French (it was when he called at Naples that he met Emma Hamilton). Napoleon had taken Malta from the Knights of St John of Jerusalem. The British captured it later, but Napoleon's action offended the Tsar of Russia, who was patron of the Order. This gave Pitt the opportunity to form a Second Coalition (1798–1801) with Russia, Austria and Naples. Meanwhile, Napoleon landed in Egypt and rapidly conquered the country. Nelson came upon his fleet at anchor in Aboukir Bay and destroyed it (1798). Napoleon was isolated. He marched into Palestine and besieged Acre, but could not capture it because Sir Sydney Smith supplied it by sea (1799). Soon afterwards Napoleon returned to France (once more evading the blockade), but without his army. This army was later defeated in Egypt. But Napoleon had returned

partly because of the news from France (Smith had cleverly allowed French newspapers to reach Acre), for the Russian and Austrian troops were victorious in northern Italy and about to invade France. Shortly after his return, he seized power by **a coup d'état** and was soon named First Consul.

Napoleon launched a second Italian Campaign which was successful, and Austria made peace at Lunéville (1801). Meanwhile, Russia had withdrawn from the Coalition, partly because British warships insisted on searching all merchant vessels for contraband that might be of advantage to the French. Together with Denmark, Sweden and Prussia, Russia formed the Second Armed Neutrality of the North in 1801 (the First had been in 1780, see page 45) to resist such action and to close the Baltic to Britain. A fleet was sent to the Baltic under Sir Hyde Parker, but it was Nelson who engaged the Danish fleet at Copenhagen (1801) and so destroyed the Armed Neutrality.

Fig. 14 The Revolutionary and Napoleonic Wars

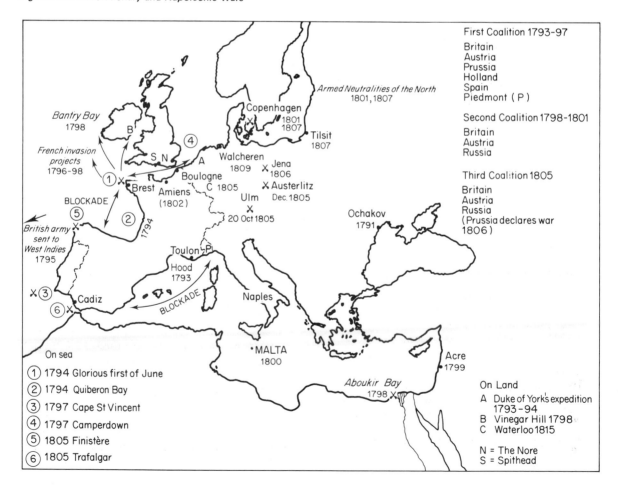

Striving for peace

Once more, Britain was alone, but Pitt would not make peace, for the terms were not acceptable. He was under great pressure to do so, for the war was again at a deadlock and was costing a great deal. Opinion favoured peace, but Pitt was not convinced. Here is a question set exactly on this point:

War aims

In February 1800 George Tierney challenged Pitt to state the reasons for the war against France:

'I would wish the Right Honourable Gentle-
5 man in one sentence to state, if he can, without his *ifs* and *buts* and special pleading and ambiguity, what this object is. I am persuaded he cannot, and that he calls us to prosecute a war, and to lavish our treasure and blood in its
10 support, when no one plain satisfactory reason can be given for its continuance.

Pitt replied: 'The observation with which the Honourable Gentleman concluded his speech appears to me one of the strangest I ever heard advanced. He defies me to state, in one sentence, what is the object of the war. I know not whether I can do it in one sentence; but in one word I can tell him that it is *security*: security against a danger, the greatest that ever threatened the
20 world . . . against a danger which has been resisted by all the nations of Europe, and resisted by none with so much success as by this nation, because by none has it been resisted so uniformly and with so much energy.'

(a) Why did men like Tierney think that there was no 'satisfactory reason' for continuing the war? (5)
(b) Was Pitt justified in claiming at this time that the 'security' of Britain was threatened by the greatest danger the world had ever known (lines 18–19)? (5)
(c) What 'success' had Britain so far had in resisting this danger (lines 22–25)? (5)
(d) The Second Coalition had been formed in 1798. What did Britain contribute to this phase of the war? When and why did she make peace? (5)

O & C

Note the firmness of Pitt's opinions – his comment about 'security' has become deservedly famous. The question asks you to review the situation in 1800, when France once more was victorious on land, and to relate how Britain had resisted France since 1793.

Britain did make peace – at Amiens in 1802. But this was after Pitt had resigned (1801) over Roman Catholic Emancipation for Ireland (see page 70). He was succeeded by Lord Addington, who signed the peace. The terms were straightforward: Britain agreed to return all her colonial conquests to France, Holland and Spain, except for Trinidad and Ceylon (Sri Lanka), and to restore Malta to the Knights of St John. (She also agreed to give up the claim to the French throne that British kings had made since Edward III and to remove the *fleurs de lys* from the royal coat of arms.) France agreed to withdraw from Italy. It was not a glorious treaty – rather one-sided, one might say. But Britain had grown tired of war and there was a great deal of admiration for the achievements of Bonaparte. Indeed, as soon as peace was declared there was a flood of interested English visitors to France.

Bonaparte, however, was less happy. To him the peace was only a truce during which many reforms were made in France and a great army began to be formed. Relations were soon strained, and Britain refused to give up Malta. War was resumed in 1803, and in the following year Pitt returned as leading minister. It was clear that the struggle would now go on to the bitter end.

Napoleon threatens to invade Britain

Bonaparte began to build up a huge army for the invasion of Britain: it could be seen from the Kent coast, for its camp was at Boulogne. (A good impression of the British people's fear of a French invasion is given in Thomas Hardy's novel, *The Trumpet Major*.) Britain made active preparations to defend the coast, including building a canal at Dungeness, and constructing forts, known as the Martello Towers, at vantage points along the coast. Volunteers were enrolled and the army increased in size. A line of beacons was erected for early warning (a number of false alarms caused moments of panic!). But Britain's main defence was the navy.

In 1804, Bonaparte crowned himself Napoleon I, Emperor of the French. It was clear he intended to be the leader of Europe. He also had the Spanish fleet at his disposal. He planned an ambitious scheme to confuse the British navy and allow him temporary control of the Channel so that he could transport his army in barges. It came near to success and showed how skilled the French navy was, despite their defeats – they were worthy opponents of Nelson. The plan was for the Toulon fleet to *rendez-vous* with the Spanish and part of the Brest fleet in the West Indies. The British would give chase, and then the French would return to the Channel and be masters for a moment – which would be enough to transport the army across. The French evaded the blockades and set off across the Atlantic. Nelson gave chase, but guessed at the real intention and sent a fast ship to warn the Admiralty. A scratch fleet under Calder checked the returning French off Cape Finistere on 22 July 1805, and the French put into Spanish harbours. Much later the combined Franco–Spanish fleet emerged from Cadiz – not to invade Britain, but to return to the Mediterranean. It was intercepted off Cape Trafalgar, south of Cadiz, and destroyed in the Battle of Trafalgar on 21 October 1805. Nelson was killed, and his death cast a shadow over Britain's greatest naval victory. It was the end of French naval power for the rest of the war – there would be no more fear of invasion.

Britain stands alone

This was not the end of naval operations, however, Britain was in command of the seas, but this did not mean that French **privateers** could not prove troublesome. Their activities increased to such a point that merchantmen were required to sail in convoy; British shipping found itself under pressure for the rest of the war, and the navy was not able to guarantee safety on the high seas.

Trafalgar did not save England from invasion. The danger had already passed, for Pitt had formed the Third Coalition (1805) with Russia and Austria.

Napoleon's invasion plans, 1804
   The cartoon was only half in jest: the Channel had been crossed by balloon in 1785! The invasion threat was real, but the Navy was there to defend England.

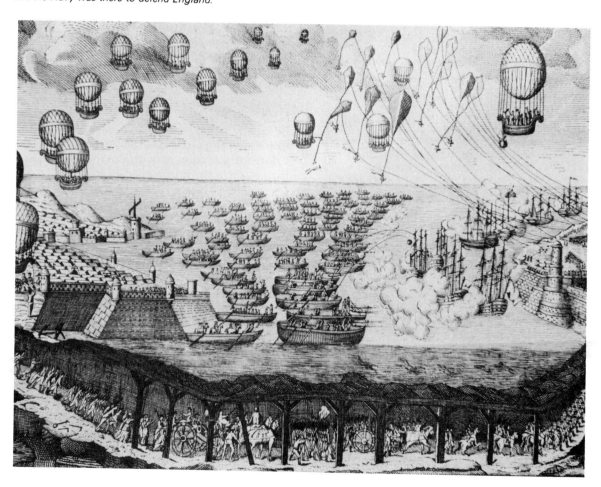

Fearing an attack from Central Europe, Napoleon struck camp and marched into Germany. Within eighteen months he was master of the whole of continental Europe, a tribute to his genius and to the army he had been able to train those few months of comparative peace. The Austrians surrendered at Ulm (on the day *before* Trafalgar), and in December the combined Russian and remaining Austrian armies were destroyed at Austerlitz, Napoleon's greatest victory. This was a dreadful blow to Pitt – Britain was alone again. But Pitt was very ill, and in January 1806 he died, worn out with work and worry.

His father had been a great war minister, but a failure as a peace minister. Pitt was a far better politician and a great peace minister. Was he a failure as a war minister? Some say he was, and it is true that all his coalitions failed – they all lacked common aims, and France had no difficulty defeating their members separately. But the war was a different one from that fought by his father. It was fought against the French Revolution and then Napoleon, against a country able to deploy the full resources of a powerful and wealthy country for its own defence and then for the defeat of Europe. Only by close agreement among the allies not to make a separate peace could Napoleon be defeated. Perhaps this was Pitt's only real failure: he could not make his coalitions 'tight' enough. He was not a great war minister and did not inspire the country to tremendous effort, as his father had. However, he worked long and hard to defeat France, and his refusal to make a dishonourable peace marked him as a great patriot, worthy of the respect a grateful country paid him at his death. He had striven for 'security – security against a danger the greatest that ever threatened the world'.

The period covered by this chapter is a very dramatic one. There were great orators in Parliament: you might like to read some parts of their speeches, and you will find selections in appropriate biographies. Important books were written – like those of Burke and Paine and others – that have influenced ideas ever since. There was a movement among working-class thinkers to try to achieve reform by themselves: the movement was smothered by Pitt's repression of the 'English Jacobins' but it left memories that inspired the next generation.

You have been asked to do some work on the radical movement of the 1790s: you might like to read Iona McGregor's *Tree of Liberty*, which deals with the movement in Scotland – it might strike you as odd that leading politicians should support the American colonists in their demands for political liberty, yet the working class radicals found little support for *their* ideas: can you suggest reasons why?

The French Revolution was a movement of tremendous importance which most thinkers in Britain quite failed to understand at the time. There have been many novels written about it – Baroness Orczy's books about the Scarlet Pimpernel are still worth reading; they are full of adventure, but do they tell you much, or help to explain about the Revolution? Anatole France's *The Gods are Athirst* is an adult book that is also a very good guide to the Revolution. You might contrast it with Charles Dickens' *Tale of Two Cities*. There is a good book by R. Welch, *Escape from France*; another about French exiles in Britain is G. Beardmore's *Jack o'Lantern and the Fighting Cock*. French spies feature in R. Moss' *Black Patch* and D. S. Daniell's *Hideaway Johnny*. Aylmer Hall's *The Devilish Plot* is about Napoleon's invasion plans, and there is a good deal about the war, culminating in Trafalgar, in J. K. Cross' *Blackadder*. Sometimes, one's appreciation of a period is made much deeper and broader by reading an historical novel. The better ones can be very good secondary sources, after all.

Pitt and Ireland

At the time of the American War, Ireland had been given a good deal of independence with her own free House of Commons (see page 52). This had not satisfied Irish opinion, because Irish trade was still controlled in the interests of British merchants and the political power was still retained by the small class of wealthy Protestant landlords. Pitt tried to reform trade regulations, but was prevented by the opposition of Lancashire merchants. Then the ideals of political liberty that inspired the French Revolution began to work like yeast among the Irish in the 1790s. Grattan declared, 'The Irish Parliament can never be free until the Irish Catholic has ceased to be a slave'. In 1793, Irish Roman Catholics were allowed to vote on the same basis as Protestants, but this was not enough. Roman Catholic Emancipation – full rights of citizenship – was demanded.

The influence of the French Revolution was very important: it inspired a new generation of Irish leaders. At their head was Wolfe Tone, a Protestant who looked forward to an Irish nation free and united, without the bitter divisions over religion.

Wolfe Tone's career is full of interest, not least because he scarcely features in many British textbooks, although he was such a great leader. This is a further example of national (in this case English) bias. Make a study of his career.

In 1791 Wolfe Tone formed the Society of United Irishmen to secure Roman Catholic Emancipation – soon, however, his movement was taken over by extreme Catholics who sought the overthrow of the Protestant ascendancy in Ireland. In an attempt to calm things, Pitt even prepared a Bill for Roman Catholic Emancipation in 1795, but there was too much opposition at Westminster, and the measure was dropped.

Disorder was soon widespread, with acts of terrorism and severe punishments: public floggings, even of women, and the destruction of Irish peasant farmsteads. The situation was dangerous, because Britain was at war. Wolfe Tone, fascinated by the Revolution, sought help from France. In 1796 General Hoche sailed into Bantry Bay with a large invasion fleet from France (does this suggest that the British were good at blockading the French navy)? Severe weather prevented his landing – it was perhaps as well for him, because the Irish were not organised. Martial law was declared and vigorously enforced in 1797, but the United Irishmen, confident of French help, raised an open rebellion. However, French help failed to arrive, and the rebellion was crushed at Vinegar Hill (1798). Some French troops did land, but they were quickly defeated and a further French fleet was intercepted. Among the prisoners taken was Wolfe Tone (now elected an honorary French citizen): he committed suicide before he could be hanged for treason. Great ferocity was used to put down the rebellion. It left extremely bitter memories.

Pitt's solution was two-fold: first to gain Irish goodwill by granting Roman Catholic Emancipation, and then to unite the English and Irish Parliaments (as the English and Scottish had been united in 1707). Do you think it a sound solution? Do you think it would satisfy the Irish? Bribery on a quite unprecedented scale, with Castlereagh, one of Pitt's particular supporters, leading the campaign, was used to get the Irish Parliament to vote itself out of existence and to pass the Act of Union 1800 (it came into force in 1801). The United Kingdom was created (with the Union Jack as its flag). The Irish peerage was to elect twenty-eight life peers to the House of Lords, and a hundred members were to be elected to the House of Commons. There was to be free trade between the two countries, and England would pay most of the cost of administering Ireland.

Was this a statesmanlike measure that would solve the Irish Problem? Some historians have praised it, but was it sufficiently imaginative and forward-looking? What do you think the Irish would say of it? Did it change the land laws that were so weighted against Irish peasants? Did it ensure that Roman Catholics would have free access to government office? Did it do anything to change the nature of the Protestant ascendancy and the close control of Dublin Castle (the centre of administration) by the English? If you had been an Irish Roman Catholic at the time, would you have welcomed Pitt's solution?

As it was, the package deal failed, for George III refused to contemplate granting Roman Catholic Emancipation. Did Pitt try hard enough to persuade him? It is true that there was opposition in the *cabinet* and many of his supporters in the House were hostile. George also hinted that if Pitt persisted it might have the effect of bringing back his 'madness'. At any rate, Pitt accepted the King's refusal and resigned, departing from office with good grace and well aware that the King still retained great confidence in him. When he returned to office, he promised never again to raise the issue. The refusal was final.

The Irish regarded this as a betrayal; very quickly groups appeared, working to achieve Roman Catholic Emancipation and the repeal of the Act of Union. For the Union had solved nothing at all (save to bring Ireland even more closely under English rule); indeed, it had made things worse, for not only did the Irish resent it, but there were now a hundred Irish MPs at Westminster. They could present a problem for the House of Commons, especially if their interests were Irish rather than British: some eighty years later parliamentary life was disrupted by the Irish Problem (see page 153), and it played an important part in twentieth-century history. Pitt could not have known this – but was his solution statesmanlike? Try to imagine the conditions of 1800 (Britain was still at war) and suggest what solution you would have produced.

Anglo–Irish history is full of bloodshed and prejudice on both sides, right down to our own days. It is difficult to take a dispassionate view, but the historian must try to do so. There are many records that give heart-rending accounts of the suffering, especially of the Irish peasants – rarely did English opinion take much note of such records.

You might like to glance at the novels of two authors, neither of them great political writers, but both giving a good idea of conditions: Aylmer Hall's *Beware of Moonlight* deals with the 1760s, and the same author's *The Marked Man* is about the French invasions of the 1790s. The revolt of 1797–1798 is the subject of three novels by Alexander Cordell: *The White Cockade*, *Witches' Sabbath* and *The Healing Blade*.

The eighteenth-century navy

Types of ships

Britain's victories in the wars of the eighteenth century were to a great extent due to the navy: by controlling the seas, Britain was able to increase her trade and her empire – when she lost control temporarily, about 1780, she lost the American colonies. It was a navy of which she could justifiably be proud, but it was not particularly more advanced than those of her enemies. Indeed, a British admiral always hoped to capture a French first-rate ship of the line and take it as his flag ship, for they were more comfortable. (Since the French navy had been refitted after the Seven Years' War, her navy was at least the equal of the British, as she had proved in the American War.)

There were two types of ships of the line. The major fighting vessels – a small number of a hundred gunships with three gun-decks and a crew of perhaps a thousand men-were the first-rate ships. There were a larger number of third-rate ships with seventy-four guns on two decks. Both types were very expensive and took a long time to construct – the *Victory*'s keel was laid in 1754, but she was not launched until 1765. Since they were so costly, and since there were not many of them, you did not risk giving battle unless the advantage lay with you. To lose just one of these ships could mean losing control of the ocean in the vicinity. So there was no disgrace if, caught in an unfavourable position, you sought to escape and avoid action.

With the ships of the line went frigates, much smaller vessels of only thirty-two guns on a single deck. They were fast and served as scouts for the battleships. The fleet also had numerous sloops and brigs for carrying supplies. The larger vessels might be copper-bottomed: this improved their speed and stopped weed, barnacles and ship-worm attacking the hulls when the ships were in warm waters. A fleet was a major weapon of war that involved a great deal of careful organisation and support if it was to operate effectively. In putting so much store by her navy, Britain tended, in comparison, to neglect her army.

Discipline in the navy

The officer in the navy had to know what he was doing: much depended on his orders, even in a normal sea voyage without action (whereas the army officer need know very little about military matters). Even so, you had to have influence and a strong patron if you hoped to rise to be an admiral. Some ordinary sailors eventually gained commissions, but there were very few of these: most officers were middle-class, occasionally an aristocrat. However, they had the respect of their men and there was a well-developed sense of trust between them. Even so, discipline was severe – and the men expected it.

It was a hard, brutal life, but a man's life that sailors took a great pride in. Floggings were fairly common, and for serious offences a man might be flogged round the fleet – he would be tied to a frame in a rowing boat and given so many lashes beside each of the ships of the line, perhaps as many as three hundred lashes in all. Such punishments had to be confirmed by the Admiralty (rarely were they over-ruled) and were normally carried out when the fleet was back in harbour. The sailor's back would be a bloody mass of torn flesh, the bones laid bare. He frequently died during the punishment, and the punishment was usually completed on the corpse. Those who survived would not live long. Of course, one could not afford to punish too many in this way – the ships had to be manned, after all! But you can see why marines were necessary on the larger ships – it was not merely to man the carronades in the forecastle!

Mutiny was the most severely punished offence. A crew guilty of mutiny would be pursued literally to the ends of the earth and then hanged without mercy. It was no wonder that the mutineers of the *Bounty* sought to hide on Pacific islands (Captain Bligh was well-known as a cruel man, and the mutiny attracted great attention, but he did not lose his command – indeed, he had shown himself a magnificent sailor in navigating the Pacific in an open boat, so that he could return to seek out the mutineers. You might like to make a study of this famous mutiny.) The wonder was that mutinies actually occurred.

Naval battles

Sailing ships have to respond to the prevailing conditions of wind and weather. Furthermore, battleships, among the largest vessels afloat, could only make a set number of responses to changes in wind direction, for the technology of all such vessels was the same. In a battle, both sides knew pretty well what the other could do and roughly how long it would take. The weather controlled everything – and on a clear day you could see for several miles. It was no wonder that naval battles took a long time: both sides had to get into the most favourable position and then come near enough to engage. The guns were amazingly accurate (though even the largest vessels pitched and rolled in the swell); but the guns had to be within range. This meant that even on the clearest of days a fog of smoke would envelop the fleets as they drew close and went into action. You can imagine the conditions on the narrow gun-decks, even if your deck was not hit! French gunners aimed for the rigging, in order to immobilise an enemy; British gunners went for the hull and caused many more casualties.

If you were very lucky, you would come upon your enemy with a favourable wind behind you, so that the enemy fleet could not escape. You would then take them in line, ship by ship, each blasting broadsides. If it was your really lucky day – and you had enough ships – you could 'double' the enemy, so that your broadsides struck their decks from both sides: they would not sustain such a bombardment for long. But, in certain conditions, you might go straight between the ships of the line. This was a very dangerous manoeuvre. All your big guns were along the sides: you had only a very few small guns in the forecastle. As you came round into position, the enemy ships could blast you with their broadsides. If you survived this fire, then it was your turn to be between two battleships at a point where they could not effectively fire at you, but where you could 'rake' them – your shot penetrating the bows or stern and rolling down the gun decks, killing and maiming all the way. It *could* be worth it! But at that very moment the ship ahead of you would shield the wind, and the vessel approaching you would be right on top of you – and there was no stopping her! You could be rammed, or get your rigging entangled so that you could not emerge on the other side, having 'broken the line'. This is what happened to the *Victory* at Trafalgar, and why a French marksman was able to shoot Nelson. The *Victory* was so very severely damaged that she had to be towed home. 'Breaking the line' was the most dangerous of tactics.

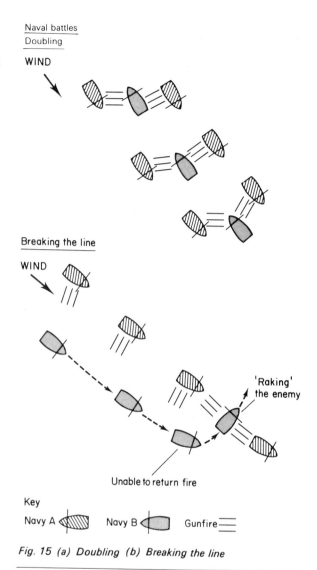

Fig. 15 (a) Doubling (b) Breaking the line

Naval commanders had to know what they were doing. Too much depended on the loss of a single ship – and the Admiralty was severe on any captain or admiral who failed in his task. You needed to know what the plan of action was. There was ample time to prepare it as you got into line and cleared the decks for action. Signalling by flags had to be at a minimum (because your enemy could read the signal too) and had to be passed down the line so that all ships in the line got the order (the admiral often sailed in the centre of the line in order to signal more rapidly). Once firing began, the smoke blotted out the signals, so you had to avoid getting in each other's way. You could not leave things to chance; a silly manoeuvre might mean a collision of two ships of the line and you would lose the battle. Hard experience had taught the Admiralty that it was safer to get captains to follow precise instructions – even when the other side knew exactly what those instructions were. A Rule Book was produced that laid down the necessary action to take in a battle. If you disobeyed the Rule Book, you would be court-martialled.

The French had their Rule Book too. Each side knew well what the other would do. If the wind changed, and your favourable position suddenly became impossible, so that you could only lose, you knew you had to disengage – to escape somehow. There were very few great sea battles in the eighteenth century (can you now see why?). Right at the beginning of the century the Admiralty had regularised Prize Money, the long-established practice of sharing out the money gained from capturing an enemy battleship. The captain got three-eighths, the senior officers one-eighth, the juniors also one-eighth, the crew the rest. After Trafalgar, Admirals received £3362.7.6; each seaman £6.10.0. Such inequality was accepted as a fact of life.

However, there were a large number of important sea-battles in the 1790s. Why? And why did the French navy (which had gained control of the Channel in 1780) do so badly? Their ships were at least as good, and the ordinary seaman as skilled, as the British. There were four reasons. Firstly, the practical knowledge of the officers, especially in navigation, could not be learnt overnight – and a great many French naval officers had gone to join the *émigrés* (the French aristocrats who preferred to leave France during the Revolution), so the navy was immediately at a disadvantage. Secondly, all British ships of the line carried a chronometer (find out about Harrison, the inventor, and Captain Cook, who demonstrated how accurate it was) and so could navigate very much more certainly than the French, who did not have this piece of equipment. Thirdly, there was a touch of desperation on the British side – they felt the French must be beaten at all costs. Fourthly, there was Nelson. It was not only that he had a wonderful power to inspire his men (strong sailors wept openly at his death), but he took incredible risks by disobeying the rules. He was successful, but the risks were great. Read about his battles – how at Cape St Vincent he broke the line, how at Aboukir Bay he sent ships across shoals on which one actually stuck, a sitting target. What if these risky decisions had not worked? The French were worthy opponents – just think of the seamanship involved in the voyages leading to the Trafalgar defeat. Do you believe the story found in some books that the French were unskilled, because they had been bottled up in harbour for so long? They seemed to be able to get out very frequently indeed!

There are many novels about Nelson's navy. You will know the Hornblower series by C. S. Forester. You might like to read *Hurricane Harbour* by G. Hackforth-Jones, or *Sixteen Sail in Aboukir Bay* by S. Plowman – both about Nelson. C. Fox Smith's *Painted Ports* is about French privateers – they were successful even after Trafalgar! There are several books by S. Styles, *Sea Road to Camperdown*, *Midshipman Quinn*, *Quinn of the Fury*, *Quinn at Trafalgar*. Two useful volumes about navy are *Sea Life in Nelson's Time* by J. Masefield and *England Expects* by Roger Hart.

The mutinies

For the British navy, this was a heroic time. But there was another side to the story. We know that discipline was harsh. It proved difficult to get the men to sail the ships. Recruits came from volunteers, often from coastal towns, or boys from charity societies (like Jonas Hanway's Marine Society, which provided 31 000 boys for the navy between 1755 and 1815). In the 1790s many more volunteers came in response to a *bounty*. On the high seas, merchantmen were stopped and sailors forcibly removed – this was one of the causes of the 1812 war with USA. The Press Gang trapped many a poor man into service – woe betide the fellow who tried to escape. No wonder there were riots against the Gangs. Gentlemen, being well dressed, would not be 'pressed'; commoners were. What was the use of all the talk of English liberties, when the Press Gang was at work? Even the courts refused to intervene and release men 'pressed' to serve in foreign parts against their will. Those who were 'pressed' were not all British: at Trafalgar, Nelson's ship carried more foreigners than British men! Finally (since the government would not contemplate conscription), an Act of 1795 required each county to supply a quota of skilled men for service in the navy. These were not willing recruits, but they were of a different quality. Many could read, and many were not prepared to accept the brutal and degrading traditions of the navy. It was men of this type who were behind the well-organised and well-conducted mutinies of 1797 at Spithead and the Nore.

These mutinies were the most serious of all – they occurred when there was great fear of invasion from the Spanish and the Dutch fleets. They were technically not mutinies, since the fleets were in port: they were more in the nature of strikes. At Spithead, pay was the first grievance (here was the influence of the quota-men, for they were used to higher wages on land). Then there were complaints about harsh discipline in general and against particular officers. The men were well-led and they wrote good letters about their grievances: they were not cowards, they did not shrink from action, they did not even ask that flogging be abolished – but they acted with great solidarity and deliberation. They sent letters to Lord Howe, the Commander-in-Chief and victor of the Glorious First of June, and to the Admirality, and appointed deputies to represent the men. Throughout they behaved with great seriousness and respect towards their officers – a notable thing, considering that a number of sailors must have received harsh and perhaps unjustified punishments at their hands. Lady Spencer, whose husband was engaged negotiating with the men, noted

> The quietness of the men, tho' comfortable in some respects, yet in others is most alarming – it proves a steadiness in them to accomplish their object, which overpowers *me*, whatever it may do to other people.

The Admiralty acted quickly and wisely. A Royal Pardon was secured and wages raised. The Spithead fleet sailed out to meet the Franco–Spanish fleet.

Things were different at the Nore. Here, the mutineers were led by Richard Parker, and there were clear signs of the influence of French Revolutionary ideas. Much more radical demands

---

The Delegates in Council; Cruikshank's Cartoon
  This mocks the idea of common sailors holding a council as though they were gentlemen, interviewing the officer sent to know their demands. Only the officer is properly dressed and there is much evidence of firearms. Britannia's picture hangs crookedly and upside-down, while Fox and his friends sit under the table saying 'We are at the bottom of it'.

  Both this and the drawing on page 75 are contemporary primary sources: both portray the same incident. Which is more likely to be what happened? Give reasons for your answer. On page 75 two marines are on guard with rifles— as they would normally be; Cruikshank shows the Council with pistols all over the place. As with the difference in dress, this is a shrewd piece of propaganda; can you explain why? What other ways does Cruikshank use to discredit the mutineers? Were they unpatriotic? If not, why does Cruikshank suggest it so forcefully? What is the meaning of putting Fox under the table?

The DELEGATES in COUNCIL or BEGGARS on HORSEBACK

Parker presenting his demands
This contemporary drawing shows the good discipline on the ships during the mutiny. Note that Parker and his two assistants are wearing their hats as though they were officers and that everyone is properly dressed.

were made than at Spithead and the government acted much more vigorously. If the Nore fleet blockaded the Thames, London would be quickly short of food and coal. Two regiments of militia were sent to Sheerness and shots were exchanged. Captain Bligh (formerly of the *Bounty*) carried an order to Admiral Duncan to bring his still loyal ships to blockade the mutineers. The Nore men lacked the solidarity of those at Spithead, and soon the mutineers surrendered and Parker was arrested. In prison, he wrote:

> Remember never to make yourself the busybody of the lower classes, for they are cowardly, selfish and ungrateful, the least trifle will intimidate them, and him whom they have exalted one moment, the next they will not scruple to exalt upon the gallows. I have experimentally proved it, and am very soon to be made the example of it.

Parker was quite right. He was hanged at the yard-arm, and the Admirality refused his widow permission to take the body for burial. Twenty-nine other mutineers were also hanged and some thirty more flogged. The Nore fleet put to sea under Duncan and won the victory at Camperdown. However, the mutinies were not over: there were mutinies in the Mediterranean fleet (Jarvis put them down severely), in the West Indies and at the Cape of Good Hope – all within a year. And mutinies continued until Trafalgar.

6 The defeat of Napoleon

The war and trade

Trafalgar ensured that Britain maintained control of the seas. But on the continent Napoleon was victorious. Austria was defeated, and Prussia, who joined the war in 1806, was annihilated at Jena. Finally, Russia was defeated at Friedland and made the peace of Tilsit, 1807. Napoleon was master of the continent. Meanwhile, he had begun a new policy to destroy Britain's wealth: if he could not get his army across the Channel, then he would strangle British trade and bring that proud country, bankrupt, to her knees. He controlled the major ports of the continent and so could control continental trade. If the British fleet blockaded France, he would blockade British trade from the land – this is what is meant by the Continental System, for he extended it across the whole of Europe, including Russia. In war, it is usual to damage the enemy's trade and supplies – Britain and France had been doing this since 1793. What was new was enforcing a land blockade against Britain on so huge a scale.

The Continental System

The System was launched by the Berlin Decree, 1806, which closed all French-controlled ports to British shipping. Trade with Britain was also forbidden, except under special licence. British goods were to be destroyed and any neutral ship calling at a British port was to be refused admission to a French-controlled port. At Tilsit, Tsar Alexander I agreed to enforce the decrees in Russia. In reply, the British issued from 1807 onwards Orders in Council preventing any ship entering ports from which British ships were excluded. These Orders in Council disrupted trade and were to lead to the war with the United States between 1812 and 1814. They had their place, too, in the forming of the Third Armed Neutrality of the North, 1807, by Baltic traders angry at the continued searches made by British naval vessels on their own neutral ships. In order to prevent Napoleon seizing the Danish fleet, and in the hope of keeping the Baltic open to British shipping, Admiral Gambier seized the Danish fleet

at the second Battle of Copenhagen, 1807. Naturally, Denmark joined Napoleon.

To make the System bite harder, Napoleon issued further Decrees that were increasingly severe, eventually ordering the confiscation of any vessel that had on board any article of British manufacture (even a chronometer!). Neutral and allied nations found that their trade and prosperity were suffering badly, and this helped to increase popular resentment against the French, so that in 1813 there was a popular rising in what has been called the War of Liberation in Germany. It was partly to enforce the System that Napoleon was led into the Moscow Campaign (1812) which proved so disastrous to him. Meanwhile, one of the reasons for the Peninsular War (see page 78) was to close Spanish and Portuguese ports to British trade. The System was damaging his interests and, by 1812, beginning to damage France as well. Napoleon abandoned it: the System was a failure.

Many books give the impression that the whole idea was silly – particularly as Napoleon had to issue many licences to permit trade, because British manufactured goods were essential to him (the army that marched to Moscow wore British-made overcoats and boots). There was very extensive smuggling, and huge numbers of troops were engaged enforcing the System in North Germany. But it has to be admitted that the System came very close to success and caused two very severe economic crises in Britain. (This underlines how important it is to present both sides of the picture.)

The first crisis was in 1808–1809 and prevented Britain successfully conducting the Walcheren Expedition to help the Dutch. The second crisis, in 1811, was so severe that Britain almost came out of the war. Exports were hit, imports dropped to very low levels, corn prices rocketed and short-time working or unemployment helped to provoke Luddism (see page 77). There was a severe drain on gold, and many bankruptcies. If Napoleon had pressed home his advantage, Britain might have capitulated – the war with France, for the first time, became unpopular. A peace party was active: read the speech of Henry Brougham (later to become an important reformer). It shows how unpopular the war had become, and how Pitt's reputation had suffered so soon after his death.

The bottomless Pitt

Gentlemen, I stand up in this contest against the friends and followers of Mr. Pitt, or, as they partially designate him, the immortal statesman now no more. Immortal in the miseries of his
5 devoted country! Immortal in the wounds of her bleeding liberties! Immortal in the cruel wars which sprang from his cold miscalculating ambition! Immortal in the intolerable taxes and countless loads of debt which these wars have
10 flung upon us! . . . Immortal in the afflictions of England, and the humiliation of her friends, through the whole results of his twenty years' reign, from the first rays of favour with which a delighted Court gilded his early apostasy [ab-
15 andonment of principles or allegiance] to the deadly glare which is at this instant cast upon his name by the burning metropolis of our last ally! But may no such immortality ever fall to my lot. Let me rather live innocent and inglorious; and
20 when at last I cease to serve you, and to feel for your wrongs, may I have a humble monument in some nameless stone, to tell that beneath it there rests from his labours in your service, '*An enemy of the immortal statesman – a friend of peace and*
25 *of the people.*'

Henry Brougham in an election speech at Liverpool in October 1812

(a) Explain 'a delighted Court gilded his early apostasy' (lines 11–12) and 'the burning metropolis of our last ally' (lines 14–15). (4)
(b) What loss of liberties (line 5) and increases in taxation and the national debt (lines 7–8) occurred during the French wars? (7)
(c) Is there any justice in the criticisms of Pitt contained in lines 4–15? Were the wars caused by 'his cold miscalculating ambition' (line 6)? (6)
(d) What were your feelings about Brougham after reading this passage? (13)

O & C

If you did not know of the economic plight of many merchants and the suffering of many workers, you might easily condemn Brougham as being unfair and unpatriotic. The questions ask you to make an assessment of what Brougham has said. Remember – you must judge it in terms of what people were thinking at the time (Brougham had a good deal of support).

Why did Napoleon not persist? There were four reasons. Firstly, by issuing licences for Britain to import corn he drew off great quantities of gold – according to best *mercantilist* principles, Britain should have gone bankrupt. Secondly, the System was beginning to affect France, and Napoleon's principle had always been 'France first' – Europe should pay for France's wars. Thirdly, the cost of enforcing it, and the need to assemble a huge army for the Moscow campaign of 1812, persuaded him to relax the System. In this way, for example, he remained at peace with USA, whilst the British were engaged in a new war with the States. Finally, there was so much evasion and smuggling, that the System was not proving sufficiently water-tight.

Conditions for Britain improved in 1812 – the Russian market was opened again to British goods, and successes in the Peninsula (see page 78) meant that Spain and Portugal provided a big trading opportunity: goods could percolate into Europe from the Peninsula. After Napoleon's retreat from Russia, the markets of North Germany were opened again, trade recovered and prosperity returned.

The Luddites

But the crisis in Britain must not be under-rated. Had Napoleon had the time and the opportunity to extend his System, it would have worked. As it was, the economic crisis was severe and produced a fresh demand for reform, especially parliamentary reform, that was to be repeated yearly until the Reform Act of 1832. It helped to produce the **Luddite movement** as well. This was a working-class reaction to high food prices and short-time working. It was highly secret, and the government learnt of their activities from spies and **agents provocateurs,** some of whom encouraged workers to plan riots in the hope of finding out about the Luddites. One of the spies was called Oliver and he became well known some years later for activities like this.

It is possible to piece together bits of evidence to reveal something of the Luddites. They got their name from Ned Ludd, a name used in various parts of the country in the notes sent by Luddites warning of their coming. They were very well organised – that is how they were able to be so secretive – and they seem to have been skilled workers who broke machines that were producing sub-standard cloth and stockings. They were also very selective in what they broke: a manufacturer who agreed not to use his machinery would be left alone; another would have only the offending machines destroyed. For the most part, their raids damaged only particular machines; they were quickly over and no one told who was responsible. The government feared that these were the beginnings of a radical movement that might cause a revolution, and used more troops to suppress them than it allowed to Wellington in the Peninsular War. That was a measure of the seriousness of the problem!

However, we cannot really talk of a Luddite movement. It varied in different parts of the country. In the East Midlands, from Nottingham to Northampton, it was largely a protest against low wages and some machines (not always new ones), and by and large only the machines suffered. In Lancashire, Cheshire and South Yorkshire it had much more of a political flavour, and demands for parliamentary reform also accompanied the call for better wages and the destruction of certain machines.

Disorder was surprisingly limited – the raids on machines were very disciplined. But the government made machine-breaking a capital offence. There was a famous trial of several Luddites for the murder of William Horsfield in Yorkshire, but Luddites were not interested in murder and they enjoyed tremendous popular support – that is why they could continue to be so secret. However, there were violent raids, and the Luddites have become a part of working-class tradition. You can tell whether an historian is on the side of the rich or the workers by the way he or she deals with the Luddites. In 1849 – nearly thirty years later – Charlotte Brontë described a Luddite raid on a hostile employer in her novel, *Shirley*:

A crash-smash-shiver-stopped their whispers. A simultaneous hurled volley of stones had saluted the broad front of the mill, with all its windows; and now every pane of every lattice lay in scattered and pounded fragments. A yell followed this demonstration – a rioters' yell – a North of England – a Yorkshire – a West Riding – a West-Riding-clothing-district-of-Yorkshire rioters' yell . . . Caste stands up, wilful against Caste; and the indignant, wrong spirit of the Middle Rank [i.e. the Middle Classes] bears down in zeal and scorn on the famished and furious mass of Operative class. It is difficult to be tolerant – difficult to be just – in such moments.

Whose side do you think Charlotte Brontë was on? You can catch a flavour of the feeling that Luddism provoked in this passage, but the Luddites were quietened as quickly as they began: by 1813 there were very few incidents. Prosperity had returned.

It is important to remember that, whilst Britain (once more alone) was fighting her war against

Napoleon and, from 1812 to 1814 against the USA, she was also troubled by serious difficulties at home. (And you can also see that the Luddites were not merely ignorant workers trying to prevent progress by breaking up new machines, as one tradition represents them.)

> You might like to read Phyllis Bentley's *Ned Carver in Danger*, a novel about Luddism in Yorkshire; if you like the book, you might try the same author's *Inheritance*, a powerful adult novel.

The Peninsular War, 1808–14

In order to enforce the Continental System, Napoleon had sent an ultimatum to Portugal demanding that she close her ports to British goods, for Britain was exporting considerable quantities to Portugal and the goods were finding their way all over Europe. He also sent Marshal Junot with a French army to seize the Portuguese fleet. When Junot arrived at Lisbon in November 1807, he saw the fleet leaving to join the British under a British escort! But in order to invade Portugal, Junot had to cross Spain. Napoleon was determined to take full control of Spain, for its Government, under the Queen's lover, Godoy, was very corrupt. He secured the *abdication* of the Spanish king at a meeting at Bayonne (March 1808) and imposed his own brother, Joseph Bonaparte, as King of Spain. This insult to Spain, together with *anti-clerical* measures that the French introduced, produced a fierce rising of the Spanish people, backed by the priests. Many Spanish nobles and the royal army joined the rebellion, but these people generally proved very ineffective. It was the Spanish peasants whose grim determination and fierce methods of fighting gradually wasted away the French forces. In 1808 a surprising victory was achieved – Marshal Dupont was cornered at Baylen and surrendered. This was the first major reverse the French army had suffered for ten years: clearly a major war was about to begin, and Napoleon had no other land war to fight at that moment.

Britain intervenes

Why did Britain intervene? Portugal was Britain's oldest ally; Britain already had secured the Portuguese fleet, and she hoped to keep Portuguese ports open to her trade. Portugal also gave a good base for action against the French, a base secured by the fleet – which could evacuate any British troops if need be – and one that in 1808 would clearly be helped by the Spanish rising.

Sir Arthur Wellesley was sent with an army to Portugal. He defeated Junot and the French at Vimiero (August 1808). At that very moment a more senior officer arrived, Burrard, who superseded Wellesley, and almost immediately was superseded in his turn by Sir Hew Dalrymple. Negotiations for surrender began and the Convention of Cintra was signed, allowing the French to be withdrawn from Portugal, with their guns, provided they did not return. This provoked a tremendous outcry in London – George Canning said, 'I will spell *humiliation* with a HEW!' – and the three commanders were recalled and court-martialled (but Wellesley was allowed to return to take command in April 1809).

Meanwhile, Napoleon himself invaded Spain and by November 1808 was in control of northern Spain: the south lay open to him. Sir John Moore, a very popular and efficient officer, had been appointed to command the British forces in Portugal. He decided the only way to save Spain was to invade the country and draw Napoleon off by attacking his supply routes. But in December 1808, Napoleon swung round and chased him, forcing him to withdraw in haste across very poor roads towards Corunna. The weather was dreadful and the discipline of the troops was only maintained by severe measures – hanging for looting, for example. Even so, the local people had no love for the British, who helped themselves to what food they could find. But if things were bad for the British, they were far worse for the French. There was no food to be had. The roads were bad anyway, and a retreating British army had just marched over them, making them impassable – no wonder the French failed to catch up and many guns were simply left abandoned if they got stuck. Only rigid discipline prevented the British retreat becoming a rout. At Corunna, the French caught up the rear-guard and, in the ensuing battle, Sir John Moore was killed – but the majority of the British force was taken off by the navy (January 1809).

Masters of Spain, the French now prepared to invade Portugal. Napoleon had returned to central Europe, to deal with an Austrian war. He never returned to Spain – had he realised what the war in the Peninsula would be like? Wellesley, restored to his command, invaded Spain and defeated the new French commander, Victor, at Talavera (July 1809). It was a narrow victory and Wellesley

decided he could not rely on Spanish commanders as a result of their conduct. He retired quickly to Portugal and threw up the defensive lines of the Torres Vedras to defend Lisbon. It was Masséna who now led the French into Portugal: he was stopped at the Torres Vedras in 1810 and was obliged to return to Spain in March 1811 because he could not penetrate them. Wellesley, created Duke of Wellington after Talavera, pursued him, but only checked him at Fuentes d'Onoro in 1811. He retired to Portugal. (Note how careful a commander Wellington was. He took no risks and always ensured his supplies were properly in order. It was close organisational work – staff work – like this that helped him to victory. He was a great soldier, a fine organiser – not a brilliant general, but his careful methods, his coolness and his determination won in the end.)

In 1812, the British captured Ciudad Rodrigo and Badajoz which secured all the routes from Portugal into Spain. A full-scale attack on Spain could now be launched. Note the date. There were severe disturbances at home: a war with the USA had begun. Was the situation favourable?

Guerrilla warfare

Was the situation favourable to the French? The year 1812 was when Napoleon gathered his huge army to march to Moscow. He regarded the war in the Peninsula as a side-issue and actually withdrew troops for the Moscow campaign, so the new French commander, Marmont, saw his army weakened. There were other troubles, too. Morale was very low. French troops tried hard *not* to be sent to Spain. They had to garrison the towns, which meant large numbers were locked away and not available for major battles. There were long lines of communication across hot and difficult country with little food and water. But the worst thing was the peasant war – a guerrilla war of the utmost ferocity. Any straggler would be killed. Dispatch riders were sometimes pinned alive to trees with bayonets and left to die. The guerrillas were merciless, and the French were unable to control the country (just like the Americans in Vietnam in the 1960s). Nowhere else were the French faced with such fierce national resistance, and they lacked the means to control the situation. Their morale was low and they got few reinforcements, for the huge army that marched to Moscow was shattered by January 1813, and the few supplies that were sent to Spain were badly needed elsewhere. Well might Napoleon complain 'It was the Spanish ulcer that destroyed me'. (But it would be a mistake to suppose it was the cause of his downfall – Napoleon was defeated in central Europe and then in eastern France. The Peninsular War, though it features large in British history, was something of a side-issue for Europe as a whole. Is this another case of bias in history?)

Once more Wellington invaded Spain and won a victory at Salamanca. He then entered Madrid, but he was afraid he would be cut off, so once more he marched back to Portugal. The war was no simple affair! In 1813 he invaded again and this time won a decisive victory at Vitoria, defeating Marshal Jourdan, a fine veteran French commander of the Revolutionary Army of 1792. King Joseph fled and the French withdrew to the Pyrenees. Wellington pursued them, but found resistance very strong. At last he defeated Soult at Orthez and then later at Toulouse (1814). By that time, Napoleon had been defeated in eastern France and had abdicated. The war was over. Napoleon was sent to rule over the tiny isle of Elba in the Mediterranean, and Louis XVIII, younger brother of Louis XVI, was put on the French throne.

It was clear that the French had lost the war because of their commitments elsewhere, and because of the long lines of communication that gave guerrillas ample opportunity to harrass them. They had frequent changes of command, too. The British had won because of their fine, competent commander. The local population (save in the north-

'And there is no remedy', from Goya's The Disasters of War
Goya was an outstanding artist of the time, whose sketches show the horrors of the guerrilla warfare. It was no wonder that French soldiers tried hard to avoid a posting to Spain! Spanish resistance was patriotic and in support of the Church; it was largely due to the peasants, who proved excellent guerrillas but who could not face an organised battallion. This is why Napoleon had to tie down so many troops in Spain, troops he badly needed elsewhere.

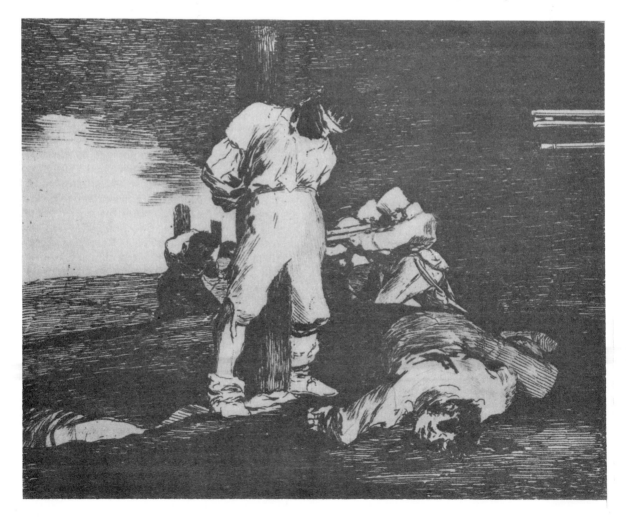

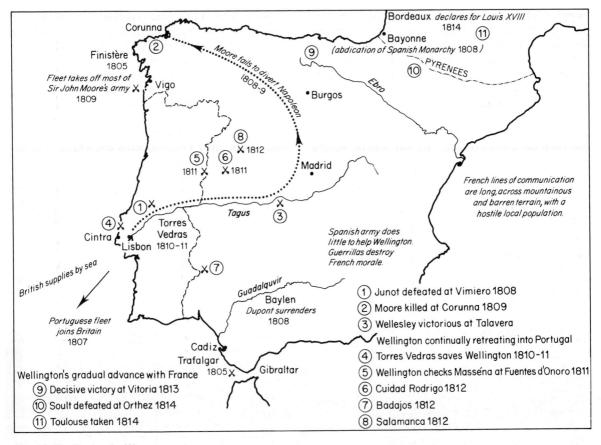

Fig. 16 The Peninsular War

west) generally supported them (Wellington's discipline was severe against looters). Also, British lines of communications ran along river valleys and were fairly short. Furthermore, the navy kept the troops supplied and could take them off if need be (as at Corunna). British troops fought an enemy growing increasingly weak (even so, they found it hard to make progress in southern France!). Wellington's reputation stood high. He was loved by his troops – and, in his own way, he loved them, too. But he had no illusions about his men – fifty years later he still insisted that flogging was the best thing for them!

> The scum of the earth, the mere scum of the earth . . . The English soldiers are fellows who have all enlisted for drink . . . people talk of their enlisting from their fine military feeling – all stuff – no such thing. Some of our men enlist from having got bastard children – some for minor offences – many more for drink; but you can hardly conceive such a set brought together, and it really is wonderful that we should have made them the fine fellows they are.

The Peninsular War is a popular subject and many history books deal with it without mentioning what was happening at home or elsewhere in Europe! It should be seen in context and its importance judged accordingly. It played a big part in the defeat of Napoleon. You might like to read Philip Guedella's life of Wellington *The Duke*. A fine novelist is C. S. Forester whose book *The Gun* gives you some idea of the Spanish peasant soldiers. Find a volume of Goya's paintings and drawings and see how they portray the bitter horrors of war. Three books giving the writings of soldiers of the time are worth reading: *Thomas Morris* (edited by John Selby), *Edward Costello* (edited by A. Brett James) and *Recollections of Rifleman Harris* (edited by C. Hibbert). Read them and then ask yourself how justified Wellington was in saying 'scum of the earth . . . enlisted for drink' (but remember that these were very gifted soldiers!).

The Congress of Vienna

Napoleon was defeated, but his career was not yet over. The allies who gathered at the great Congress of Vienna to settle the affairs of Europe after sending Napoleon to Elba were soon quarrelling. Castlereagh, one of Pitt's young supporters, was now the British Foreign Secretary. In 1812 he had been instrumental in keeping Britain in the war and ensuring Wellington got his reinforcements. With the Moscow campaign of 1812, Castlereagh was able to follow Pitt's example and form the Fourth Coalition (1813). But it was a coalition with a difference. Pitt's had all fallen apart – the members followed their own advantage. Castlereagh was not going to allow this to happen. He provided war aims for the allies and got the members of the Fourth Coalition (Britain, Russia, Austria, Prussia and Sweden; others joined later) to agree not to make a separate peace with Napoleon. He also bound them together by the Treaty of Chaumont (1814). This was very necessary, because Austria had been prepared to make peace, fearing that Russia would become too powerful.

At Vienna, in 1814, the Congress that was to decide the future of Europe was a brilliant assembly. The proceedings were dominated by Metternich, the Austrian Chancellor, a very clever man indeed. But Castlereagh, also a clever man, made his mark and he was the representative of the country which alone had withstood the French for so long, a country that was unchallenged in its wealth and its power at sea. However, the allies could not agree among themselves. Their disputes and the unpopularity of returning *émigrés* in France encouraged Napoleon to return from Elba.

Napoleon's Hundred Days and Waterloo

He was greeted ecstatically, and Louis XVIII wisely fled from Paris. Napoleon had returned to France as Emperor of the French – for the Hundred Days (1815). His vigour was incredible, for he had a fully supplied army in the field before the allies were ready. Boldly he struck against the forces in the north, intending to defeat the allies separately. The Waterloo Campaign was a brilliant piece of strategy, showing that his genius had not diminished. But it failed. Was it the rain on the last night before Waterloo? Was it his own illness on that night? Was it that the strategy was too brilliant for his commanders to follow properly? Was it that he faced stolid British troops – for the first, and only, time – troops that simply refused to give way? Was it because of Wellington? Or was it that the

Prussians, under Blücher, appeared on the French right wing at the crucial moment, when Napoleon expected to see Frenchmen?

> The Waterloo Campaign is well known and deserves a full study. Follow not only the Battles of Ligny and Quatre Bras which preceded the final battle, but the whole strategy of the campaign. Study also the weapons and the tactics used. Then you will be in a position to make an unprejudiced and well-informed judgement as to who deserves most credit in the campaign. There are many books: the very best is a big and adult volume by G. D. Chandler, *The Campaigns of Napoleon*. (Ask your teacher to advise on other books.)

Waterloo was a total defeat for Napoleon. The war was over at last and Napoleon sent off to St Helena in the South Atlantic, where he died in 1822. Wellington was greeted as a national hero. Britain, in the words of Pitt, had at last 'saved herself by her endeavours, and Europe by her example'. British prestige had never stood higher. But now what she wanted was to return to peace and leave the affairs of Europe to take care of themselves – provided her own interests were safe and that there was no threat to the future peace and security of the continent.

Foreign policy, 1815–30

Britain emerged from the Napoleonic Wars as one of the leading European powers, recognised as the equal of Austria and of Russia. Castlereagh, the Foreign Secretary, was seen as a very well informed and powerful expert on foreign affairs – perhaps the equal of the great Austrian Chancellor, Metternich. Already, he had shown his skill with the Fourth Coalition, binding the allies together with the Treaty of Chaumont, 1814. This treaty was, in effect, a Quadruple Alliance, since it not only required the four allies not to make a separate peace, but also required them to protect the peace settlement once it had been established and reserved 'to themselves to concert together on the conclusion of a peace with France, as to the means best adopted to guarantee to Europe, and to themselves reciprocally, the continuance of the peace'.

The Congress of Vienna in 1814 and 1815 settled the affairs of Europe (incidentally adopting many of the frontier changes Napoleon had introduced). Castlereagh obtained a declaration against the slave trade at the Congress, and he also made clear that the basis of his policy towards Europe was to prevent any one power dominating as France had done. But he intended to avoid interference in the internal affairs of other nations as far as possible, provided British interests were not affected. It was to be a policy continued by his two great successors as Foreign Secretary, Canning and Palmerston.

The Congress System

The Quadruple Alliance was renewed at Vienna, but the Congress was more than a meeting of victors to divide the spoils: there was much idealism – a great wish on all sides to achieve as sound a settlement as possible and to create a diplomatic system that would make it possible to avoid the horror of war in future. This came to be called the *Congress System* and was designed so that the Great Powers (Britain, Austria, Russia and Prussia), together with all the other countries whose interests were affected, might meet periodically and especially when any crisis arose, so that discussion might take the place of war. A century later the League of Nations, which was formed to prevent further war after the First World War, looked back to the Congress System as a model.

It was criticised very shrewdly by the Opposition in the House of Commons as replacing the dominance of Napoleon with that of the great powers:

> The object of the new system is to crush the weak by the combination of the strong – to subject Europe in the first place to an oligarchy of sovereigns, and ultimately to swallow it up in the gulf of universal monarchy.

The Opposition had a point: this is indeed what happened to the Congress System in the hands of Metternich. In 1815, Tsar Alexander I, who had undergone a religious conversion at the time of the Moscow Campaign, introduced the Holy Alliance – a league of monarchs who agreed to rule their country in accordance with Christian principles. Castlereagh would have nothing to do with so vague an undertaking – 'a piece of sublime mysticism and nonsense', he called it. But nearly all the monarchs of the continent signed it, and Metternich was soon able to convert it into a union of Austria, Prussia and Russia to repress liberal ideas. He used the Alliance to transform the Congress System into a means of suppressing liberalism everywhere he could. As a result, Castlereagh gradually withdrew from the System.

The first meeting of the Powers after Vienna was at the Congress of Aachen (Aix-la-Chapelle) in 1818. France had been occupied after Waterloo by an allied army under the command of Wellington until a very heavy **indemnity** had been paid. By 1818, against all calculations, that indemnity had been paid off and France asked for the army to be withdrawn. The Congress agreed and formed the Quintuple Alliance (adding France to their existing alliance; but at the same time they secretly renewed their Quadruple Alliance just in case France misbehaved!). But, thereafter, disputes divided Castlereagh from his former allies. Metternich feared liberalism would destroy the stability of Europe, and when liberal revolts broke out in Naples and north Italy, he called a Congress at Troppau in 1820. Castlereagh sent an observer only, and the Congress issued the Protocol of Troppau by which the powers declared their right to intervene in the affairs of any state in order to suppress liberal revolts. Castlereagh protested. This was not what he had intended. For the Cabinet at home, he produced on 5 May 1820 a State Paper that laid down the basis of foreign policy that was, in effect, to be followed by Britain until the First World War: Britain would not interfere in the internal affairs of other nations – that would be going too far – but:

> We shall be found in our place when actual danger menaces the System of Europe, but this Country cannot, and will not, act upon abstract and speculative Principles of Precaution – The Alliance which exists had no such purpose in view in its original formation – It was never so explained to Parliament; if it had, most assuredly the sanction of Parliament would never have been given to it.

Britain took no part in the suppression of the liberal revolts and was ignored by Metternich; he moved the Congress to Laibach (1821) because plague had broken out in Troppau, and was permitted to put down the revolts in Italy.

Spain and Portugal

Meanwhile, a very serious revolt had taken place in Spain. Britain had no very important interest in Italy, but she had recently fought a long and successful war in Spain to free the country from the French; she had trading interests there as well. More than this, British interests in the Spanish Empire were considerable – she wanted to extend her trade in what we now call Latin America. The Spanish Empire had begun to break up about 1810 and there were a whole series of revolutions that resulted in the creation of new Latin American republics. Britain played a big part in helping the new republics to establish themselves (statues to several

British admirals still stand in Latin American capitals today, testifying to this help) and Britain gained much trade as a result.

However, the revolt in Spain caused a Congress to be called at Verona, 1822. Castlereagh prepared to go himself: the danger was that France would be allowed to put down the revolt – and then what might happen? By the Protocol of Troppau, France might go on to defeat the liberals in the Spanish Empire in the Americas. It was a testing moment, but Castlereagh committed suicide (see page 94) and his rival, George Canning, succeeded him. Canning followed much the same policy as Castlereagh had laid down, but he lacked Castlereagh's ability in diplomacy and his vision of using the Congress System as a means of preventing war. He was much more prepared to pursue actively the obvious interests of Britain, whatever the consequences.

The Congress of Verona permitted France to put down the liberal revolt in Spain. Canning warned France to go no further. At the same time the President of the United States, President Monroe, issued his famous Monroe Doctrine in 1823. This declared the whole American continent to be the special interest of the USA, who would oppose any armed intervention by foreign powers. It was a Declaration that made clear to Europe that it would have to fight the USA as well as Britain if it intervened in the Spanish Empire. The British fleet was available, after all, to give support to Monroe if need be; France went no further. But Canning pushed his advantage further by recognising the independence of the Latin American republics in 1825. (George IV was so angry at this that he refused to read the King's Speech to Parliament containing this decision!) Looking back in 1826, Canning justified his acceptance of French action in Spain on the grounds that it had not extended to the Americas:

> Contemplating Spain, such as our ancestors had known her, I resolved that if France had Spain, it should not be Spain 'with the Indies'. I called the New World into existence to redress the balance of the Old!

It is no wonder that the Canning Society exists today to further links between Britain and Latin America.

An attempt to impose a reactionary regime on Portugal in the 1820s was prevented by Canning first sending a naval squadron to Lisbon – as a warning to the French not to interfere – and in 1826 landing four thousand troops to preserve Portuguese independence. But the Portuguese colony of Brazil also secured its independence because of British help. Canning's policy seemed rather more concerned with expanding trade than with securing the stability of world diplomacy.

The Greek Revolt

Canning's greatest test was the Greek Revolt. This began in the Morea (south Greece) in 1821 against the Greeks' overlords, the Turks. Europe was immediately interested – for two very different reasons. In the first place, Greece was considered to be the cradle of European civilisation and there was a tremendous revival of interest in Greek thought, literature, art and architecture in the late eighteenth century. People thought of the Greeks as though they were the heroes of whom Homer had written. They were Christian people, too, and this also helped to inspire support for the Revolt. Many people went to fight for the Greeks, and when Byron, a poet with a European reputation, died after the Battle of Missolonghi in 1824, there was an emotional wave of support for the Greeks.

However, there was another reason for Europe's interest: Russia wanted to help the Greeks because the Greek Orthodox religion was very close to Russian Orthodox – and because a friendly, independent Greece could be of great help to Russia in securing a port in the Mediterranean. Austria was not happy about this, for it would mean greatly increased Russian influence in the Balkans and this could provoke revolt among her own Slav territories. It might also seriously affect her economic interests, for she made great use of the Danube for trade. Canning, for his part, could not accept a pro-Russian Greece lest this mean increased Russian influence in the Mediterranean – it was, in fact, what the Victorians were soon to call the Eastern Question: how to hold Russia back (see page 129).

By 1825 the Sultan of Turkey was winning: he had employed Ibrahim Pasha (son of Mehemet Ali of Egypt) to crush the Greeks in the Morea. Canning showed considerable ability in this crisis: he could not defend the Greeks himself, nor was Britain alone strong enough to hold back Russia. But he could control Russia by co-operating with her. In 1827 the Treaty of London was signed by Russia, France and Britain to impose terms on the Sultan requiring him to grant the Greeks self-government. He refused, so a combined British, French and Russian fleet was sent to blockade the Morea.

At this vital moment, Canning died (1827), and for three years British policy lacked a firm guiding hand. However, the situation was changed by a

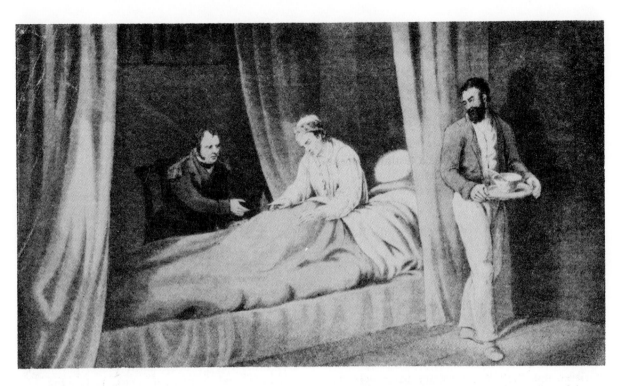

Byron's death in Greece
  Byron had a reputation throughout Europe as a great poet, though in England his personal reputation was not so great! But he represented much of the idealism of the rising generation seeking to reform existing institutions. His death made the Greek Revolt a European problem.

quite unexpected development: the combined fleet under Admiral Codrington was engaged in the Battle of Navarino Bay, October 1827, as a result of which Turkish naval power was destroyed and Ibrahim Pasha was isolated in the Morea. French troops landed and soon defeated him; the Greeks were saved. Meanwhile, Russia had begun to advance down the Black Sea coast towards Constantinople. The crisis was ended by the London Protocol of 1830 establishing an independent Greece–though it was far smaller than what the Greeks had hoped to achieve. The following year Greece accepted Prince Otho of Bavaria as King – an unlikely choice, but one imposed on Greece by the Powers. What interested Britain was not to increase trade with Greece, but to secure her established interests in the Mediterranean without allowing Russia to become influential in the area: it was not to be another case of the Spanish Empire. Latin America could be helped towards complete independence; Greece had to be kept small so that Turkey could continue to exist as a bastion against Russian advances towards the Mediterranean. At least there was no general European war as a result of the Greek Revolt, but neither was there any clear settlement of the eastern Mediterranean, and this was to disturb European diplomacy for the rest of the century.

7 Revolution averted

Conditions after the war

'Boney was beat!' Waterloo was recognised as one of the decisive battles of the world. Rarely had British prestige stood so high. Victory bonfires greeted the news – now there would be peace and prosperity . . . But the rejoicing was short-lived: more bonfires were soon started by angry, starving workers burning hay-ricks. For fully five years after the war, popular discontent and agitation was such that the wealthy, continuing their life of ease and indulgence, feared a revolution quite as destructive as the French that had ushered in twenty years of war.

Why was this? When we try to explain why important things were happening, we look for causes. These can be roughly divided into two types: those of a temporary, passing nature, and those that were more deep-seated. The temporary causes sprang from the war itself. Europe had suffered badly, and it was a little while before it could afford to purchase large quantities of manufactured goods, so exports did not leap ahead as some people had hoped. Government contracts to supply the navy and army (with food, boots, clothing, armaments, equipment) quickly ran out, and it was suddenly difficult to find alternative markets. Manufacturers found life was hard. There was short-time working and unemployment, which was made worse by the rapid demobilisation of soldiers and sailors. If manufacturers felt the pinch, workers felt it more, for without work they had no money and suffered deprivation and hunger. There was no 'unemployment pay' and the Poor Law gave relief at little above starvation levels. Even so, the rising cost of the Poor Rate caused resentment among the landed classes.

What should the government do? It did not see it as its duty to interfere with industry or the 'national economy' (the term would not have been recognised). Increasingly, the government was coming to believe that the most effective and economic methods would be found by allowing as much free and open competition as possible. (Do you recognise the influence of Adam Smith's ideas here?) It preferred to let things alone and so encourage manufacturers to find the best and cheapest methods – giving an *incentive* to look for improvements and to become rich through personal effort and hard work. This has been called 'individualism'. The idea of interfering as little as possible became the dominant idea of Victorian politics: it was known by the French phrase, *laissez-faire*. So the government did nothing to plan the switch from war-time to peace-time production. It reduced expenditure and left others to solve the problems of adjusting to the changed conditions. For the worker and those out of work alike, things got worse. Wages fell and the price of bread rose (see Fig. 17). There were riots, and in some areas brief outbreaks of *Luddism* returned. Desperate men trudged miles in search of work. For ten years after Waterloo, the standard of living for many people must have dropped; some historians argue that workers suffered for a whole generation.

In the field of finance the government felt confident and experienced, but its position was serious. The National Debt stood at the unheard-of figure of £831 million, and people had much more cause to fear government bankruptcy than in 1783 under Pitt (see page 56). Some £30 million (nearly half the assessed revenue) went on interest charges on the Debt. No wonder the government cut expenditure – but even in peace-time its costs were great. Looking ahead to 1816, Castlereagh complained: 'taking the future peace establishment at 20 millions a year, there will exist a serious deficiency of means to meet the charge.' But in 1816, the government, despite its need of revenue, was forced to abolish income tax. Pitt had adopted it in 1798 as a war tax: it had proved effective as a **progressive tax** paid by the wealthy. Now the war was over, the tax had to be repealed. (Note this carefully. The government had no wish to abolish the tax, but the MPs forced it to – does this suggest it was a powerful government in control of affairs?). The government was obliged to turn to indirect taxation (**regressive taxes**) that bore most heavily upon the poor, those least able to afford them.

The countryside

Landowners had run up heavy debts during the war for agricultural improvements. They feared that peace would open British markets to a flood of cheap grain from Europe, which would bring down the price of British corn catastrophically. They demanded protection. They got the 1815 Corn Law, which excluded foreign corn until British corn had reached the famine level of eighty shillings a quarter. This guaranteed a high price to the farmer. (Only landowners could sit in the House of Commons at this time. They looked after their own interests, preferring to do little about the needs of others. If you were a manufacturer or a worker, what would you think?) Of course, the poor paid dearly, for bread was a staple part of their diet for which there were few substitutes then. It seemed the scales were weighted heavily against the poor.

The poor were also the chief sufferers from the deep-seated changes that were transforming British society (see Chapter 1). The increasing population made the impact of agricultural change greater. Enclosure frequently deprived the poor of the 'wastes' from which they might supplement their meagre diet and income. They had to seek relief from the parish, according to the old Elizabethan Poor Law. There were many different ways of dealing with paupers and no single approved system. Some villages used the labour rate – a landowner could either pay his share of the poor rate or give able-bodied poor work to do, paying at an agreed rate and contributing to the cost of feeding the pauper. Some used the Roundsman System where groups of paupers were sent round to landowners who paid a proportion of their wages, the parish making up the rest.

The Privy Council, 1816
   Cruikshank here shows how the government was disturbed at having to repeal income tax. Castlereagh is on the left, Vansittart on the right and the Prince Regent on the 'throne'. On whose side was Cruikshank—government or opposition?

Contrast this cartoon with the one on p. 88. Is Cruikshank reliable as a primary source? (Remember, it is not enough to say simply that he was biased). Discuss with your teacher the use of cartoons as evidence.

The Blessings of Peace or the Curse of the Corn Bill

Cruikshank's comment on the 1815 Corn Law
  Cruikshank shows the rich landowners refusing
permission for cheap food to be imported–John Bull and

his family emigrate! Would contemporaries think this a fair
comment on the 1815 Corn Law? What do you think, from
the evidence available to you today?

The best known method was the Speenhamland System (introduced in 1795 by the Berkshire magistrates meeting at the Pelican Inn, Speenhamland, near Newbury). It was not new; it supplemented wages to bring them up to an agreed level based on the price of bread:

When the Gallon Loaf of Second (quality) Flour, weighing 8lb 11oz, shall cost 1/-; then every poor and industrious man shall have for his own support 3/- weekly, either produced by his own or his family's labour, or an allowance from the poor rates, and for the support of his wife and every other of his family, 1/6.

Read the extract again. What does it tell you? It was not a minimum wage but an allowance, and it varied with the price of bread. If the labourer had a family, he got more according to the number in the family. (Some argued at the time that this encouraged labourers to have large families – can you see why?

Do you agree with the argument?) If the labourer had work, then he would get nothing if his wage took him above the level laid down, or his wage would be made up to that level. But it was an allowance at starvation level designed to keep the poor alive in a very bad year. No one dreamt that that poor relief would become a continuing necessity throughout each year. The idea had become widely adopted by 1797 and remained a common method of poor relief in many counties of southern England and the Midlands (rarely in the North, where wages were higher), and it tended to keep wages low. Even so, the poor rate went up – partly because of rising prices, partly because of the rising population. Large farmers paid proportionately more, but tended to get the advantage of using labour at very low rates. Small farmers had less need of labour and suffered from the high poor rate – quite a number of them went bankrupt.

The poor themselves often turned to petty theft

and poaching to supplement their meagre allowances, and the magistrates (all landowners) replied with savage sentences, hangings, transportation and imprisonment, all of which left the labourer's family destitute. In 1815, severe Game Laws were introduced, increasing penalties and producing almost open warfare between gamekeepers and poachers. Property was regarded as much more valuable than human life. (Is that the same today?) It must have been a dreadful time, for memories of the suffering survive even into our own day. The rich, in contrast, suffered very little. Traditional society was being torn assunder: there were bitter feelings that could easily lead to class war.

Historians have looked carefully at this period and have often blamed the politicians of the times. You might like to glance at *The Village Labourer* by the Hammonds, or that great reflection on social changes, E. P. Thompson's *The Making of the English Working Class*. They are history books of high reputation, but they are written with passion and a deep sympathy for the sufferings of the rural poor. Other historians have been more guarded in their conclusions, but the experience of the years after Waterloo did much to alter people's attitude to traditional society and values.

Poacher caught in a 'humane' man-trap

Towns

Conditions in the growing towns, both for work and living, were also very bad. To the shortage of work was added overcrowding in slums, frequent epidemics, and poor relief that was badly organised, for many growing towns had been villages a generation before. Severe discipline, bad working conditions, long hours and low pay gave plenty of problems for those who were lucky enough to have work. The government did not interfere, for it adopted the principle of *laissez-faire*: but it had banned trade unions (the Combination Acts, see page 61), which might have done something about working conditions, at least for the skilled men. If the countryside had its problems, these were dwarfed by those of the growing industrial towns, for the greater concentration of people presented a serious problem.

The fear of revolution

Tales of rick-burning, Luddism and disorder, and of men drilling as soldiers in the North, made the government fear revolution. It is easy to condemn the ministers, but consider the difficulties they faced. There was no police force: outside London, local constables were amateurs and often unpaid. The local yeomanry, composed of young land-owners with little respect for the 'lower orders', could not be relied on for keeping the peace. (Can you see why?) The army was small and could not be sent all over the country. The Home Office had a very tiny staff. In these circumstances, the government simply supported the action of local magistrates in enforcing the severity of the penal code. There was a reliance on spies and *agents provocateurs*, whose reports filled the shelves of the Home Office and terrified the government into supposing that a Jacobin revolution was in the making, especially as there were societies with links in different towns that raised the old fears of the Corresponding Societies of the 1790s (see p. 60). Spies encouraged simple men to commit acts that led to riots, or worse – and sometimes they simply invented stories. One spy (known as Oliver) earned a reputation for this sort of thing. You get a good idea of how successful these spies were from A. J. White's *Waterloo to Peterloo*. But the government saw revolution in every large gathering of working men and every demand for reform: it was determined not to lose control.

Did the government have reasonable cause to suppose a revolution threatened? Certainly the distress in country and in town came together in working-class agitation that soon developed an organisation all its own. It was almost as though a new working-class consciousness was appearing that demanded reforms and the cutting out of corruption in government. (The Whigs did not approve of workers demanding such things on their own account, even if they themselves favoured the proposals. There were few men in Parliament prepared to take the workers' side.) In the country, popular agitation was encouraged by great orators such as Henry Hunt and by journalists of the genius of William Cobbett, whose forthright style earned him great popularity. The government became so anxious about the *radical* press that it raised the stamp duty to 4d in hopes of making journals too expensive for working men. But a flood of un-stamped papers appeared, such as Cobbett's *Twopenny Trash*, a cheap version of his *Political Register*. The agitation was given a programme for radical reform, because it was argued that, since the House of Commons was composed solely of wealthy landowners who were ignorant of the

actual working and living conditions of the poor, no serious change was likely until parliamentary reform had changed the Commons into a House representing the working man. Huge meetings were held and many petitions signed demanding par-liamentary reform. At the meetings there was plenty of wild talk and some advanced views were put forward, like those of the Spencean socialists, followers of Thomas Spence, who advocated equal distribution of land (he died in 1814). The govern-ment could be forgiven for fearing Jacobinism and turning to repression to keep order, since reform could only increase agitation for more. A Report of the Secret Committee into the Disturbed State of the Country (1817) noted:

> Attempts have been made, in various parts of the country, as well as in the metropolis, to take advantage of the distress in which the labouring and manufacturing classes of the Community are at present involved, to induce them to look for immediate relief not only in a reform of

A Radical Reformer
Cruikshank produced this cartoon in 1819, showing the ministry's fears of revolution. They flee before the monster that recalls the guillotine and the French Revolution. Is it a fair representation of the ministry's fears? On whose side is Cruikshank in this cartoon? Remember to give your reasons!

Parliament . . . but in a total overthrow of all existing establishments.

'Tory Repressors'

If you glance at some text books, you will see members of the government between 1815 and 1822 labelled as 'Repressors' and between 1822 and 1830 as 'Reformers'. You will know that this is far too simple a judgement: it needs serious correction, not only because it takes little account of the problems facing a government at that time, but also because it fails to look at the position of the cabinet itself. The government had been hastily formed in 1812 on the assassination of Spencer Percival. It was not expected to last long; indeed, the only reason it was not composed of Whigs was because they favoured Roman Catholic Emancipation (see page 70) and the Prince Regent did not. However, its leader, Lord Liverpool, remained Prime Minister from 1812 to 1827. If he was no great parliamentarian, he was a capable politician, trained by the Younger Pitt himself, and skilled in holding together a talented team of ministers. Sidmouth was Home Secretary (you have met him as Addington who took over from Pitt in 1801) and he did not use spies deliberately to provoke rebellion; he was a kindly man, courteous and sincere, doing his best to administer well – not the ogre of popular tradition. Lord Eldon, Lord Chancellor from 1807 to 1828, had been Lord Chancellor from 1801 to 1806 and had served with Pitt; he was a noted lawyer. The chief spokesman in the Commons was Castlereagh, the Foreign Secretary (it is worth mentioning that his rival, George Canning, leader of the 'Tory Reformers' was in the ministry as President of the Board of Control for India from 1816 to 1820). Castlereagh, being the chief spokesman, was closely associated with government policies: he was pilloried by Cobbett and (from a safe distance) by poets like Byron and Shelley. It is worth quoting a little from Shelley's *Masque of Anarchy*:

I met Murder on the Way –
He had a mask like Castlereagh –
Very smooth he looked, yet grim;
Seven blood-hounds followed him: . . .

Next came Fraud, and he had on,
Like Eldon, an ermine gown;
His big tears, for he wept well,
Turned to mill-stones as they fell.

Like Sidmouth, next, Hypocrisy
On a crocodile rode by. . . .

It is a long poem that was read throughout the nineteenth century by working-class radicals. It ends with a line that has often been quoted:

Shake your chains to earth like dew
Which in sleep had fallen on you –
Ye are many – they are few!

The line came naturally to the lips of **Chartists** twenty years later. When you re-assess historical judgements, as we are doing with the 'Tory Repressors', it is as well to remember such contemporary poems, for they are evidence of pretty strong feelings – even if they are exaggerated.

The government lasted a long time, but it was not always sure of its position. The Prince Regent frequently threatened to dismiss the ministers and they could not always control the House of Commons. You have already seen the House repeal Income Tax, against Castlereagh's wishes. Here is another point to bear in mind, when judging the government's actions. As a government, they did not altogether control the House of Commons.

When the ministers considered news of rickburning, machine-breaking, monster meetings and workers' societies in different towns, linked by correspondance and exchanging fraternal delegates, they wondered where it would lead. Then in 1816 a huge meeting, addressed by Henry 'Orator' Hunt, at Spa Fields in London ended in a violent riot. Was this the beginning of Jacobin revolution? Was the riot linked with those workers drilling like soldiers in Lancashire? The ministers suspended Habeas Corpus (thus allowing arrest and imprisonment without a charge being brought) and passed the Seditious Meetings Act (1817). Sidmouth justified himself:

To suspend the Habeas Corpus Act at the present moment would obstruct the commission of the most flagrant crimes and check the hands of the sacriligeous despoilers of the sacred fabric of the constitution.

Over a hundred leading agitators were arrested.

Samuel Bamford, a radical who later wrote an autobiography, had been at the Spa Fields meeting as a delegate from the Midlands. He recalled the atmosphere in London:

. . . many of the leading reformers were induced to quit their homes, and seek concealment where they could obtain it. Those who could muster a few pounds, or who had friends to give them a frugal welcome, or had trades with which they could travel, disappeared like swallows at the close of summer, no one knew whither . . . Cobbett, in terror of imprisonment, had fled to America.

But the climax came on 16 August 1819, at St Peter's Fields in Manchester. It was one of many monster meetings at which petitions demanding parliamentary reform were signed. This one had been well publicised and people came from some distance in holiday spirit to hear Orator Hunt. The magistrates were nervous that the meeting might turn into a riot and had called out a detachment of cavalry and the local Yeomanry 'just in case'. At the outset of the meeting, the cavalry moved into the crowd to arrest Hunt. They did so, but the crush of people was so great that the yeomanry, supposing the cavalry was under attack, drew their swords and charged the peaceful crowd. Panic ensued and many were injured. Eleven people were killed. The public reaction was immediate: many condemned the act as the culmination of repression, and it was soon called 'Peterloo' in hollow mockery of the great national victory. A new class hatred had entered English politics, and for well over a century Peterloo was the rallying cry of working-class resistance to oppression. It has become almost a national myth.

In 1819, the government leapt to the defence of the magistrates. The Lord-Lieutenant of Yorkshire was dismissed for criticising them. Even Canning (leader of the 'Tory Reformers') acknowledged, 'To let down the magistrates would be to invite their resignations and to lose all gratuitous service in the counties liable to disturbance for ever.' Quickly, the government passed the Six Acts 1819, clamping down on popular agitation by restricting public meetings, the possession of fire-arms and the carrying out of military training, and by raising the stamp duty on journals.

In Scotland, agitation continued. There was what amounted to a general strike in Glasgow and an unsuccessful rebellion by some weavers in 1820. Andrew Hardie unsuccessfully led a group of radicals against the Carron Iron Works; a special commission tried them for treason and twenty were transported, but Hardie and John Baird were executed.

Oliver the Spy had no part in Peterloo or the Scottish disturbances, but he was concerned with a hare-brained scheme to assassinate the whole Cabinet as they sat at dinner – it was called the Cato Street Conspiracy, 1820. It failed dismally, and the conspirators (except Oliver) were either killed or captured. At their trial, their defence counsel remarked, 'If all the circumstances could be investigated, it would prove that the treasonable part

is altogether the brewing of a spy and an informer.' It did not help the conspirators: they were condemned. Their leader, a young idealist, Arthur Thistlewood, who had been an organiser at the great Spa Fields meeting, declared on the scaffold, 'I die in the cause of liberty.' But the conspiracy marked the end of the post-war disturbances, for conditions were beginning to improve and social tensions generally relaxed for the moment. The 'Tory Repressors' were giving way to the 'Tory Reformers', and the Six Acts were not renewed.

Here are two examples of documentary questions based on Peterloo. They differ in their approach, but both are exemplars of types you may well encounter. The Carlyle question uses the quotation simply as stimulus, allowing the questions to spring from it, so that the quotation is not essential to the questions. Note that the important questions are (*b*) and (*d*), and (*d*) is not really concerned with the quotation as such. Carlyle was a noted critic of Victorian times. Look him up in the index and in reference books. You might like to dip into some of his writings – they are always very vigorous – and to visit the museum in Cheyne Walk, London, in the house he occupied.

The other question uses the documents more fully and needs more careful reading: it tries to get you to use the passages as sources in the way an historian might. The answer to (*a*) clearly begins with listing the disagreements over the numbers attending, but there are other points to note; (*c*) calls for the exercise of common sense and historical judgement – bias comes into this; (*d*) refers to the Six Acts and the government support of magistrates.

These questions are not difficult or demanding. Do you think they are good examples of the way to use documentary extracts in examinations? Make use of the same extracts and produce your own questions (total marks of 20, but you may divide them as you wish). Try out your questions on the form and see whether they prefer yours to the ones set by the Examining Boards.

Peterloo

Who shall compute the waste and loss, the obstruction of every sort, that was produced in the Manchester region by Peterloo alone! Some thirteen unarmed men and women were cut
5 down. The number of the slain and maimed is very countable: but the treasury of rage, burning hidden or visible in all hearts ever since, more or less perverting the effort and aim of all hearts ever

since, is of unknown extent. 'How ye came
10 among us, in your cruel armed blindness, ye
unspeakable County Yeomanry, sabres flourishing, hoofs prancing, and slashed us down at your
brute pleasure; deaf, blind to all our claims and
woes and wrongs, of quick sight and sense to
15 your own claims only! There lie poor sallow
work-worn weavers, and complain no more
now; women themselves are slashed and sabred,
howling terror fills the air; and ye ride prosperous,
very victorious, – ye unspeakable: give us sabres
20 too, and then come-on a little!' Such are
Peterloos . . .

Carlyle

(a) Why was Peterloo so called? In what year
did it take place?
(b) What circumstances led to this incident?
(c) What sort of person might have said the
imaginary words in lines 9–20?
(d) What were the causes of discontent in the
period after 1815?
(e) Do you think the passage exaggerates the
significance of Peterloo?
(f) What do you know of Carlyle?

Note that Carlyle says 13 were killed (line 4) and
their number was 'very countable', yet the figure
generally given is 11. Can you suggest why there is
this difference? – Carlyle was alive at the time of
Peterloo. Does this make you distrust Carlyle as a
source?

O & C

Study the following four extracts. All are about
the Peterloo massacre in 1819.

Extract 1
'It was an orderly demonstration of men,
women and children, some 80,000 strong which
marched to St Peter's Fields, Manchester, to
listen to Orator Hunt making demands for political reform. The organisers took the utmost care
that there should be no violence, but the days
before the meeting were full of tension and
suspicion on behalf of the authorities. The legality of the coming meeting was questioned;
yeomanry were held ready for action.
. . . In order to make certain there would be no
trouble, Hunt offered to give himself up before
the meeting. Then, while Hunt was addressing a
vast but silent crowd, the magistrates decided
the meeting was illegal and sent the yeomanry to
arrest him. The mounted soldiers forced their way
through the dense crowd to the platform and
Hunt allowed himself to be arrested.
Then, either panic at being surrounded by a
crowd of 80,000 or deliberate vindictiveness

caused the yeomanry to raise the cry, 'Have at
their flags', and strike out right and left with their
swords . . . Over 400 people were wounded,
113 being women. Eleven died, including two
women and a child.
It was an unprovoked attack by a Government
using armed force upon unarmed people exercis-
ing their right to meet together.

Social and Economic History of Britain,
P. Gregg (Harrap), 1965

Extract 2
'The events of yesterday will bring down
shame upon the name of Hunt and his ac-
complices. They openly defied the warnings of
the Magistracy and having invited the attendance of a mass of people over 100,000 in
number, proceeded to address them with language of the usual malevolent nature. They
astounded all ears with continued shouting and
clapping of hands . . .
The Yeomanry advanced in full charge through
the multitude and surrounded the Orators who
were taken into custody . . .
Now ensues a most painful and melancholy
part of our recital. The necessary ardour of the
troops in the discharge of their duty led to some
fatal and many serious accidents . . . A very
worthy young member of the Yeomanry is linger-
ing in the Infirmary every moment expecting to
draw his last. During the charge he was assailed
by a brickbat which brought him off his horse and
had his skull fractured. The extent of his injuries
is heart-rending'

Report in the *Manchester Mercury,*
17 August, 1819

Extract 3
'On the cavalry drawing up they were received
with shouts of good-will as I understood it but
they waved their sabres over their heads, darted
forward and began cutting down the people. The
cavalry were in confusion for they could not,
with the weight of man and horse, penetrate the
compact mass of human beings to reach Hunt.
Sabres were used to hack a way through defenceless limbs and heads . . . Their cries were
piteous and heart-rending but all appeals were in
vain . . .
. . . It was near this place that one of the
yeomanry was dangerously wounded and un-
horsed by a blow from a fragment of brick,
supposed to have been thrown by a woman.'

Passages in the Life of a Radical, S. Bamford
published 1839

Extract 4

'Whatever may be our feelings at the assembly of 50,000 people, half employed and half starved . . . the fact is nearly 100 of the King's unarmed subjects have been sabred by cavalry in the streets of their own town in the presence of those Magistrates whose sworn duty it is to protect the life of the meanest Englishman . . . Of the crowd a large portion consisted of women. About 8 or 10 were killed and above 50 wounded were taken to hospitals; but the gross number of injured is not supposed to have fallen short of 80 or 100. Such are the facts . . . The Riot Act limits the Magistrates' right of interference to 'unlawful assemblies' and no other. Was that at Manchester an unlawful assembly? We believe not. Was the subject proposed for discussion unlawful? Assuredly not.

Editorial in *The Times*, 19th August, 1819

(a) What differences of fact and opinion do you detect between these extracts?   (5 marks)
(b) In what ways do any of the extracts agree with one another?   (5 marks)
(c) How do you account for the differences and similarities, in view of the fact that they are all describing the same event?   (5 marks)
(d) What measures did the Government take to curb popular discontent after the Peterloo massacre?   (5 marks)

AEB, November 1980

It is easy to see the bias in the *Manchester Mercury* report, but on whose side was *The Times*? Note that the Editorial does not exaggerate the number killed. Which of extracts 2, 3 and 4 is the most trustworthy, do you suppose? – Bamford was present at Peterloo.

'Tory Reformers'

Conditions were different in the 1820s, and there were a number of reforms. Most of these were straightforward and simple, but since they followed a period when reform was rare, they have attracted a good deal of attention. You have already realised it is too simple to divide Liverpool's ministry into 'Repressors' and 'Reformers', for there was no sudden change either of attitudes or of men – Canning had sat with Castlereagh in the ministry, remember. Economic conditions improved and agitation diminished, making the idea of moderate changes acceptable. The most dramatic incident was Castlereagh's suicide. Read Montgomery

Hyde's little book, *The Strange Death of Lord Castlereagh*, to try and discover the reasons behind it. Castlereagh had proved himself a fine Foreign Secretary (see Chapter 6), but as chief spokesman in the Commons he was popularly associated with repressive measures. Cobbett wrote delightedly of his death, and there were some cheers at his funeral.

However, the ministry had already begun to break up before Castlereagh's death, especially over the affair of Queen Caroline (you might like to pursue her story—start with what T. H. White says in *The Age of Scandal*). In 1820, George III, that poor old man, died and was succeeded by the Prince Regent, now George IV. His estranged wife returned against his wishes and demanded to be treated as Queen. George hated her, excluded her publicly from the coronation and demanded a divorce. The Whigs and Radicals leapt to her aid, representing her as a deeply wronged woman and she became very popular. Very quickly the ministry realised that the Commons would not agree to a royal divorce (which would be necessary because of the law at the time). Croker, an active political observer, noted: 'The King wants the Ministers to pledge themselves to a divorce, which they will not do . . . The King has certainly intimated his intentions of looking for new and more useful servants.' Do you see how important the King still was in politics? But the Whigs would not do: they had taken Caroline's side and wanted Roman Catholic Emancipation. So Liverpool remained in office and the Queen's carefully stage-manged popularity dropped when she accepted a handsome pension to live privately abroad. Liverpool's ministry survived.

Sir Robert Peel showed how things were moving when he wrote to Croker as early as February, 1820: 'Do you think that . . . public opinion is more liberal (to use an odious but intelligible phrase) than the policy of the government?' There were some changes of minister. Liverpool remained Prime Minister until his stroke in 1827, Eldon was Lord Chancellor until 1828, Sidmouth was replaced as Home Secretary by Peel in 1821, but he remained in the cabinet at the King's especial request until 1824. Canning became Foreign Secretary in 1822. He was the leader of the 'Reformers' but he had served in the 'Repressors' ministry and in 1819 had boldly stated that Parliamentary Reform was the first step to Revolution. In 1823 Robinson became Chancellor of the Exchequer; more importantly, perhaps, William Huskisson, who had held minor office before, became President of the Board of Trade in 1822. The change in personnel was gradual—and taken from men who had served the 'Repressors'. The measures the new ministry pro-

Consider this extract:

Castlereagh

The ruffians who continue to praise this man
tell us that the history of his life is found in the
measures of the Government for the last twenty-
seven years; and that is true enough; it is found in
5 all the various acts that have been passed to shut
the Irish up in their houses from sunset to sunrise,
and to transport them without trial by jury. It is
found in the Power-of-imprisonment Bill of
1817. It is found in those terrible Six Acts . . . His
10 history is in the figure of eight and eight cyphers,
which represent the amount of the National
Debt. It is written in those measures which have
reduced the most industrious and enterprising
farmers in the world to a state of beggary . . . It is
15 written in a mass of pauperism hitherto wholly
unknown in England, and it is written in starvation to Ireland amidst over-production.
(WILLIAM COBBETT in *The Weekly Register*,
1822.)

(a) Explain the references to Ireland (lines 5
6 and 16–17), the Six Acts (line 9), the
National Debt (lines 11–12), the plight of
British farmers (lines 13–14) and a mass
of pauperism' (line 14).   (12)
(b) Is this passage fair to Castlereagh? To what
extent was he personally responsible for the
matters of which the writer accuses him?
(8)

O & C

In the passage, Cobbett gives his assessment of
Castlereagh and puts the blame for the unpopular
measures of the government firmly on his shoul-
ders. The questions that follow the passage ask
you (a) to explain references, and (b) to give your
judgement on Cobbett's assessment. Cobbett was
well known and lived through all the events he
records – he is a primary source. Here you are
asked to question whether such an important
source can be wrong. You know him to be biased,
and so you can expect him to paint the worst
possible picture. But there is much more to judgement in history than spotting bias.

duced were not sweeping, but such as their predecessors would have favoured. Already, in 1819,
William Hazlitt, the essayist, had written: 'A
modern Whig is but the fag-end of a Tory . . . which
reminds one of Opposition coaches, that raise a
great dust or spatter through the mud, but both
travel the same road and arrive at the same
destination.' It was a point Tierney put on behalf of
the Whigs in 1826: 'though the gentlemen opposite
are in office, we are in power, the measures are ours,
but all the emoluments are theirs . . . If we take
away our support, out Canning must go tomorrow.'

Reforms did not await the new ministry: already
in 1819 a Factory Act had been passed – no more
effective than that of 1802, but at least an indication
of government concern. In 1819, also, Peel secured a
'return to cash payments' (restoring the gold standard from which Pitt had been forced to depart in
1797, see page 64). It was to be effected by 1821, and
was welcomed by the bankers as leading to more
secure credit. But it coincided with good harvests
(which meant low prices for farmers). Farmers are
businessmen, not economists: they blamed Peel for
their drop in incomes and were to remember this in
the 1840s. These two measures deserve to be listed
with those of the 'Tory Repressors'.

Trade, trade unions and penal reform are the
three areas in which reform occurred in the 1820s,
though 1829 saw a new development.

Trade

There were distinct moves towards free trade.
Huskisson was the main force behind the measures,
but opinion generally was beginning to favour free
trade. In 1820 some merchants of the City of
London petitioned for the repeal of tariffs, arguing
shrewdly that: 'Nothing would more tend to
counteract the commercial hostility of foreign states
than the adoption of a more enlightened and more
conciliatory policy.' There was little to fear from
foreign competition at this time, and with
Robinson's help Huskisson secured tariff reductions on a wide range of articles by 1825. Canning's
recognition of the Latin American Republics (1825;
see page 84) certainly encouraged trade, and
Huskisson helped further by modifying the
Navigation Acts 1823, which were finally repealed

in 1849. Between 1824 and 1825 a series of Reciprocity Treaties with certain other countries provided for equal treatment of ships in port. These measures all pointed towards freer trade, but before you decide Huskisson had really changed policy, read this extract from the Committee on Import Duties, 1840:

> The Tariff of the United Kingdom presents neither congruity nor unity of purpose . . . no fewer than 1150 different rates of duty are chargeable on imported articles . . . In the year 1839, out of a total customs revenue of £22,962,000, there were only 17 articles which produced 94% of that revenue . . .

Remember that the 1815 Corn Law was a perfect example of **protectionism.** It was attacked for this very reason. A Radical meeting in Manchester in January 1819, condemned it as:

> being neither more nor less than a vile conspiracy between Great Landlords and the Ministers, to extort from the industrious labourer, through the very bread they eat, an immense portion of Taxes . . . and to enrich themselves and their pensioned minions, by the sweat of the poor man's brow.

But MPs were landowners who would defend their *vested interests*: Peel had already encountered their disapproval over the return to cash payments. All Huskisson was prepared to do was to modify the Corn Law by a *sliding scale* that allowed small quantities of foreign corn to be imported as British corn reached the famine limits of eighty shillings a quarter. This helped stabilise prices a little and prevented corn merchants from making a quick profit by holding back supplies as they approached the limit and then releasing them in order to get maximum prices while preventing foreign imports. So the merchants, not the farmers, lost money. In any case the sliding scale did not come in until 1828, after Huskisson's resignation.

Trade unions

Trade unions were made legal by the repeal of the Combination Acts in 1824. It was Francis Place who was responsible for this. He was a Radical, a tailor of Charing Cross, who did much to influence opinion by his activities and writings. He was helped by the economist McCullock and by a radical MP, Joseph Hume, who cleverly stage-managed witnesses before the committee enquiring into the Combination Acts. But there was a wave of strikes, some with violence, and the government hastened to reimpose restrictions on trade unions (1825) although they were not banned. Both Huskisson and Lord Liverpool admitted that the repeal provisions of 1824 had just 'slipped through' without their realising!

Penal reform

Peel was the man responsible for penal reform. The penal code was savage, with death sentences for trifling offences.

> Arrange a visit to the County Records Office, or get the relevant pages photocopied, in order to note the many death sentences and heavy prison sentences passed at the County Court. You will see that property was more valued than life – and that social class mattered, for sentences varied greatly according to the 'quality' of the prisoner!

By 1827 Peel had reduced death sentences for over a hundred crimes. He was greatly helped by reformers such as Romilly and Mackintosh. But he went further and turned his attention to prisons, many of which were still privately owned and provided an income to gaoler and owner. Peel was helped by humanitarians such as John Howard, Elizabeth Fry and Foxwell Buxton to pass his Gaol Acts 1823 and 1825. These increased powers of inspection and regulation of prisons, but the main programme of prison-building lay in the future.

> Look carefully at these figures: what do they suggest about the effectiveness of Peel's modifications to the penal code?

Year	Number convicted	Sentenced to death	Executed	Executed for murder
1820	9 318	1236	107	10
1830	12 805	1397	46	14
1840	19 927	77	9	9

> Consider the problems that are involved in using figures like these to make such judgements. Do you think Peel's reputation as a reformer, on the basis of the evidence given above, has been exaggerated? Christopher Hibbert's book, *Roots of Evil*, gives a good review of these, and other reforms.

Speculation in 1825

This cartoon satirises the scramble to buy shares in 1825. It led to a serious slump and to the bank legislation of 1826 that permitted joint stock banks outside of London—banks that helped entrepreneurs build their factories. The 'bubble' recalls the South Sea Bubble of 1720 that was still remembered with horror in banking circles. Balloons had been used since the 1780s for short flights, but they were never considered safe.

The police force

Peel's most important reform whilst he was Home Secretary was the establishment of the Metropolitan Police Force in 1829. Problems of policing without a trained and established force were great, especially in the growing towns. Even so, any suggestion of a national police force was rejected out of hand as being a direct threat to the liberty of an Englishman, and savouring too much of the undesirable practices of continental countries. But when Peel was Chief Secretary for Ireland (1812–18) he had already established the Royal Irish Constabulary, and now, with Wellington's active help, he turned his attention to the metropolitan area, establishing the Metroplitan Police Force in 1829. It was under a Commissioner directly responsible to the Home Secretary and was run on military lines: many of the early recruits were former NCOs from Wellington's army. But they were unpopular, these 'Peelers' or 'Bobbies', and suspected of being government spies – it was not ten years since Oliver had been active, after all! The *Standard*, a Tory journal, roundly attacked this first British permanent paid police force:

> It is professedly a corps of spies . . . of free government . . . We would much prefer even an actual military police with red coats and bright muskets.

It was so unpopular that in 1834 a London jury brought in a verdict of justified homicide after a 'Peeler' had been knifed at the Copenhagen Fields demonstration. But the discipline, discretion and dignity of the new force, together with its efficiency, soon earned it respect. Its organisation was copied by many forces as they were established in the towns during the next decades and in the country areas under the Rural Police Act 1839. A contemporary writer noted in 1838 that the new Metropolitan Police Force had made its mark:

> The experience of nine years has confirmed the predictions of good from it, made by the authors of the measure. Person and property are now incomparably safer than they were under the old system. The new police are objects of universal approbation and most deservedly so.

Now that you have covered the reforms between 1819 and 1829, discuss in class whether the main political figures deserve the name that historians have normally given them – the 'Tory Reformers'. Remember that these reforms came after a long war and a period of unusual social tension: they set a pattern, but compared to what was very shortly to come, they must appear almost trivial.

Victorian police forces and the prisons of Victorian Britain make good subjects for project work. There are many specialist books available, but remember to visit the Records Office for information on your local force in Victorian times. Ask the archivist if there are quarterly reports to the police authority, and reports of prison visitors. These sources may be more valuable than a general account given in a book. Always try to make your projects genuine research exercises; go to as many different sources as you can. If you can look at some contemporary primary sources, try to make full use of them.

Lincoln prison chapel
Note the careful planning of the chapel—each prisoner has an individual place, partitioned off from his neighbour. All can be seen easily from the front. Why was this expensive arrangement adopted? Does it suggest the prison authorities at Lincoln castle were kind, or harsh, men? Could they have been humanitarians?

Roman Catholic Emancipation, 1829

The end of the decade was a time of crisis for the Tories. In 1827, Lord Liverpool, who had held the ministry together, had a stroke and retired. George IV flatly refused to have Canning as Prime Minister, but Canning was so well supported in the House of Commons that George had to accept him. Several prominent Tories refused to serve under him, particularly as he favoured Roman Catholic Emancipation. Both Peel and Wellington resigned, but Canning continued undaunted. When he died suddenly of a chill (1827), the King chose Lord Goderich (formerly Robinson of the Exchequer), who proved so incapable of holding squabbling politicians together that he begged, tearfully, to be allowed to resign – George had to lend him his handkerchief! Then the King called Wellington.

Wellington's two years as Prime Minister (1828–30) were stormy. He was no politician and expected the Commons to behave like a regiment; even with Peel as Home Secretary and principal spokesman, the government was not always in control. Very soon the surviving Canningites, such as Huskisson and Palmerston, resigned. Indeed, Wellington helped them to go. But in 1828, Lord John Russell, a Whig, secured the repeal of the Test and Corporation Acts (despite the efforts of Lord Eldon) so that dissenters might now hold public office. Naturally, the Irish Roman Catholics expected to enjoy the same relief.

Roman Catholic Emancipation had disturbed English politics since Pitt failed to get it as the price of the Act of Union (see page 70). Every year in the Commons, motions for emancipation were presented, but those that passed were rejected by the Lords. However, in 1828 Vesey Fitzgerald, appointed to succeed Huskisson at the Board of

Daniel O'Connell expected at Whitehall
  This contemporary cartoon shows the Speaker ready to hit O'Connell back to Ireland, since he could not take his seat. However, a game of shuttlecock did not take place: instead Welligton decided on Roman Catholic Emancipation, 1829.

A Parliamentary Game of Shuttlecock

Trade, sought re-election. Until 1918 it was the custom for all ministers to seek re-election on accepting office and so there was to be a by-election in County Clare. It was won by Daniel O'Connell, a Roman Catholic, who could not take up his seat. The crisis had come. The *Annual Register* put the Emancipation case (1828):

> Above all, it is absolutely necessary to grant the demands of the Catholics, because otherwise the Catholics would not allow Ireland to enjoy a moment's repose, and, exposing us every moment to the danger of rebellion, would render that part of the United Kingdom . . . the source of alarm, of discord . . . of positive weakness. It was added, that the concession was due, as being the consummator in the hope of which alone the people of Ireland had been brought to consent to the Union.

In Ireland there had been extensive disorder since the previous century. Its cause was partly the poverty of the people and the harsh land laws, but religious differences were always to the fore. Agrarian crime, cattle-maiming, arson, torture, beatings and murder were common in the countryside. There were also many secret societies, such as the Catholic Defenders who opposed the Ulster Peep o' Day Boys, or the Whiteboys in the South, or the Moonlighters or the Threshers. But the disorders were on a local scale. It was Daniel O'Connell's achievement to make a national movement out of these local disorders. A tall, handsome orator, he soon earned the title 'Liberator' for his demand for the repeal of the Union. But, first, he wanted Roman Catholic Emancipation, and for this purpose he formed the Catholic Association (1823). The following year the society was collecting substantial funds as 'rents' – soon £1000 a year. As soon as the government suppressed it, it reappeared under a slightly changed name. O'Connell was fast becoming the national leader. His victory at County Clare (1828), aided by the priesthood, forced a decision on Wellington. He knew that civil war threatened in Ireland: he had seen enough bloodshed, so he resolved, much against his will, to press for Roman Catholic Emancipation.

Peel, with six years as Chief Secretary for Ireland behind him, had always opposed such a measure and did so again in 1828. Wellington persuaded him that it was his duty to help to pass it and so save Ireland from further disorder. With great courage,

Peel piloted Emancipation through the Commons in 1829. The Tory Party split and Peel was blamed (as he had been in 1821 over Cash Payments). But Peel had an old-fashioned eighteenth century view of government: a minister was the King's minister governing in the best interests of the nation and this should override party considerations. The measure passed: Roman Catholics could now be MPs and hold public office. Peel was bitterly attacked: he lost his seat at Oxford University at the 1830 election. He was accused of breaking his party, an accusation that was to be made again in 1846 (see p. 121).

Wellington's ministry tottered on to its fall, hastened by the economic depression of 1829–30. In 1830 George IV died and this required a general election. Wellington just managed to survive as Prime Minister for the new King, William IV, but there were many demands for further reform, especially Parliamentary Reform. Wellington would have none of this, and boldly asserted in November, 1830 'that the legislature and system of representation possessed the full and entire confidence of the country'. Within a fortnight the ministry had been defeated in the Commons and resigned. The long Tory dominance was at an end and the old Tory Party was to be refashioned by Peel into a new 'Conservative Party' over the next ten years.

Wellington was a great general whose coolness and judgement in battle, and close attention to detail, earned him the admiration of his enemies. But he was no politician. Read through the parts of this volume dealing with Ireland up to 1829 and then hold a class debate on the question: Was Wellington right to go for Emancipation and risk breaking up the Party?

After the debate, try a piece of empathetic imaginary writing. Suppose you were producing a BBC radio programme of the crisis of 1829–30. Write the script of the broadcast using four characters: yourself as narrator; a Tory voter from Oxford University; an Irish Roman Catholic politician delighted to be returned at last to Westminster; and an English society lady, a friend of Wellington and supporter of Peel – Mrs Arbuthnot, for example, who left a revealing journal. The characters meet to discuss or give their opinions at Christmastide, 1830.

8 Reform, not revolution

Parliamentary reform: the 1830–32 crisis

Next time you are in central London, visit Cartwright Gardens, close to St Pancras Station. There you will find a statue of Major Cartwright (1740–1824) with a plaque recording that he was a 'consistent and persevering advocate of Universal Suffrage, Equal Representation, Vote by Ballot and Annual Parliaments.' This was a programme for Parliamentary Reform that went back at least to the days of John Wilkes in the 1770s. The Younger Pitt had tried to get a reform measure passed in the 1780s (see page 57). He failed because too many people with *vested interests,* fearful of losing influence and money, opposed him. Then came the French Revolution and twenty years of war. Demands for reform were often condemned as the first step to social revolution – a reaction that continued after the war.

Demands for reform

These came from the Old Whigs led by Lord Grey, whose long, active political life stretched back to his association with Charles James Fox. Grey disapproved of the 'mob' but he remained faithful to the idea of reform. Demands for reform also came from the Radicals who led the great meetings and agitation in the years between Waterloo and Peterloo. During the 1820s the attitude to moderate reform was very favourable, and after the Tory Party split over Roman Catholic Emancipation (1829), Parliamentary Reform was only a matter of time. The death of George IV in 1830 meant a general election at which Wellington and the Tories were returned. (Some history books say the election was influenced by news of the July Revolution in France which replaced Charles X with the constitutional monarch, Louis Philippe, but a glance at the dates will show you that the English election was largely over before news of the revolution in Paris was received.) By November, Wellington had been obliged to resign.

There was tremendous popular enthusiasm for parliamentary reform, with a number of societies being formed. In Birmingham, Thomas Attwood formed a Political Union that was soon in correspondence with similar societies in other towns, and did much to direct popular agitation for reform during the coming crisis. As Cobbett put it: 'In short, the game is up, unless the aristocracy hasten forward and conciliate the people.' King William IV asked Grey to form a ministry. It was the first Whig ministry for over twenty years: Parliamentary Reform would follow.

The Reformers' programme had not changed much since the 1770s, but conditions in Britain had changed a good deal. Firstly, there had been a huge increase in the population, with little increase in the number of voters. Secondly, there had been an increase in the country's wealth, but it was no longer only landed and merchant wealth – it was now also wealth from trade and the industrial north. Landowners and merchants had a vote, though industrialists (who regarded themselves as the wealth of the future and wanted the vote to promote their interests) might well not have a vote: they were anxious for a political voice and were quite prepared to support their workers in a vigorous, if not violent, campaign to get it.

The electoral system

What was wrong with the system of election in 1830? There were three things.

1. The distribution of the parliamentary seats:

England & Wales:	513 members (of whom 94 sat for counties, 419 for boroughs)
Scotland:	45 members (under the Act of Union 1707)
Ireland:	100 members (under the Act of Union 1800).

In England, constituencies had two members each. The parliamentary boroughs were the problem, since their distribution was related neither to population nor the wealth of the country – boroughs in Cornwall and the south accounted for over half the seats, with tiny fishing villages returning two members, while gigantic towns such as Manchester,

Birmingham, Leeds, Sheffield had no members. Scotland had eight times the population of Cornwall, yet returned one member fewer.

2. The *franchise* (qualification for the vote) varied between constituencies. Women did not have the vote, and only the most idealistic people suggested they should be enfranchised. For adult males, the counties had the fairest system – a forty-shilling freehold. Landowners enjoyed a great influence as a result. All counties, regardless of size and population, returned two members, except for Yorkshire which had four from 1821 (when the Cornish borough of Grampound had been disfranchised for corruption). Welsh constituencies had only one member each.

There was no uniform system in the boroughs. A few were fairly democratic, having a large electorate – like Westminster or Preston, where residents who paid the old 'scot and lot' tax had the vote, or the 'potwalloper' boroughs where the vote went to those who could claim the possession of a hearth. Some of these had declined to small villages, yet still returned two members. There was a large number of *nomination* boroughs, so called because they were rarely or never contested, since the local lord or squire owned most of the property. Some were almost deserted, like Old Sarum near Salisbury, or had disappeared, like Dunwich, which had sunk beneath the waves off Suffolk yet still returned two members. There were also a large number of *rotten* boroughs, in which the franchise varied considerably: in some 'close' boroughs it was confined to the corporation; in 'freeman' boroughs it was confined to freemen of the borough (many of whom would be created immediately before an election); in 'burgage' boroughs certain householders had the vote. When there was an election that was contested in these *rotten* boroughs, there was usually a great deal of bribery. The MPs from these boroughs could scarcely call themselves representatives of the opinion of the people.

3. Bribery and corruption. This arose partly from the fact that voting took place in public at the *hustings*, so that everyone knew who voted and for whom. Landlords were known to evict tenants who voted against their wishes; each candidate employed thugs to help 'persuade' voters. Votes were openly bought and sold, and not only did electors get a good deal of money from each candidate, but it was the custom to 'feast' electors to help them make up their minds! A tradesman voter would find candidates very anxious to buy his wares, and a publican would be in his element. Elections could be riotous and cost a lot of money, but despite this the idea of secret voting was rejected in 1830.

Here is an example of a question set on intimidation at elections. Study the poster and cartoon opposite and then answer the questions. (The cartoon is a caricature by George Cruikshank showing evictions at Tregony in Cornwall in 1820. The Treasury frequently bought this pocket borough for government candidates; the tenants were kept in debt so that evictions could be used as a threat to make them support the landlord's candidate. The defeated candidate is shown on the right.)

(a) Taunton was a 'potwalloper' borough in 1819. Explain this term.   (4)
(b) What does the poster tell us about the electors?   (6)
(c) Tregony was a Cornish borough. Why did Cruickshank choose Cornwall as an example to make his point?   (4)
(d) Explain the phrase used above in the description of the cartoon 'the Treasury frequently bought this pocket borough for government candidates'.   (6)
(e) The landlord (far left) in the cartoon is saying, 'they'll vote according to conscience, will they?!! I'll let 'em know they are nothing but his lordship's slaves'. How do the poster and the cartoon explain the conduct of a contested election in a rotten borough in the period before 1832?   (10)
                                                    Maximum: 30 marks

UCLES

Look at the way the marks are distributed: they tell you how much you are expected to write and give you a good idea of what the examiners think important. In this case, they are more interested in what you know than in whether you can make use of your knowledge. The questions may start with 'explain' or 'why', but they are really only asking for basic knowledge (*a*, *b* and *c* (14 marks) ask for this, and *d* relies heavily on knowledge). You must know your facts. Question *e* is the difficult one. Here you must draw together all you can remember and use the evidence from the two sources. You may dismiss Cruickshank's cartoon as being biased, but the list of dispossessed artisans and workers cannot be so easily discounted. It was published as a poster at the time for all to see and would have been challenged in the courts if it had been untrue. Taunton was small enough for electors to know the persons named. This piece of evidence seems trustworthy and its message is obvious.

TO

TENDER HEARTED

LANDLORDS

ILCHESTER

TO WIT

Names of the Independent Voters in the Borough of Taunton, Somerset, who live in Houses belonging to Sir T. B. Lethbridge, Bart. but did not vote for the Baronet's Brother-in-Law, H. P. Collins, Esq. at the last election and who have received Notices to quit their houses, signed by the Honourable Baronet:—

MOSHACK	COOK	Labourer
JAMES	STICKEY	Mason
WM	MAULE	Cordwainer
WM	UPHARE	Cordwainer
WM	BRAGG	Labourer
JOSEPH	CLARKE	Taylor
SAMUEL	BALE	Coachmaker
RICHARD	THOMAS	Mason
ANDREW	GOODMAN	Weaver
JAMES	TRUDE JUN.	Weaver
JOHN	GOODMAN	Weaver
JOHN	BOLLOM	Weaver
JOSEPH	GREY	Weaver

Dated 26th June 1819

Marmott, Printer, East St., Taunton.

(a) *Poster from Somerset Record Office*

(b) *Cartoon from Jackdaw, No. 16. 'Freedom and Purity of Election: showing Necessity of Reform in the close boroughs'.*

The crisis develops

What was the attitude of the new Whig cabinet? Grey had no love for democracy and preferred that reform be carried through by the ruling class, not by popular clamour. His Cabinet agreed with his prejudices, for it was one of the most aristocratic cabinets of the century (although it also contained a number of Canningites who had left the Tories in 1828). It was clear to them that the Tories and the House of Lords would oppose Reform, but they were well aware of the considerable pressure for Reform in the country. A crisis was expected. It proved a very serious crisis that put tremendous strain on Lord Grey and on the new King, William IV, a friendly, approachable fellow whose naval background had not well equipped him for the subtleties of politics – some called him 'Sailor Bill', others 'Silly Billy'.

However, behind the agitation for reform lay a deeper feeling – popular distress, hastened by the slump and bad harvests of 1829 and 1830. There were disturbances in the countryside, beginning suddenly in Kent and spreading quickly across the country as far as Wiltshire and the Humber. Farm labourers gathered and burnt hayricks and barns and destroyed threshing machines (which had recently become generally available and were threatening the labourers' autumn employment). In various counties notes were delivered to farmers, threatening attacks if the machines were not destroyed or if wages were not raised – many were signed 'Captain Swing'. Were these events the beginnings of an organised rising? The authorities acted swiftly. Lord Melbourne, Grey's Home Secretary, urged magistrates to be severe against all who were caught, and a special commission, appointed in December 1830, hanged nine labourers and transported 457. Melbourne was ruthless in suppression – more so, perhaps, than the Tories fifteen years before. The 'Swing Riots' were not directly concerned with Reform, but they frightened the wealthy and added to the tensions of the crisis. The Hammonds, two noted historians, have called the riots 'the last revolt of the rural poor'.

You might glance at an advanced history book, *Captain Swing*, by Professors Hobsbawm and Rudé, to get a good idea of the extent and nature of the disturbances. Hester Burton's novel, *No Beat of Drum*, shows clearly how the social distress affected the poor. Traditional rural society was being torn apart.

Read the following extract and answer the questions below.

'During the autumn of 1830 the agitation in the country was deeper than political. Economic misery, pauperism, starvation and class injustice had brought society to the verge of dissolution.
5 Rick burning *under orders of "Captain Swing"*, kept the rural south in terror. In the industrial north the workmen were drilling and preparing for social war. The middle classes clamoured for Reform, equally *to pacify the revolutionary spirit*
10 *below*, and to secure their own rights against an aristocracy they had ceased to trust . . .

In the first fortnight in November 1830, when Wellington met the recently elected Parliament, came the most important political crisis of the
15 century. On 2 November, when Lord Grey called attention to the absence of any promise of Reform in the King's speech, Wellington replied that '*the system of representation possessed the full and entire confidence of the country*'. The Duke had
20 challenged the nation . . . and the King sent for Lord Grey. In choosing his Ministry, Grey was constituting a new party. He was fusing the Canningites and reforming Tories with Whigs. The object that Grey had in view in constructing
25 his Cabinet was to carry a Reform Bill extensive enough to give peace to the land.'

Adapted from G. M. TREVELYAN: *British History in the Nineteenth Century*

(a) What factors led to the agrarian unrest 'under orders of "Captain Swing"' (line 5) and where did the outbreaks of violence occur?

(b) Why did the middle classes think that it was necessary 'to pacify the revolutionary spirit below' (lines 9–10)?

(c) What were the respective posts of the Duke of Wellington and Lord Grey when the King delivered his speech on 2 November 1830?

(d) Write a paragraph of about 15 lines describing the 'system of representation' which Wellington considered 'possessed the full and entire confidence of the country' (lines 17–19).

(e) Why, from their political record, did Lord Grey believe that the Canningites and reforming Tories would give him their support for the reform of Parliament?

UCLES

This question reveals skilfully why the passing of the Reform Act has been considered a major event. It points to the social distress (*a*), the agitation in the country (*b*) and the line-up of support among the politicians (*e*). Note that once again the questions rely heavily on information — you must know your facts.

But there is more to questions like this than knowing facts. After you have got these answers right, try adding a couple of your own questions designed to make more use of the quotation — something along the lines of 'How accurate is it?', or 'How valid are the points it makes?' or 'Is it "good history" or a biased account?'

This additional exercise is very useful, for it helps to prepare you for the unexpected question. As examiners become more skilled in making up documentary questions, and as teachers and candidates get used to the technique, the questions tend to become less obvious, less obvious, less a simple matter of recalling information, and more a matter of thinking about the passage quoted or about the problem with which it is dealing.

THE MORNING CHRONICLE.

LONDON:

SATURDAY, OCTOBER 8, 1831.

The Reform Bill is lost by a Majority of 41. The votes in favour of the Bill were in all 158, including 30 proxies; the votes against it were 199, including 49 proxies.

The triumph of the wicked does not endure for ever. Thank God, there are ways by which the invaders of the rights and properties of the people can be managed. When a House of Commons leaves the Government and the nation—the remedy is a dissolution. When the House of Lords stands out against the KING and the nation, the remedy is a fresh creation of Peers. Without this remedy the Constitution would fall to pieces, and the people would be left a prey to anarchy.

The speeches last night of the LORD CHANCELLOR and Earl GREY in reply were masterly—of Lord BROUGHAM'S speech, it was said by an opponent (Lord LYNDHURST), that it was perhaps the most masterly he had ever made.

It would be offering an insult to the understanding of our readers were we to argue farther a question which no one can misunderstand. The enemies of the Bill are the creatures of corruption, who wish to retain the element in which they have been generated, & in which they find support. As Lord BROUGHAM observed, the real Aristocracy of the country, the old Peers possessing estates which will allow them to be upright, are generally in favour of the Bill. The present Ministry them-

The Morning Chronicle announces the loss of the Bill
Which party did the Morning Chronicle support? Does this extract suggest it made a good case for supporting that party?

The government appointed a committee of four (Lord John Russell and Lord Durham were the most active) to produce proposals for Parliamentary Reform. In a crowded, tense House, Russell revealed the secrets of the Reform Bill. Some members gasped, others laughed at what proved to be a series of proposals far more sweeping than any had anticipated. After vigorous debate, the Bill passed its second reading on 23 March, 1831 by a majority of one vote (302–301, the largest recorded vote of the unreformed House of Commons). Soon afterwards, it was defeated in committee. Grey demanded a dissolution of parliament and a new general election.

The country was in uproar: 'the Bill, the whole Bill and nothing but the Bill' was the popular cry, and the Whigs were returned with a good majority, claiming that they had 'appealed to the people'. A Second Reform Bill was passed by the Commons, but was defeated by the Lords. The response in the country was immediate. At least one national newspaper reported the news between heavy black lines, as though mourning for a sovereign. Throughout the country there were vigorous demonstrations and agitation, with fears of widespread disturbances. In London, Francis Place was responsible for organising agitation through the National Political Union; elsewhere other Political Unions, following Thomas Attwood's lead, took charge, and where this happened there were no serious disturbances. But in Nottingham, Derby and Bristol there were serious riots. Nottingham castle and the Bishop's Palace at Bristol were burnt; the military were called out. Many petitions supporting Reform were presented, and once again there were ominous rumours of men doing military training in the North. The workers were determined to have Reform – and hoped to profit by it. William Cobbett observed in his *Political Register* (1833): 'What did we want the Reform Bill for? . . . that it might do us some good, that it might better our situation . . . not for the gratification of any abstract or metaphysical whim.'

The situation was serious, and a Third Reform Bill was presented. To secure its passage through the Lords, Grey had to get the King's agreement to the creation of sufficient Whig peers to ensure a majority: in April 1832, he demanded that fifty peers be created. The King refused and Grey resigned. Wellington was called to form a government, but he could not do so. Agitation in the country rose to a climax and there were genuine fears of revolutionary outbreaks. In London, Place posted his slogan 'To stop the Duke, go for gold', hoping a run on the Bank of England would force reform through. Grey returned to office with the King's reluctant promise to create as many peers as might prove necessary. None were needed, for Wellington led sufficient peers out of the Lords to allow the Third Reform Bill to pass in June and become the First Reform Act 1832. It was greeted with hysterical joy throughout the country. Bonfires were lit, and it was realised that popular pressure had played a significant part in getting the Bill through.

Consequences of the Reform Act 1832

The Act altered the franchise: the county franchise of forty shillings remained, but the vote was also given to £10-copyholders and long-lease holders and to £50-leaseholders. In the boroughs there was a uniform male franchise of £10-householders, provided they placed their names on the voters' register. The distribution of seats was altered: 56 boroughs with fewer than 2000 inhabitants lost both seats, and 31 boroughs with between 2000 and 4000 lost one seat. The 143 seats were distributed among the new large towns and counties. In addition, eight seats were given to Scotland and five to Ireland. This was clearly a partial solution to the problem of distribution of seats. It was fairer than before, but a surprising number of tiny boroughs remained with one or two members.

The Act was greeted as a great triumph. Lord John Russell believed it would be the only Reform Act and soon earned the nickname 'Finality Jack'. But when the dust had settled, people realised that a new era had not dawned. If the Act had saved Britain from revolution, the important aspect was the way it had been passed, not its content. Parliamentary seats were still far from fairly distributed and elections could be just as corrupt as before. The franchise changes were far from radical; the new property qualifications actually deprived a number of working men in 'potwalloper' boroughs of their vote. The new Act underlined the importance of property and antagonised the working men: they had risked much in their agitation for the Bill. They got no reward. Soon they were openly talking of the 'Whig betrayal' and many joined the Chartists (see page 123). The electorate was merely doubled to a total of about 800 000 out of a population of 24 million. Clearly, a new Reform Act would be called for. It came in 1867 (see page 138). The Whigs were well satisfied: they had avoided passing too radical a measure and, although industrialists now had the vote, the landed interest remained in control and 'democracy' had been defeated. Whatever some historians have said, the First Reform Act was not a great turning point.

Sir Robert Peel had opposed Reform vigorously, and had thereby regained much of his former reputation among his party (though he had had to seek a new seat at Tamworth). He argued that the old balanced constitution of the eighteenth century had been destroyed by the Reform, and that the old constitution had worked well, carrying Britain through twenty years of war to victory. Furthermore, he said there was a risk of a new type of politician, a demagogue, intent on personal ambition rather than carrying out the government of the country in the best way. Governments would become vote-conscious and seek cheap popularity, anxious to be re-elected rather than do unpopular things, and in the new House of Commons there would be little chance for very young men, like the Younger Pitt, or Sir Robert himself, to give the best years of their lives to Parliament and the country as young ministers, because the enlarged electorate would be unlikely to vote for them until they were much older. The Act itself would open the floodgates of reform in every walk of life and begin a rapid change in society, and a further Reform Act would soon be demanded.

Discuss amongst yourselves whether Peel was right and try to puzzle out what one historian of the period meant by writing that 'what the Tories said was true, but what the Whigs did was right'.

What differences did the Reform Act make? The following is an exercise in making a judgement.

1. Traditionally, 1832 has been seen as a great watershed, a triumph for democracy permitting the passing of major reforms that might otherwise have been denied or delayed.

2. G. M. Trevelyan, *History of England*, p. 636:

> This final crisis, that secured the actual passage of the Reform Act, gave dramatic emphasis to the popular element in the 'new constitution'. The people, as a whole, had wrenched the modern Magna Carta from the governing class. The nation thenceforth master in its own house . . .

3. The United Kingdom population in 1831 was 24 028 584.

Elec-torate:	England and Wales	Scotland	Ireland	Total
1830	435,000	4,000	39,000	478,000
1832	657,000	64,000	93,000	814,000

4. Major reforms:
1832 Reform Act
1833 Factory Act, Abolition of Slavery
1834 Poor Law Amendment Act
1835 Municipal Corporations Act (no others before 1841)

5. The franchise changes were far from radical; the new property qualifications actually deprived a number of working men in 'potwalloper' boroughs of their vote. It underlined the importance of property and it antagonised working men: they had risked much in their agitation for the Bill. They got no reward. Soon they were openly talking of the 'Whig betrayal' and many joined the Chartists in 1838.

Was Trevelyan right? If you disagree with him, would you trust his other judgements?

Before 1832 a great landed family might so control a seat as to make it effectively their own – reserved for the family. Take, as an example, Reigate in Kent, a borough returning two members.

1796	Hon. John Somers Cocks (heir to Lord Somers, whom he succeeded in 1806)
	Capt. Joseph Sydney Yorke (son of the Lord Chancellor)
Feb. 1806	Hon. Philip James Cocks
	Capt. Joseph Sydney Yorke (son of the Lord Chancellor)
Dec. 1806	Hon. Edward Charles Cocks (heir to Lord Somers)
	Rt. Hon. Philip Yorke (later drowned at sea)
Jun. 1807	Hon. Edward Charles Cocks (heir to Lord Somers)
	James Cocks of Charing Cross
Nov. 1812	Hon. James Somers Cocks
	James Cocks of Charing Cross
Jan. 1819	Hon. James Somers Cocks
	Vice-Admiral Sir Joseph Sydney Yorke
Apr. 1820	Hon. James Somers Cocks
	Vice-Admiral Sir Joseph Sydney Yorke
1823	James Cocks of Charing Cross
	Vice-Admiral Sir Joseph Sydney Yorke
1826	James Cocks of Charing Cross
	Vice-Admiral Sir Joseph Sydney Yorke
1830	James Cocks of Charing Cross
	Vice-Admiral Sir Joseph Sydney Yorke

The population in 1830 was 3397 (in 1861 it was 9975). The electorate in 1830 is unknown; in 1832 it was 152 (in 1861 it was 835).

Apr. 1831	Joseph Yorke of Forthampton
	Vice-Admiral Sir Joseph Sydney Yorke
1832	John Somers Cocks (Viscount Eastnor) (Died in July and was succeeded by Capt. Charles Philip Yorke.)
1835	Capt. Charles Philip Yorke (A 'Chartist' candidate gained 14 votes to Viscount Eastnor's 85)
1837	Capt. Charles Philip Yorke (NB; a tiny electorate – bribery?)
1841	Charles Somers Cocks (Conservative) (Viscount Eastnor)
1847	Thomas Somers Cocks (Conservative)
1852	Thomas Somers Cocks (Conservative)
1857	William Hackblock of Reigate (Liberal)
1858	William Monson (Liberal)
1859	William Monson (Liberal)
1863	Granville Leverson Gower (Liberal)
1865	Granville Leverson Gower (Liberal)
1867	The election was declared void and the constituency disfranchised for gross corruption.

Now, did the 1832 Act make any difference at Reigate?

Try to trace results in your local constituency at this period – the *Victoria County History* might help your researches. The Records Office may have details of electoral returns as well.

The Whig Reformers

A fresh election on the new franchise in 1832 produced a substantial majority of Whigs and Radicals. This did not add to Grey's strength, for there was serious disagreement between the two groups. The Radicals had much to do with the sudden rush of important reforms, but the Whigs would have preferred to have rested on their laurels. The Radicals were helped by a strange ally, a group of humanitarian Tories such as Oastler, Sadler and Shaftesbury.

Abolition of slavery

The first great measure was the abolition of slavery in the British Empire in 1833. This was the culmination of a highly successful campaign by the Anti-Slavery Society (1823), and its veteran evangelical leader William Wilberforce, friend of the Younger Pitt (see page 57), who lived just long enough to witness the passing of the measure. (You could organise a class visit to Wilberforce House in Hull and arrange to consult some of the documents there.) The slave trade had been abolished in 1807 (see page 2), but in 1833 the status of slavery was ended at a cost of £20 million in compensation to the slave owners. A scheme of apprenticeship was adopted to help former slaves, but it was not well run and there was much disorder and distress in some Caribbean islands. Nevertheless, the measure was a selfless, expensive and humanitarian act.

Improvement of working conditions: the Factory Act 1833

It was one thing to free the slaves in the New World, but what of working conditions at home, especially in the new factories? These were so harsh that Richard Oastler published a famous letter in the *Leeds Mercury*, 1830, in which he bitterly contrasted the concern some humanitarians showed for Negro slaves, with their indifference to the conditions under which children and adults were employed in textile factories. He addressed the letter to Wilberforce himself – a telling point, for Wilberforce was MP for Yorkshire. An extract from the letter has been used in the question below.

Two types of slavery

The pious and able champions of *negro* liberty and *colonial* rights should, if I mistake not, have gone farther than they did: or perhaps, to speak more correctly, before they had
5 travelled so far as the West Indies, have sojourned in our own immediate neighbourhood . . .
   Let truth speak out, appalling as the statement may appear. The fact is true. Thousands
10 of our fellow-creatures and fellow-subjects, both male and female, the miserable inhabitants of a *Yorkshire town* (Yorkshire now represented in Parliament by the giant of anti-slavery principles) are this moment existing in
15 a state of slavery *more horrid* than are the victims of that hellish system '*colonial slavery*' . . . The very streets which receive the droppings of an 'Anti-Slavery Society' are every morning wet by the tears of innocent
20 victims at the accursed shrine of avarice, who

are *compelled* (not by the cartwhip of the negro slave-driver but by the dread of the equally appalling thong or strap of the overlooker) to hasten, half-dressed *but not half-*
25 *fed*, to those magazines of British infantile slavery – *the worsted mills in the town and neighbourhood of Bradford*! . . .
   Thousands of little children, both male and female *but principally female*, from seven to
30 fourteen years of age, are daily *compelled* to labour from six o'clock in the morning to seven in the evening, with only – Britons, blush while you read it! – *with only thirty minutes allowed for eating and recreation.*

(a) Explain 'the giant of anti-slavery principles' (lines 3–14), 'the accursed shrine of avarice' (line 20), 'the over-looker' (lines 23–4) and 'the worsted mills' (line 26)   (4)
(b) Do you find this passage effective – exaggerated – just – too emotional? Were factory conditions '*more horrid*' than those on the slave plantations (line 15)?   (4).
(c) Who besides Oastler led the campaign for factory reform? Briefly summarise the factory legislation passed during the period, and show the particular importance of the Act of 1833.   (8)
(d) What objections were raised against this legislation?   (4)

O & C

Questions (a), (c) and (d) seek information, but (b) is different. It asks you to judge the passage in terms of its effectiveness as evidence – remember that in your answer it is not good enough simply to say that the passage is biased. You need to think hard about it, and to say a good deal more. Do you think it should have earned more than 4 marks (20 per cent)?

Do some research and make a list of the principal factory reforms up to 1876. Also track down the arguments factory owners used to defend their factory methods and resist factory legislation. Some of them were sensible; some were fine examples of 'special pleading' and some were simply nonsense.

There was nothing new about child labour. On farms and in the cottages of domestic workers, children at a very early age were set to long hours of tedious and tiring work by parents who proved harsh task masters. This was traditional. But factories called for an abundance of cheap labour, and the simple fact that there were so many people of all ages crowded into one mill made the bad conditions more obvious. What might have gone unnoticed in the 'domestic system' was quickly deplored in the harsh conditions of the new factories.

It was the children who attracted most attention, for in an age favouring *laissez-faire*, adults were expected to look after their own interests themselves. It was a common practice for parishes to send pauper children as apprentices to distant mills. This removed the cost of their keep from the rates. Sir Robert Peel's father, himself a mill owner, had tried to regulate the conditions under which such children lived and worked in the 1802 Factory Act, and again, helped by Robert Owen, in that of 1819; but neither Act was successful, partly because enforcement was left to local magistrates, some of whom were mill owners themselves!

It was generally the small factories where conditions were worst. Some of the owners of large mills were well-known humanitarians: Peel, Owen, Arkwright, Salt were only the better-known among many successful mill owners who found it possible to make a fortune and still provide excellent conditions for their workers. Several Royal Commissions revealed the extent and nature of the worst conditions: long hours for little pay; harsh labour relations, including beatings by the overseer, and heavy fines, especially for lateness; little attention to health and safety; exploitation of children and especially of women. Frederick Engels, himself a mill owner, drew on his own observations in Manchester and on those reported by several Royal Commissions, in order to produce a famous book, *The Condition of the English Working Class in England in 1844* (note the date). He revealed frightful living conditions as well as bad working conditions. The book gives a realistic picture founded on respectable primary sources and should be available in your local library. (Engels went on to help Karl Marx in his researches and contributed to the development of ideas that were later espoused by communists.)

After the failure of another Factory Act in 1832, a Royal Commission was appointed to investigate conditions in factories. It reported in 1833. This began a new feature of legislation: important reforms were often the result of a Royal Commission's actual recommendations; the problem was investigated and a solution attempted. The Factory Act 1833 (Althorpe's Act) was the first effective factory Act: it applied to all textile factories (apart from silk and lace) and banned the employment of children under the age of nine. Children aged nine to thirteen were not to work more than 9 hours a day or 48 hours a week. Young persons (aged 13–18) were not to work more than 12 hours

daily or 69 hours a week. (That these rules were considered very radical shows what must have been happening at some factories!) Not less than two hours schooling daily was to be provided for children under fifteen. But the most remarkable thing was the appointment of inspectors to enforce the Act. At first there were only four of them and they met with hostility, but these inspectors soon began to make their presence felt, despite the efforts of some mill owners to obstruct their work. (Note that this was a clear case of the government interfering, despite the accepted ideas of *laissez-faire*). Adults were left out of the Act – they could look after themselves. Almost immediately an important movement grew up, promoted by Oastler and Stephens, called the Ten Hours' Movement. It was well organised and began to agitate and influence opinion. Clearly, other Factory Acts would have to come.

Trade unions in the 1830s

Since the repeal of the Combination Acts (see page 61), trade unions had been growing. They had been small and local affairs, though often with links with other unions in distant towns to help members who were tramping round in search of work. But by 1830 some remarkable attempts were being made to bring together all the skilled workers of a particular trade. John Doherty formed the Grand General Union of All Spinners (1829) and a National Association for the Protection of Labour (1830) that claimed a membership of 100 000. His hope was to gather existing unions of skilled men to bring considerable pressure to bear on the employers: his concerns were spreading beyond simple trade matters into politics. Doherty's ideas were strongly influenced by Robert Owen, a self-made industrialist who developed a model industrial community at New Lanark (near Glasgow). His ideas were advanced, and Owen has been called 'the father of British socialism', but these ideas were not confined to radical political views. He was an outspoken humanitarian and also held advanced views about education. His ideas influenced important thinkers of the time and the early Labour Party at the end of the century. In the 1820s he went to America to establish an ideal community at New Harmony, based on his own theories. It was not particularly successful under him, and he returned to England. Owen then took up Doherty's lead, planning to form a huge union.

In 1832 he opened a 'labour exchange' in Gray's Inn Road, London, with branches in the provinces.

The idea was for members to deposit goods they had made that might be exchanged for other goods they needed. The idea proved immediately successful, but lack of good management led to its failure in 1834. In 1833 Owen established the Grand National Consolidated Trades Union (GNCTU) bringing together many trades in a single co-operative venture. The GNCTU had ambitious plans extending to workers' control of industry and a workers' parliament. But it failed, partly because of a trade slump, but more particularly because the employers, backed by the government, broke the Union by lock-outs and by requiring workmen to sign 'The Document' declaring they were not and would not be members of the Union. However, skilled men continued to form and maintain unions on a smaller scale, and Owen's ideas lived on to the next generation and beyond.

The farm workers of Tolpuddle

The unions were for skilled workers, generally in towns. There was little done to help the rural worker. After the severity of Melbourne's suppression of the 'Swing Riots' (see page 104), farm labourers remained sullen. Direct action had failed, but they were not crushed. Some turned to trade unionism to promote their interests. This led to one of the most famous cases of the century – the Tolpuddle Martyrs.

Tolpuddle is in Dorset, and you may visit the court-house where the 'martyrs' were sentenced. They were farm workers who had dared to form a trade union for the purpose of helping each other and pressing for better pay and conditions. Landowners were generally hostile to any unions among agricultural workers, and it does appear that these men were harshly dealt with in order to destroy their union and to be an example to anyone else in the neighbourhood. (Remember that it was only because of the intense campaign fought on their behalf that the country even heard of Tolpuddle – the magistrates were not necessarily striking a blow on behalf of landowners throughout the nation. Remember, too, that the 'Swing Riots' and the popular disturbances over the Reform Bill were very recent, and the magistrates no doubt wanted to make sure there was no repetition of these events. When you make a judgement in history, try to see as many sides of an issue as you can.)

At that time it was common practice among private societies, especially if a need was felt for secrecy, for members to take an oath of loyalty and to perform a series of actions that marked their entry into the society. The men at Tolpuddle did just

this, and the magistrates proceeded against them as if these men were criminals. They were tried for taking a secret and illegal oath under an Act of 1797 passed at the time of the naval mutinies (see page 73) and scarcely remembered since. Six labourers were sentenced to transportation to Australia. Important men outside Dorset heard of the case. It was widely interpreted by Radicals as a deliberate attempt to destroy trade unions and to undermine the liberty of the subject – so long as he was a poor man. (It was noted that wealthy men who joined, for example, the Freemasons took a secret oath and were not tried for it!) If the government intended the sentence as a stern warning, and Melbourne was anxious to encourage repression, it misfired, for there was tremendous popular agitation on behalf of the men who had been sentenced. They were men of good character, one at least a locally-known Methodist lay preacher. Robert Owen put himself at the head of demonstrations, and in London the GNCTU set up a Dorchester Committee, with William Lovett as chairman. Before the decade was over the sentences had been annulled and the labourers returned to England. For trade unionists, the Tolpuddle Martyrs remained a symbol to inspire future generations.

Here is a question that covers trade unionism in some of its aspects up to the 1830s; it is good for revision, too. Look up references and questions (i)–(iv) in other parts of this book.

Trade Unions

(a) ... May it please your Majesty that it may be enacted that all contracts, covenants, and agreements whatsoever, in writing or not
... made or entered into by any journeymen
5 manufacturers or other workmen, or other persons within this kingdom, for obtaining an advance of wages of them, or for lessening or altering their usual hours or for decreasing the quantity of work, shall be and the same are
10 hereby declared to be illegal, null, and void, to all intents and purposes whatsoever. Combination Act, 1799

(b) Spring Assizes, Western Circuit, Dorchester. Monday, March 17, Crown Court.
15 John Lock.—I live at Half Puddle. I went to Toll Puddle a fortnight before Christmas. I know the prisoner James Brine. He asked me if I would go to Toll Puddle with him. I agreed to do so. Edward Legg, Richard Peary, Henry Courtney,
20 and Elias Riggs were with us. They joined us as we were going along. One of them asked if there would not be something to pay, and one said

there would be 1*s*. to pay on entering, and 1*d*. a week after. We all went into Thomas Stanfield's
25 house into a room upstairs. One of the men asked if we were ready. We said, yes. One of them said, 'Then bind your eyes', and we took out handkerchiefs and bound them over our eyes. They then led us into another room on the same floor.
30 Someone then read a paper, but I don't know what the meaning of it was. After that we were asked to kneel down which we did. Then there was some more reading: I don't know what it was about. It seemed to be out of some part of the Bible. Then we got up and took off the bandages from our eyes.

The Times, 1834

(i) What led to the passing of this Combination Act (line 11)?   (5)
(ii) What was a 'journeyman' (line 4)?   (1)
(iii) Why were the Combination Acts repealed in 1824?   (3)
(iv) In what ways were trade unions still restricted in their activities (up to 1875)?   (3)
(v) What charge was made against the men of Toll Puddle?   (2)
(vi) What effect did the subsequent sentence of transportation have on trade unionism?   (3)
(vii) Why did these early unions attach importance to initiation ceremonies such as this (lines 23–36)?   (3)

O & C

The Co-operative Movement

Owen's ideas were on a grand scale, but they did not all fail. The idea of co-operation led to the Rochdale Pioneers (1844) who opened a co-operative shop in Toad Lane, (now a museum) and began the Co-operative Movement that was to be an important influence upon the working class for well over a hundred years. The 'pioneers' subscribed to a fund for the purchase of good-quality food which was sold to members and others at a fair price. A *dividend* based on the amount purchased was paid and this was an incentive to purchase more, especially as the goods were not in any way adulterated. (It was very common for foodstuffs to be seriously adulterated; you can read about this in John Burnett's *Plenty and Want*). The Co-operative charged fair prices, in contrast to the high prices forced on workers in the 'Tommy Shops' run by employers at which their employees were frequently forced to purchase inferior goods (see Disraeli's novel, *Sybil*). No credit, however, was allowed: it

was cash sales only. The Co-operative provided an illustration of Victorian self-help: it was thrift in action, but it also gave experience in organisation and democratic processes, for every member had a vote to elect the management committee. The Co-operatives that grew up in the next decades were to become large institutions (their turnover exceeded £13 million by the 1880s) and to have an influence upon the Labour Party in due course.

The Poor Law

For some time the high cost of the poor rate had been causing great concern and this was increased by the fears raised by the 'Swing Riots'. Landowners hoped to bring down the cost of poor relief, and they were supported by a group of reformers known as Utilitarians, or Benthamites, followers of an important political philosopher, Jeremy Bentham. These Benthamites were fearless reformers and great opponents of inefficiency in government: they believed in examining the principal institutions of the country and were quite prepared to scrap them if they were found wanting. One of their famous slogans was 'the greatest happiness for the greatest number'. They worked indefatigably and had tremendous influence on nineteenth-century opinion and reform. Their methods were often hasty and harsh, but they were anxious to get quick results to benefit the community and the poor. One of their leaders was Edwin Chadwick. He had been Bentham's private secretary and he became very active in social reform, especially the Poor Law and public health. His vigorous methods made him one of the most hated men in England and since he offended so many influential people he slipped out of public life, but his influence was considerable and his ideas were often very sound (though sometimes they were simply wrong). His reputation has suffered, perhaps unjustly.

You might like to make a study of his career to decide whether he was really misunderstood or deserved the hatred of rich and poor. Roger Watson has written a useful pamphlet, *Edwin Chadwick, Poor Law and Public Health*, but the best book is an advanced work, S. E. Finer's *Edwin Chadwick*.

The Poor Law Amendment Act 1834 was largely Chadwick's work: it was the most important reform of the Whigs. A Royal Commission was set up to enquire into the Poor Law, and Melbourne required it to report quickly because of the 'Swing Riots'. Chadwick was the Secretary to the Commission, and it was because of shortage of time that he had to confine the final published Report largely to the agricultural South (consequently, his proposals were quite inappropriate for the industrial North, where conditions were very different). Chadwick was particularly hostile to the Speenhamland system (see page 88), arguing that it was wasteful, demoralised the pauper, kept wages low and encouraged 'improvident marriages and large families' and so produced the high Poor Rate. (He exaggerated both the effects of the system and the extent to which it was still in use by 1832.) His solution was intentionally severe. No one opposed the principle that society had a responsibility towards the poor, but there was a widespread belief that many who sought poor relief were lazy or feckless: their poverty was their own fault. As yet there was little awareness of the real causes of poverty (although Chadwick showed some insight here) and few people had understood that the rapid population rise had produced too many hands for too few jobs.

Here is an example of a different sort of question to the ones given earlier. Instead of using the extracts as a basis for questions requiring you to remember facts, the examiner asks you to use the extracts as *evidence*. You are asked to *examine* the extracts and to think about them, to test their *validity* and reliability. Note that they contrast primary sources with secondary sources. Contemporary sources make up the raw material of history, but sometimes a good secondary source can correct a misleading impression given by contemporary writing. Do the two secondary sources give an adequate summary of the effects of the Speenhamland system? What are the dangers of relying heavily on contemporary written evidence? How would you check such evidence for reliability? Discuss this problem with the class and make a list of the suggestions that are worth noting. The problem is a very important one, and one that you might well be asked to discuss in an examination.

Study the following five extracts about the effects of the Speenhamland system in the early nineteenth century.

Extract A
"In Coggeshall, Essex, weekly wages are 8s. (40p) but by piecework a good labourer may earn 10s. (50p). Now, consider the case of a labourer with four children for the maintenance of which family according to the Speenhamland scale, 11s. 6d. (57½p) is required. Of this sum the good worker can earn 10s. (50p) and receives the remainder, 1s. 6d. (7½p), from the Parish. But the idle man who will not work at all and whom no one will employ, receives the whole amount from the Parish. Where then is the incentive for the good labourer to work? He would fare just as well being idle."

Evidence of a witness before the Royal Commission of Enquiry into the operation of the Poor Law, 1833

Extract B
"The Speenhamland system encourages early and improvident marriages for it is to a labourer's advantage to marry as young as possible and have many children. The more mouths he has to feed the greater the supplement he receives from the parish. Thus, the population increases more rapidly than ever."

A statement by David Ricardo, the early economist, in his book *Principles of Political Economy and Taxation*, 1819

Extract C
"Four men were working near the farm-house and upon questioning them about their wages one among them who was 30 years old and unmarried, complained greatly about the lowness of his wages and added that had he been married with a parcel of children he would be better, not worse, off as he would receive allowances for the children, or else get greater opportunity for piece work and therefore earn more money."

Evidence given by a Mr. Hickson, a landowner in Kent, to Edwin Chadwick in 1834

Extract D
"The Speenhamland system was intended as an insurance against unrest and restrained any tendency to violent revolution by saving families from starvation. However, it had a depressing effect on wages as employers realised that these would be raised to the minimum from the parish poor rates . . . The Speenhamland system was also thought to encourage the poor to have large families."

From *The Age of Industrial Expansion*, A. J. Holland (Nelson), 1979

Extract E

"The Speenhamland system demoralised the countryman for no matter how hard he worked he would not get more than the fixed wage; it deprived him of all incentive . . . Many contemporaries believed the system encouraged larger families and there seems to be some evidence that it undoubtedly encouraged earlier marriages . . . Some historians think this may have prevented the spread of revolutionary ideas among the poor at this time."

From *British Economic and Social History, 1700–1975,* C. P. Hill (Edward Arnold), 1979

(a) Which of the extracts are secondary sources? Give reasons for your answer. (*2 marks*)

(b) In Extract E it is stated that 'Many contemporaries believed the system encouraged larger families'. What evidence is there from the other extracts that this statement is true? (*4 marks*)

(c) Extract E does *not* say the system actually *did* encourage larger families only that many contemporaries believed it did. How could the historian verify whether or not the system did encourage larger families? (*2 marks*)

(d) What difference is there between Extract D and Extract E on the subject of violent revolution? How do you account for this difference? How, if at all, could you verify which one is correct? (*6 marks*)

(e) What difference is there between Extract A and Extract C on the subject of piece work? (*3 marks*)

(f) What was the Speenhamland system? (*3 marks*)

AEB, June 1981

'Indoor relief': work houses

It was necessary to distinguish between those truly in need (the sick, aged or very young), those who were 'swinging the lead', and those who desperately wanted work but could find none. The method was simple: 'outdoor relief' was banned except for the aged, sick and poor in their own homes, while relief to the able-bodied poor was to be 'indoor' only (i.e. the poor must enter an institution). In order to ensure that families should not idly apply for 'indoor relief', conditions in institutions were to be worse than those endured by the poorest labourer. Chadwick called this the 'less eligibility' principle; 'the condition of the recipient should not, on the whole, be more eligible than that of any labourer living on the fruits of his own industry' and the poor bitterly hated it.

'Indoor relief' required that special houses be built for the poor, and in order that this might be done cheaply, quickly and efficiently the Act grouped parishes into unions (so that the poor houses were called the 'Union'). A huge building programme quickly produced a series of strong, prison-like buildings, some of which still survive today (they are often used as hospitals). Of course, it took several years before most of the 'Unions' were ready. New boards of guardians were to be elected to run each Union. This was a new development in local government, and it reduced the powers of the JPs. But the new guardians were very closely supervised by the three Poor Law Commissioners, appointed by the Act (Chadwick was appointed their Secretary) so that no Union might be slack or too extravagant. This direct control of local government was new, and it was a development of great importance for the future.

Conditions in the new 'Unions' were bearable but inhumane: food was plain and monotonous, meals taken in silence, families were divided up (males and females in different wings of the building 'to prevent them breeding') and there was a workhouse dress – a good idea, since it clothed inmates adequately and hygienically, but it was degrading to the wearers. There was no segregation of the poor (as Chadwick had planned), so that able-bodied poor mixed with vagrants, the sick, the old, the mentally ill, the very young. Harsh and difficult work, sometimes almost impossible to perform within the allotted time, and often of a degrading character, was common – at Andover those set to grind bones for fertilisers actually fought over the putrid gristle still adhering to the bones. No wonder the poor hated the Unions, calling them Poor Law 'Bastilles' and the Commissioners the 'bashaws of Somerset House'. The 'Union' entered working-class folklore; the shame of being a pauper ate deeply into working-class consciousness well into the present century. It is no wonder that the poor were driven to do almost any work rather than be forced to enter the workhouse. When Oliver Twist, in Charles Dickens' novel, cries lustily when he is born, Dickens comments: 'If he could have known that he was an orphan, left to the tender mercies of churchwardens and over-seers, perhaps he would have cried louder.'

Occasionally there were riots and sometimes a Union workhouse was burnt down. But the Act seems to have been effective, however brutal, in the agricultural South. The real trouble lay in the North, for urban poverty was quite a different problem. Work in the factories was often only on a casual hourly basis, and a family might well be employed for part of a week and unemployed for the rest, with no work to be had. What was needed in such conditions was short-term outdoor relief to tide a family over brief periods of enforced unemployment. Relentlessly, the Commissioners moved North to impose a policy of indoor relief only. There were riots; at Huddersfield the Commissioners were turned out of the town. Organisations opposed to the New Poor Law appeared, such as that led by the factory reformers, John Fielden and Richard Oastler, and by such Radicals as Stephens, who declared that the country was divided between 'the rich oppressors and the poor oppressed'. The impact of the New Poor Law on the North was the greater because the Commissioners came just as one of the deepest slumps of the century began (1838–1842), so that there was often no work to be had and distress was very widespread (forcing the authorities to continue the usual outdoor relief). It is not surprising that Chartism became so active in the North, or that the Poor Law played a part in the causes of this working-class movement.

Visit the local Records Office and ask about archives for the Poor Law and for the Minutes of the local Poor Law Guardians' meetings. You will find a great store of material waiting to be read and thought about. You may be lucky enough to see copies of letters sent to the Commissioners and their replies, or to see accounts or the dietary sheets (which will show that generally paupers were not starved). After examining a selection of these documents, write a study of conditions in the local 'Union' and try to decide whether the popular stories of dreadful treatment and degrading rules are well supported, or exaggerated.

Municipal reform

Local government at this time was not a single system. What operated in the counties and the smaller divisions, the parishes, had roots going back to Saxon times, but some degree of control was exercised through Justices of the Peace at their quarter sessions. What operated in the towns was different. Some towns, even some large ones, were still local parishes; others had at some stage received charters from the Crown that gave them certain rights of self-government. The system was very

complex and quite out of date, given the huge increase in population and the growth of large towns that lacked the power to run their own affairs. There was also much evidence of corruption in the conduct of business by the towns with charters, known as borough corporations, and this was so not only in the very small boroughs.

The extent of corruption and ineffectiveness was revealed by a Royal Commission, as a result of which the Municipal Corporations Act 1835 (actually passed during Peel's short ministry) ended the 'closed corporations'. Town corporations were now to be elected by ratepayers to serve for three years (one third being re-elected every year to allow for greater continuity); the elected council could then in its turn elect a certain number of aldermen for a six-year term of office. In addition, specialist officers were to be employed for important administrative posts and a Watch Committee was to establish and organise an efficient police force. The Act brought a new standard of conduct to local government and established a pattern that was later extended to other towns and to the counties. It was to dominate local government for nearly a century and a half. This was the last great reform of the 1830s. Why? Pressure for reform was not slackening, but the Whigs were becoming worried by the pace and extent of reform. They had no intention of allowing the Radicals to push them into undermining the social influence of the great landowners. The aged Grey hoped that the tide of reform might ebb, and took the opportunity of resigning over a crisis in the cabinet in 1834. William IV had no love for the Whigs, and when their new leader, Lord Melbourne, an aristocrat with little interest in reform, offered his government's resignation, the King leapt at the opportunity to recall Wellington and the Tories. Wellington advised the King to ask Peel to form a ministry.

Peel, Melbourne and the late 1830s

Peel's reputation had been restored among the Tories by his vigorous attack on the Reform Bill. He was in Italy at the time of Melbourne's resignation, but rushed back and published in *The Times* a letter to his constituents at Tamworth. There was nothing unusual in this, but it was clearly accepted as a declaration of policy for the general election. Some historians have made much of the letter, pointing to its acceptance of the Whig reforms and of a policy of moderate reform in the future, and claiming that it made Peel the father of a new Conservative Party. They have called it the Tamworth Manifesto.

Examine the following extract and the Comment that follows. The questions are designed to help you research the career of Peel as much as to encourage you to think about the political changes that were taking place.

To the Electors of the Borough of Tamworth.

GENTLEMEN, . . . I feel it incumbent upon me to enter into a declaration of my views of public policy. . . . I will never admit that I have been, either before or after the Reform Bill, the defender of abuses, or the enemy of judicious reforms. I appeal with confidence, in denial of the charge, to the active part I took in the great question of the Currency—in the consolidation and amendment of the Criminal Law—in the revisal of the whole system of Trial by Jury . . .

With respect to the Reform Bill itself, I will repeat now the declaration which I made when I entered the House of Commons as a Member of the Reformed Parliament, that I consider the Reform Bill a final and irrevocable settlement of a great Constitutional question—a settlement which no friend to the peace and welfare of this country would attempt to disturb, either by direct or insidious means.

Then, as to the spirit of the Reform Bill, and the willingness to adopt and enforce it as a rule of government; if, by adopting the spirit of the Reform Bill, it be meant that we are to live in a perpetual whirlwind of agitation; that public men can only support themselves in public estimation by adopting every impression of the day—by promising the instant redress of anything which anybody may call an abuse . . . if this be the spirit of the Reform Bill, I will not undertake to adopt it. But if the spirit of the Reform Bill implies merely a careful review of institutions, civil and ecclesiastical, undertaken in a friendly temper, combining, with the firm maintenance of established rights, the correction of proved abuses and the redress of real grievances—in that case, I can for myself and colleagues undertake to act in such a spirit and with such intentions.

The Tamworth Manifesto, 1834

Comment

Although Peel had advocated a number of important reforms during the 1820s, he had nevertheless been a firm opponent of Parliamentary Reform in 1832. When, however, Peel was invited by William IV to form a government in 1834, he took the opportunity to restate his views in a letter addressed to his own constituency at Tamworth. This 'Tamworth Manifesto' outlined the new *Conservative* policy, as opposed to the old *Tory* policy of men like Liverpool and Wellington. Although his first ministry only lasted a few months, the years between 1835 and 1841 were spent in building up this new Conservative party.

Questions

(a) What was Peel's attitude to the Reform Bill by 1835?

(b) When had he first announced his changed views?

(c) Why had he taken up this new position?

(d) What had been Peel's attitude to other reforms during the early part of his career?

(e) What did Peel fear might happen as a result of the success of the Reform Bill?

(f) What *was* Peel prepared to reform in the future?

(g) What conditions did he lay down as the basis for any such reform?

(h) In what way does the Tamworth Manifesto illustrate the difference in policy between the old Tory Party and the new Conservative party?

Peel failed to win the election – it was the first time the King had failed to get his choice of minister returned, and this was an important pointer to the future. The Crown stopped actively influencing elections; in a sense, it was a delayed effect of the Reform Act.

Melbourne returned in April 1835 to head a ministry increasingly embarrassed by disputes between Whigs and Radicals. He was soon weary of these squabbles (which help to account for the few reforms passed), but he suddenly gained a new zest for political life when the young Victoria became Queen in 1837. She was a sharp contrast to her uncles and did much to make the monarchy popular. Young and vivacious, she brought a breath of fresh air to court life and seemed to usher in a new, more respectable, more responsible age. She had a great affection for Melbourne and regarded him as her principal adviser, convinced that she was a Whig at heart. Melbourne responded happily, giving her the advantage of his long experience in political affairs; generally, his advice was shrewd and very proper. (Lord David Cecil has written a fine book on Melbourne, called *Lord M*, which shows that Melbourne was an amusing and talented man, quite different from what you might expect of the repressor of the 'Swing' rioters.)

In 1839 the government fell and Peel was called upon to form a government. The Queen did not like Peel. He was cold and formal – such a contrast to 'Uncle Mel'. He was also a Tory. Now, Peel was well aware that she would continue to seek advice form Melbourne behind the scenes, but more important was the realisation that almost *all* the advice reaching the Queen would come from the Whigs, since the ladies officially appointed to her bed-chamber were wives and daughters of great Whig families. Peel requested a token change among her ladies involving the appointment of a Tory lady or two. It was a natural request, and Melbourne supported it, but the Queen showed her obstinacy and refused, choosing to regard it as an affront to her. As expected, Peel interpreted this as lack of confidence and refused to take office without a change of ladies. This 'Bedchamber Crisis' brought Melbourne back as Prime Minister, but now he was dependent on Peel's support in the Commons to remain in office. At the time, he was described as Peel's pensioner. Peel was happy to bide his time until he felt confident that the electorate had had enough of the Whigs. In this, he was helped by the severe slump for which the Whigs were by no means responsible, but for which they were blamed. They ended, indeed, with a reputation for being hopeless in financial matters.

Melbourne's reforms

The reforms of Melbourne's ministry were not as important as those of Grey's. This was partly because Melbourne's ministry was not strong and was disunited, for one group of Radicals sought to push the ministry into measures that it feared to introduce; therefore, few reforms were passed. In 1836 came the Tithe Commutation Act permitting the *tithe* to be paid in cash rather than in kind, a method which farmers preferred. There were other administrative reforms affecting the Church of England, for example making the income of dif-ferent *livings* more equal, which helped the poorer clergyman. More important, perhaps, was the Compulsory Registration of Births and Deaths (1836). This made possible – eventually – the proper enforcement of the Factory Act 1833. (Do you see why?) As the *cause* of death had to be recorded, it now became possible to spot public health problems and the onset of epidemics at an earlier stage (see page 206).

In 1840 Rowland Hill persuaded the government to adopt the penny postage. Formerly postage was paid on letters according to the distance they had travelled when they were received. The penny stamp

The Penny Black

was also paid by the sender, but it was same cost whatever the distance. This made postage much cheaper and may have even encouraged people to write more to each other (but remember that even a penny was a lot when your daily wage was five shillings or less!). Business certainly benefited, and so did political organisations, who could now send literature very cheaply all over the country – something the Anti-Corn Law League took full advantage of! Penny postage lost money for four years, but then made a profit, which assured its own future and that of the hobby of stamp collecting!

By far the most important of Melbourne's re-forms was the 1840 Reunion Act for Canada. In 1791 Pitt had divided Canada into two parts but had placed both parts under a single Governor-General (see page 49). Pitt's Act had not worked well. Increased emigration into Upper Canada and Nova Scotia put an added strain on what was already an unhappy situation, especially as the French Canadians in Quebec felt threatened. In 1837 rebellion broke out in both Canadas, and 'Radical Jack' Durham was sent out as Governor-General. Some say he was sent to get him out of Melbourne's way! Nevertheless, with the help of a remarkable man, Edward Gibbon Wakefield, he produced the important Durham Report (1839), suggesting that the two Canadas should be united to avoid the rising racial tension between French Canadians and others. He further suggested that a railway should be built to cement this union and to encourage economic development. For the new Canada, he recommended responsible government that would cover all internal affairs, with Westminster reserving control over constitutional issues, defence, regulation of trade and foreign affairs. It was an important Report of which the principles were extended to other 'White' areas of the Empire during the century. The Reunion Act

1840 adopted the proposals and gave Canada internal self-government (ultimately secured under Lord Elgin in 1848). The Act can be seen as a milestone in the development of the Empire into the Commonwealth. But it did not end the tension between the French and other Canadians – a movement for an independent Quebec became important in the 1960s! Westminster retained control of the Canadian constitution (at least in theory) until 1981.

Peel's great ministry, 1841–6

Sir Robert Peel (1788–1850) represented a new age, for he was the son of a self-made calico printer from Bury, Lancashire, and he was never allowed to forget this. Melbourne unkindly observed he could not be in the same room as Peel without hearing the grinding of mill-wheels! But no expense had been spared on Peel's education: he went to Harrow and Oxford, where he mixed with the sons of the aristocracy and where his fine quality of mind was noted. He became a Tory MP (in 1809) when he was still very young, and his maiden speech was a triumph, like that of the Younger Pitt. Within a year he was given junior office and in 1812 was raised to the difficult post of Chief Secretary for Ireland. Ireland was to be the cause of the two greatest challenges of his career, in 1829 (see page100) and 1846. It was in Ireland that he developed his cold reserve, as a shield against politicians 'on the make'. And this cold exterior remained with him: backbenchers respected him, but could not rejoice in his company, as they might have done with Fox. Lord Ashley compared him to 'an iceberg with a slight thaw on the surface', and Daniel O'Connell said his smile was 'like the silver plate on a coffin'. His reserve was a problem in politics, but in private he could relax and be affectionate. He earned the devoted friendship of a group of outstanding young men such as Gladstone, Graham, and Sydney Herbert, the friend of Florence Nightingale (after 1846 they were known as 'Peelites').

Gather together the earlier references to Peel in this volume, and you will see why he was regarded as the rising man of the Tory Party, and why he became its leader (despite those grinding mill-wheels!) in the 1830s. Historians have always had a deep respect for Peel and have sometimes attributed to him achievements for which he was not responsible. He was a political leader whose words could inspire, but he was no party organiser. The new Conservative Party, which some have credited him with creating, was really the work of the careful organiser, F. R. Bonham. Indeed, the party he led in 1841 was far from united. The many country squires, who formed its backbone, found the party discipline irksome; they were also suspicious of his evident intellectual powers and worried about where his ideas on Free Trade might lead. Throughout his great ministry, Peel had to take care to prevent disunity; after its collapse in 1846 he said he was 'much more surprised that the union was so long maintained than that it was ultimately severed'.

Peel's victory in 1841 was more a repudiation of the Whigs than a vote for his policies. He had three broad aims: to restore finances (for there was a serious trade slump, with considerable unemployment), to pass necessary social reforms, and to conduct an efficient and economical administration. His ministry was one of the strongest of the century: it contained six men who had been or were to become Prime Minister and five who were to become Viceroy of India. (It did not contain Benjamin Disraeli; some say he took his revenge on Peel in 1846.)

Financial measures

In 1841 Peel was at the height of his powers as a financier and parliamentarian. He turned first to finance to wipe out the deficit left by the Whigs and to restore prosperity. He realised that Britain was rapidly changing from an agricultural to an industrial economy. 'We must make this country a cheap country to live in', he said. His solution was to follow Huskisson's example and go for free trade. He would have liked a further modification of the Corn Laws, for, after a good deal of research, he had already realised by 1841 that they were not necessary for the protection of agriculture; but his party represented the landed interest and he was far too wily a politician to risk touching the one policy upon which country squires were agreed – the maintenance of the Corn Laws to preserve the landed interest.

Instead, helped by two good harvests and a return of prosperity, Peel restored confidence with the Free Trade Budgets of 1842 and 1845, in which he reduced the tariff on raw materials, foodstuffs and manufactured goods and so reduced the cost of living, especially for the poor. The loss of revenue was more than made up by reintroducing income tax at 7d in the pound on all incomes over £150 a year. This tax affected the well-off (it is called a *progressive* tax) but was regarded as a temporary measure. (Gladstone, Peel's great successor, strove to abolish income tax, but it is with us still!)

Improvements in conditions at work

Lord Ashley (Shaftesbury) had secured the appointment of a Royal Commission on the working conditions of women and children in mines. Its Report was illustrated and the descriptions shocked public opinion: the Collieries and Mines Act 1842 forbade the employment underground of women, girls, and boys under the age of ten. There was some provision for inspection of mines, but not enough, and further measures were needed, like the Mines Act 1850 appointing paid inspectors and requiring the reporting of accidents, and the Mines Regulations Act 1860. (Shaftesbury was no supporter of 'women's liberation' – he believed very firmly that a woman's place was in the home.)

The Commission had also reported on conditions in certain factories, but a new Factory Act was lost in 1842 because Nonconformists objected to factory schools coming under Church of England dominance (the Victorians took their religion very seriously, and violent disputes between denominations did much to delay educational provision and reform). The Mines Act 1844 dropped the educational proposals, but required the fencing-in of dangerous machinery and forbade its being cleaned by youngsters whilst it was in motion. Children's hours were reduced to 'half-time' ($6\frac{1}{2}$ hours a day) and women's hours were reduced to twelve daily. A public clock was to be provided to prevent arguments! In 1845 Ashley secured a Print Works Act excluding children under eight from calico-printing works and banning night work for women and children. It also extended education requirements and increased the powers of inspectors. (The Ten Hours' Movement had not yet achieved its aim: this came in 1847, after Peel's fall, with a Factory Act limiting women and young persons to ten hours – even so, employers were able to keep machinery in production throughout the day by the 'relay system' that had to be prohibited by an Act of 1850.)

Banking

In 1844 Peel passed the important Bank Charter Act that did much to regularise the country's banking system and increase the reputation of London as an international financial centre. The Act brought the issue of bank notes ultimately into the hands of the Bank of England (but the last note-issuing bank did not cease issuing until 1921) and divided it into two quite separate parts, the Banking Department for ordinary banking business and the Issue Department that could issue up to £14 million in notes backed by securities, but any notes beyond this figure had to be backed by gold.

> Look back over the whole of this chapter and count up the number of factory and mines Acts giving protection to children and others. More acts were needed in the 1860s extending that protection to workers in other trades and extending the powers of inspectors. Carry your list through to the end of the century. Does this support the idea that this was a period of *laissez-faire*? Some historians – and many contemporaries – said it was.

Ireland and the Corn Laws

In Ireland, Daniel O'Connor, the Liberator, continued to agitate for a repeal of the Union. He organised a monster meeting at Clontarf (1843) as a climax to his campaign. Peel forbade it and O'Connor gave way – this was a momentous decision, for it broke the Liberator's reputation in Ireland: he was to die a pilgrim on the way to Rome in 1847. Meanwhile, Peel attempted reform. A Royal Commission (1844) recommended Irish tenants should be compensated for any improvements they had made, and a land Bill was introduced in 1845 for this purpose – Peel's fall prevented its passing, and Gladstone was to take up the measure again some thirty years later (see page 139). But in 1845 Peel increased the grant to the Roman Catholic Training College for Priests at Maynooth. This was vigorously opposed by Protestants in Peel's own party and (to everyone's surprise) Gladstone resigned, arguing that the grant was not consistent with the views he had expressed in his book, *Church and State*. Disraeli was quick to seize on the open divisions in the party and began a series of attacks that culminated in the ruin of Peel's career.

'Let us tell persons in high places that cunning is not caution, and that habitual perfidy is not high policy . . .' Disraeli's extravagant oratory inflamed passions among the Tory backbenchers, squires 'who spend their time in hunting and shooting and eating and drinking'. Soon Disraeli had gathered around him a group of discontented Tories, young idealists with romantic fancies of recapturing a long-lost England. They called themselves Young England and their leader was Lord George Cavendish-Bentinck. As the crisis in the party deepened, their influence (for a brief period) increased.

The 1845 potato crop in Ireland began well, but by the summer it had been attacked by a fungus that destroyed potato crops throughout Western Europe. Ireland suffered terribly, for the rural population had been increasing rapidly and the poor labourers and peasant farmers depended on the potato. Famine and disease stalked the land. Peel imported cheap maize (which the Irish called 'Peel's brimstone') and started a programme of public works. These relief measures were not enough: it was the suffering in Ireland that forced Peel into repealing the Corn Laws. 'Rotten potatoes have done it all; they have put Peel in his damned fright', declared the Duke of Wellington. But things got much worse in 1846, for the crop failed again. Mass emigration followed, and the population of Ireland fell. Bitterness and resentment remained both in Ireland and among the Irish who had emigrated, mostly to the USA. Thirty years later Gladstone was to try to reform conditions, but he had to face a new and deeper hatred than previous generations.

The Anti-Corn Law League

There was another influence urging Peel to repeal the Corn Laws. In 1838 in Manchester three remarkable men, Prentice, Wilson and J. B. Smith, founded the Anti-Corn Law League. It proved to be one of the most successful *pressure groups* of the century and by 1840 had recruited Richard Cobden as its principal spokesman, who gained the support of John Bright, one of the finest orators and moral leaders of the century. Together, they toured the country and repeatedly demanded the repeal of the Laws in the House of Commons (for both became MPs). The League had a number of advantages. Opinion was shifting markedly towards Free Trade, and wealthy industrialists were happy to subscribe large sums. A Liverpool merchant frankly admitted in 1842,

> He had gladly given his £100 for the next year to accomplish the objects of the League; he had hopes he was promoting his own individual good to no small extent by extending Free Trade principles; he was not ashamed to avow his belief, that his £100 subscription would bring him back a hundred times £100, if the objects of the League should happen to be attended by success.

The League used every available means of spreading its views, sending lecturers, organising demonst-

rations, tea-parties and petitions and making full use of the new penny postage (1840) for campaign literature. The support of the wealthy and 'respectable' was a distinct advantage, and under Cobden's guidance the League concentrated exclusively on the single negative aim of Repeal (so they need not risk disagreements as to what further policies to follow). In each of these things the League scored over its most serious rival, the Chartist organisation (see page 123).

Here is another question that makes full use of the extracts (only (e) asks you to repeat things you have learned before seeing the extracts). The questions provoke careful thought about checking the validity of the arguments used – an important part of the historian's task.

Study the following two extracts and then answer the questions.

Extract A

"Our opponents say that our object in bringing about the repeal of the Corn Laws is, by reducing the price of corn, to lower the rate of wages. I state it most emphatically as a truth that, for the last twenty years, whenever corn has been cheap wages have been high in Lancashire. On the other hand, when bread has been dear wages have been greatly reduced.

We do not want cheap corn merely that we may have low money prices. What we desire is plenty of corn, and we do not care what its price is, provided we obtain it at its natural price.

To pay for that corn more manufactures would be required from this country which would lead to an increased demand for labour which would be necessarily accompanied by a *rise* in wages."

Part of a speech made by Richard Cobden on 8th February, 1844, on behalf of the Anti-Corn Law League

Extract B

"The Anti-Corn Law League had a number of advantages. The movement of opinion was towards free trade and the League was well supported by industrialists who regarded their subscriptions as well spent. The support of wealthy men gave an aura of respectability, so important in the politics of the time. The League's chief rival as a movement for popular support was the Chartist movement. The Chartists argued, with good cause, that the League's interest in the cost of bread sprang from a wish to reduce wages, not from a concern for the welfare of the poor. It is no wonder the two movements were hostile. Finally, under Cobden's direction, the League concentrated solely on the negative aim of repeal, thus attracting support from all those who saw the Corn Law as an obstacle to reform, without having to worry about the disagreements which existed between their different supporters."

From *Economic and Social History of England, 1770–1977*, R. B. Jones (Longman), 1977

(a) Which one, if any, of these extracts is a primary source? Give reasons for your answer.   (2 *marks*)
(b) Which of these two extracts provides the most reliable historical evidence about the Anti-Corn Law League? Give reasons for your answer.   (3 *marks*)
(c) Both extracts agree that the opponents of the Anti-Corn Law League accused it of wanting to reduce wages. Because they agree, does this mean that the accusation is true? Give reasons for your answer.   (4 *marks*)
(d) What is meant by "with good cause" (Extract B, line 10)? How would the historian check that the statement "with good cause" is historically correct?   (4 *marks*)
(e) Describe, briefly, the methods used by the Anti-Corn Law League to obtain its aim.   (7 *marks*)

AEB, November 1981

The League argued that the Corn Laws kept food prices high artificially, so that rich landowners could get richer at the expense of the hardships of the poor (you can check this argument for validity by looking at graph 17). They exhibited a 'big loaf' which they said would replace the present Corn Law loaf, and that a policy of Free Trade would cheapen goods and increase trade and prosperity.

Peel needed no convincing: he had come to similar conclusions in 1841. But he knew his Party would not agree to Repeal, for they had come to regard the Corn Laws as the symbol of the power of the landed interest – and they realised the League was attacking this quite as much as the Corn Laws. Peel might move towards Free Trade, but he would not touch the Corn Laws. On one famous occasion in 1845 he crumpled his notes whilst listening to a further appeal by Cobden and, whispering to Sydney Herbert that he must answer the speech, hurriedly left the Chamber. But it was not the League that persuaded him: whatever the legend that grew up at the time, the League was as far from success in 1845 as in 1841 – they were planning a monster campaign for the election they expected to come two years later. It was the Irish crisis that forced Peel to risk his own future by repealing the Corn Laws. In 1846, Cobden admitted,

'. . . the League would not have carried the repeal of the Corn Laws when they did, had it not been for the Irish famine and the circumstance that we had a Minister who thought more of the lives of the people than his own continuance in power.'

The Laws are repealed

Disraeli seized his chance. Perceiving that Peel would push through some measure against the Corn Laws, he rose again and again to attack Peel, accusing him of holding on the office by betraying his party. 'Dissolve . . . the Parliament you have betrayed . . . a Conservative Government is an Organised Hypocrisy', he declared. The cheers that greeted this insult came not only from the Opposition benches. Disraeli's speeches became increasingly personal, and at one point Peel was goaded into implying that it was all in revenge for not being given office in 1841. Disraeli denied it. Peel had Disraeli's letter of 1841 in his pocket – why did he not produce it?

These debates are famous. Look them up in a good biography of Peel and in Robert Blake's *Life of Disraeli* and try to reconstruct them so that you can show what each side thought was at stake – and why Peel did not unmask Disraeli at that moment.

In November 1845, Peel proposed to his Cabinet that the Corn Laws be suspended to permit cheap grain to be imported for the relief of Ireland. The Cabinet split and Peel resigned, hoping that the Whigs under Lord John Russell would repeal the Act for him. Russell had, indeed, issued a Letter from Edinburgh (4 December) to his constituents in the City of London calling for Repeal. But he failed to form a ministry, and Peel had once again to take up office, but now openly committed to Repeal. The 'Peelites', the leading younger men of his party, supported him, but the party was split. With Whig support he carried Repeal in June 1846, but was defeated three days later on a measure for coercion in Ireland. He resigned, his political career at an end, once again blamed for breaking his Party.

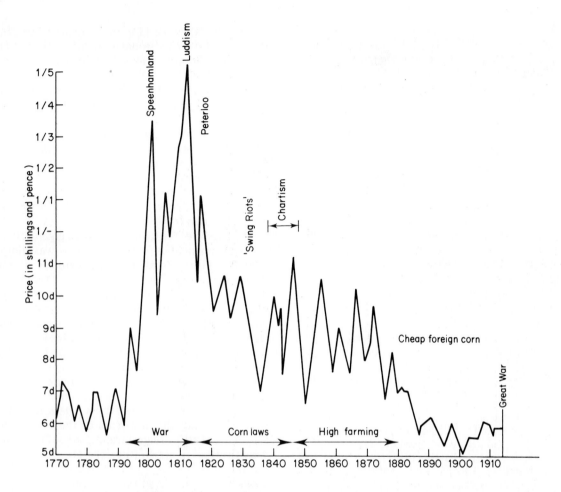

Fig. 17 Price of 41b loaf, 1770–1910
Judging by the price of a loaf to the workers, the Corn Laws seem to have made little difference. But people firmly believed they kept bread prices high; here is a reason for treating what contemporaries said with caution and checking it as far as you are able.

The following question uses extracts simply as a means of asking straightforward factual questions. It is not a difficult question, but it is useful for revision, getting your ideas sorted out and deciding the views of each side.

Read the two extracts printed below. Extract A is taken from a speech given before the House of Commons on 16 February 1846. Extract B is from a speech made to the House of Commons on 15 May 1846. Answer the questions which follow the extracts.

A
"While I retained the hope of acting with a united administration, while I thought there was a prospect of bringing this question to a settle-
5 ment, I determined to retain office and incur its responsibilities. When I was compelled to abandon that hope . . . I took the earliest opportunity, consistent with a sense of duty and public honour, of tendering my resignation to the queen.
10 . . . This night is to decide between the policy of continued relaxation of restriction or return to restraint and prohibition. This night you will select the motto which is to indicate the commercial policy of England. Shall it be 'advance' or
15 recede'? . . . Is this the country to shrink from competition? . . . Is this the country which can flourish in the sickly, artificial atmosphere of prohibition? Is this the country to stand shivering on the brink of exposure to the healthful breezes
20 of competition?"

B

"If we think the opinions of the anti-Corn Law League are dangerous . . . it is open in a free country like England for men who hold opposite views to resist them with the same
25 earnestness . . . . But what happens in this country? . . . We trusted to others . . . to one who by accepting, or rather by seizing that post, obtained the greatest place in the country, and at this moment governs England. . . . I think the
30 Right Honourable Baronet may congratulate himself on his complete success in having entirely deceived his party."

(a) Who made the speech from which extract A is taken?   1
(b) What was "this question" (line 3) to which the speaker referred?   1
(c) Who attempted and failed to form a government on the "resignation" (line 8) of the speaker in the first extract?   1
(d) Explain fully what the speaker meant by "the policy of continued relaxation of restriction or return to restraint and prohibition" (lines 10–12).   4
(e) What commercial policy is being advocated by the speaker in lines 12–20?   1
(f) Name one politician who favoured this commercial policy and indicate how he supported it. (Be sure to name a different politician from your answer to (a).)   2
(g) Name the speaker of extract B.   1
(h) Name two leaders of the "anti-Corn Law League" (extract B line 21).   2
(i) Give two argumets used by the members of the anti-Corn Law League in support of their opinions.   2
(j) Who was "the Right Honourable Baronet" (line 30) and how had he "deceived his party" (line 32)?   2
(k) What happened to the Conservative party in 1846?   3

UCLES

Peel left the Commons, but retained much influence behind the scenes, especially with the Queen, who had (on Albert's advice), come to respect him He died in 1850 from a chill after a fall from his horse; it is reported that the poor in Lancashire openly wept in the streets at the news. They had taken him to their hearts. Willingly, they paid their hard-earned pennies to erect the many statues to Peel that you can see in many northern towns. (Chartist leaders noted with regret that the poor were less prepared to donate pennies to their working-class political movement.)

Disraeli blamed Peel for breaking his Party – but Peel looked back to an older tradition, that of the eighteenth century, where the minister served the monarch in the interests of the nation as a whole. Despite all the vilification, he was able to claim that Repeal was a great Conservative act, since, once more, as over Parliamentary Reform, the landed interest had been prepared to sacrifice its vested interest: it remained socially and politically powerful, and the new industrialists, who had paid so much to the League, had to join the landed interest on its own terms. By Peel's sacrifice of placing principle above party, disorder and distress had been alleviated.

The Repeal of the Corn Laws was a gigantic crisis in Victorian politics. The Tory press was almost unanimous in condemning Peel as a guilty man who had broken up the Conservative Party. The effect on the House of Commons was considerable, as party lines became blurred, and for the next twenty years governments were, in effect, coalitions and their legislative programmes were small. Disraeli had to wait until the 1860s before he could begin to put his idea of a Conservative Party into operation.

Despite the fears of the landed interest, Repeal did not mean the collapse of British agriculture – on the contrary, for the next thirty years it was so prosperous that the mid-years of the century are known as years of 'high farming' when huge sums were invested in agriculture. The price of corn did not fall: it seems that from the late 1820s the Corn Laws had not greatly affected the price of corn after all. But Repeal had been a triumph for Free Trade. Even Disraeli admitted (in 1852) that Protection was dead, and Gladstone as Chancellor of the Exchequer in the 1850s systematically removed tariffs until the 1860 Budget left only small revenue tariffs. That year Cobden was responsible for a Free Trade Treaty with France: England was effectively a Free Trade country, and this coincided with an immense growth in wealth that characterised Victorian prosperity.

The repeal of the Corn Laws has attracted a great deal of attention among historians, as much because of the personalities involved as because of the political and economic changes that are associated with it. Read up about the repeal and the part played by Peel, Cobden and Disraeli. Then have a class debate, as though you were in the House of Commons, with one person taking the part of each of these three major figures. The rest of you should join in by making your own speeches and questioning the three principal speakers. At the end you should take a vote on whether to repeal the Corn Laws.

Chartism

At least some of the wealthy industrialists who supported the Anti-Corn Law League wanted to break the political power of the landed classes. They did not succeed, but they already had a parliamentary vote and might seek election to the Commons. The working class had no vote and lacked the ownership of land that would qualify them to sit in the Commons if they were elected. The Reform Act, for which they had toiled, had excluded them from a direct political voice. Bitterly disappointed at this 'Whig betrayal', working-class leaders began a movement to gain the vote, believing that if they could elect working-class MPs, then governments would properly understand working-class problems and pass measures to reform social conditions.

The origins of this idea can be traced back at least to Major Cartwright's proposals of 1776. By the 1830s, large factories and developing industrial towns were making the working class a strong political force that could no longer be simply ignored or suppressed. Living and working conditions may have been at their lowest point of the century in the 1830s, and one cause of Chartism was the hope of improving these conditions. One of the more violent leaders, J. R. Stephens, declared,

> Chartism is no political movement, where the main question is getting the ballot . . . This question of universal suffrage is a knife and fork question, after all . . . a bread and cheese question, notwithstanding all that has been said against it.

But Chartism was more than a protest movement: there were many idealists who were working to establish a 'New Jerusalem', where men might be proud of their labour and have both a sense of dignity and actual security of employment with adequate wages. Carlyle, the political philosopher and critic, put the point well in *Past and Present* (1843):

> It is not to die, or even to die of hunger, that makes a man wretched . . . But it is to live miserable; to be heart-worn, weary, yet isolated, unrelated, girt-in with a cold universal '*Laissez-Faire*'. This is and remains forever intolerable to all men whom God has made.

The movement gathered strength from the popular reaction against the harshness of the Poor Law Amendment Act 1834 and gained further support in the great slump between 1837 and 1842 when distress and unemployment was extremely widespread. But Chartism was much more than a protest from industrial northern towns: there were many facets to Chartism. Rural Chartism had distinctive features of its own, and there were many towns with declining industries that had strong Chartist groups. There were Chartist organisations that looked after social and educational activities and strove for a social enlightenment among the working classes – organisations that continued to exist long after the political movement had collapsed.

Chartism actually began in London when William Lovett formed the London Working Men's Association (1836) and produced a petition with six points: universal manhood suffrage, secret ballot voting, payment of MPs, no property qualification for MPs, equal electoral districts, annual Parliaments.

> Discover the meaning of each of these points and discuss among the class their importance. Find out the dates when five of the six were secured and decide why one was never achieved.

Chartist petitions

The petition became the symbol of the movement, and Daniel O'Connell called it 'the People's Charter' (hence the name Chartism). A vigorous campaign was launched and a 'People's Convention' with members elected from all over the country met in Birmingham. But already divisions were appearing among the leaders: Lovett believed in the 'moral force' of persuasion, if possible in co-operation with moderate middle-class opinion. He was opposed by a vigorous orator, Feargus O'Connor, who led the more militant Chartists in Lancashire and Yorkshire. In January, 1838, he declared, 'the time for physical force had arrived, and he would maintain . . . it was high time to lay down the spade and take up the sword'. He believed in 'physical force' to bring pressure to bear on the government. He was a good journalist, and his *Northern Star* became the principal Chartist newspaper.

In July 1839, Parliament rejected Chartism's first petition, although it had one and a half million signatures. There were immediate riots and a demand for a general strike (a 'sacred month', as they called it). In Newport, Monmouthshire, John Frost led an armed attack, believing that there would be a simultaneous rising in the North. There was no northern rising. Frost was transported, and both Attwood and O'Connor were imprisoned. Lord John Russell, the Home Secretary (in marked contrast to Melbourne earlier in the decade) sent General Napier to control the North. It was a good choice, for Napier did not seek confrontation. He sympathised with the workers and invited their leaders to demonstrations of artillery fire: it was sufficient to discourage a rising.

A second petition, signed by some three million people, was rejected in 1842. Once again there were riots and disorder, and in Lancashire and the West Midlands there was a spontaneous protest that took the form of men drawing the plugs from steam engine boilers, making the engine useless. It was called the 'Plug Plot', though there is no great evidence to suggest it was centrally organised. O'Connor, for all his fiery words, failed to make use of the protests and Chartism died down, especially as employment and prosperity improved after 1842. Instead, he spent much time, energy and money organising a Land Scheme by which he hoped to settle workers on small-holdings. It was a romantic idea with little chance of success, considering the numbers of workers who would want to have a small-holding; the scheme soon got into serious financial difficulties and had to be wound up.

In 1848 there was a world-wide slump that caused many revolutions throughout Europe. There was serious fear of an outbreak in Ireland. O'Connor planned a monster petition to be presented in London. He claimed 5 700 000 signatures, and a huge crowd gathered at Kennington Common to march with it to Westminster. The government was alarmed. It put the defence of the capital in the hands of the veteran Duke of Wellington, who drafted in large numbers of troops and artillery and enrolled 170 000 special constables (one of them was Louis Napoleon, the future Emperor of the French). Very serious trouble, if not a rising, was anticipated, for the defence preparations were on a huge scale. But they were not necessary, since O'Connor would not fight. The great petition was delivered by cab and found to contain fewer than two million signatures, many of them frivolous, like 'Queen Victoria', 'Pug Nose', 'No Cheese', and Chartism collapsed in a burst of ridicule and widespread arrests. It was soon popular to treat the 1848 petition as a joke – but Wellington was certainly taking no chances! The government was frightened.

Chartists in London, 1848

The influence of Chartism

Chartism collapsed, but it did not disappear, for it remained as an inspiration to later generations, and in some areas its social organisations remained active. Old Chartists turned to the Co-operative Movement and the New Unionism of the 1880s (see page 178) and the early organisations that grew into the Labour Party at the turn of the century. Chartism failed because the full weight of the governing classes was thrown against it. The movement was divided in leadership and was never a concentrated national movement with a single political aim (like the Anti-Corn Law League). Once its petitions had been rejected, more or less out of hand, by Parliament, its only hope of success lay in revolution – and the English working class solidly refused to rebel. Prosperity returned soon after 1848 (symbolised by the Great Exhibition of 1851) but it was twenty years before further major reforms were introduced. Working-class leaders turned elsewhere in those twenty years. Some emigrated, others joined the important 'self-help' movements of the time, others became leaders in the Temperance Movement and in local Nonconformist chapels, some joined the New Model Unions (see page 178).

It is easy to dismiss Chartism as a failure, or as a working-class movement that was in advance of its time. But the political ideas of the Chartists, their search for a more equitable society and their social organisations continued to have an influence into our own century.

> There are many books about Chartism and a number of collections of documents, including biographies of Chartist leaders. It is helpful to dip into these to get a stronger appreciation of the movement. There are a number of historical novels dealing with Chartism, for example, Mabel Ferrett's *The Angry Men, Comrades for the Charter* by Geoffrey Trease and Alice Hadfield's *Williver's Return* – you might contrast this with the same author's *Williver's Quest* which deals with South Wales and Luddism in 1818.

> Examination questions often use stimulus material from the Chartist period. Here are three examples that show how the material is used to permit questions that ask for information beyond the actual sources quoted. It is a common technique and one that need present no problems. Note particularly the tone of the extract in the second question – a Leicester Chartist in 1840. Was he a 'physical force' Chartist? What arguments did he use?

Chartism 1836–48

1. The work of the LWMA reflected the belief that ignorance was the greatest evil. Its many committees supported the campaign for 'a cheap and honest press', and encouraged the establish-
5 ment of libraries and the collection of social statistics. Through pamphlets such as the famous *Rotten House of Commons*, and through petitions and addresses, the LWMA reached a national audience. These calls for reform were
10 interwoven with practical advice: 'With union everything will be achieved; without union nothing'. In 1837 the LWMA took its first hesitant steps towards creating an organised national movement. Excursions by its missionaries
15 (James Watson, Hetherington, Vincent, John Cleave and John Hartwell) into Wales and the North produced an associated membership of some 136 clubs.

O'Connor ridiculed their achievement. It is prob-
20 ably impossible to estimate the number of Radical Associations which he established, but in the North of England and western Scotland he found a keen response to his campaign for 'a new radical party'.

25 The differences between O'Connor and Lovett's men now came into the open, and several northern WMAs changed their allegiance. The delighted Irishman chose Leeds as the base from which to launch a second front, and the publi-
30 cation of the *Northern Star* was followed in April 1838 by the setting up of the Great Northern Union.

(a) What do the initials LWMA stand for (line 1)? (1)
(b) What features of the House of Commons in 1837 would have led the LWMA to describe it as 'rotten' (line 7)? (5)
(c) What significance does the author attach to the existence of '136 clubs' (line 18)? (2)
(d) Why were the LWMA anxious to see 'a cheap and honest press, the establishment of libraries and the collection of social statistics' (lines 3–6)? (4)
(e) What was the importance of the *Northern Star* in promoting the Chartist point of view (line 30)? (3)
(f) Contrast the main demands of O'Connor's 'new radical party' (line 24) in the North of England and western Scotland with those of the LWMA. (5)

Total marks (20)

2. The passage below is part of a speech made in 1840 by a Leicester Chartist.

Not that Corn Law repeal is wrong; when we get the Charter we shall repeal the Corn Laws and all the other bad laws. But if you give up your agitation for the Charter to help the Free Traders,
5 they will not help you in return to get the Charter. Don't be deceived by the middle class again. You helped them to get their votes . . . you swelled their cry of 'the Bill, the whole Bill and nothing but the Bill'. But where are the fine promises they made
10 you? Gone to the winds! They said when they had gotten their votes, they would help you to get yours. But they and the rotten Whigs never remembered you. Municipal reform has also been for the benefit of the middle classes – not for
15 yours. And now they want to get the Corn Laws repealed – not for your benefit – but for their own. 'Cheap bread', they cry. But they mean 'low wages'. Do not listen to their cant and humbug. Stick to your Charter. Forget the failures of last
20 year. Next time will be different! Be prepared to take up arms to secure your just rights. Force can be justified against tyranny. You are veritable slaves without your votes.

(a) (i) Name the Bill (line 8) and the year in which it became law. (1)
   (ii) What was meant by Free Trade (line 4)? (1)
(b) (i) What is meant by 'the rotten Whigs' (line 12)? (1)
   (ii) What is meant by 'municipal reform' (line 13)? (1)
(c) What does the speaker mean by 'Forget the failures of last year' (line 19)? What had happened 'last year'? (4)
(d) There were two main groups of Chartists. What were they called? To which do you think the speaker belonged? Give your reasons. (3)
(e) Suggest what the Chartists would have considered as 'other bad laws' (line 3). What other reasons were there for the rise of the Chartist movement? (5)
(f) 'Next time will be different' (line 20). Describe what happened 'next time'. (4)

Total marks (20)

3. The Conservative government arrested and transported many Chartists. The divisions in the movement now became sharper than ever. Most of the middle classes were frightened away by
5 the events of 1842 and turned their attention to the rival movement. Lovett abandoned the cause and turned his energies to promoting working-class education.

The field was clear for the leadership of Feargus
10 O'Connor. He was a capable journalist whose paper did much for Chartism. In 1845 he started a land company to set up Chartist settlements of smallholders; in 1847 he was elected an MP and in 1848 under the impulse of European events of
15 that year, the last Chartist petition was drawn up. It was to be presented to Parliament by a procession, marching to Westminster after a great meeting.

The petition arrived at Parliament in three cabs; it
20 was found to contain not the 5 million signatures O'Connor claimed but under 2 million. Parliament declined to discuss it and the movement ended in fiasco.

(a) (i) Who was the leader of the Conservative government (line 1)? (1)
   (ii) What was the name of O'Connor's paper (line 11)? (1)
(b) What was the 'rival movement' (line 6)? Who were its leaders ? (3)
(c) What were the 'events of 1842' (line 5)? Why had they frightened away the middle classes? (3)
(d) What was the aim of O'Connor's land company (line 12)? What happened to it? (3)
(e) What precautions did the government take to deal with the great meeting? (line 18) Were these precautions justified? (4)
(f) Why did the movement end 'in fiasco' (line 23)? What other reasons were there for the failure of Chartism? (5)

Total marks (20)

O & C

9 Palmerston and a confident foreign policy

Palmerston as Foreign Secretary

Lord Palmerston (1784–1865) became Foreign Secretary in 1830. For the next thirty-five years he was to prove a dominant presence in the House of Commons (as he was an Irish peer, he could be elected to the Commons) for he held high office, (except for the years of Peel's ministries) throughout the period. Indeed, in the twenty years of confused party politics that followed Peel's fall, Palmerston and Russell were the two principal rivals for leadership of the government. The Queen called them 'two dreadful old men' and tried hard to escape from them, but as they dominated the Commons she was obliged to accept them as leading ministers. Not surprisingly, the years 1856 to 1865 have been called the 'years of Palmerston' – a decade when Britain's prosperity seemed to give her an unchallenged position in the world, so that she could pursue a confident policy that appeared to be above the petty squabbles of lesser powers. This atmosphere of accepted authority backed by a power sufficient to intimidate any possible rival is typical of what contemporaries came to associate with Palmerston's foreign policy. It reflected Britain's greatness, and so seemed only right and proper to most Victorians.

Palmerston had entered the Commons as a Tory and held office as Secretary of War under Liverpool, but he was a Canningite and broke with the Tories over Roman Catholic Emancipation. Three years later, Lord Grey surprised his colleagues by making him Foreign Secretary, for Palmerston was no orator. Nevertheless, it was Grey's happiest appointment: Palmerston proved a statesman of consequence, able to carry on the basic policies of Castlereagh and Canning. His success depended on Britain's evident strength, but also upon his understanding of foreign affairs, an understanding that came from long hours of hard work poring over reports so that he might have a full mastery of the details involved in relations with each important country. To get these details as reliably as possible, he employed a host of agents, from diplomats to traders and travellers (some engaged to check on the activities of other agents!) who kept him closely informed of opinion and policy across Europe. The tiny Foreign Office staff was kept as busy as he with the voluminous correspondence, but this meant that Palmerston was very well informed – as well informed as Metternich, the Austrian Chancellor, whose spies were as active as Palmerston's agents.

At home, he went out of his way to court popularity, and went about this with the same close attention to detail as he gave to policy matters. He made full use of the press – when he wanted to promote support for a particular policy, some favoured editors might well obtain confidential information to help them mould public opinion. With the ordinary Englishman he was wildly popular, for he openly adopted a bellicose patriotism in order to advance British interests at the expense of others – especially the French. He seemed to be the British lion, king of beasts, simply dictating terms to the world: when he growled, other powers crept away. The popular image (which he did much to encourage) was that he sent a gun-boat to enforce any British interests that might be questioned. As a result, he was the darling of the populace, who called him 'Pam' for short, and he proved almost irremovable. Leading politicians in other countries feared him and called him 'Lord Pumicestone', and this added to his popularity at home. His happy personality was in sharp contrast to the high moral tone adopted by his political rivals. He lived the life of a regency beau, and his evident success with women may have shocked 'society', but it was an additional reason why the British public took him to their hearts.

Palmerston's foreign policy

Palmerston was no fool. Sending a gun-boat would be likely to succeed only against small powers, and he was careful to make full use of diplomacy where great powers were involved. Nevertheless, his vigorous pursuit of British interests (a policy that ultimately depended on Britain's wealth and her powerful navy) gave some people the impression that he was something of a bully in foreign affairs. Cobden, particularly, hoping that the spread of Free Trade would bring an era of peace and stability, was a constant critic of his methods. But Cobden may have misinterpreted those methods: gun-boats were not sent against major powers, and even with the favourable circumstances of a wealthy country and powerful navy, Palmerston was always at pains to gain allies to secure his position. In fact, for all his 'sabre-rattling' in public, he was anxious to continue that balance of power that had inspired Castlereagh. The aim was that no single power should dominate in Europe, but stability be attained by as equal a distribution of strength among the great powers as might conveniently be achieved (see page 82). Europe, in Palmerston's day, was the centre of the political world: countries elsewhere, even the young United States, seemed to matter little.

Generally, Palmerston wanted to preserve and extend Britain's commercial interests against her rivals – and here the navy was especially useful. 'Our interests are eternal and those interests it is our duty to follow', he declared in 1848. The next generation was to find it increasingly difficult to maintain such a position, for by the 1860s powerful rivals were appearing. However, in the middle years of the century Britain was feared and respected abroad, and this was due to Palmerston's skill and understanding in foreign affairs. We can see examples of his skill by examining the various crises with which he was faced, either as Foreign Secretary or Prime Minister – for it is at a crisis that one can best judge the effectiveness of a policy. Only at the end of his life was his success checked and his judgement impaired, for by that time new circumstances were emerging and a new power was coming to dominate Europe – Bismarckian Germany.

Your task is to imagine that you are writing the obituary article in *The Times*, an article intended to establish authoritatively Palmerston's place as a diplomat. You will have to examine the circumstances of each crisis in turn and make a list of important points about them. Then you will have to judge whether or not Palmerston followed a consistent policy in the succession of crises. Was the policy a sound one, based on realistic principles? Did it maintain Britain's *best* interests throughout and leave her in a strong position to face the future? It would be helpful to have a paragraph on each main point: relations with other great powers, balance of power, maintaining prestige, promoting commercial interests, for example. Don't fall into the mistake of telling the whole story of each crisis in turn – the obituary is intended to be an *assessment*, not an account. And remember that in 1865, your readers would have known most of the detail, for they would have lived through it. Remember also that they would know nothing of what happened afterwards: you do – it is easier for you to judge, therefore, but you must be careful to judge historically and not to use your knowledge of later events too much. (You might discuss this problem with your teacher before you begin.)

Palmerston and the Belgian Question

As soon as he became Foreign Secretary in 1830, Palmerston was faced with a major diplomatic problem. In July 1830, Louis Philippe had become King of the French after a three days' revolution – it was a decided change from the arrangements that had been made at Vienna in 1815 (see page 82). Louis Philippe was known as a liberal: would he support the many liberal movements that were growing in influence all over Europe, and so threaten to overturn that Vienna Settlement?

In 1815 Belgium had been annexed to Holland in order to form a stronger buffer against any French advance into Europe. From the first there had been difficulties over race, religion and language (these differences are still very real in Belgium today) and in 1830, inspired by the July Revolution in France, the Belgians had driven the Dutch from many parts of their territory. Clearly, this involved British interests, for she would not contemplate France controlling Belgium. Palmerston called a conference of great powers in London, 1830–31, which agreed to establish an independent kingdom of Belgium under Leopold of Coburg, Queen Victoria's uncle. The Dutch rejected the idea and invaded Belgium. A dangerous diplomatic situation resulted – would there be a European war? When the Belgians, hoping for French aid, elected as king the second son of Louis Philippe, Palmerston exerted all his efforts to block any French gains. 'Union with France we cannot permit', he frankly asserted. The immediate crisis was over by 1832; France would not secure control of Belgium, but the problem continued to trouble European diplomacy until the Treaty of London, 1839, which guaranteed Belgian neutrality and integrity. This was a triumph for Palmerston's diplomacy. (Incidentally, it was the violation of this Treaty which brought Britain into the Great War – see page 169 – for this was the Kaiser's 'scrap of paper'.)

Over Belgium, Palmerston had supported the

liberal movement, even though he opposed the French. But it would be quite wrong to suppose he was interested in supporting liberals as such: he simply pursued British interests within the context of the balance of power. When the reactionaries, Metternich and Tsar Nicholas, tried to increase their influence in the Iberian Peninsula, Palmerston managed to block it a little by his Quadruple Alliance of 1834, which he called 'a capital hit and all my own doing'. But Spain and Portugal remained open to foreign interference.

The Eastern Question

Palmerston's most important success in the 1830s was over the Eastern Question, the problem of what to do about the declining Ottoman Empire and the conflicting interests in the Near and the Middle East. The Eastern Question was one of the central problems of European diplomacy throughout the nineteenth century, and the failure to settle it was one of the factors which led to the First World War. Palmerston pursued the policy begun by Pitt and Castlereagh (see page 83): he supported Turkey (the Ottoman Empire under its Sultan) as a buffer state against the advancing influence of Tsarist Russia. Ultimately, this may well not have been Britain's best interests, but until the Crimean War in the 1850s, it made very good sense. Palmerston could not have foreseen later developments, so we must be on our guard against judging him in terms of our knowledge of later events.

In the sixteenth and seventeenth centuries, the Ottoman Turks had been feared as the scourge of Eastern Europe – on two occasions they had besieged Vienna. But by the nineteenth century their power was declining and they were finding it difficult to control their vast empire. They allowed local rulers a relatively free hand, so long as taxes were paid. It was at this very time that Russia was expanding her territories at Turkish expense. The Younger Pitt had already protested against Catherine the Great's seizure of Ochakov (1791), fearful that this might ultimately lead to Russian control of the Dardanelles Straits and thus give her free access to the seas of the world. If this happened, British trade routes and commercial interests in the Levant would be threatened. But it was not merely

Fig. 18 The Eastern Question

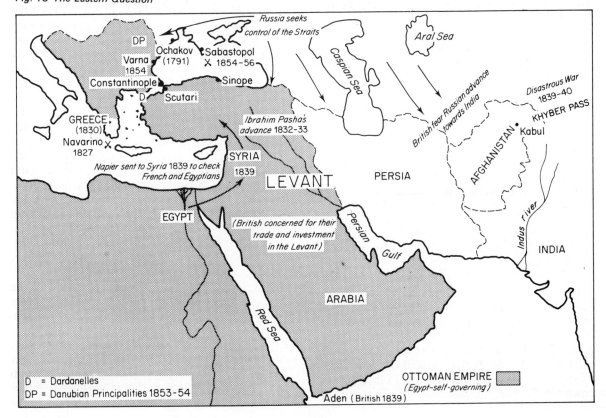

the question of the Straits; many of the peoples living in the Balkans were Slavs and most were Greek Orthodox. They looked for protection to Russia on gounds of similarity of race and religion. Austria's trade routes lay across the Balkans and down the Danube: any Russian expansion into the Balkans, or Russian help to Balkan nationalism, would affect the delicate European balance of power in the area and so present an additional threat to British interests in the eastern Mediterranean. France also had interests there. So all the Great Powers had an interest in the Balkans. Finally, Russian expansion beyond the Caucasus and into Afghanistan presented a possible threat to India, the centre of British imperial interests. For all these reasons successive British governments supported Turkey – keeping the 'sick man of Europe' alive, as they said – against Russian ambitions. The Russian threat had been contained over the Greek Revolt (see page 84), but it had not been removed.

Egypt was nominally part of the Turkish Empire; its ruler, the Pasha Mehemet Ali, had not been paid by the Sultan for the help he had given during the Greek Revolt. He claimed Syria as payment, and his son, Ibrahim Pasha, began a march on Constantinople to enforce the claim. Desperately, the Sultan sought aid from Russia and so checked the Pasha – but the price was high, for by the Treaty of Unkiar Skelessi (1833), Turkey became Russia's ally and agreed to close the Straits to foreign warships on Russian demand.

Britain and France had been much occupied by the problems of Belgium and Portugal and had allowed this 'tremendous blunder', as Palmerston called it, to happen. It was not until 1839 that Palmerston got the opportunity to reverse the situation, for then war once more broke out between the Sultan and Mehemet Ali. This time it was the Sultan who attacked, hoping to regain Syria. Ali was sure of French support, and Palmerston was worried lest Russia and France agreed a settlement to Britain's disadvantage. He therefore secured, in July 1839 an understanding between the great powers (Britain, France, Russia, Austria and Prussia) to settle the matter together. But in 1840 a new minister, Thiers, came to power in France, and his support of Mehemet Ali opened the question once more. There was distinct hostility between Thiers and Palmerston, and in July 1840 Palmerston secured a new agreement (called the Quadruple Alliance) to settle the question of Syria among Britain, Russia, Austria and Prussia. France was excluded. Insulted, Thiers talked of war, and Palmerston confidently declared, 'If France throws down the gauntlet, we shall not hesitate to pick it

up'. British and Austrian troops were sent to Syria under Sir Charles Napier as a warning to France and to secure the Egyptian defeat. Ali gave way: he had to surrender Syria, but was confirmed as hereditary ruler of Egypt. This was what the Quadruple Alliance of 1840 had required.

In July 1841, all the powers (including France) signed the Straits Convention closing the Dardanelles to foreign warships in peace time. The 'blunder' of 1833 had been reversed, and Palmerston represented it as a great triumph for his careful diplomacy. But it had not been an easy thing: the Cabinet had been far from convinced that his methods were right – they felt that risking war with France was going too far. At one moment in 1840, Palmerston had threatened to resign: the Cabinet let him continue and the crisis was resolved.

In this incident you can see that, although Palmerston succeeded in the end, his methods could be risky, and his colleagues were by no means convinced that they were sound. The country backed Palmerston in what he called his 'firm and stout language' against France, but his colleagues had a point.

Look at the following examination question: Macaulay certainly favoured Palmerston – if you had only his view as evidence, would you have supposed the Cabinet had some doubts? (Does this show you one of the dangers in relying on contemporary sources?) Note how the passage is used to ask some very detailed questions.

The Eastern Question

I will not plague you with arguments about the Eastern Question. My own opinion has long been made up. Unless England meant to permit a virtual partition of the Ottoman Empire between
5   France and Russia, she had no choice but to act as she has acted. Had the treaty of July (the treaty of London or the Quadruple Alliance) not been signed, Nicholas would have been really master of Constantinople and Thiers of
10 Alexandria. The treaty once made, I never would have consented to flinch from it, whatever had been the danger. I am satisfied that the War party in France is insatiable and unappeasable . . . The policy which has been followed I believe to be
15 not only a just and honourable, but eminently a pacific policy . . . For my own part, I will tell you plainly that, if the course of events had driven Palmerston to resign, I would have resigned with him.

T. B. Macaulay in a letter of December 1840

(a) What was 'the Eastern Question' (line 2)? Briefly explain Britain's interest in it.   (5)

(b) What events in 1839 had caused concern to the European powers?   (3)

(c) State the terms of 'the treaty of July' (line 6) and name the four powers that signed it. (4)

(d) What were the two international agreements in 1841 that brought this crisis to an end?   (4)

(e) Discuss Palmerston's handling of the crisis. Was he obliged to resign as a result of it (lines 17–18)?   (4)

O & C

Relations with France were severely strained. During Peel's great ministry (1842–6) Aberdeen was Foreign Secretary, and he did much to repair Anglo-French understanding, eventually arranging an entente cordiale, or an agreement to work together. But relations remained troubled. There was disagreement over Tahiti; and when, in 1846, Louis Philippe tried to unite his family by marriage to the Spanish royal family, the entente broke down.

The China trade

The opening of the China trade owed little to diplomacy. For some time the East India Company had been extending its trading links with China, but the Chinese Empire showed no inclination to encourage such contacts. Some of the European traders involved in trade with China were smugglers and their profits were high, especially in opium. But opium was a government monopoly, and in an effort to stamp out illegal trade the Chinese authorities seized some British opium at Canton (1839). In the subsequent disputes, shots were fired at a British warship. Palmerston promptly replied by sending a squadron to bombard Canton. The war was quickly ended by the Treaty of Nanking (1842) by which the Chinese agreed to pay for the war, cede Hong Kong to Britain, open their ports to British trade and grant treaty rights in Canton, Ningpo, Amoy, Fouchow and Shanghai. The 'Opium War' was an inglorious affair, but it opened up a profitable trade at the demand of gun-boats.

Two further wars with China followed. In 1856 the Chinese arrested the *Arrow* on a charge of piracy. Since the ship's captain claimed (somewhat dubiously) to be sailing under British colours, Palmerston (now Prime Minister) sent gun-boats to bombard Canton once again. By the Treaty of Tienshin (1858) China agreed to make further concessions and pay an indemnity. There was much opposition in the House of Commons to what was widely regarded as a quite unjustified war, and Cobden and Bright secured a vote of censure against the government. Palmerston promptly dissolved the House and won a resounding victory at the ensuing general election (1859) – both Cobden and Bright lost their seats. Whatever the rights of the matter, the British voters clearly approved of 'gun-boat diplomacy' – provided it was successful! As the Chinese refused to ratify the treaty, a third Chinese War was necessary (1859–60) which ended when the Treaty of Peking, 1860, enforced the previous treaty.

Palmerston and important incidents, 1848–51

In 1848 there were revolutions all over Europe that threatened the continuance of reactionary regimes. Palmerston generally sympathised with the liberal revolutionaries and certainly encouraged the Sicilian rebels. By 1849, however, the reactionaries were successful everywhere, except perhaps in France. In 1850 one of the more repressive of the reactionaries, the Austrian General Haynau (popularly called the Hyena of Brescia because of his actions in Italy) visited London and was much abused by draymen at Southwark Brewery. Austria demanded an apology, and after much pressure Palmerston issued a formal one in insulting terms. The Queen and foreign governments disapproved, but Palmerston's popularity was such that he could not be removed. The following year Kossuth, the exiled leader of the defeated Hungarian revolution of 1848–9, was received with great honour by Palmerston – the Queen had personally to intervene to prevent him receiving Kossuth at the Foreign Office itself. Austria was insulted – was this wise? Certainly, it showed Palmerston's independent attitude!

The most blatant example of Palmerston's 'gun-boat diplomacy' was the Don Pacifico incident of 1850. Don Pacifico had only a tenuous claim to British citizenship, but when his outrageously inflated claim for compensation for damage to his house arising from a riot in Athens was turned down by the Greek government, Palmerston sent gun-boats to blockade the city. (There had previously been a succession of formal notes sent to the Greek government, but the British public was not to

Marshal Haynau escapes the London workmen
Note the uniform of the policemen who are helping Haynau to escape the mob. The bridge and buildings are clearly shown.

How would you set about identifying the actual place shown? Was the Embarkment constructed at this time?

know this.) France promptly supported the Greeks and there was real fear of war. But the Greeks paid up – which increased Palmerston's popularity, since it was widely interpreted as a reproof to the French. There was a different reaction in the House of Commons where Gladstone joined with Cobden and Bright in an outright attack on Palmerston for his action. Palmerston prepared a long speech showing that his policy was consistent with what had been followed by Castlereagh and Canning, and ending with the confident assertion, '*civis Romanus sum*', meaning that any British citizen could expect that same protection as had been accorded Roman citizens in the Roman Empire. It was a personal triumph, as Gladstone reluctantly acknowledged, but it had been the methods, not the policy, that were under attack, and this got lost in the debate. Palmerston survived.

In 1840, the Queen had married Prince Albert, a keen student of politics and foreign affairs, who soon gained considerable influence behind the scenes. When Palmerston returned as Foreign Secretary in 1846, he found that he was expected to inform the sovereign far more than had been the case before. He found this irksome, not only because he rightly regarded himself as the expert, but because he was used to working on his own.

Frequently he would not even inform his colleagues – sometimes the first the Cabinet knew of a vital move in an important crisis was what they read that morning in the newspapers – some of which Palmerston controlled! His habit of informing the Queen *after* an action had been taken in her name had annoyed her in the past, and after 1846 she required to be informed *before* an action was taken. This irritated Palmerston, but in 1850, Prince Albert prepared a memorandum to settle the matter: all diplomatic dispatches were to be shown to the Queen, none was to be sent without her consent, and 'having *once given* her sanction to a measure . . . it be not arbitrarily altered or modified by the Minister'. It was clear what had been happening!

This effort to control Palmerston was not effective, for in December 1851, he sent an official telegram without consulting anyone, congratulating Louis Napoleon Bonaparte upon the success of his *coup d'état* when he seized control of the government of France. Palmerston clearly believed the French needed firm handling and that Louis Napoleon would supply it and remain on friendly terms with Britain. But Bonaparte was a name of which British public opinion disapproved: Palmerston had taken a wrong decision and he was momentarily very unpopular. The Queen seized her chance and demanded his dismissal for ignoring the 1850 Memorandum. Within a year he was back as Home Secretary in Aberdeen's ministry of 1852–5.

The Crimean War

Most of the original immediate causes of the Crimean War were settled before hostlities began: the war was largely the result of popular pressure on governments at home.

The conflict was really another chapter in the story of the Eastern Question (see page 84). In 1844 Tsar Nicholas had suggested a partitioning of the Ottoman Empire between Britain and Russia; he repeated the suggestion in 1853, adding that Russia should control the Straits. Though the suggestion was rejected, Louis Napoleon of France felt left out of things, and it was for this reason that he took advantage of a dispute in Palestine to assert the French position. The Roman Catholics claimed the right to guard the Holy Places in Palestine, and France backed them against a counter-claim by the Greek Orthodox, whom Russia backed. To support the Catholics, Napoleon sent the iron-clad *Charlemagne* to Constantinople, where the Sultan was also strengthened in a resolve to resist any Russian demands by the British Ambassador, Stratford de Redcliffe. To make things quite clear, an Anglo-French fleet was sent to the Dardanelles.

By July 1853, Russia had invaded the Danubian Principalities and the British fleet had passed through the Dardanelles. When a Russian Squadron defeated the Turks in the Bay of Sinope, there was tremendous anti-Russian feeling in France and Britain, the fleets entered the Black Sea (January 1854) and troops were landed at Varna. But Austrian diplomacy had already secured the withdrawal of the Russian troops from the Danubian Principalities. War fever was at such a pitch that the British and French troops were not returned home, but transported to the Crimea where, after a somewhat indecisive battle at Alma, they besieged the Russian naval base of Sebastopol. This was defended with great ability and courage by Todleben.

A war fought so far from home called for great powers of organisation. These were lacking. The senior officers were elderly and their staff work and planning appears to have been minimal. Within a few months, organisation got much better – but by then it was too late, for the damage had been done and the tale of stupendous military incompetence had been graphically reported in the columns of *The Times* by a war correspondent of genius, W. H. Russell. The allies were lucky that their incompetence was matched by that of the Russian high command, and the war dragged on with displays of personal heroism in the field and rising public complaint at home. The winter of 1854 – 5 proved a severe test and added to the problem of supplies. At the same time, across the Black Sea at Scutari, near Constantinople, Florence Nightingale was making her reputation and ensuring that the lack of provision by the War Office would not be forgotten.

> The Crimean War is a good topic for project work, for much has been published on it. Florence Nightingale similarly makes an excellent topic; you may like to read Woodham-Smith's biography, and some may want to contrast it with Lytton Strachey's famous hostile essay. You might arrange a class visit to Claydon House, Buckinghamshire, where Florence spent a great deal of her retirement. You will find some of her papers there.

At home, the sorry tale of incompetence provoked Roebuck, a Radical MP, to press for a Commission of Enquiry (1855). Aberdeen resigned and Palmerston became Prime Minister. The Commission's Report (1855) blamed the Cabinet, the senior civil service, the army staff and the War Office. Clearly, important reforms would have to follow, but they did not come quickly – some of them had to wait until Gladstone's ministry of 1868–74 (see page 139).

Peace was signed at Paris (1856). The Straits Convention (1841) was reaffirmed, and the Black Sea was neutralised – Russia could not sail her fleet there! Russia's claim to protect the Sultan's Christian subjects was set aside and the powers guaranteed the independence and the integrity of the Ottoman Empire. The Danubian Principalities were given self-government (they united in 1859 and later became the Kingdom of Romania). The Sultan undertook to make much-needed reforms – but, as no machinery was established for carrying these out, they were forgotten. The terms were insulting to Russia, and the Peace tended to disturb the whole balance of power – within fifteen years two new powers had appeared in Central Europe, Italy (1860) and Germany (1871). Palmerston had maintained the 'sick man of Europe' as a barrier against Russia and a means of strengthening British interests in the Middle East – this situation outlasted him, but it was to be no permanent solution.

Palmerston's last years

As Prime Minister, Palmerston was no reformer: he had no wish to add to the Statute Book. At the same time, the prosperity of mid-Victorian Britain brought a sense of security and stability that may have been misplaced. A crisis broke in 1858 when Orsini, an Italian revolutionary, threw a bomb at Louis Napoleon in order to draw attention to the Italian Question. The bomb had been made in Birmingham and the Emperor vigorously protested to Britain. Somewhat surprisingly, Palmerston introduced the Conspiracy to Murder Bill which made it a serious offence to plot murders in England that would be carried out abroad. This seemed to be bowing to French demands and Palmerston lost popularity – he was even hooted by the mob in Hyde Park. The Bill failed and he resigned.

Palmerston was back again as Prime Minister in 1859, much to the Queen's displeasure. He did much to make the final stages of the struggle for Italian unity possible during 1859 and 1860. At this time, Britain's fear of a French threat led to active rebuilding of naval defences, refitting the fleet with iron-clads, and the Volunteer Movement (county regiment rifle corps) began. Throughout the century resentment and fear led to much hostility towards France: any anti-French policy was always popular in Britain.

In 1861 the Civil War began in the United States. It soon had very serious effects in Britain. The government and upper classes tended to support the Southern Confederacy, but the working class solidly supported the North as being anti-slavery – and this despite the 'cotton famine' in Lancashire, produced by the Northern blockade of Southern ports in America, so that there was great suffering among half a million British textile workers. Soon after the war began, a Northern US frigate intercepted the British steamer *Trent* (1861) and compelled the captain to surrender two Southern agents, Mason and Sidell, who were on their way to London to enlist support for the Confederacy. Palmerston sprang to the defence of neutral shipping on the high seas and demanded in insulting terms that the two men be returned. Fortunately, the Prince Consort saw the note before it was dispatched and toned it down to make it sound less like an ultimatum. This gave President Lincoln the opportunity gracefully to release the prisoners and so the possibility of a war with the Northern States was averted. This was the last action of importance of the Prince, for he died shortly afterwards of typhoid, leaving a Queen so griefstricken that she retired from active public life for some years.

The Northern States had a further point of complaint: a warship, one of several built for the Southern States at Liverpool, and so one that could not be delivered once hostilities had begun, disappeared on its sea trials (1862). It was known as No. 290, and the order forbidding it to sail actually lay on the desk of the Secretary of the Admiralty. The ship re-appeared, now called *Alabama*, and caused considerable loss and damage to Northern shipping before she was herself destroyed (1864) off Cherbourg by the US Cruiser, *Kearsafe*. Was the British government responsible? Other vessels that could be used against Northern shipping were prevented from leaving port after they had been built, which implied the government was liable. The United States claimed compensation for loss of its shipping. Palmerston refused. Eventually, after the matter had been placed before an international arbitration court, Gladstone paid £$3\frac{1}{4}$ million compensation in 1872! (See page 143.)

Palmerston's last years were clouded by his declining ability in international affairs. A different world was dawning, in which Britain's supremacy would not go unchallenged. At the time few people recognised the signs. In 1863, a major rebellion in Poland against Russia brought the possibility of a European war, but Britain was not prepared to support France in such a war. Instead, the Tsar, with the help of the Prussian Minister, Bismarck, defeated the Poles, and the possibility of closer relations between Britain and France was reduced – a point not lost on Bismarck!

The last major problem with which Palmerston had to deal was a highly complex one concerning Schleswig-Holstein. The crisis was finally precipitated by the Danes, who began to incorporate Schleswig in 1863. German nationalists, led by Prussia, objected. Rashly, Palmerston implied Britain would help the Danes, and they appealed to him for help when Bismarck invaded in 1864. Bismarck had called Palmerston's bluff: the Cabinet refused to go to war and Denmark was easily defeated. It was a sad end to a glorious career; he had misjudged the rising power of Prussia and failed to recognise in Bismarck a master of diplomacy who was at least his equal. Six years later, Bismarck was responsible for establishing the new German Empire. But Palmerston had not lost his touch with the electorate, for he won the general election of 1865. He died of a chill before Parliament met.

Now you have covered his career, use this chapter and as many other sources as you wish to write up your task on Palmerston. Remember to judge him in the context of his time and not to rely too much on a knowledge of what happened shortly after his death. You will find useful this question set on a tribute written at the time of Palmerston's death.

A tribute to a statesman

One of the most popular statesman, and one of the truest Englishmen that ever filled the Office of Premier, is today lost to the country. The news of Lord Palmerston's death will be received in every
5 home throughout these islands, from the palace to the cottage, with a feeling like that of personal bereavement.

He has left none like him – none who can rally round him so many followers of various
10 opinions, none who can give us so happy a respite from the violence of party-warfare, none who can bring to the work of statesmanship so precious a store of recollections. It is impossible not to feel that Lord Palmerston's death marks an
15 epoch in English politics. Other Ministers may carry into successful effect reforms from which he shrunk. Others may introduce a new spirit into our foreign relations, and abandon the secret diplomacy which he never failed to support.

20 Others may advise Her Majesty with equal sagacity, and sway the House of Commons with equal or greater eloquence; but his place in the hearts of the people will not be filled so easily. The name of Lord Palmerston, once the terror of
25 the Continent, will long be connected in the minds of Englishmen with an epoch of unbroken peace and unparalleled prosperity.

The Times, October 19, 1865

(a) The passage speaks of bereavement 'from the palace to the cottage' (lines 5–6). What was the attitude of Queen Victoria to Palmerston? Why would he have been mourned by the humbler people in the nation?   (6)

(b) Why does *The Times* suggest that Palmerston's death was the end of 'an epoch in English politics' (lines 14–15)? Does later history support this view?   (6)

(c) In the period you have studied, show how far Palmerston was still 'the terror of the Continent' (lines 24–25).   (2)

(d) What grounds has *The Times* for connecting him with 'an epoch of unbroken peace and unparalleled prosperity' (lines 26–27)   (6)

O & C

10 Gladstone and Disraeli: political duellists

The 'Age of Equipoise'

The idea of the two-party system (Whigs and Tories alternating in power) is thought to be typical of Victorian politics. But for twenty years after 1846 there was no such clear division – Peel had not created a lasting party. This was to happen under Disraeli after the Second Reform Act.

During these twenty years there were few major reforms, although many problems remained to be solved. There are many reasons why there should have been this twenty years' delay – prosperity had drained much of the vigour of political protest: the Great Exhibition replaced the Chartist challenge as the symbol of the time, and these prosperous years have been called the 'age of equipoise'. No great point of principle divided the politicians. By 1852 Disraeli had accepted free trade and admitted that protection was dead, and most people agreed with Palmerston that they 'had no desire to go on adding to the Statute Book'. Instead, the politicians formed and re-formed ministries with no very clear policies. After Palmerston had been dismissed in 1851, he brought down Russell as a 'tit-for-tat' measure the following year. A brief Derby–Disraeli ministry followed. It was called the 'Who Who' ministry because Wellington, who was getting deaf, kept asking who the ministers were when they were read out to him. Aberdeen next formed a ministry with most of the Peelites, but it collapsed in 1855 amid the disclosures of the Crimean War, and Palmerston emerged as Prime Minister to dominate the politics of the next ten years.

From the extract in the following question you will gather how little party allegiance counted: it was much more a matter of personalities. Note the date – it was the middle of the Crimean War. Can you blame Derby for not leaping at the opportunity of office? Of course, Disraeli was angry, for it meant another chance lost to fuse sufficient support to form a government behind which a party might be built up. Russell was not a decisive Prime Minister; indeed, he found himself continually seeking support rather than leading a ministry.

A man of froth

I was so annoyed and worn out yesterday that I could not send you two lines to say that our chief (Lord Derby) has again bolted! . . . What is most annoying is that, this time, we had actually the Court with us, for of the two Court favourites, Aberdeen was extinct and Newcastle in a hopeless condition; and our rivals were Johnny in disgrace and Palmerston ever detested. The last, however, seems now the inevitable man; and although he is really an impostor, utterly exhausted, and at the best only ginger-beer and not champagne, and now an old painted pantaloon, very deaf, very blind, and with false teeth which would fall out of his mouth when speaking if he did not hesitate and halt so in his talk, here is a man which the country resolves to associate with energy, wisdom and eloquence, and will until he has tried and failed.

DISRAELI in a letter in February 1855

(a) Why was there a political crisis in 1855? What had caused the previous ministry to resign? (3)
(b) Explain Disraeli's exasperation with Lord Derby (lines 2–3). (3)
(c) Who was 'Johnny' (line 7)? Why was he 'in disgrace', and why was Palmerston 'ever detested' by the court? (4)
(d) Do you think that Palmerston's career and policies after 1855 warrant this description of him as an exhausted impostor, 'only ginger-beer and not champagne' (lines 11–12), who did not deserve the country's confidence? (10)

O & C

The twenty years following the fall of Peel did see a host of minor reforms, all of them gradually increasing the authority of the State to supervise conditions in many aspects of life and work. This came to be called 'collectivism' and it was to lead quite naturally into the measures that laid the foundation of the Welfare State of the twentieth century. Yet this happened at a time when the popular concept of government was dominated by *laissez-faire* ideas (as little government interference as possible). This is another indication of the danger of relying uncritically on contemporary sources.

Parliamentary Reform itself, despite the Chartist failure, was not dead – even 'Finality Jack' Russell developed an ambition to pass a further measure to reform Parliament. His opponents realised they might lose support if they stood in his way and so, urged on by Disraeli, they also tried their hand at reform. But there was no agreement as to what the reform might be, and there were many suggestions involving 'fancy franchises' – voting qualifications of a complicated type.

During these years, Gladstone was increasing his reputation and moving towards important reforms. Palmerston became quite alarmed; in 1860 he exclaimed, 'Wait till I'm dead. If Gladstone gets my place you'll see some strange things.' For Gladstone was coming to respect the artisan class (skilled workers), believing them sufficiently responsible to be given the vote. (Victorians were not patronising by habit – they just had different ideas from ourselves. We find their ideas quaint; they would have found ours very shocking.) Most people with the vote, however, firmly believed that only those with 'a stake in the community' (i.e. those who had property) deserved the franchise. In 1864, Gladstone amazed his friends by declaring: 'I venture to say that every man who is not personally incapacitated by some consideration of personal fitness or of political danger, is morally entitled to come within the pale of the Constitution.' The following year, in an emotional speech at the Free Trade Hall in Manchester, he assured his audience, 'I come amongst you . . . unmuzzled'. Now, Gladstone was recognised as a great moral leader, but he was a consummate politician as well, and he was building up a solid base of support for any future bid for leadership. He began a quite new feature of political life: he, a leading politician, toured the country making long speeches full of moral appeal to the working man. It was a sign of the future.

Many informed commentators feared the effect of increasing the number of Parliamentary electors. As you complete the following question, note how skilfully it has been constructed.

Opposition to Democracy, 1866–67

A. Uncoerced by any external force, not borne down by any internal calamity, but in the full plethora of our wealth, with our own rash and inconsiderate hands, we are about to pluck down

5 upon our heads the venerable temple of our liberty and our glory. History may tell of other acts as signally disastrous, but of none more wanton, none more disgraceful.   ROBERT LOWE

B. If you once permit the ignorant class to
10 begin to rule, you may bid farewell to deference for ever.   WALTER BAGEHOT

C. I fear that persons who are unwilling to shape their every idea and feeling to the test of party will be entirely excluded from the House of
15. Commons.

LORD CRANBORNE (later LORD SALISBURY)

D. The equality of men, any man equal to any other; Judas Iscariot to Jesus Christ; the calling in of new supplies of blockheadism, gullibility,
20 bribeability.   THOMAS CARLYLE

(a) These four men were all critics of the proposals for parliamentary reform. Write a sentence on each of them.   (6)
(b) Explain 'Uncoerced by any external force, not borne down by any internal calamity' (lines 1–2).   (2)
(c) What did Bagehot mean by saying 'you may bid farewell to deference for ever' (lines 10–11)   (2)
(d) Were Cranborne's fears, in the third section, justified after 1867?   (2)
(e) What was done to reduce the possibility of 'bribeability' (line 20) in elections?   (2)
(f) Write a paragraph explaining any one argument in favour of reform presented by politicians in 1866–67.   (6)

O & C

To answer (a) you will need to give a very brief mention of the career and importance of each man – and this will involve a little research (remember, it is *why* they should have been selected that is the key). Only one of them, despite the points made, was a definite Tory or Conservative – which one?

The language which the Victorians used was different from our own. Puzzle out the meaning of the words and phrases – they are not as difficult as they might seem on first reading. When you use contemporary documents, you must come to terms with differences of language. Of course, if you cannot work out the meaning, you can always turn to a good dictionary – but it is best to try hard to puzzle out the meaning, and then to check in the dictionary to see if you were right!

The examiner has two measures particularly in mind for (e): they are to be found in this chapter.

The Second Reform Act

After Palmerston's death, Gladstone led in the Commons and presented Russell's last effort to achieve Parliamentary Reform (1866). The Bill proposed lowering the franchise qualification, which would have resulted in a considerable increase in the electorate. There was strong opposition, led by Robert Lowe and a group of discontented Whigs who feared the effects of giving the vote to uneducated men. They helped to defeat the Bill, and the government resigned. John Bright called Lowe and his followers the *Adullamites* (a biblical reference to the young discontents who had joined David in the wilderness cave of Adullam).

This question concentrates on Lowe's fears and asks you to explain them and to decide how justified they were.

An Adullamite's alarm

The Government are proposing to enfranchise one class of men who have been disfranchised heretofore . . . I ask the House to consider what good we are to get for the country at large by this

5 extension of the franchise. The effect will manifestly be to add a large number of persons to our constituencies, of the class from which, if there is to be anything wrong going on, we may expect to find it. It will increase the expenses of

10 candidates . . . it will very much increase the expenses of electioneering altogether. You must look for more bribery and corruption than you have hitherto had. That will be the first and instantaneous result . . . The second will be that

15 the working men of England, finding themselves in a full majority of the whole constituency, will awake to a full sense of their power. They will say, 'We can do better for ourselves. Don't let us any longer be cajoled at elections. Let us set up

20 shop for ourselves. We have objects to serve, and let us unite to carry those objects. We have machinery, we have our trade unions, we have our leaders all ready. We have the power of combination.'

ROBERT LOWE on proposals for parliamentary reform, 1866

(a) To what 'class of men' was it proposed to give a vote (lines 1–2)? When was this Reform Act passed, and in what circumstances? Outline its main provisions. (8)

(b) Why were Lowe and his supporters known as 'the Adullamites'? What was their importance at this time? (3)

(c) Why does Lowe say that the proposals would increase the expenses of candidates and electioneering (lines 10–11)? (3)

(d) To what extent had his predictions in lines 14–24 been fulfilled by 1914? (6)

O & C

You will notice that you have already used part of the answer to (c) and (d) in answering part of the previous question. These two questions were set by the same Examining Board but in different years. It is a useful exercise to go over recent examination papers – it shows you what to expect, as well as being good practice!

Derby now became Prime Minister (Disraeli took his place when he died) and the new ministry seized on Parliamentary Reform as the means of remaining in office. Disraeli demonstrated his incredibly acute judgement and skill as a politician, and with splendid disregard for consistency, but a keen sense of timing, he accepted many amendments to his proposed measure – much to Gladstone's anger. There was much popular support for Reform, and John Bright put himself at the head of a vigorous campaign, especially in the North. There were some disturbances, too; much was made of one in Hyde Park when some railings were torn down. The

The Hyde Park riots—how destructive were they?

disturbances may have been exaggerated, but they played their part in helping to pass the Second Reform Act 1867. It was a personal triumph for Disraeli and he hoped to win the subsequent election – but the new electorate preferred Gladstone, whose supporters were returned with a big majority in 1868.

The Act was far more radical than the Bill the Adullamites had defeated: it gave the franchise to the *urban* artisan – all male householders and lodgers paying £10 a year in rent. In the counties, those paying £12 in rates got the vote. The electorate was increased from 1 359 000 (in 1866) to 2 455 789 (in 1868). But the most important change was in the distribution of seats. Boroughs with fewer than 10 000 inhabitants were reduced to one MP. Constituency boundaries were altered so that smaller boroughs were included in rural seats. Rural seats tended to return Conservatives, so that they had a built-in advantage, for there were more rural than urban seats. It would be going too far to suggest Disraeli realised this in 1867, but it certainly played a part in his electoral victory of 1874!

A third member was added to the very large towns (Manchester, Liverpool, Birmingham and Leeds) and London University gained a member. The Act opened a new chapter in political affairs. Disraeli and the Conservatives grasped its significance before Gladstone and the Liberals. Local party organisations now became important, and a group of young Disraelians, led by J. E. Gorst, formed the National Union of Conservative and Constitutional Associations (November 1867) to give the new electors the opportunity of conveniently bringing their ideas before their leaders and so perhaps influencing party policy. Party organisation at local level was to become one of the keys to electoral success. In the three-member constituencies it was crucial, for electors had only two votes for three candidates.

		A	B			A	B
(a)	1	7000	3050	(b)	1	5050	3050
	2	3000	2400		2	4000	2400
	3	2550	1500		3	3500	1500
		12 550	6 950			12 550	6 950

There are 19 500 valid votes. In example (a) party A has nearly twice the votes of B but only two candidates returned. In example (b) it has the same number of votes but better distributed – and gains all three seats!

Disraeli showed great political skill – he had 'dished the Whigs'. But many people were troubled by the new large electorate. Derby had spoken of 'a leap in the dark', Carlyle of 'shooting Niagara'. How would this new electorate behave? Robert Lowe urged that 'we must educate our new masters'. But, as John Stuart Mill put it, when Disraeli told the working class he had given them the vote, they replied, 'Thank you, Mr Gladstone'. The new voters proved responsible enough, after all.

William Ewart Gladstone, 1809–98

Gladstone began as a Tory but ended as a Liberal. Some of his ideas have proved important to our own century. He dominated late Victorian Britain and was held in awe by many people, especially among the poor. They called him the 'People's William' and the 'Grand Old Man' – GOM for short. Ask how many of your family and their relations now in their sixties or seventies are called W. E.!

Born in Liverpool of a merchant family, Gladstone was sent to Eton and Christ Church, Oxford, where he proved himself a brilliant scholar and became well acquainted with the aristocracy. He was deeply religious, high-minded and moral, with tremendous physical and mental powers. His capacity to persuade others was unusual and he was an outstanding orator. Disraeli distrusted him profoundly – either because he suspected he was as devious as he was himself, or because he was simply jealous of his only obvious rival: he spoke of 'that sophistical rhetorician, inebriated with the exuberance of his own verbosity'.

Gladstone's rise was slow, but, as Vice-President of the Board of Trade under Peel, he gained a reputation for dealing with complex matters in a way that back-benchers could understand.

Can you work out why it was crucial? It could easily happen that many votes could be 'wasted' on a popular candidate which might have secured all three seats. It was the Radicals who first worked this out – in 1865 Schnadhorst had founded the Birmingham Association. It began to organise the constituencies so well that they always returned Liberals – they formed a party *caucus*: the politics of the twentieth century were beginning to appear.

Suppose an electorate of 10 000 (20 000 votes), six candidates, three per party (A and B).

However, he resigned in 1845 over the Maynooth Grant (see page 118), which he saw as being in conflict with his book, *Church and State* (1838). He returned to help Peel repeal the Corn Laws and became a leading Peelite – he never forgave Disraeli for attacking his hero, Peel. He became a convinced Free Trader and an outstanding Chancellor of the Exchequer from 1853, after he had personally destroyed Disraeli's poor attempts at a budget in 1852. England became a Free Trade country under Gladstone (he regarded it as completing Peel's work), but he was never able to abolish income tax. Disraeli tried to get him to join the Tories again in 1858, but he refused. Gladstone then travelled in Italy, where he confirmed his growing liberal beliefs because of what he witnessed in Naples – the reactionary government there he called 'the negation of God' and he became a firm supporter of Italian nationalism and unification.

Gladstone was Chancellor again under Palmerston and Russell, and won a substantial victory against the House of Lords by repealing the duties on newspapers in the 1861 Budget against their wishes. During the 1860s he was responsible for major Treasury reforms that established the system of House of Commons control of expenditure that was to last until the 1960s.

It was during these years that he established his claim to leadership of what became the Gladstonian Liberal Party. But he was quite out-manoeuvred by Disraeli over the Second Reform Act; nevertheless, he won the 1868 election. During the campaign he shocked polite opinion by stomping up and down the country appealing directly to the common people. He regarded the election result as giving him a *mandate* to carry through his programme of reforms. This was a new departure in British politics and showed that Gladstone was more aware than many of his contemporaries of the growth of democratic ideas in the country.

As Prime Minister, Gladstone proved himself a very capable administrator, in full control of his Cabinet, and he pushed through his programme vigorously. But with each reform he found his popularity waning; Disraeli quickly picked up the support he had lost in the country. Gladstone found that the Queen disapproved of him – she complained he addressed her like a public meeting. He found his relations with her increasingly difficult. She much preferred Disraeli (whom she permitted actually to sit down in her presence at a formal audience!). Track down the stories of Gladstone's worsening relations with the Queen: they reveal a good deal of the character of both.

Gladstone's first ministry, 1868—74

Ireland

The ministry began with the Irish problem, and Irish affairs were to consume an increasing amount of Gladstone's time as the years passed. Conditions for Irish peasants had not improved much since the horrors of the famine of the 1840s: the peasantry existed only just above starvation level. Nassau Senior observed (in 1862),

> Some of the cabins in Ballintry seemed to be without windows or chimneys, the smoke coming out of the door. The population, as far as we saw it, consisted of half-naked children and half-starved dogs . . . The explanation is that these wretched villages are the property of a good-natured, careless landlord. He never comes near them, does nothing, and forbids nothing.

Absentee landlords left estates in the hands of bailiffs, who employed harsh methods to extort the exhorbitant rents: tenants who fell into arrears were frequently evicted, without compensation for any improvements they had made – they had no security of tenure. Landlords were also turning to profitable cattle grazing, so that they were happy to see tenants evicted. Years before, Peel had appointed the Devon Commission (1842) to assess the conditions of Irish peasants. The Commission reported 'It would be impossible to describe adequately the privations which they and their families habitually endure.' But the few improvements that had been made were often to the advantage of the landlords – roads were constructed for their convenience. Apart from semi-starvation, the peasants had to pay Church rates to the Anglican Church (though the people were Roman Catholic) and their pigs might be seized if they failed to pay. The English, to the Irish peasants, represented an alien rule that was resented and hated. Disorder, violence, cattle-maiming were common in Ireland. Isaac Butt noted (1866)

> The various illegal societies, the agrarian crimes, which have so consistently disturbed Ireland, have all resulted from the conviction of the people that, under the present system of landed property, they needed some protection beyond that given them by the law.

The rural outrages served to increase anti-British feeling and to raise a repugnance among the British, who replied with coercion. Intimidation on both sides was common and there was a long tradition of secret societies like the Whiteboys.

Gladstone studied the Irish problem keenly. He recognised (as many Englishmen did not) that the system of agriculture in Ireland was quite different from that existing in England. What produced profitable and efficient farming in England, in Ireland produced exploitation, hatred and a farming that was barely at subsistence level. Many Irish had emigrated, taking with them a hatred of the British, and among the Irish societies that grew up in the USA the Fenian Brotherhood (1858) was one of the most extreme. Its members planned to free Ireland of the British yoke. After the American Civil War they attempted to invade Canada (1866), but failed, and many returned to Ireland, well supplied with US dollars. The government reacted promptly, imprisoning their leaders, especially their founder, James Stephens. In 1867 there were several outrages in Britain that forced the Irish problem to the public's notice. The first was an attack on Chester Castle: troops were sent down by rail from London and the attack failed. Then a policeman was killed in an attempt to rescue two Fenians from jail. Three of the attackers were hanged for murder and were called the 'Manchester martyrs'. Then came an attempt to rescue Fenians

from Clerkenwell Gaol: a wall was damaged, but many innocent people were injured and twelve killed. The Fenians established a pattern that was to be followed for the next century and more.

The violence died down, the more so as the Irish priesthood refused to support the Fenians, but Gladstone was anxious to solve the problem. When he won the election in 1868 he declared, 'My mission is to pacify Ireland'. He began with the Irish Church Act 1869 which disestablished the Anglican Church of Ireland on the grounds that its privileges and official position were unreasonable when less than 20 per cent of the population belonged to it. Its endowments were given to Irish education and charities, and £13½ million was provided for the upkeep of the Church of Ireland. This meant that the peasants no longer paid tithes to an alien church – but it offended many Englishmen and antagonised many Anglicans who had formerly supported Gladstone.

After much study of the Irish problem, Gladstone next passed the First Irish Land Act 1870 establishing the principle of compensation for improvements by tenants and limiting powers of arbitrary eviction. There was also a limited scheme to help peasants

Fenian prisoners, 1868

buy their land. But the Act proved unworkable: it offended landowners and failed to pacify the Irish peasants. It was in 1870 that Isaac Butt founded the Home Rule League to promote repeal of the Union and gain self-government for Ireland.

Education

The year 1870 was a landmark in British education, for W. E. Forster, after a great deal of negotiation with Anglicans and Nonconformists, passed his Education Act. It provided for the election of School Boards to establish elementary schools in those areas where there was inadequate provision. The School Boards were empowered to levy an education rate to pay for their schools. Government grants were increased to those denominational schools which provided education for children where School Boards were not necessary, but there was to be no compulsory denominational religious teaching. Education was neither free nor compulsory (although there was provision for School Boards to pay the fees of poor children, and there were restricted powers available to compel attendance if it was desired). The Act was a great step forward and marked the beginning of a State system of education, but it met with tremendous opposition. It is difficult for us today to appreciate the intensity of the conflict: it sprang from the Nonconformist feeling that the Anglicans had got the better of the deal, for they feared wholesale conversions to Anglicanism, since there were more Anglican schools than schools of other denominations. It was a pity that so many Nonconformists were Liberal Party supporters. Gladstone himself was not over-enthusiastic about the reform, but a radical wing of the party, strongly influenced by Joseph Chamberlain, organised the National Education League to press for universal free and compulsory education, independent of religious denominational control.

The People's William: a cartoon by Spy of Vanity Fair, 1879

A Punch cartoon on the 1870 Education Act

Civil service and the army

In 1871 the religious tests that restricted Oxford and Cambridge colleges to Anglicans were repealed – to the anger of Anglicans of the upper and middle classes. Many of these people had already been offended by the opening of the civil service to entry by competitive examination (1870): a fruitful avenue of employment was curtailed for many sons of wealthy families (although the Foreign Office was not similarly thrown open!). The same classes were offended by the Cardwell army reforms of 1870–1. These, like the civil service reforms, sprang from the revelations of the Crimean War, but an added reason was the recognition that Bismarck's Germany had produced a highly efficient army capable of destroying the French army in a very short time in the Franco-Prussian War, 1870–1. Purchase of commissions was abolished, though there was so much opposition from the Lords that Gladstone had to persuade the Queen to pass this measure by Royal Warrant. Flogging of soldiers was abolished, and there were extensive organis-ational reforms, a short service enlistment for six years, with a further six in the reserve, was intro-duced. This allowed the formation of 'linked bat-talions', with one serving abroad and the other at home – the latter was primarily concerned with training recruits. The general staff was reorganised by subordinating the Commander in Chief to a unified War Office under the Secretary of State for War. It was hoped that an efficient military machine would result from these reforms.

Trade unions

Trade unions had grown in influence since the 1830s and had played their part in the agitation for the Second Reform Act. They were beginning to play a part in politics, and a deputation had visited Gladstone after his electoral victory, for they looked to him for reform. They wanted protection of their funds, for in 1867 the Queen's Bench Court had ruled in the case of *Hornby v Close* that they were not protected by the Friendly Society Act and thus a trade union could not recover funds embez-zled by its secretary. This was remedied by the Trade Union (Protection of Funds) Act 1869, and the Trade Union Act 1870 secured their full legal recognition (which offended manufacturers). In order to secure the passage of the Act, Gladstone had to agree to the Criminal Law Amendment Act 1871 which made it almost impossible to picket a strike, thus rendering the strike weapon rather ineffective. Gladstone lost much union support.

Other reforms

Greater efficiency was brought to local government by the creation of the Local Government Board (1871) and the Urban and Sanitary Rural Districts provisions (1872). In 1872 came the Ballot Act providing secret voting by ballot (one of the Chartist aims). It reduced intimidation at elections (which offended the aristocracy, who feared their electoral influence would be severely curtailed). The Act did not stop bribery, corruption or disorder at elections. The year 1872 also saw the Licensing Act, a much-needed reform reducing the number of beer houses and pubs – drunkenness, with its attendant social problems, was a serious problem in Victorian Britain. But many great brewing and distilling families had been Whigs and Liberals; they now switched to the Conservatives, and their consider-able funds and influence were used against the Liberals at the next election (when Gladstone complained he had been swept away in 'a torrent of gin and beer').

In 1873, the Supreme Court of Judicature Act carried through a major reform of the law courts, simplifying their structure, but causing many lawyers to complain at interference with their vested interests. By 1873, the powerful ministry that had so confidently taken office and launched itself upon so extensive a programme of reform was clearly flag-ging. Disraeli mockingly called the front bench 'exhausted volcanoes'. It was no surprise when the government was defeated over the Bill to create a Roman Catholic University in Ireland (1873).

Problems abroad

In foreign affairs there were problems. Gladstone had hoped to continue the Castlereagh tradition of working through a concert of Europe, but the sudden rise of Bismarckian Germany changed matters, and the German victory over France quite altered any balance of power that might have existed. Gladstone was unable to prevent Bismarck annexing the two French provinces of Alsace and Lorraine, nor was he able to do more than protest when Russia simply denounced (October 1870) the Black Sea clauses of the 1856 Treaty of Paris. Clearly, Britain was no longer dictating to the world and the contrast with Palmerston's day reduced Gladstone's popularity. Worse was to follow, for Gladstone accepted the arbitration of an inter-national court and paid £3$\frac{1}{4}$ million (in 1872) to the USA in compensation for the damage to her shipping caused by the *Alabama* (see page 134). It mattered little that Russell had first put the matter to arbitration in 1865, and that these negotiations had been continued by the Derby – Disraeli ministry, 1867 – 8: the public blamed Gladstone for what it interpreted as weakness.

In January 1874, Gladstone decided to appeal to the country, but Disraeli gained a clear majority. Can you see why? Make a list of the reforms of Gladstone's ministry and besides each note down those interests that were offended. It is easy to see why Gladstone's support fell away: Disraeli did not so much win the election as Gladstone lost it. He withdrew from politics and turned to an active retirement (how old was he?).

Benjamin Disraeli, 1804–81

Both Gladstone and Disraeli were outstandingly shrewd politicians, but there the similarity ended. Disraeli was a Christian from a Jewish family, a middle-class intellectual: it was incredible that he should become the leader of the Victorian Conservative Party. His father, Isaac, was a man of letters, but as he was not wealthy, the young Disraeli had to make his own way in the world. From the first he was a dandy, noted for his flamboyant waistcoats and delicate curls (you might like *Don't Mr Disraeli*, an historical novel by Carol Brahms and S. J. Simon.) A ladies' man, he was a decided social success. He became a novelist; some of his books showed a distinct social conscience – for example, *Sybil*, subtitled 'The Two Nations'. His ambitions equalled his undoubted talents and he turned confidently to politics. His efforts to secure election as a Radical were unavailing, but after a successful marriage to a wealthy widow he became MP for Maidstone (1837). His maiden speech was a celebrated fiasco (try to find out why, and write your own account as though you were reporting for *Punch*).

Disraeli was always brilliant; his wit and sarcasm and the speed of his repartee made him a very effective debater. But it is difficult to get at his real ideas, for they frequently changed. He took up different causes – for example, the Young England

Disraeli—overdressed

THE RISING GENERATION—IN PARLIAMENT.

Peel. "WELL, MY LITTLE MAN, WHAT ARE YOU GOING TO DO THIS SESSION, EH?"

D——li (the Juvenile). "WHY—AW—AW—I 'VE MADE ARRANGEMENTS—AW—TO SMASH—AW—EVERYBODY."

group of romantic Tory squires under Lord George Bentinck, who hoped to re-establish social harmony as they supposed it existed in times past. He wrote of 'Tory Democracy', a phrase that became very popular, but which he never defined. He espoused Protection, especially when his determined attacks did much to bring down Peel (1846), but by 1852 he had acknowledged Protection was dead. In the 1850s he was complaining that the colonies were not worth keeping, yet in the 1870s he had become the great proponent of imperialism – was it in order to oppose Gladstone?

In 1852 Disraeli was Chancellor of the Exchequer in Derby's government, but his Budget was not a success. At this time, the Queen disapproved of him, partly because Albert distrusted him. But after Albert's death Disraeli overcame her dislike, largely through his extravagant expressions of concern and sympathy – unlike Gladstone, he realised the Queen had feelings! She commented that his Cabinet reports were like reading a novel, and he was always careful to 'lay on flattery with a trowel'. He won her over completely – when he died she sent a small bunch of primroses, 'his favourite flower' (it was a signal honour for the Queen to send flowers to a subject, even a prime minister). In Victorian England, relations with the monarch were very important and Disraeli's success was a tribute to his social capacities.

His unusual political insight was demonstrated by the way he guided the Second Reform Act 1867 through Parliament, but the size of Gladstone's electoral victory put his leadership in doubt. He restored his reputation by the brilliance of his destructive debate as Leader of the Opposition. Nothing exemplifies the contrast between Gladstone and Disraeli better than their reaction when they took office as Prime Minister. Gladstone wrote in his diary (1868), 'I ascend a steepening path, with a burden of ever-growing weight. The Almighty seems to sustain and spare me for some purpose of His own, deeply unworthy I know myself to be. Glory be to his name.' Earlier that year, Disraeli had succeeded Derby as Prime Minister: he responded jauntily to congratulations, 'Yes! I have climbed to the top of the greasy pole.'

Rarely did Disraeli make great public speeches – unlike Gladstone – but in 1872 he made two, at the Free Trade Hall, Manchester, and at the Crystal Palace. They made a huge impression and launched a new view of Conservatism, so that they are still recalled by political leaders today. He declared he would strive to make Britain predominant in the world (Gladstone's foreign policy had been inglorious), he would make the Conservatives the 'imperial party' (Gladstone was no imperialist) and they would seek social reform on behalf of the whole community, not of separate groups (as he accused Gladstone of doing). The Conservative Party was to be the party of the nation as a whole. There was little hint of actual policy measures, but the speeches established the basis of the party's appeal for the next hundred years or more: far more than Peel, Disraeli was the founder of the Conservative Party.

This question takes one of Disraeli's 1872 speeches and uses it to ask some shrewd and widely-ranging questions.

Conservative objectives

Gentlemen I have referred to what I look upon as the first object of the Tory party – namely, to maintain the institutions of the country, and reviewing what has occurred, and referring to the
5 present temper of the times upon these subjects. I think that the Tory party, or, as I will venture to call it, the National party, has everything to encourage it. I think that the nation has arrived at the conclusion which we have always main-
10 tained that it is the first duty of England to maintain its institutions. There is another and second great object of the Tory party. If the first is to maintain the institutions of the country, the second is, in my opinion, to uphold the Empire of
15 England. If you look to the history of this country since the advent of Liberalism you will find that there has been no effort so continuous, so subtle, supported by so much energy, and carried on with so much ability and acumen, as the attempts
20 of Liberalism to effect the disintegration of the Empire of England. Another great object of the Tory party is the elevation of the condition of the people.

A speech by Disraeli in 1872

(a) On what grounds might Disraeli call the Tory party 'the National party' (line 7)? (2)
(b) What did Disraeli mean by the 'institutions' (line 11) of the country? Why might the Conservatives regard it as their particular task to 'maintain' (line 13) them? (4)
(c) Can you justify Disraeli's accusation that the Liberals had attempted 'to effect the disintegration of the Empire of England (line 21)? (6)
(d) What concern had Disraeli shown, earlier on in his career, for 'the condition of the people' (lines 22–23)? What, when he came to power in 1874, did he do about it? (8)

O & C

Imagine how horrified Disraeli's Cabinet was to discover in 1874 that he had little idea of policy – they were expected to make up their own! (Read Robert Blake's celebrated biography on this point.) He was fortunate that he had able ministers to help – such as Richard Cross, the Home Secretary. Perhaps Disraeli was already tired as well as old – in 1874 he sighed 'Power, it has come to me too late. There were days when on waking I felt I could move dynasties and governments; but that has passed away.' Apart from foreign affairs, he took little part in framing the measures of his ministry.

Disraeli's ministry, 1874–80

There were great achievements at home – indeed, Alexander Macdonald, a trade union MP, said in 1879 'the Conservative Party has done more for the working classes in five years than the Liberals have in fifty'. What did he mean?

Domestic reforms

In 1874 Richard Cross pushed through the Factory Act which restricted the working week to $56\frac{1}{2}$ hours (how many hours a day?) and disallowed the employment of children below the age of ten. Another Factory and Workshops Act (1878) consolidated the various regulations for different types of factories and made it illegal for children over ten to be employed for more than half-time – the other half of the time was supposed to be spent on education. (This half-time system remained until the Education Act 1918. (Can you see any advantages or disadvantages in a half-time system? Try to discover how it worked in your area.)

The great year for reforms was 1875. Gladstone's trade union legislation of 1871 had failed to grant the right of peaceful picketing: Cross removed this grievance by the Conspiracy and Protection of Property Act 1875. The Employers and Workmen Act brought equality in contracts between worker and employer (hitherto a worker, but not his employer, could be liable to criminal charges if he was in breach of contract). Next came the Artisans Dwellings Act which permitted certain large towns compulsorily to purchase, demolish and rebuild insanitary houses. (Here was a breach of *laissez-faire* and of property rights! Can you see how it could be justified?) Cross was helped in preparing this measure by Joseph Chamberlain, radical mayor of Birmingham, who made use of it to improve slum areas in the centre of his city. The Public Health Act

1875 consolidated the public health regulations and established a system that local authorities were obliged to enforce, appointing a medical officer and supervising a whole range of building regulations. Medical officers were given special powers to deal with infectious diseases. The same year the Sale of Food and Drugs Act gave public analysts power to prosecute merchants and manufacturers who adulterated foodstuffs. (Note how *laissez-faire* was being eroded.)

After 1875 the pace of reform slackened, partly because of the pressure of foreign and imperial affairs, and partly because the Irish MPs began an organised obstruction of business. They had learnt a great deal from the tactics of Samuel Plimsoll, whose protests against 'coffin ships' and the unnecessary loss of seamen's lives so disrupted business that the House was glad to pass the Merchant Shipping Act 1876, establishing the Plimsoll Line to prevent overloading (more Acts in 1894 and 1906 were needed to improve conditions further). In 1876, also, Lord Sandon's Education Act required children to attend school full-time to the age of ten, and half-time thereafter to thirteen, unless they gained a certificate in proficiency in the 'three Rs': it was enforced through the School Boards by Mundella's Act of 1880. (Now, was Macdonald right in his judgement of 1879?)

Imperialism

Disraeli certainly associated the Conservative Party with imperialism, but he seems to have had little idea of any positive policy. Things simply happened, often because overseas the man on the spot acted on his own initiative. When things began to go wrong, the Liberals claimed this was retribution for a wanton 'forward' policy adopted without regard for the consequences.

The purchase of the Suez Canal shares in 1875, which gave Britain a majority holding, was the first important achievement for the Empire by the ministry, since it increased Britain's influence over the major new routeway to the East. But Disraeli had acted largely because he feared the French might get the shares first. The Khedive Ismail of Egypt had huge debts because of his extravagant ways and offered for sale his holding of seven-sixteenths of the share capital of the Suez Canal Company. Disraeli, without parliamentary permission, bought them for £4 million with money advanced by his friend Rothschild. 'It is settled: you have it, Madame' an excited Disraeli wrote to the Queen – she regarded it as a great triumph. Parliament was less impressed, and there was a stormy debate in which the Opposition was ably led by Robert Lowe who objected to the exorbitant interest charge of £100000. The purchase was approved, however, and British directors were appointed to the board of the Company – though they did not control it.

In 1876 came another imaginative move. Disraeli persuaded Parliament to confer the title 'Empress of India' on the Queen. She was delighted – indeed, she had an Indian servant who gained considerable influence at the palace. The title may have raised British prestige, but its impact on conditions in India was less obvious.

Disraeli left the Colonial Secretary, Carnavon, a free hand, particularly in South Africa – 'In all these affairs I trust you . . . Do what you think wisest'. Trouble with the Zulus and a dispute with the Boers in the Transvaal prompted Carnavon to annexe the territory in 1877 – the discovery of gold and diamonds in the area also increased interest! The Boers, not unnaturally, objected, but the menace from the Zulus had first to be contained. These splendid fighters had built up a large empire and constituted a real threat to the Whites. A series of incidents led to the Zulu War of 1879 during which a British force was defeated at Isandlwana (the Prince Imperial, son of the former French Emperor, Louis Napoleon III, was killed). A full-scale war had to be waged to defeat the Zulus. (H. Rider Haggard has written several books, once very popular, about the Zulus. You might like to read them and to go on to read other books about the wars in South Africa. Ask the librarian to suggest titles to you.)

Meanwhile, in Afghanistan Russian influence was growing, and it was feared that there might be a threat to the north-west frontier of India. In 1878 a second Afghan War was launched, and the British Resident with his staff were massacred at Kabul. Here was another example of the 'forward' policy leading to defeat and costly wars.

Foreign policy

If Disraeli had disappointed his Cabinet in other areas, in foreign affairs he took a very personal interest. The main problem was a revival of the Eastern Question (see page 84). A series of risings by the Balkan Christian subjects of the Sultan brought a direct appeal for help to Russia. If Russia helped gain these peoples' independence, this would greatly increase her influence and might threaten Britain's interests in the eastern Mediterranean. Disraeli determined to support the Sultan. But Turkish irregular troops, the Bashi-Bazouks, in 1876

EMPRESS AND EARL;
OR, ONE GOOD TURN DESERVES ANOTHER.

Lord Beaconsfield. "THANKS, YOUR MAJESTY! I MIGHT HAVE HAD IT BEFORE! *NOW* I THINK I HAVE EARNED IT!"

'Tit for Tat': a Punch cartoon
When Disraeli passed the Imperial Titles Act making the Queen an Empress, it seemed only natural for her Imperial Majesty to return the compliment and create him Earl of Beaconsfield. Punch makes the obvious point: It is very gentle satire compared with Gillray or Cruikshank. Do you think Punch is on Disraeli's side, or is he indicating that feeling in the country is hostile to this playing with titles? How would you try to find out which opinion is correct?

massacred some 12000 Balkan Christians. Misled by the British ambassador at Constantinople, Disraeli dismissed reports of the massacres as 'bazaar gossip'. But the massacres caused Gladstone to erupt like a volcano and to publish his pamphlet *The Bulgarian Horrors and the Question of the East* (1876) which sold 200000 copies in a month. He called for vengeance on the Turks, 'Their Zaptiehs and their Mudirs, their Bimbashis and their Yuzbashis, their Kaimakams and their Pashas, one and all, bag and baggage, shall, I hope, clear out from the province they have desolated and profaned.' Public opinion was instantly with Gladstone, and the simmering hatred between him and Disraeli blazed out. Disraeli complained, 'That unprincipled maniac, and with one commanding characteristic – whether preaching, praying, speechifying or scribbling – never a gentleman.' But when the Sultan refused to make concessions to his Christian subjects or to reform his administration, Russia declared war in 1877. The Russian advance was held up at Plevna by Osman Pasha – a decisive moment, for otherwise Constantinople would have fallen. Disraeli ordered the British fleet to the Straits and on to Constantinople to defend the Sultan. Opinion swung heavily in his favour, and a popular song caught the feeling:

> We don't want to fight, but by Jingo, if we do,
> We've got the men, we've got the ships, we've got the money too.

This 'jingoism' was nothing new – it revived the patriotic fervour that Palmerston had encouraged so successfully.

The Russians imposed the Treaty of San Stefano (1878) almost excluding Turkey from Europe and creating a huge Bulgaria stretching to the Aegean Sea. This was not acceptable to Britain (or to the other European powers, especially Austria, whose Balkan interests were directly threatened). Disraeli demanded a revision of the Treaty, called up the army reserves and transferred 7000 Indian troops to Malta as a sign of strength. Bismarck, the German Chancellor, cynically declaring that he would be an 'honest broker', called a conference at Berlin. Disraeli represented Britain and behaved in best Palmerstonian fashion, even calling for a special train to leave Berlin if some of the British demands were not conceded. Bismarck was much impressed: 'The Old Jew – that is the man!' he remarked. But, for all the drama, the real work had already been done behind the scenes before the Congress met, largely by Salisbury, the new Foreign Secretary. The Congress permitted Russia to regain Bessarabia, and Batum on the South Eastern shore of the Black Sea. Bulgaria was reduced in size, the north part coming under Russian influence, and Eastern Rumelia under Turkish control but with a Christian governor. Macedonia was to remain Turkish. Austria was to occupy Bosnia and Hercegovina and garrison the Sanjak of Novibazar. Britain gained the right to send a fleet into the Black Sea whenever it was necessary (this was a guarantee to Turkey) and gained Cyprus.

The Treaty of San Stefano had been destroyed, Turkey preserved and Russia checked. Disraeli returned to Britain to announce that he had brought back 'peace, and a peace, I hope, not without honour'. His popularity rose to new heights.

Fig. 19 The Congress of Berlin

(a) Treaty of San Stefano 1878
Before the war, Turkish lands included Bosnia and all of Bulgaria. The treaty gave Bulgaria access to the Aegean and thus gave Russia access also, for Russia was Bulgaria's protector.

(b) 1878 Congress of Berlin
Turkey regained much of Bulgaria and so cut Bulgaria's and Russia's access to the sea. There was continual trouble in the Balkans until, in 1914, the assassination at Sarajevo led to the First World War (see page 169). Did the statesmen at Berlin get it wrong in 1878?

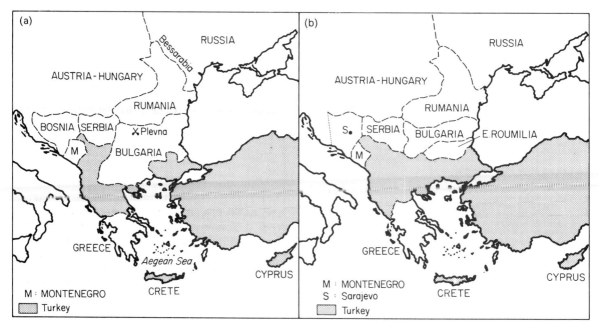

This extract from Gladstone's pamphlet presents a different picture from what Disraeli wished the British public to see. The Sultan (the Porte) was scarcely a reliable ally whom Britain should happily protect. The questions that follow use the passage to ask about the crisis leading to the war and the Congress of Berlin, 1878. Be careful in answering (d), for opinion sided with both – at different times!

Balkan troubles

It may seem that one who is no more than a private individual is guilty of presumption in dealing with so great and perilous a question. But I have great faith in the power of opinion, of
5 the opinion of civilised and Christian Europe. It can remove mountains. Six months ago England and Europe had just learned, upon official authority, the reality and extent of the Massacres, and of outrages far worse than Massacre, in
10 Bulgaria . . . The belief that a government in alliance with her Majesty could stand in close complicity with crimes so foul was a belief so startling, nay, so horrible, that it was not fit to be entertained, unless upon the clearest and fullest
15 evidence . . . The acts of the Porte, through nine long months, demonstrate a deliberate intention. The purpose has been to cover up iniquity . . .
The British ambassador has been possessed with the belief that the condition of the subject
20 races of Turkey ought to be supremely determined by whatever our estimate of British interests may require. A little faith in the ineradicable difference between right and wrong is worth a great deal of European diplomacy.
GLADSTONE in a pamphlet on the 'Bulgarian Atrocities', 1876

(a) Explain 'a government in alliance with her Majesty' (lines 10–11) and 'the Porte' (line 15). (3)
(b) What were the 'crimes so foul' (line 12) of which Gladstone complains? Why should 'Christian Europe' (line 5) be particularly offended by them? (4)
(c) What 'British interests' (line 21) were involved in the Balkan question? How was the issue settled in 1878? (10)
(d) Did public opinion in Britain side with Gladstone or with Disraeli? Why? (3)

O & C

Disraeli's defeat

Eighteen months after his tremendous triumph, Disraeli suffered a shattering defeat at the polls. Why? Partly because of a wave of economic troubles at home. In the late 1870s there was a depression that resulted in significant unemployment which had its effect on public opinion. At the same time, other countries were beginning to raise tariffs against British goods, whilst Britain's policy of Free Trade left British industries wide open to foreign competition. Again, because of developments in transport and technology, cheap food began to flood in from the mid-west of Canada and the United States, and Disraeli, who had defended Protection for the farmers in 1846, now refused to grant it when they were in most need of it. They suffered badly from the competition – and the agricultural interest was presumed to be strongly Conservative. In addition, bad harvests in 1878 and 1879, together with widespread cattle and sheep diseases combined with the cheap foreign corn imports to force many farmers into bankruptcy. It was no consolation to them to know that cheap imports meant lower cost of food for everyone.

Ireland suffered an even worse depression in agriculture and this increased the agitation for Home Rule. By 1878 a new and forceful Irish leader, Charles Stewart Parnell (1846–91), a Protestant landowner and an MP since 1875, had organised the Irish Nationalist MPs into a disciplined body using highly effective obstructionist tactics which held up government business. In Ireland, Michael Davitt, aided by many Fenian sympathisers and money from the USA, formed the Land League (1879), of which Parnell became President. It openly attacked landlords who raised rents and evicted tenants. To the ministry's trouble at home were added the reverses suffered in South Africa and Afghanistan.

However, the main reason for Disraeli's defeat was Gladstone. He decided that he must come out of retirement and once again attack his old adversary. He launched the Midlothian campaign in November 1879, a 'pilgrimage of passion' as Disraeli described it, that concentrated opinion all over the country against the government, for although Midlothian was the constituency he intended to contest, *The Times* reported all his speeches fully and they were read throughout the land. (Look them up in your County Library.)

Gladstone's attack on the 'forward' imperial policy of the government, 'weakening the empire by needless wars, unprofitable extensions and unwise engagements' concentrated all the political and economic discontent into a moral crusade directed against 'Beaconsfieldism' (the name coined to describe Disraeli's policies after he became Lord Beaconsfield).

> Remember the rights of the savage. Remember that the happiness of his humble home, remember that the sanctity of life in the hill villages of Afghanistan, among the winter snows, is as inviolable in the eyes of Almighty God as can be your own.

Once again, Gladstone had pointed a new way in politics –no wonder the Queen was horrified. In March 1880, in the general election campaign, he repeated his triumph in a second Midlothian campaign – the Liberals won a clear majority of 137 seats in the new Parliament. Try as the Queen might to prevent Gladstone's assuming power, and she tried Lord Hartington and Lord Granville, the two Midlothian campaigns had thrust Gladstone forward as the inevitable choice for Prime Minister. Disraeli died the following year: the Queen was left with Gladstone, whom she found increasingly distasteful.

Gladstone's second ministry, 1880–85

A host of difficulties faced Gladstone. Despite its huge majority of seats, the ministry was not a success and Gladstone's handling of problems suggest his powers were in decline. His control both of the administration and his Cabinet lacked the quality of his first ministry: there were new men whom he could not persuade to his views. Many of the big towns had returned Liberals, which was often due to careful local party organisation – Joseph Chamberlain in Birmingham had established a party 'caucus' that secured control over nearly all the seats of the city. He was a new type of Radical, an industrialist who looked to the government to take a direct part in reforming conditions – the opposite of the *laissez-faire* school of thought. He wanted government intervention where necessary – and he also wanted British industries to be protected against foreign competition (a Fair Trade League had been formed to press for tariffs). Gladstone would have none of this: he was a Free Trader and believed in *individualism*; he resisted increasing the powers of the state. In a changing world, he retained many of the ideas of the previous generation – above all he would not touch Free Trade, believing it was the basis of British prosperity, despite the growth of Protection abroad and

the flood of imports from competitors – in 1882 the first refrigerated meat arrived from New Zealand.

When Chamberlain spoke of old-age pensions for the poor, Gladstone opposed him on the grounds that it would diminish thrift and self-respect. He found that the rising young radicals opposed him – Charles Dilke, Labouchere and Chamberlain – and there was a possibility of a split. He developed a personal animosity towards Chamberlain (he once admitted he had stayed longer than was wise in office in order to prevent Chamberlain becoming leader of the Liberals). But there was resistance also from the Old Whig element in the party – Hartington (soon to become Duke of Devonshire) was out of sympathy with some of Gladstone's views. In politics, men are as important as measures. Gladstone may have shown himself a less capable party leader than Disraeli, for he failed to hold his party together.

Imperial problems

There was also Disraeli's legacy of problems to trouble the ministry. The immediate problem was Afghanistan. Gladstone was no imperialist and was intent on reducing expenditure: reluctantly, the Queen had to acquiesce to Britain withdrawing from Afghanistan. In the Transvaal, the Boers were demanding their independence now that the Zulus had been defeated. The First Boer War, 1880–81, resulted in a severe British defeat at Majuba Hill in 1881. Gladstone was anxious to end the war, and by the Convention of Pretoria, 1881, the Transvaal regained its independence under certain conditions, notably that of Britain conducting its foreign relations. The easy victory gave the Boers a false impression of their strength. Certainly, the whole affair reduced Gladstone's popularity a great deal.

In Egypt, it was different: Gladstone pursued a policy as ambitious as any of Disraeli's. Britain and France had exercised 'dual control' over Egyptian finances since 1878 and their control over the Suez Canal was considerable. Angry at this foreign interference, a nationalist revolt led by Arabi Pasha threatened the position of Khedive Tewfik and of his foreign friends. An Anglo-French fleet was sent to Alexandria, and in 1881 the British bombarded Alexandria and landed troops which defeated Arabi Pasha at Tel-el-Kebir in 1882. Britain now occupied Egypt, imposing Sir Evelyn Baring (later Lord Cromer) as Consul-General. But control of Egypt involved taking on the Sudan to the south. There, a religious and nationalist leader, Mohammed Ahmed, called the Mahdi, was fast gaining control. In 1883 an Egyptian force under an English officer,

Hicks Pasha, was ambushed and destroyed. Gladstone decided to withdraw before he became involved in a major war. It was a wise decision – but he chose the wrong man to do it. He chose General Charles Gordon.

Gordon was a remarkable man. He was as profoundly religious as Gladstone and had as deep a social conscience. He was something of a legend already, having served in the Crimea, China and under Ishmail Pasha, Tewfik's father. Gladstone was obliged to choose him because of the popular demand created by the press. But when Gordon arrived at Khartoum, he did not withdraw forces – he stayed. Throughout the summer telegrams arrived from Gordon without any indication of when he intended to withdraw. Gladstone became exasperated and soon Gordon was besieged by the Mahdi's fearsome dervishes (1884). A relief force despatched immediately would have saved him, but there were unaccountable delays. Eventually relief arrived at Khartoum two days after Gordon's death and the fall of the city (January 1885). There was a tremendous outcry and many demonstrations in London against Gladstone. The Queen was at Balmoral. She sent a telegram, uncoded (so that every telegraph clerk relaying it on the way to London would read it), saying 'You have murdered Gordon'. (Was she deliberately interfering in politics? Gladstone thought so.) But Gordon's death was not avenged: the Sudan was evacuated. Once again, Disraeli's legacy had led Gladstone into unfamiliar policies that proved costly failures and reduced his popularity.

> Many books have been written on Gordon – there were scores published very soon after his death. His career and character have fascinated many writers. Try to find out more about him and his ideas; discover his ideas on the slave trade; decide what he was up to in Khartoum in 1884. You might start with Alan Morehead's *The White Nile*.

Home affairs

At home Gladstone had no better success. He was ill and often absent from the House (was this why there were delays over Gordon's relief force?). In the House itself much time was deliberately wasted by four bright young Conservatives – Lord Randolph Churchill, their leader, whose brilliance in debate matched Gladstone (look at the well-

Gordon deserted
The date of this picture is 24 May, 1884. Gordon was killed the following January. Was the picture intended to work up public pressure on Gladstone to reverse his policy of withdrawal from the Sudan? If so, this would not be bias. What would it be?

known biography of this wayward figure written by his famous son, Winston Churchill), A. J. Balfour (Lord Salisbury's nephew), Henry Drummond Wolff and Sir John Gorst. They called themselves the Fourth Party. One of their prime targets was Bradlaugh, the Radical MP for Northampton. He was an atheist – he could not swear the oath, they declared, and so could not take his seat. The debate on this issue occupied much of the first years of the ministry. Eventually, after being re-elected, he was admitted and allowed merely to affirm the oath as a member. But time wasted meant few measures were passed.

In 1890 Mundella's Act made elementary education compulsory. There was an ineffective Employers' Liability Act providing for compensation for industrial injuries (1880). In 1882 an important measure, the Married Women's Property Act, gave women for the first time the right to control their own property – formerly it had become their husband's. This was a stride towards equal rights for women. In 1883 came a Settled Land Act, allowing easier disposal of inherited estates. Also in 1883 came the Corrupt Practices (Elections) Act curbing bribery and corruption at elections by severely limiting the money that might be spent on returning a candidate during the election campaign. It was successful (although election petitions alleging corruption remained frequent).

The chief measure was the Third Reform Act. The demand for this came from the Radicals, but there was considerable opposition from the Lords. In a vigorous campaign throughout the country, Chamberlain, John Morley and the veteran John Bright attacked the Lords with phrases like 'Peers against People'. 'Mend them or end them'. This had its effect and a compromise was reached (in which the Queen played an important part). It involved two separate Acts, linked together as the Third Reform Act. The first part was the County Franchise Act 1884 which gave the vote to male householders and lodgers paying £10. This increased the electorate, especially among the agricu-

Deputation to a candidate on Women's Rights, 1880
 The fight for equality of the sexes goes back a long way: it was not a big step from a deputation like this to the demand that women should have the vote. (See p. 177).

latural labourers (and Irish peasants!). The very large electorates meant the rapid development of local party organisations in each constituency. The second part was the Redistribution Act 1885. By this Act all boroughs with fewer than 15 000 inhabitants were deprived of their MPs and merged with the counties (a move that favoured the Conservatives, it was felt). Boroughs with between 15 000 and 50 000 inhabitants lost one member. Twenty-two boroughs with between 50 000 and 100 000 inhabitants retained two members. The rest of the country was divided into single-member constituencies. The University seats remained – but the three-member seats disappeared. This gave a fairer system, but manhood suffrage had not yet been achieved. It came in 1918.

Ireland again

But what really disturbed the ministry was the Irish problem. Parnell had developed to a fine art the technique of obstructing parliamentary business – with the purpose of causing such a nuisance that Parliament in desperation would repeal the Act of Union. He led the Irish MPs brilliantly. Eventually, the obstruction caused Gladstone to bring in the 'closure' measure (1881) giving powers to end debate at a set time. It was embarrassing for him, and the Fourth Party made great play with what they represented as Gladstone deliberately restricting freedom of speech.

In Ireland the Land League had by 1880 raised a 'plan of campaign' with cattle-maiming, rick-burning, 'moonlighting', assault and murder. Anyone who occupied the land of a tenant who had been evicted was 'boycotted' (treated as if he did not exist 'by isolating him from the rest of his country as if he were a leper of old', as Parnell put it. The word comes from the name of Captain Boycott, the agent of a large landowner who was the first to suffer this fate.) In hopes of stopping the disorder, the government prosecuted Parnell and other Land League leaders for conspiracy – but the jury could not agree on the verdict. So the government resorted to the familiar pattern of coercion with wide powers of arbitrary arrest. However, they did pass the Second Irish Land Act 1881, giving some 'fixity of tenure', freedom of sale and fair rents – the 'three Fs' of the Land League's programme – and a land commission that would advance up to three-quarters of the purchase price to a tenant whose landlord agreed to sell. It was a generous measure, but not enough. Parnell continued to make provocative speeches and this led to his imprisonment in Kilmainham Gaol, Dublin in 1881.

The Land League increased their campaign of violence and enforced a 'no rent' strike until Parnell should be released. Deadlock and disorder ensued. To break this, Chamberlain, with Gladstone's connivance, arranged through Captain O'Shea what has been called the Kilmainham Treaty, 1882, by which Parnell and two other leaders were released to help stop disorders in return for an Arrears Act to help about 100 000 Irish peasants pay off their rent arrears. It seemed that some progress might be made. But shortly after Parnell's release, the new Chief Secretary for Ireland, Lord Frederick Cavendish, and the Under-Secretary, Mr Burke, were murdered in Phoenix Park, Dublin (1882) by a terrorist gang known as the 'Invincibles'. Other disturbances followed, and the government replied with the severe Coercion Act 1882. Parnell, though innocent, was blamed for the outrage and his position was weakened. He now tried to conciliate opinion and worked towards a settlement, for he was

Bombs in the House of Commons

The Invincibles were a dangerous Irish nationalist terrorist group. Bombing the House of Commons was perhaps as important as the Phoenix Park murders in concentrating opinion in England. The group was still active three years after those murders.

neither a fool nor a revolutionary and saw the opportunity for success slipping away because of the revulsion by British public opinion against disorder.

By 1885 Gladstone's ministry was divided and discredited. He resigned, and the Queen happily sent for Lord Salisbury, who formed a 'caretaker' government until a new election could be held on the new electoral registers required by the Third Reform Act. The ministry passed the Ashbourne Land Purchase Act 1885, making £5 million available for loans to Irish tenants to purchase their farms.

That summer there were many confidential negotiations. Parnell had made his position clear in 1885: 'We cannot under the British Constitution ask for more than the restitution of Grattan's Parliament. But no man has the right to fix the boundary of the march of a nation.' For the Conservatives, Lord Randolph Churchill gave Parnell to understand that they would consider granting Ireland Home Rule. Chamberlain offered a complex scheme of allowing the Irish to run their own local affairs (he called it 'devolution'). Sometime during the summer, Gladstone was converted to the need for Home Rule on the grounds that the Act of Union had manifestly failed and that the Irish people sought their freedom. (Do you remember what he had said in the Midlothian campaigns?) But Gladstone did not make this clear to Parnell, so at the election Parnell ordered his Irish supporters in England to vote Conservative, believing he would get a better deal from them.

The election resulted in the Liberals gaining a majority of 86 over the Conservatives. Many of the rural seats, surprisingly, went Liberal, and Joseph Chamberlain claimed that this was due to his own 'unauthorised programme' – it had not been officially adopted. Gladstone certainly disapproved of it. In a speech at Edinburgh, 1884, he declared,

> There is a disposition to think that Government ought to do this and that, and that the Government ought to do everything. If the Government takes into its hand that which the man ought to do for himself, it will inflict upon him greater mischiefs than all the benefits he will receive . . . The spirit of self-reliance should be preserved in the minds of the masses of the people, in the minds of every member of that class.

The 'unauthorised programme' called for just such government action. Chamberlain replied a year later in a speech at Warrington, 1885,

> It is therefore perfectly futile and ridiculous for any Rip Van Winkle* to come down from the mountain on which he has been slumbering, and to tell us that these things are to be excluded from the Liberal programme . . . I shall be told tomorrow that this is Socialism. Of course, it is Socialism. The greater part of municipal work is Socialism and every kindly act of legislation by which the community has sought to discharge its responsibilities and its obligations to the poor is Socialism, but it is none the worse for that. Our object is the elevation of the poor, of the masses of the people.

(* The reference to Gladstone is clear.)

Here was a sign of the coming split in the Liberal Party (see page 155). But the majority of 86 was balanced by Parnell's Irish Party of 86 MPs, all of whom had taken an oath of obedience to him. The election was therefore a stalemate, and Parnell held the key to the future, it seemed.

Just before Christmas, however, Gladstone's son, Herbert, told the press of his father's conversion that summer to Home Rule. This 'Howarden kite' (so called because the announcement came from Gladstone's country house at Howarden) was wilfully misinterpreted by the Conservatives, who saw the chance of office slipping away. It allowed Gladstone to form his third ministry in 1886, safe in the knowledge that the Irish would support him and that a Home Rule Bill would pass. But he had reckoned without Chamberlain or the Old Whigs of the party. The divisions of his previous ministry were reappearing.

Hartington and the Old Whigs objected to Home Rule because it would seem to be breaking up the Empire at its very centre, as well as damaging the interests of the Anglo-Irish landlords. But the real threat came from Chamberlain: he believed (correctly) that Gladstone would push through Home Rule at the expense of his own programme of extensive social reform, and he would do so in an autocratic manner. Chamberlain was also developing a new and dynamic view of the Empire as a great trading area – Irish Home Rule as such played no part in this idea. He was also well aware that Gladstone could not last for ever – was he intent on splitting the Party in order to seize the leadership? Was it no more than personal ambition? He made his position clear by announcing that about forty 'Liberal Unionists' would oppose Home Rule.

Lord Salisbury had not publicly committed the Conservatives, but Lord Randolph Churchill, who had conducted the confidential negotiations with Parnell, was quite certain what to do. In a letter of 16 February 1886, he wrote, 'I decided some time ago that if the G.O.M. went for Home Rule, the Orange Card would be the one to play. Please God it may turn out the ace of trumps.' So began that close association of the Conservative Party with Ulster Protestants that was to last a hundred years.

Gladstone presented his First Home Rule Bill in April 1886, proposing an Irish Parliament, with Westminster controlling defence, foreign and colonial matters. The Union had failed and coercion was 'morally outworn'. He answered the Liberal Unionists, 'The unity of the Empire must not be placed in jeopardy . . . There should be an equitable distribution of Imperial burdens . . .' and replied to Lord Randolph, 'Certainly, Sir, I cannot allow it to be said that a Protestant minority in Ulster, or elsewhere, is to rule the question at large for Ireland.'

Nevertheless, in June the Bill was defeated, 93 Liberals voting against it. Gladstone decided to appeal to the country, and the Queen delightedly called a general election. Gladstone told his constituents,

Two plans are before the world. There is the plan of the government: and there is the plan of Lord Salisbury. Our plan is that Ireland should transact her own affairs. His plan is to ask Parliament for new repressive laws, and to enforce them resolutely for twenty years . . .

Lord Randolph replied cuttingly that Home Rule would obstruct parliamentary business '. . . all useful and deserved reforms are to be shivered into fragments. And why? For this reason and no other; to gratify the ambition of an old man in a hurry.'

The country rejected Home Rule. A Conservative government was returned (remaining in power for almost twenty years) and Chamberlain with his Liberal Unionists remained outside the Liberal Party – to become ever more closely linked to the Conservatives (he had more chance of extending state powers to provide social reform with them than with Gladstone!).

Parnell holding the balance

The result of the election meant that both parties sought Parnell's support in order to form a government. The price was Home Rule. The Cartoon sums up the situation: Parnell's shillelagh is inscribed 'Home Rule' and neither Gladstone nor Salisbury look happy! The notice is a reference to Jesse Collings' campaign for the agricultural vote, '3 acres and a cow'.

Try to find the relevant volumes of *Punch* at the County Library, and read the appropriate sections of biographies of Gladstone, Churchill and Chamberlain. Then hold a class debate on the question, 'Was Gladstone right over Home Rule in 1886?'—or another question, 'Who split the Liberal Party, Gladstone or Chamberlain?'

There is a famous description of a Christmas dinner ruined by a family row over Parnell, Ireland and the power of the priesthood, in James Joyce's *Portrait of the Artist as a Young Man*. Have the powerful passage read out in class, for it will leave a great impression.

Lord Salisbury now took office and entrusted Ireland to his nephew, A. J. Balfour. To many people's surprise, this languid, intellectual aristocrat proved a tough administrator, combining coercion with some reform – his intention was 'killing Home Rule with kindness'. He extended government provision of funds to allow more tenants to buy their farms and improved communications by the Light Railways Act 1891. His various measures reached a culmination with Wyndham's Land Purchase Act 1903 – a bold measure encouraging landlords to sell and lending tenants the necessary purchase capital at half a per cent interest. It was successful in creating a new class of peasant proprietors. But in the 1880s the Irish replied to his intentions with a systematic plan of campaign requiring tenants to withhold rents on pain of reprisals. For his vigorous coercive measures they called him 'Bloody Balfour'.

In 1887 an attempt was made to destroy Parnell's reputation. *The Times* published letters that suggested he had approved of the Pheonix Park murders. Parnell denounced them as a forgery, and after a special commission of enquiry in 1889 an impoverished journalist, Richard Pigott, confessed to forging them. Parnell was vindicated and achieved new heights of popularity. Suddenly, (like Sir Charles Dilke before him) he was destroyed by a divorce scandal. Captain O'Shea, who had condoned a long-standing love-affair between Parnell and his wife, Kitty, demanded a divorce, citing Parnell as the co-respondent. Parnell made no defence, and Victorian society was shocked at the revelation. Anxious to retain the Nonconformist vote, Gladstone demanded that the Irish Home Rulers choose between Parnell and himself. In Ireland, the priests turned against Parnell – but he fought on. In December 1890, after a long and bitter party meeting, his leadership was rejected; he died in 1891. The Irish were never again to be led so vigorously and the nationalists broke up into feuding groups that did little to promote their real cause. The myth of Parnell, the rejected, lost leader began to grow.

The end of Gladstone's career

In the election of 1892, Gladstone won a small victory and began his fourth ministry. The Second Home Rule Bill passed through the Commons in 1893 and Gladstone was given a standing ovation. The Lords threw out the Bill by a huge majority. Gladstone wanted to appeal to the country again, but his Cabinet refused and he resigned, complaining that he had been pushed out of office. Younger men in the Party felt that Home Rule was becoming a worn-out slogan – although, like Fox a century before, Gladstone had pointed towards the aspirations of the rising generation in Ireland. It was a sad ending to a fine career, but his world was passing: Free Trade and rugged individualism were under attack. Even an attempt to rouse public opinion against the Turks over the Armenian massacres of Christians failed. Gladstone died in 1898: by remaining at the helm so long and driving out Joseph Chamberlain, had he prevented the Liberal Party from adopting new and radical policies appropriate to the twentieth century that was about to dawn? Was Gladstone one of the causes of the development of the Labour Party?

There were some able young men in his last Cabinet, such as Sir William Harcourt and H. H. Asquith. At the 1892 election, the 'Newcastle programme', calling for payment of MPs, reform of the House of Lords and of local government, showed the party still had radical ideas. Lord Rosebery became Prime Minister at the Queen's request – it was one of her last insults to Gladstone, for she did not ask his advice. It was a shrewd move on her part, since Rosebery was no radical. But Harcourt was able to introduce death duties in the 1894 Budget – he raised £14 million thereby from the wealthy. It was a sign of the coming twentieth century and the growing power of the state. The Lords let through the measure, but obstructed much of the other legislation, and in 1895 Rosebery resigned. Lord Salisbury won the ensuing election and combined with the Liberal Unionists to form his third ministry.

There have been many books praising Gladstone, for he stood like a giant among his contemporaries. Many of his opponents distrusted him and many more were fearful of his changes of course during his career. He was no simple, straightforward character. But the common people loved him, however much they disapproved of some of his actions. He represented a deep sentiment of noble morality that was characteristic of the great Victorian leaders. It is difficult to sum up his career and his importance, but you might look up the obituary notice in *The Times* and see whether you agree with its judgement. Here is a much shorter, much simpler judgement by Goldwin Smith: attempt your own obituary notice of that 'sophistical rhetorician, inebriated by the exuberance of his own verbosity', the 'People's William'.

John Morley wrote the 'official' *Life of Gladstone*. Here is a passage that sums up some of his achievements. The questions that follow are useful revision exercises, but they do not make good use of the passage. After completing them, compose three questions of your own that uses the extract directly and try them out on the class.

Gladstone's political achievements

His passion for economy, his ceaseless war against public profusion, his insistence upon rigorous keeping of the national accounts – in this great department of affairs, he led and did not
5 follow. In a survey of Mr. Gladstone's performances, some would place this of which I have last spoken, as foremost among his services to the country. Others would call him greatest in the associated service of a skilful handling and
10 adjustment of the burden of taxation; or the strengthening of the foundations of national prosperity. Yet others again choose to remember him for his share in guiding the successive extensions of popular power, and simplifying
15 and purifying electoral machinery. Irishmen at least, and others so far as they are able to comprehend the history and vile wrongs and sharp needs of Ireland, will have no doubt what rank in legislation they will assign to the es-
20 tablishment of religious equality and agrarian justice in that portion of the realm.

JOHN MORLEY

(a) What did Gladstone achieve in adjusting 'the burden of taxation' (line 10), and in strengthening 'the foundations of national prosperity' (lines 1–12)? (6)
(b) What 'successive extensions of popular power' (lines 13–14) took place under Gladstone's administrations? Explain 'purifying electoral machinery' (line 15). (4)
(c) What did Gladstone do for 'religious equality and agrarian justice' (lines 20–21) in Ireland? Do you agree with the writer's view of Gladstone's achievements in this sphere? (10)

O & C

11 Salisbury and the Conservative dominance, 1886–1906

Domestic reforms

Salisbury was a very capable Foreign Secretary and he proved a strong Prime Minister. A great aristocrat, he seemed the natural leader of the Conservative Party but, much to the Queen's horror, he was quite prepared to give office to Joseph Chamberlain. He was no reformer, but ready to pass measures that helped the poor. He was also a wily politician. Lord Randolph Churchill was anxious to press on with many social reforms; Salisbury was not prepared to go so fast. He suspected Lord Randolph of being more interested in his own advancement than in reform. Lord Randolph was probably planning to challenge Salisbury for the leadership of the party. When his reform programme was opposed by the Cabinet (1886), he made a dramatic threat to resign. Salisbury coolly accepted the resignation. It was the end of Lord Randolph's career; his health gave way and his end was a sad one.

There was little reform under Salisbury. Local government was reorganised by the County Council Act 1888, setting up 64 counties and 60 county boroughs to carry out important local services. A separate Act created the London County Council. In 1894 Urban and Rural District Councils were created and the ancient parishes were reorganised. The 1894 Act also allowed women to vote and be elected to parish and Urban and Rural District Councils. But women still could not vote at parliamentary elections or be elected to the Commons!

Other reforms were continuations of earlier measures, for Chamberlain's energies were absorbed elsewhere! The Allotments and Small Holdings Acts 1887–9 and the Housing of the Working Classes Act 1890 improved things a little for the poor. The Factory Act 1890 enforced sanitary conditions; the Shops Act 1892 reduced working hours for shop assistants. Technical education was helped by the new county councils and boroughs after 1889, and school fees in elementary schools were abolished in 1891. But these were small measures, even though people were becoming increasingly aware of social problems. It was the Empire that was attracting most attention.

Imperialism

In the 1880s the so-called 'scramble for Africa' saw almost the whole continent carved up between rival European powers. The empire-builders went in search of trade and wealth. Some were explorers of the 'dark continent', some were mere adventurers, quite a number were missionaries. There was tremendous interest and enthusiasm.

You can test this easily by asking at your local reference library if they have copies of, say, the *Illustrated London News* or *The Graphic*, popular magazines with illustrations. Note the number of articles on the Empire and the number of wars all over the globe! Note also the assumption of superiority, for the 'natives' are always shown standing while English officers are seated, and when local chieftains are captured after resisting British action in their areas, they are shown running at the heels of a common soldier's horse, a halter round their necks. You will find pictures of 'natives' being flogged for disobedience or numbers of them being shot for rebellion. Such pictures reflected and encouraged the British conviction that Britain was civilising and governing vast areas of the globe.

The Empire was popular: it provided jobs for all sections of society, and the colonies supplied cheap raw materials and provided a market for manufactured goods. Cheap foodstuffs such as sugar, tea, coffee, rice and grain meant a better diet for the British people. Canada, Australia and New Zealand provided open opportunities for many emigrants. Music-hall songs and ballads celebrated what was clearly an expression of Britain's greatness, and the two Royal Jubilees (1887 and 1897) were both used to reinforce the theme of an Empire on which the sun never set. Prime ministers of the self-governing territories came to London for colonical conferences. (The novels of G. A. Henty, R. L. Stevenson, H. Rider Haggard and Rudyard Kipling all give a flavour of British confidence at this time.)

Jubilee celebrations, 1897

Joseph Chamberlain seized on imperialism as the answer to Britain's trade rivals (see page 194). The Empire would supply the market for British goods and create the wealth from which further social reform would come. He went further: he saw the Empire as a great moral force for good: 'a larger patriotism . . . the greatest secular agency for good the world has yet seen'. In 1895, he surprised everyone by deliberately choosing the Colonial Office when Salisbury invited him to join his cabinet. Hitherto, it had been regarded as a minor office, but Chamberlain made it the centre of attention, starting programmes for financial aid and development in existing colonies and expanding Britain's influence over wide areas – a policy not without its problems.

Not everyone favoured the Empire – you will see some of the reasons if you read a funny poem by H. Belloc, *The Modern Traveller*, (1898) in which three strange adventurers seek their fortune in Africa:

Great Island! Made to be the bane
Of Mr Chamberlain.
Peninsula! Whose smouldering fights
Keep Salisbury awake at nights.

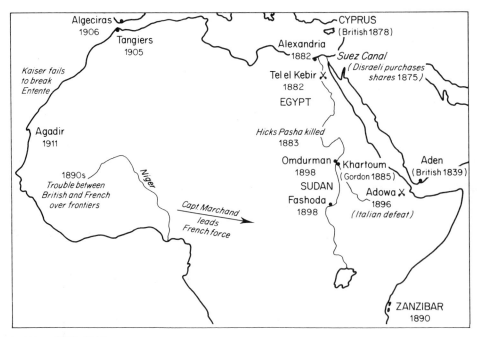

Fig. 20 North Africa, 1882–1914

Sudan

Gordon's death in 1885 had gone unavenged, but the increasing interest of European powers in the headwaters of the Nile (and Egypt depended on the Nile) made the Egyptian government worried. Britain, France, Germany and Italy were competing to control these headwaters. In 1896 the Italians were defeated at Adowa by Ethiopian troops helped by the French. Public attention centred on the area. It was known that the French Captain Marchand, was planning to march eastwards from Chad. Kitchener was sent up the Nile and routed the Dervishes at Omdurman (1898) near Khartoum. British artillery, machine guns and rapid rifle-fire wrought such a dreadful slaughter that hardened troops were sickened. (You can read an eye-witness account of the battle in Winston Churchill's *My Early Days*.) Gordon had been avenged (thirteen years late!).

Kitchener marched south and came upon the French force encamped on the reedy island of Fashoda. Marchand refused to give way. In Paris and London war-fever raged. Would the two countries fight over that marshy island? At length the French withdrew – Delcassé hoped to gain British support against Germany. There was no war: Britain occupied the whole of the Sudan south of Egypt. But war had been a serious threat. This was an indication of how imperial affairs could affect European diplomacy.

Second Boer War, 1899–1902

Meanwhile, serious trouble in South Africa was coming to a head. The discovery of gold and diamonds in the Transvaal had encouraged a host of prospectors to arrive. The Boers called them *Uitlanders*, and President Kruger of the Transvaal taxed them heavily and refused them the vote. He feared that if they had it, Cecil Rhodes, premier of Cape Province, a man with considerable mining interests, would possibly gain control of the Transvaal. The Uitlanders protested and there were plans for a rising – it was to coincide with a raid by Dr Jameson, a friend of Rhodes. The 'Jameson Raid' took place in December, 1895: there was no rising and it was a total failure. Jameson was captured and Rhodes resigned. The British government was embarrassed: did Chamberlain know of the raid? A parliamentary enquiry in 1897 failed to determine how far he was involved. Some people have suggested the enquiry was a 'cover-up' and perhaps deliberately failed to reveal Chamberlain's involvement in the raid: even while it sat, the proceedings were known as the 'lying in state at Westminster'! But the Boers regarded Kruger as a hero, and Kaiser William of Germany sent him the 'Kruger telegram' (1896) congratulating him on maintaining 'the independence of your country against attacks from without'. It was a clear sign of Britain's unpopularity abroad.

Dr Jameson as a prisoner

tactics to prevent any supplies reaching the guerrillas and imprisoned men, women and children in overcrowded camps. Somehow, the glory seemed suddenly tarnished and a reaction set in against Imperialism. In 1900, Lloyd George, a young Liberal MP, had dared to address a meeting in Chamberlain's Birmingham on behalf of the Liberal 'pro-Boers' who were against the war – he had to escape in disguise with a police escort. But opinion had changed by 1902. By then foreign powers had begun to think that Britain was weak. The treaty of Vereeniging (1902) ended the war, with the Boers accepting the sovereignty of the British Crown, but gaining the promise of self-government (it came in 1910 with the Government of South Africa Act) and £3 million to repair and restock Boer farms.

The war had cost £250 million and revealed the inefficiency of the British army: as in the Crimean War, disease had claimed more lives than battles did. The Liberals had largely opposed the war; their new leader, Campbell-Bannerman, attracted much support by condemning the anti-guerrilla tactics as 'methods of barbarism'. A new confidence returned to the Opposition, so soon after their defeat in the khaki election.

The problem of the Uitlanders remained, and relations between the Boers and the British, represented by Sir Alfred Milner, High Commissioner in South Africa, rapidly deteriorated. Both sides openly prepared for war, and on 9 October 1899, Kruger sent an ultimatum demanding Britain to stop sending reinforcements to South Africa. War began three days later. It was welcomed with tremendous enthusiasm in Britain: this was the high point of Imperialism. Those who opposed the war were sometimes ostracised.

In December 1899 came 'Black Week' when Britain suffered a series of severe defeats. Would she lose the war? Lord Roberts was sent with huge reinforcements, which were joined by contingents from India and the colonies. It seemed the whole might of the British Empire was being pitched against a small community of Boer farmers – some 400 000 troops against some 80 000 Boers. Successes came, such as the relief of Mafeking (1900), and Chamberlain was instrumental in persuading Salisbury to call a general election – the Khaki election, 1900, named after the color of the new fighting uniform. The Conservatives obtained a resounding majority to 'win the war'. But the war dragged on, with the Boers fighting a bitter guerrilla war until 1902. The British used 'scorched earth'

A. J. Balfour's ministry 1902—5

During the war Queen Victoria died (22 January 1901). In her long reign she had done much to raise the monarchy in public esteem, and her sense of duty and hard work reflected the attitudes of many of her people. Her death clearly marked the end of an era: her successor, Edward VII (1901–10) lacked her qualities of devotion to detailed work, and, although he was extremely popular at home and abroad, he contributed little to the serious political problems of his reign. Lord Salisbury was growing old, and retired in 1902. At the time Chamberlain was out of action because of a serious cab accident – cynics said he chose to resign at that time for that reason! The new Prime Minister was his nephew, Arthur J. Balfour, a dapper, withdrawn aesthete who lacked charisma and has often been thought a weak man – but he was an adroit politician with a brilliant mind, and the Irish had once called him 'Bloody Balfour'.

His government brought in a series of important reforms of the armed forces, which the Liberals carried forward and which did much to sustain Britain's efforts at the beginning of the Great War, 1914–18. In Europe, an arms race had developed

THE COMING OF ARTHUR."

Shade of Pam. "H'M! A LITTLE YOUNG FOR THE PART,—DON'T YOU THINK?"
Shade of Dizzy. "WELL, YES! WE HAD TO WAIT FOR IT A GOOD MANY YEARS.—BUT I THINK HE 'LL DO . ."

The Coming of Arthur
The 'part' is that of Prime Minister. Note the date: Balfour had to wait ten years before he succeeded his uncle in office, but Punch is already pointing to him as the likely man. It is worth remembering this in view of the reputation he gained between 1903 and 1906 (see page 165).

between Britain, Germany and France. Only a well-equipped, well-led army could hope for success in battle. Balfour established as an effective body the Committee of Imperial Defence, with the Prime Minister as chairman, members drawn from the army and navy and representatives from the new Dominions. The leader of the Opposition was also kept informed. Army reforms followed the Report of a Commission of Enquiry. More importantly, Sir John Fisher, First Sea Lord (1904), and Lord Cawdor pushed through naval reforms. The fleet was concentrated in home waters to meet the possible threat of invasion from Germany, and in 1906 the first Dreadnought battleship was launched. It was an outstanding achievement of naval architecture, built at incredible speed and capable of sinking any ship afloat because of her powerful guns. Germany retaliated by building her own ships, and a naval arms race developed, reaching a climax in the popular slogan of 1908 'We want eight and we won't wait!'

Education

Balfour's most important measure was the 1902 Education Act. The 1870 Act had provided for a state system of elementary education, but secondary education lagged behind. There had been some provision under the 1889 Technical Instruction Act by some School Boards and local authorities, but in 1900 this was declared illegal by the Cockerton Judgement on the grounds that they exceeded their legal powers. Balfour's Act cleared up the situation by abolishing the School Boards and placing elementary, technical and secondary education under the control of County Councils or County

Boroughs. The local authorities took their task very seriously, and you will see today many former grammar schools with proud buildings dating from Edwardian days. It was a major reform that established an 'education ladder' by which abler children could win scholarships to attend the secondary grammar schools. But it provoked tremendous opposition from Nonconformists because it permitted voluntary-controlled denominational schools (largely Church of England) to be aided from the rates. Their opposition was bitter and a number of them preferred to go to jail rather than pay the education rate for the support of Church of England schools.

Tariff reform

Joseph Chamberlain, himself a Nonconformist, felt this opposition very keenly. He also realised that many of his supporters were joining the Liberals who had declared they would repeal the Act. It was partly for this reason, partly to revive the flagging spirits of the ministry, partly to get Protection against foreign competition, but more particularly because of his dynamic imperialist ideas, that he launched the idea Tariff Reform – proposing a tariff against foreign manufactures, but with a special preferential tariff (a low one or none at all) for members of the Empire. This would make Imperial Preference help to unify the Empire into a great economic force – as he put it, 'The days are for great Empires, not for little states'.

During the war, a registration duty of one shilling a quarter on imported corn had been imposed: Chamberlain hoped this would be repealed so far as Empire-grown corn was concerned, but retained against foreign corn. However, the Chancellor of the Exchequer, a confirmed Free Trader, repealed the duty altogether. Angrily, Chamberlain launched his Tariff Reform campaign at a great speech in Birmingham (1903). It had an electrifying effect, especially on the young men of the party. Soon, the Conservatives were split into Free Traders and tariff reformers. Chamberlain resigned as Colonial Secretary in order to have greater freedom to press his campaign. Balfour reconstructed his cabinet and pursued a middle course – he favoured tariff reform, but realised the party was not yet convinced: it needed time to be persuaded. 'I will not play Robert Peel to my party', he declared.

However, the Conservative Party was split. Chamberlain founded a Tariff Reform League that conducted effective propaganda in the press and at public meetings, and quickly set about getting constituencies to adopt Tariff Reform candidates (for Chamberlain was well versed in the arts of political management). There was no doubt of the enthusiasm that his campaign evoked: beside it, his rivals' Unionist Free Trade League failed to arouse much emotion. There was equally no doubt that the Liberals benefited from Chamberlain's campaign: they argued that Tariff Reform would reverse British prosperity which had been built on Free Trade, and that it would mean a tax on food that would raise the cost of living (they made great play with their large Free Trade loaf contrasted with the small Tariff Reform loaf).

As his campaign gained momentum, Chamberlain found that the country preferred Free Trade and cheap food. His campaign had come too soon: not until the 1930s, in very different circumstances, was Imperial Preference achieved. But the vigour of his campaign contrasted sharply with Balfour's quiet leadership, and it frightened many Conservatives, particularly when other leaders took it up. Lord Milner, for example, developed his ideas of Empire much further, and in 1907 Lord Salisbury wrote him a revealing letter:

> My opinions are so halting, so limited, beside yours. You see the great vision of a consolidated Empire full square against the world and a national policy which will use to the uttermost the resources of the State for the common good. And I see the Conservative Party. It is a Party shackled by tradition; all the cautious, all the timid, all the unimaginative, belong to it. It stumbles slowly and painfully from precedent to precedent with its eyes fixed on the ground.

Was Balfour so mistaken in choosing to adopt an undemonstrative style of leadership? In trying to balance between Chamberlain and the Free Traders, Balfour lost a good deal of credit and gained an undeserved reputation for weakness and indecision. His government began to suffer badly at by-elections. To the reaction against the Boer War and those 'methods of barbarism' was added a new complaint when indentured Chinese labour was brought in to work the South African gold mines – these labourers were kept in bad conditions and the cry of 'Chinese slavery' united working-class and humanitarian opinion against the government.

Trade unionists also opposed the government because it refused to reverse the decision in the Taff Vale Case (1901) when the Amalgamated Society of Railway Servants had been compelled to pay substantial damages to the Taff Vale Railway Company for losses incurred during a strike. This threatened the whole basis of strike action, since it removed the protection that trade unionists sup-

Punch cartoon (1903) (cartoon of 1892)
  'History Reverses Itself': Punch made a good point with
this cartoon. Peel had split the Conservatives in going for
Free Trade in 1846; Balfour helped split his party by not
returning to a form of protection in 1903.

posed they had under the 1870 Act (see page 143).
Few unions would dare strike if they could be sued
for loss of trade by employers. There was also
continued resistance to the Education Act 1902; and
the Licensing Act 1904, which granted compensation to publicans whose pubs were closed by public
order, greatly angered Temperance Societies.

It was no wonder that the government was losing
by-elections heavily in 1905, but Chamberlain
looked forward to a general election, believing that
he could control the Conservative Party organisation. At last Balfour resigned (December 1905),
hoping that divisions among the Liberals would
prevent them forming a government. But
Campbell-Bannerman formed a ministry which in
January 1906 won the biggest party majority ever –
377 seats, a majority of 84 over all other parties.
Only 157 Conservatives were returned (Balfour was
actually defeated), but Chamberlain's Birmingham
held firm for Tariff Reform. Who would now lead the
Conservative Party? Balfour was not in the House
and was discredited. Chamberlain had tremendous

support, although many were deeply suspicious of
him – was he another 'old man in a hurry'? In July
1906, at the Birmingham celebrations for his seven-
tieth birthday, he suffered a stroke and had to retire
from public life. He died in 1914. Chamberlain
represented a new force in British politics – the
industrialist, Nonconformist from the provinces
who was a master of party organisation. It is ironic
that his greatest success was the occasion of the
Conservatives' greatest defeat.

This problem of party unity lay at the heart of
many political disputes of the time. Here is a
skilfully prepared question in which the examiner
has cleverly combined the 1886 Liberal Party split
over Home Rule (a and b) with the Conservative
Party split of 1903 over Tariff Reform (c and d). The
quotation from Lord George Hamilton (one of
those who resigned in 1903) shows what a
difficult job Balfour had! The last question (e) is
very testing: it asks you to consider people's
motives. Discuss it in class before attempting it.

Party differences

A. My public utterances and my conscientious
convictions are absolutely opposed to such a
policy and I feel that the differences which have
now been disclosed are so vital that I can no
5 longer entertain the hope of being of service in
the Government.
JOSEPH CHAMBERLAIN in 1886

B. As I anticipated we could come to no agreement at our Cabinet on Monday. The Balfour-
Chamberlain alliance is an impossible combi-
10 nation for those who are opposed to Joe's
protectionist and preferential ideas. Chamberlain
whilst ready to resign, openly states that he must
adhere, whether in office or out of it, to the
Preferential scheme, but he adds, 'I am not Prime
15 Minister and my colleagues are not necessarily
bound by what I say.' But if the Prime Minister
will not repudiate his theories we lesser men
have no alternative but to go. A. J. cannot afford
to part with Chamberlain just now, he may be
20 right, so we mediocrities must go!
LORD GEORGE HAMILTON in 1903

(a) To what 'policy' (line 3) had Chamberlain
been opposed? From whose Government
(line 6) was he resigning?   (4)
(b) What were the political consequences of
his resignation in 1886?   (4)

(c) Explain 'The Balfour-Chamberlain alliance' (lines 9–10). What were 'Joe's protectionist and preferential ideas' (lines 10–11)?   (4)

(d) Why did 'lesser men have no alternative but to go' (lines 18–19)?   (2)

(e) Why did Balfour not want to lose Chamberlain? What did Chamberlain decide to do and how did his decision affect the fortunes of the party?   (6)

O & C

Balfour's government had to face a number of problems and it became very unpopular. This question examines the reasons for the unpopularity.

A Government in decline

The Conservatives had been in office continuously for ten years. Towards the end their Education Act had thoroughly aroused the latent hostility of the Free Church part of the nation. A
5   licensing Act had had the remarkable result of offending, at one and the same time, both the Liquor Trade and the Temperance Movement. The Trade Unions were angered by a decision of the Law Courts which had cut at the root of their
10   long-established status, and which the Government had refused to redress by legislation. Industries had flourished on Free Trade and were alarmed and alienated by Chamberlain's protectionist campaign. At the end, Chinese Labour
15   had added fresh volume to the current of un-

popularity. More important, perhaps, than any of these was the division in the ranks of the Conservatives themselves. The resignation of several of the best-known members of the
20   Cabinet was paralleled in the constituencies by dissensions among the local leaders and the rank-and-file. Our modern political history shows no exception to the rule that a party which goes to the polls with open and serious divisions
25   in its own ranks is doomed to defeat.

All these causes in combination brought the Conservatives to complete disaster.

Viscount Samuel, *Memoirs*

(a) To what 'ten years' (line 2) does the writer refer?   (1)

(b) Indicate the main importance of the 'Education Act' (line 3). Why had it 'aroused the latent hostility of the Free Church part of the nation' (lines 3–4)?   (4)

(c) What 'decision of the Law Courts' (line 9) had been taken? Why were Trade Unions 'angered' (line 8) and what was eventually done 'to redress' (line 11) the matter?   (4)

(d) What was 'Chamberlain's protectionist campaign' (lines 13–14)? Mention an industry which 'had flourished on Free Trade' (line 12).   (4)

(e) Explain the reference to 'Chinese Labour' (line 14).   (4)

(f) When did the General Election take place? Indicate how it was a 'complete disaster' (line 27) to the Conservatives.   (4)

O & C

Changes in foreign policy

Salisbury had combined the offices of Foreign Secretary and Prime Minister until 1900. During his ministries important developments took place. One of the most important was the creation of the modern Foreign Office where reports from agents all over the world were concentrated in order to keep the permanent staff well informed. Salisbury, like Palmerston, always remained in complete control – but can you see how this development could easily lead to the permanent staff having a very great influence on the making of foreign policy?

Salisbury had to face a different situation from that which had faced Palmerston. In Europe, France might still be the traditional enemy, but a new power had arisen since 1870 – Bismarck's Germany. Bismarck dominated European dip-

lomacy and sought to strengthen his position by a Triple Alliance (1881) of Germany, Austria-Hungary and Italy. He hoped to isolate France, his bitter rival, and prevent any agreement between France and Russia – can you see why? As an expanding industrial power, Germany was thought to rival Britain, but Bismarck hoped to gain British friendship. Salisbury was not prepared to get involved in European affairs unless British interests were directly involved. This did not mean disregarding Europe, since that would have been foolish. But it has become popular to call Salisbury's period one of 'splendid isolation' in which Britain, confident of her wealth and power stood haughtily aside from the petty squabbles of Europe. However, this is too simple an interpretation. Britain's interests were far too closely linked with stability in Europe for her to take up such a position. Similarly, it would have been a mistake to join Bismarck against France, lest

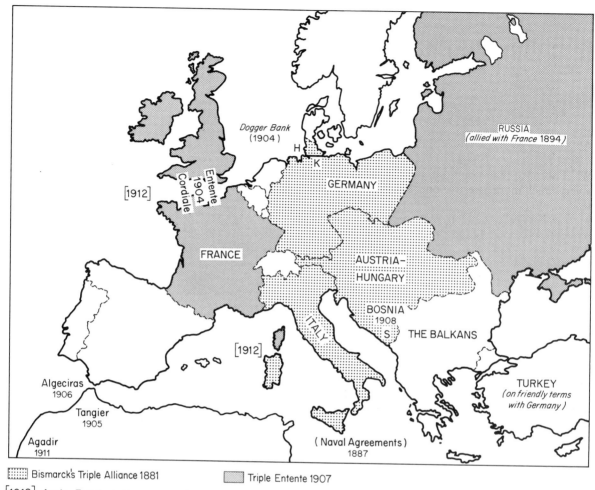

Bismarck's Triple Alliance 1881   Triple Entente 1907

[1912] Anglo-French naval arrangement
  S = Sarajevo (1914)
  H = Heligoland 1890 exchanged for Zanzibar and made into a German naval base
  K = Keil Canal, enlarged for 'Dreadnought' sized battleships by 1914

Fig. 21 European diplomacy in the early 20th century
By 1912, Germany was encircled by the Entente powers, and Britain and France were working closely together in the military and naval sectors. Europe was divided into two armed camps. The final crisis came in the Balkans in 1914.

Britain be drawn into conflicts that did not directly concern her. When Bismarck offered an alliance in 1889, Salisbury excused himself by saying that all treaties had to be approved by Parliament and he could not himself commit the country (as Bismarck seemed to expect).

At the Congress of Berlin, 1878 (see page 148) Disraeli had supported the Sultan. Salisbury very soon came to the conclusion that he had 'backed the wrong horse' and began looking for ways of modifying the 1878 settlement. The opportunity came in 1885–7 when he agreed to a united Bulgaria

under a German, Frederick of Coburg, as King, in order to block Russian influence in the Balkans. But when Bismarck, anxious to prevent Russia forming an alliance with France, himself made a Reinsurance Treaty with Russia (1887), Salisbury became anxious not to commit Britain too closely with Germany. The furthest he would go was the Anglo-German Treaty (1890) exchanging Heligoland (when did Britain gain Heligoland?) for Zanzibar and Uganda in Africa. The Germans soon made Heligoland a heavily-defended naval base guarding the newly constructed Kiel Canal.

Anxious to strengthen British interests, Salisbury made two Mediterranean Agreements (1887). The first, with Italy, effectively guaranteed her against any attack from France; the second offered similar support to Austria-Hungary if she was attacked by Russia. These Agreements were not very precise, but were the closest Britain had yet come to any formal alliance in peacetime since 1815. They clearly showed support of Bismarck and his Triple Alliance.

In 1890 Bismarck resigned, for the new Kaiser William II was intent on following his own policy – a very much more assertive one. Salisbury began a reappraisal of British foreign policy. The Kaiser was anxious to make Germany an imperial power with 'a place in the sun' – this could conflict with Britain, and there was a close link between her imperial conflicts and European diplomacy. There was a growing concern about Germany. In 1895 the Kaiser had sent the Kruger Telegram, which Britain regarded as an insult. There were disputes over African colonies, especially in the area of what was to become Nigeria. In 1895 Britain declared that any foreign penetration into the Upper Nile Valley would be regarded as an unfriendly act – you can see now why the Fashoda Crisis (see page 160) was thought so important, and why Delcassé might be anxious to come to an agreement with Britain! In China, Germany forced the government to grant her the port of Kiao-Chow (1897) and Russia secured the important ice-free Port Arthur (1898). Britain obtained the lease of Wei-hai-Wei in order to keep abreast of other powers in China. During the Boer War hostility towards Britain among European powers was widespread. This caused many people in Britain to worry about the future.

However, there was more than colonial conflict. Germany had become an important manufacturing rival and there were popular fears that she would flood Britain with cheap goods, thus bankrupting many firms (see page 194). Worse still, in 1899 and 1900 Germany passed Navy Laws that clearly showed she intended to challenge British naval supremacy. There was widespread concern. (Erskine Childers's famous spy thriller, *The Riddle of the Sands*, is set in 1901 on the sandy islands of Germany's North Sea coast. It was one of a number of popular novels that provoked anti-German feeling. Earlier there had been Colonel Chesney's *The Battle of Dorking* (1871), a book about a future German invasion of Britain. Both books are worth reading, for, like H. G. Wells' *The Land Ironclads* (1901), they foretold the type of war that was to come in 1914 at a time when most people thought only in terms of Napoleonic warfare!)

In 1900 Salisbury appointed Lansdowne as Foreign Secretary: he had already set the course of British foreign policy and Lansdowne simply followed it. You might like to hold a class debate on whether Salisbury should be remembered as a more important influence on foreign policy than Disraeli – or even Palmerston.

Joseph Chamberlain was particulary anxious to form an alliance with Germany (and also with the USA), and between 1898 and 1901 made unofficial approaches on his own initiative. But Salisbury was less sure that this was the best idea. He was conscious that German influence with the Sultan was increasing and that Turkey was an unreliable ally – in private, he agreed the Porte might well soon collapse. At the same time, he realised that Britain's interests might, after all, not be so badly affected if Russia did gain access to the Mediterranean through the Straits – particularly when France and Russia signed a Dual Alliance in 1894. The following year he wrote to the First Lord of the Admiralty, 'I am not at all a bigot to the policy of keeping Russia out of Constantinople. On the contrary, I think that the English statesmen who brought on the Crimean War made a mistake.' By 1897, he had decided it was better to relax the hold on Constantinople and to concentrate on the Suez Canal and Egypt (again, you can see why Fashoda was so important). During the 1890s Germany had pushed forward the idea of a Berlin-to-Baghdad railway: this posed a threat to British interests in the Levant and in India. Salisbury became convinced that Chamberlain was wrong: Germany was more a threat than a friend. He had already made overtures to France.

Britain's alliances

Europe was now divided into two hostile camps: the German Triple Alliance (1881) and the French Dual Alliance (1894). Britain was a party to neither and was beginning to feel the need to have allies. She looked first beyond Europe. In 1902 came the Anglo-Japanese Alliance providing for mutual aid if either were attacked by more than one power (in 1905 it was extended to cover India and South-East Asia as well as the Far East). This publicly marked a change in Britain's position.

A far bigger change came over relations with France. Both Britain and France now saw Germany as a growing threat and, despite a tradition of hostility and more recent rivalry in Africa, discussions took place over several years that resulted in the Anglo-French Entente Cordiale of 1904 (an entente is an agreement to work in co-operation, but it is not binding as is a treaty). Lansdowne and Delcassé were the chief negotiators, but King Edward VII's state visit to Paris (1903) may have helped. Opinion differs as to whether the King played any actual part in the making of the Entente. Some historians say he did, but Balfour, who was Prime Minister at the time, wrote to Lansdowne in 1915 when the official *Life* of the King appeared, 'so far as I remember, during the years which you and I were his ministers, he never made an important suggestion of any sort on large questions of policy'.

The Entente was concerned with imperial affairs: France recognised Britain's special position in Egypt and Britain recognised that France had a similar position in Morocco. In return for giving up her claim to fishing rights off Newfoundland, France received compensation in territory in West Africa. But if the Entente was concerned with imperial affairs, Europe interpreted it (correctly) as Britain backing France against Germany.

In 1904–5 there was a Russo-Japanese War (can you see why Britain did not have to intervene under the 1902 Treaty?). Russia was shatteringly defeated, and people wondered how effective an ally she could be for France. During the war the Russian Baltic fleet had sailed around the world to be sunk in Tsiushima Bay, but as it sailed across the Dogger Bank in the North Sea, it fired on some British trawlers, believing them to be Japanese torpedo boats (or so the officer of the watch claimed!) (You can see part of one of the trawlers, complete with shell holes from this Dogger Bank Incident (1904) in Hull Museum.) The Kaiser felt confident of breaking the new Anglo-French Entente after this incident. In March, 1905 he made a speech at Tangiers promising the Sultan of Morocco aid against the French. Germany then demanded a conference which met at Algeciras (in January 1906). But Germany gained no advantages. This First Moroccan Crisis (1905–6) only served to strengthen the Entente. Britain stood firmly behind France (indeed, very secret military talks began between the high command of both armies to discuss British aid to France if she were attacked).

In Germany the naval arms race (following the launching of the Dreadnought) became serious, and the Kiel Canal was widened in order to take vessels of this size – the task was completed by 1914. It was in vain that an international conference on disarmament at The Hague (1907) called for a halt. Public

Damage to a Hull trawler by Russian shells, 1904

opinion in Germany and Britain moved in favour of hostilities – as the years passed, British fears of German spies grew to hysterical proportions. (John Buchan's *Thirty-Nine Steps* catches the atmosphere well and makes good reading.) In 1908 the new German Navy Law provoked a howl of protest in Britain, and relations were worsened by the Kaiser giving a provocative interview to the *Daily Telegraph* (in October 1908).

In 1906 the new Liberal Foreign Secretary was Sir Edward Grey. He followed the policy already begun, and strengthened it with the Anglo-Russian Convention (1907), regulating the position of Russia and Britain in Persia by dividing that country into three spheres of influence, the centre being neutral, the southern part under British influence and the northern part under Russian influence. Afghanistan was recognised as coming within the British sphere of influence. Once again, it was a matter of imperial interests, in this case the defence of India – but the Convention was seen as linking Britain with the Franco-Russian alliance and is generally known as the Triple Entente.

Almost immediately, the Triple Entente was challenged by Austria-Hungary. The Berlin Congress (1878) had allowed Austria-Hungary to administer Bosnia-Herzogovina: in 1908 Austria annexed the two territories. Russia was anxious to recover her prestige after the disastrous war with Japan. She was prepared to go to war in defence of Serbia, who believed herself threatened by Austria (see Fig. 19). There was considerable pan-Slavist agitation, but both Britain and France urged caution and so Russia did not take any action. This was regarded as a blow to the prestige of the Triple Entente. (George Bernard Shaw's play *Arms and the Man* is a light-hearted look at the many small wars in the Balkans.)

In 1911 came the Second Moroccan Crisis. France had been extending her interests in Morocco and Germany demanded compensation, sending a gun-boat, the *Panther*, to Agadir in an effort to secure some form of naval base on the Atlantic coast. The Anglo-French Entente held firm – it was strengthened by the Chancellor of the Exchequer, Lloyd George, publicly warning Germany in an important speech at the Mansion House in the City of London in July 1911. The speech was doubly significant, for it came at the height of the constitutional crisis (see page 172) and was made by Lloyd George, who was not known as a war-monger (he had opposed the Boer War at some risk to himself – see page 161). The Committee of Imperial Defence was called and decided to dispatch an expeditionary force to France should war result. The crisis ended with Germany backing down (in September) but gaining compensation in the Congo area of Africa.

The cost of the arms race caused considerable concern, and Lord Haldane made an attempt to reach an arms limitation agreement with Germany (1912). This failed, but 1912 saw a further agreement between Britain and France: the British fleet assumed responsibility for the Channel and North Sea, the French fleet for the Mediterranean (Salisbury's Mediterranean Agreements were now reversed!), but there was still no formal alliance between the two countries.

The First World War

The Balkans provided the occasion for the outbreak of the First World War. Turkey could not control her Empire – Italy had seized two whole provinces in 1911 – and her Balkan lands were in open disorder. Russia sought to control the Straits and to help the Slav peoples in the Balkans. Austria sought to exclude Russian influence from the Balkans, and Germany had become the supporter of the 'sick man of Europe', Turkey. In 1912 Greece, Serbia and Bulgaria, with Russian help, formed the Balkan League and utterly defeated Turkey in the First Balkan War. Austria was angry at this increase of Russian influence and so Grey, the British Foreign Secretary, called a conference in London (1913). It was overtaken by the Second Balkan War, in which Serbia's territories and ambitions were increased. Austria was alarmed, especially as she feared a rising amongst her own Slav peoples which would be helped by Serbia and Russia. There was good cause for such a fear, since there were many nationalist movements and secret societies.

On 28 June 1914, the heir to the Austrian Empire, the Archduke Franz Ferdinand, and his wife, were assassinated by members of a secret Serbian society at Sarajevo, capital of Bosnia. With the Kaiser's support, Austria sent Serbia a humiliating ultimatum and on 28 July declared war. Russia and France mobilised. Germany, well prepared, declared war on Russia on 2 August and on France on 3 August. She was confident: her famous Schlieffen Plan was designed to sweep through Belgium and northern France to encircle Paris and so precipitate French surrender – all within three weeks. It would then be possible to transfer the bulk of the army to the Russian front to defeat the enemy there, for Russia, it was estimated, would take many weeks to mobilise fully. The speed of the operations would, in effect, mean that Germany avoided the danger of being caught in a war on two fronts. The Plan assumed Britain would be neutral (and in the summer of 1914 the Kaiser was convinced that Britain was on the verge of very serious civil disorder, see page 183).

Britain had no formal treaty with France or with Russia, but for ten years her planning had centred on helping France against Germany. At the beginning of August the cabinet was divided: should Britain go to war, send naval help only, or remain neutral? What decided the issue was the German invasion of Belgium in violation of the 1839 Treaty of London. An ultimatum was dispatched to Berlin. No reply was received and by midnight on 4 August 1914 Britain was at war with Germany. The Kaiser complained that Britain had gone to war over 'a scrap of paper' – but the British Expeditionary Force, perhaps the best-trained troops in the world at the time, played a vital part in defeating the Schlieffen Plan and so ruining German hopes of a quick victory.

Meanwhile, Grey wrote in his diary 'The lamps are going out all over Europe; we shall not see them lit again in our lifetime'.

The latter half of this section has been concerned with diplomatic history. When dealing with diplomatic history one has to remember what is happening in different parts of the world, for this may affect things happening elsewhere. Diplomatic history is complicated. But the causes of war do not only lie in diplomacy. Look back over those sections of the volume dealing with foreign affairs since Palmerston and see if you can trace any definite pattern in British foreign policy. Then look at references to trade rivalry and to imperial rivalry among the European powers. When you have made a list of each of these things, set out a series of points to show what were the causes of the First World War. You will be able to list quite a number of separate causes!

You will find this documentary question will help a little, especially with the details of the final crisis in the summer of 1914. It is clear that Beatrice Webb (a leading Fabian) had considerable respect for Grey, whose speech put the point that Britain had to defend Belgium under her treaty obligations. The war was tremendously popular at first; even so, there were many people who did not want war – quite a few pacifists. Many of these were Liberals and supporters of the Labour Party, and this helps to explain the last two lines of Beatrice Webb's extract.

The outbreak of war

A. The War which is now shaking to its foundations the whole European system originated in a quarrel in which this country had no direct concern. We strove with all our might, as
5 everyone knows, to prevent its outbreak. It was only when we were confronted with the choice between keeping and breaking solemn obligations—between the discharge of a binding trust and of shameless subservience to naked
10 force—that we threw away the scabbard. We do not repent our decision. We were bound by our obligations, plain and paramount, to assert and maintain the threatened independence of a small and neutral State. Belgium had no interests of her
15 own to serve, save and except the one supreme and over-riding interest of every State great or little, which is worthy of the name, the preservation of her integrity and of her national life.

ASQUITH, August 1914

20 B. It was a strange London on Sunday: crowded with excursionists to London and baulked would-be travellers to the continent, all in a state of suppressed uneasiness and excitement. We sauntered through the crowd to Trafalgar Square
25 where Labour, Socialist, pacifist demonstrators—with a few Trade Union flags—were gesticulating from the steps of the monuments to a mixed crowd of admirers, hooligan warmongers and merely curious holiday-makers. On
30 Monday the public mind was cleared and solidified by Grey's speech. Even staunch Liberals agree that we had to stand by Belgium. But there is no enthusiasm about the war.

BEATRICE WEBB, August 1914

(a) What was the 'quarrel' (line 3)? (4)
(b) What 'obligations' (lines 7–8) had Britain to Belgium? (3)
(c) What was the attitude of 'Labour, Socialist (and) pacifist demonstrators' (lines 25–26) to the outbreak of war? (3)
(d) Why was 'the public mind . . . cleared' (line 30) by Grey's speech? Who was Grey? (4)
(e) Why does the writer say 'Even staunch Liberals . . . (lines 31–32)? How united was the Liberal Government in 1914 about going to war? (4)
(f) Write a note on Beatrice Webb. (2)

O & C

12 The Liberals, 1906–14

Domestic reforms

In January 1906, the Liberals won the biggest landslide victory since the Reform Act. Go through the last chapter and make your list of the reasons why. People voted Liberal not simply because they disliked the Conservatives; they looked to the Liberals to reform some sections of society, particularly to improve the provision for the poor. Victorian attitudes were changing: poverty was no longer regarded as the just reward of idleness and intemperance. A 'New Liberalism' was emerging.

Campbell-Bannerman was the Prime Minister and he had an able cabinet, which included John Burns as President of the Local Government Boards – this was a bid to secure support from the 29 Labour members (there were also 24 'Lib–

'Forced Fellowship'

Labs' – what do you think the term meant?). Great reforms were expected of these men (though significant social reform had to wait until H. H. Asquith became Prime Minister in 1908). But they reckoned without the House of Lords.

Balfour was soon back in the House. He planned to direct Conservative tactics in the Lords by giving the peers clear signals from the Commons. He wrote to Lord Lansdowne suggesting the Government probably hoped the Lords would throw out the more extreme measures it put forward to satisfy its Radical followers. This would give it the excuse to attack the Lords for obstruction. (Do you see how shrewd a political leader Balfour was?) He suggested,

> . . . we should fight all points of importance very stiffly in the Commons, and should make the House of Lords the theatre of compromise. It is evident that *you* can never fight for a position that *we* have surrendered; while, on the other hand, the fact that we have strenuously fought for the position and been severely beaten may afford adequate ground for your making a graceful concession to the Representative Chamber.

It was a clever scheme: it meant that the Lords could in effect control what the Commons did – they would allow to pass only those measures they thought appropriate. So, much of the Liberal legislation failed – even the Education Bill they had been elected to pass. The huge majority in the Commons was blocked. There had been a long history, since at least the 1861 Paper Duties, of the Lords blocking Liberal measures whilst passing Conservative Bills, and in 1907 Campbell-Bannerman passed a series of Resolutions of the Commons warning the Lords that if this continued there would be legislation to limit their powers of *veto* to a suspensive one only. The warning was not heeded.

Even so, a number of important measures were passed. In 1906 came the Trade Disputes Act – this was proposed by the Labour members, and Balfour advised the Lords to pass it! It reversed the Taff Vale judgement (see page 164). There was also a

Workmen's Compensation Act 1906 obliging employers to compensate workers earning less than £250 a year if they were injured at work.

The Education Bill failed, but the Schools Meals Act 1906 allowed local rates to be used for providing meals for 'necessitous children' – it was a small beginning to what became the Schools Meals Service. Even so, it drew opposition from those who argued it was destroying the responsibility of the individual parent – it was an argument Gladstone had once used. There was also the Schools Medical Inspection Act 1907 which allowed some check on children's health by regular medical inspection. Many of the recruits at the time of the Boer War had been rejected as medically unfit and this was an effort to improve general levels of health among the poor. In 1912 grants were made available for specialist treatment of children's eye, ear, and teeth complaints. In 1907 also came a 'free places' scheme to allow poor children to take up places in secondary (grammar) schools. This was not to provide equality of opportunity, but it did give the chance to a few fortunate children (usually boys) to 'get on' through educational success.

The year 1907 was important for other measures concerning children. Juvenile courts, where the atmosphere was less forbidding and sentences less severe, were introduced. The Borstal system began, and it was greeted at the time as a great new stage in treating young offenders. The Probation Service was introduced. An Act prohibited the sale of alcohol, tobacco and fireworks to children, and there were further measures regulating children's working hours after school and at weekends. In 1908 the Children's Act, called the 'Children's Charter', consolidated previous legislation relating to the treatment of children and dealt with cruelty by parents and others.

In 1908 the miners secured an eight-hour day by the Coal Mines Regulation Act – the first Act to regulate the hours of adult male workers. That year Labour Exchanges were started. They were intended to tell working men in search of work about the vacancies in the area, instead of them having to tramp literally miles in search of a job, often on the rumour that hands were wanted at a factory, only to discover that the rumour was false. Spending a day walking round without food was a demoralising thing. Here was a sign that the government was coming to terms with the problem of unemployment. In 1909 the Trade Boards Act protected workers in 'sweated' trades' such as tailoring' from bad conditions and inadequate pay – such workers had few trade union members and were badly exploited. Often they were immigrants from

Eastern Europe working in the tailoring trades. Trade Boards were set up, consisting of employers and workers, and these fixed a legal minimum wage – one that could be enforced if an employer failed to pay it. In 1911 the Shops Act provided a half-day off a week for shop assistants and further regulated working hours. You can see how this legislation meant that the State was taking an increasing part in the running of people's lives. Clearly, the nineteenth century was being replaced by the 'New Liberalism'.

The naval programme continued (see page 167) and was greatly increased after 1908. Further reforms of the army were made by Haldane (1907–8) which created a small but highly trained Expeditionary Force with its own supplies. Home defence was based on the Territorial Army of 300 000 formed from the old militia and the Volunteers. A general staff was formed for overall planning, and in universities and public schools an Officers' Training Corps was formed to provide a reserve of officer material. Conscription, which was common on the continent, was firmly rejected.

In 1908 Asquith became Prime Minister and Lloyd George Chancellor of the Exchequer, with Winston Churchill as president of the Board of Trade. New measures were proposed and a new vigour disturbed the surface of politics. The most important measure of 1908 was the Old Age Pension Act (to come into force in 1909) providing a pension of five shillings weekly to those over seventy whose income was less than eight shillings weekly. There were reductions for those whose income was between eight shillings and twelve shillings. The payments were small, but pensioners no longer had to fear the workhouse and a pauper's grave at the end of their lives. The pensions were non-contributory: over 650 000 people applied for pensions in the first year (this cost £8 million) – by 1914 there were nearly a million pensioners.

The Constitutional Crisis

In 1908 another important Government Bill, the Licensing Bill, was rejected by the Lords in a very off-hand manner. Passions were enflamed, and moderate Conservatives were worried at the effect on the country. The stage was set for direct confrontation with the Lords.

It came over the 1909 Budget. Lloyd George did not frame his Budget to provoke a crisis – he hoped to secure further social reform through the Budget, for there was a *constitutional convention* that the Lords did not amend a money Bill, and no one seriously contemplated them throwing out the Budget! Certainly, Lloyd George aimed to tax rich landowners for the benefit of the poor. At the time his proposals were thought swingeing – though by later standards of taxation they seem surprisingly moderate: after all, he had to raise an additional £15 million for old-age pensions, and more to cover the naval costs, and the health and unemployment insurance scheme that was proposed. He suggested a maximum of 5 per cent for income tax (in 1982 the *standard* rate was 30 per cent) and to introduce a 'surtax' of $2\frac{1}{2}$ per cent on incomes over £3000. There were to be higher duties on tobacco and alcohol. The main opposition, however, concentrated on important new land taxes. These involved a complete revaluation of property (which annoyed the landed interest even more).

The Lords headed the opposition. It was easy to represent them as defenders of privilege and property against a Chancellor whose Budget sought to raise money 'to wage implacable warfare against poverty and squalidness'. Lloyd George put his tremendous oratorical gifts to great effect. At Limehouse he delivered a speech that set the tone for a campaign that had something of the class struggle about it. The King sent a private letter reproving him and Lansdowne called him a ' robber gull'. Opinion in the country seemed to concentrate behind the government: it was 'Peers against People' all over again and when, in November 1909, the Lords rejected the Budget, Asquith triumphantly demanded a general election.

At this point it might be useful to recall the issues at stake. This question helps to do it: read the section on the constitutional Crisis up to the passing of the Parliament Act and note the points that will help you to answer the questions which follow the passage – the last one requires careful thought!

A constitutional crisis

We are living under a system of false balances and loaded dice. When the democracy votes Tory we are submitted to the uncontrolled domination of a single Chamber. When the democracy votes
5 Liberal, a dormant Second Chamber wakes up from its slumbers and is able to frustrate and nullify our efforts. They proceed to frustrate and nullify the clearest and most plainly expressed intention of the elective House. The House of
10 Lords have deliberately chosen their ground. They have elected to set at nought in regard to finance the unwritten and time-honoured conventions of our Constitution. In so doing, whether they foresaw it or not, they have opened
15 out a wider and more far-reaching issue. We have not provoked the challenge, but we welcome it. We believe that the first principles of representative government are at stake and we shall ask the constituencies of the country to
20 declare that the organ, the voice of the free people of this country, is to be found in the elective representatives of the nation.

ASQUITH in 1909

(a) What did Asquith mean by 'They have elected to set at nought ... (line 11)? Give illustrations. (8)
(b) What was the 'wider and more far-reaching issue' (line 15)? (4)
(c) What happened when the Government asked 'the constituencies of the country' (line 19)? Why were there two elections in 1910? (4)
(d) Summarise the results of this crisis. What did the Parliament Act do to prevent 'the uncontrolled domination of a single Chamber' (lines 3–4)? (4)

O & C

The January 1910 election proved a shock to the Liberals. Only 275 Liberals were returned and there were 273 Conservatives. After all that effort, the great campaign had failed to convert the electorate. There were 40 Labour members returned, but more important were the 82 Irish Nationalists. These men, as in 1886, now held the balance of power. Did you notice that there was no mention of Home Rule between 1906 and 1910? Now it was to become a central issue. The Budget could only pass with Irish support – and the Irish members disliked the liquor duties. Clearly, they would demand Home Rule as the price of their support. More than this, they would need to limit the powers of the House of Lords in order to ensure that Home Rule actually reached the Statute Book.

Politics now took on quite a different aspect. The Conservatives were able to represent the Liberals' attack on the Lords as a purely party measure demanded by the Irish so that they could stay in power. It was clearly not the wish of the people – the election had shown that – and the Lords were truly the 'guardians of the constitution'. Lloyd George might well retort that the Lords were 'not the watchdog of the Constitution, but Mr Balfour's

'Rich Fare'
There is no doubt of Bernard Partridge's sympathies. Lloyd George is shown as an ogre with his mace, the 1909 'Budget' seeking out the defenceless middleclass English person.

poodle' – but the electorate had given the Liberals no clear majority. They were the 'prisoners' of the Irish members!

As the dispute grew, both sides became increasingly violent in their attitudes. The atmosphere was reflected in the country at large, and over the next four years it seemed that the Irish Question would provoke civil war. Agitation by trade unions for better pay, and by women for the parliamentary vote, added to the atmosphere of violence, which rose to a climax in 1914. No wonder the Kaiser supposed Britain was too involved with internal disputes to be able to intervene in a continental war! (You might like to glance at a famous book by George Dangerfield, *The Strange Death of Liberal England*, that covers this period.)

In April 1910, Asquith published a Bill to limit the powers of the House of Lords, and the 1909 Budget was passed through both Houses. A week later Edward VII died suddenly. It was a tribute to Edward that this death should have been such a shock to the nation. George V was advised to call a constitutional conference to try to resolve the differences between the parties. It met between June

and November, and we know from the Asquith Papers (for its proceedings were confidential) that it came very close to agreement. But, in the end, Balfour had to admit that the Conservatives in the country would never accept this agreement, and so the Conference ended and the public was told that no agreement had been reached. A new election was called for December 1910. It gave almost the same result as the January one. Asquith returned as Prime Minister, but he was the 'prisoner' of the Irish, led by John Redmond – the Lords would be reformed and Home Rule would follow. What had been a remarkably violent campaign since 1909 now became almost hysterical.

Unknown to the public, before the December election Asquith had secured from George V a 'contingent guarantee' that, should the Liberals be returned, sufficient peers would be created to ensure the passing of the Parliament Bill (it was the same trump card that Lord Grey had held in 1832, see page 105). The violent Conservative campaign was waged in ignorance of this guarantee. By late spring, however, Balfour had realised that Asquith was certain to get his Bill through: the King would create the necessary peers (an actual list exists in the Asquith Papers of those who were to be ennobled to secure its passage, should this prove necessary).

Balfour tried to convince his party that it was better to have the Bill than to have the Lords swamped so that all Liberal legislation would pass in future. His advice was rejected scornfully by a large section of the party, who, led by Lord Willoughby de Broke and the aged Lord Halsbury, proudly took the name of 'Ditchers' – they would defend the Constitution to the last ditch! They formed the Halsbury Club to organise their activities. Another group who were prepared to compromise by letting the Bill pass were called the 'Hedgers'. Until the very last moment, on a hot August night in 1911, it was uncertain whether the Bill would pass. Eventually, with Lansdowne officially announcing there would be a creation of peers if necessary, the Lords passed the Bill by 131 to 114. It was a moment of great triumph for Asquith, the Prime Minister, whose careful handling of the long crisis had proved a success in the end.

The *Preamble* to the Parliament Act 1911 indicates that a proper reform of the Lords would have to wait (we are still waiting!), but they lost the right to amend or reject any money bill at all (the Speaker was to certify what was a money bill). In addition, if the Lords rejected a government bill in three successive sessions then it would receive the royal assent regardless. However, the maximum life of a parliament was reduced from seven to five years, thus the Lords retained a *suspensive* veto of up to three years, but as parliament could last only five years no government would be able to get a huge legislative programme through in its lifetime. Clearly, further reduction of the Lords' power of veto would be likely in the future.

On that same hot night (10 August) the House of Commons passed a Resolution to pay MPs a salary of £400 a year, which was regarded as a perfectly adequate income for a middle-class gentleman. Working people could now afford to be MPs. This was one of the six points of the Chartists (see page 123).

Aftermath of the crisis

The Conservative Party had been through a severe crisis, though they had not lost badly. But they turned savagely upon their leader, whom some openly accused of betraying their cause. Leo Maxse, editor of the *National Review*, ran a special 'hate Balfour' campaign with the slogan B.M.G. (Balfour

Must Go). Balfour was angry and disgusted: he resigned. He was succeeded by Bonar Law, a very different sort of leader (you might like to glance at Robert Blake's biography of Bonar Law). He was a dour Scot and a former industrialist, and adopted a very aggressive manner. The Conservative Party was behaving very strangely, lurching further into violent opposition. They believed Asquith was betraying the Constitution and the Empire and they were prepared to fight to save them.

Rudyard Kipling was a keen Ditcher and caught the antagonism towards Balfour cleverly in a little mock manuscript that he wrote to Lord Milner shortly after Balfour's resignation in October 1911:

> From the Stele of Bal-Phour Dunforusal: (circa 1910 BC)
> 1. . . . . said It was a matter of purely Historical Interest . . . to   be   left   to   Future . . . agez . . . and   sat   down . . . in   large   part surrounded   by   family   of   matured   views . . . not   understanding   he   had   done

Bonar Law, arriving at a Unionist gathering at Blenheim, 1912

... or said anything unusual *damnin.*

2. To which they made answer: *Not by a domsite* and took steps ... very pronouncedly ... but always with the most loyal intentions ... and ... collecting the *Verri Worstofhern* some which had called him every *namunder Thesun* ...
3. made as you might say a fragrant bunch of 'em ... a nosegay of withered Roses. ...
4. Thrust it under his nose *first* and then
5. in case he should jibble a second time cut a large and spiky Khlub for ... the other End ... Holding it *in Terrorem* (what you might call an ...
6. *arrière pensée*). The most devoted *adherentz* so long as he kept running in front of them ... in the way he should go. ... sweating big drops ... without an ounce of Conviction ...
7. but actually concerned for his position which is ...
8. that of a *Natural Leader.*

It was intended as a joke – if you puzzle through it, you can distinguish the events that are recorded here – but it reveals the extent to which Balfour had been rejected by a powerful section of his party.

National Insurance

Another great measure of 1911 was the National Insurance Act covering health and unemployment insurance. Its aim was to make medical services available to workers who could not normally afford them. The Act fixed weekly contributious from workers, employers and the State to pay for a stamp that would qualify contributors for sick pay and medical attention. It was to be administered by existing Friendly Societies and trade unions so long as they were registered as 'Approved'. The scheme was closely related to the successful German scheme, but was limited in three respects: it did not include the worker's family, it did not include hospital or consultancy fees and it was confined to workers earning less than £160 a year. It has been claimed as the beginning of the present-day National Health Service: would you agree?

As to unemployment, it was widely agreed that the existing Poor Law could not cope – in 1905 a Royal Commission had examined the whole problem and its Report (1909) proved very influential. The Webbs (see page 181) contributed a Minority

The Liberal Party summarises the National Insurance Act, 1911
  Is this anything more than party propaganda?

Report that was very forward-looking. The 1911 scheme did not implement the Report, but allowed a small benefit of seven shillings weekly for a maximum of 15 weeks in any one year, depending on contributions. It was confined to trades in which employment was not regular, as for example, building, iron-founding, shipbuilding and engineering, and covered about $2\frac{1}{4}$ million workers. It was not extended to all manual workers until 1920, and even then farm labourers and domestic servants were excluded. Many history books praise the scheme: do you agree it deserves a great deal of praise?

Irish Home Rule

With the publishing of the Third Home Rule Bill (1912) – which was bound to pass under the Parliament Act – the Irish problem took a new and dangerous turn. Resistance to Home Rule centred on Ulster, where an Ulster Volunteer Force had been formed to defend the Union by any means. It was useless for John Redmond, the Irish Nationalist leader, to urge (1912), 'We on these benches stand precisely where Parnell stood. We want peace with this country. We deny that we are separatists . . .' Ulstermen simply would not accept the idea of rule by a Roman Catholic dominated government in Dublin. Their leader, Sir Edward 'King' Carson KC, left no doubts as to what was intended. In 1911, at a great meeting at Craigavon, he declared,

> We must be prepared, in the event of Home Rule passing, with such measures as will carry on for ourselves the government of those districts of which we have control. We must be prepared – and time is precious in these things – the morning Home Rule passes, ourselves to become responsible for the government of the Protestant Province of Ulster.

In September 1912, scores of thousands of Ulstermen led by Carson, signed a solemn Covenant pledging resistance to Home Rule. The Conservative Party, under Bonar Law, gave ample support. At a huge meeting at Blenheim (1912) Bonar Law called the Home Rule Bill a 'corrupt Parliamentary bargain' (can you see why?) and urged resistance by all possible means, including force: 'I can imagine no length of resistance to which Ulster will go in which I shall not be ready to support them and in which they will not be supported by the overwhelming majority of the British people'.

These were provocative words: he appeared to be condoning civil war. The Irish desired to have the whole of Ireland as a unity – especially as northern Ireland was then prosperous and industrial: they formed their own volunteers. By 1914 both sides were armed, and a bloody struggle seemed imminent. In March 1914, Asquith decided to test the loyalty of the British garrison at the Curragh (the barracks at Dublin), for they would have to enforce Home Rule, and many of the officers were from Protestant Anglo-Irish families. The officers publicly declared they would prefer to resign rather than have to fight to enforce Home Rule. This was a great shock: the 'Curragh Munity' appeared to show that the government could not rely on the army (this is another reason why the Kaiser supposed Britian would not fight in 1914). George V, anxious to avoid a crisis, summoned a conference at Buckingham Palace in July 1914. It failed. But the outbreak of war in August saved the situation, for Redmond promised Irish support, and the Irish Question – just for the moment – was lost in the wave of hysterical patriotism with which the outbreak of war was greeted. (The Home Rule Act was duly placed on the Statute Book – amid many Conservative protests – during the war, but was postponed until the peace, when a different solution had to be worked out!.)

The suffragettes

The example of the Conservative leaders was readily followed by workers and the women. For at least a generation, the movement had been growing for the emancipation of women from legal disabilities and for access to the professions and higher education. Parliament was an obvious bastion of male supremacy and an equally obvious target. Like the Chartists before them, women demanded the vote in order to achieve some equality with men and the opportunity to express their political voice, and possibly serve as ministers. The movement to get women the vote (the suffrage) was called the Suffragette Movement. But there was vigorous opposition to the idea of women having the vote – Queen Victoria had deplored the idea – and some leading Liberals agreed with her, including Asquith.

In 1903 the Women's Social and Political Union was founded by Mrs Emmeline Pankhurst for the purpose of securing the suffrage. The movement was divided between those believing in violent means and those advocating more peaceful persuasion. Some of the latter broke away to form the Women's Freedom League (1908). After 1909 the agitation become more violent, for little progress was being made. Suffragettes openly damaged property, from cutting the grass on golf courses (which particularly offended politicians) to setting houses on fire. They happily went to prison, calling out 'Votes for Women'. In 1913, Emily Davison threw herself to her death in front of the King's horse in the Derby. She was the movement's first martyr. Many suffragettes in prison went on hunger strike and were forcibly fed – so many that the government resorted to the 'Cat and Mouse' Act 1913 allowing the release of suffragettes on licence, to be imprisoned again immediately if they were involved in further disruption. The violence gained them little sympathy – some people questioned what they really wanted, saying 'Votes for Women' was something for ladies, but what of ordinary women themselves? (Can you see what they meant?)

It was the first World War that really changed matters. In the great national effort for victory, women had more than proved their worth, and in 1918 the Representation of the People Act gave manhood suffrage from the age of twenty-one and suffrage for women over thirty. Women gained the vote almost on the same basis as men. Two further Acts in 1918 enabled women to be elected – Lady Astor was the first woman to take her seat as an MP (in 1919) – and the Sex Disqualification (Removal) Act permitted women to practise any civil profession and to hold any civil or judicial office.

There are many books on the fight for equal rights: make a special study of it. You could use the following questions as the framework of your research, but try to use as much contemporary material as possible (journals, posters, speeches, letters) rather than confining yourself to secondary sources. Remember to indicate why some of the sources you use are more *reliable* than others.

Forcible feeding of a suffragette
What is there about this picture that tells you it is a piece of propaganda? Suggest reasons why you think it effective.

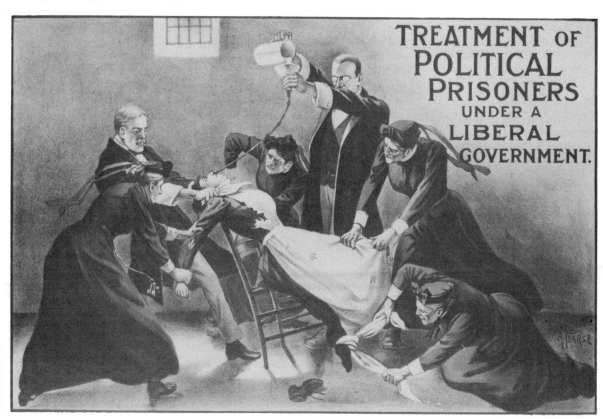

This question is a particular challenge, for you will have to do some research beyond this text-book in order to answer it fully.

The suffragettes

The Liberal government was slowly converted to the side of the women, but it was faced with much more urgent problems in 1912–14.

The violent suffragette movement ended within a
5 month of the outbreak of the First World War in August 1914. All suffragette prisoners were released from goal and Mrs Pankhurst and Christabel threw their energies loyally into re-cruiting women for the war effort. What then had
10 they achieve? They had not advanced the vote for women; in fact they had probably delayed it. A huge, peaceful demonstration by the con-stitutionalists in Hyde Park in the summer of 1914 was treated everywhere with great respect;
15 dignified argument in support of women's votes was clearly overcoming outdated, Victorian pre-judices. But the unbalanced, hysterical acts of the suffragettes made many people feel that women would never be able to use the vote
20 sensibly.

(a) Which suffragette association was led by Mrs Pankhurst? (1)
(b) (i) Why did some suffragettes take violent action during their campaign for votes? (2)
   (ii) Give *four* examples of the sort of violent action taken. (2)
   (iii) "Suffragettes were released from goal" (line 10) without completing their sentences on the outbreak of war. In what other circumstances were some suffragettes released from goal without completing their sentences? (2)
(c) What were the 'urgent problems' (line 3) facing the Liberal government which made them neglect the suffrage question? (3)
(d) Explain why some people believed that the suffragettes 'had probably delayed it (the vote for women)' (line 12). (3)
(e) What kinds of 'dignified argument' (lines 15–16) were put forward in support of women's votes? (3)
(f) What were the 'Victorian prejudices' (line 17) about women which were becoming outdated by 1914? (4)

UCLES

Total marks (20)

The Labour Party

The Labour Party has its roots deep in the tradition of English radicalism and the wish to build a 'New Jerusalem' – a wish strengthened by the experience of destitution and distress during the nineteenth century. Even in 1900, the idea that the 'humbler orders' might aspire to be national politicians seemed absurd to many people – try to imagine what an achievement it was for a working man to do this. Victorian England was characterised by deference towards one's social superiors, who were expected to govern the country. But throughout the period working men had shown themselves capable of considerable organisational skill – for example, the Chartists, whose influence lasted long after 1848 (see page 123) among working-class families.

Trade unions

Trade unions were another example of a movement with long-lasting influence. After the failures of the 1830s (see page 109), trade unions tended to be formed among skilled craftsmen – artisans, the 'aristocracy of labour' – because they had money and were rarely out of work. By the middle of the century they had developed a pattern that has been called 'New Model' trade unionism: skilled crafts-men in a union for their craft, whatever industry they worked in. They often adopted the name 'amalgamated', for example the Amalgamated Society of Engineers (1851). Skilled craftsmen were essential workers who were reasonably paid and rarely resorted to strike action (though they would strike in a good cause and support a brother union). The New Model Unions did much to make unionism respectable. They charged high fees and concen-trated on Friendly Society and other benefits. The Amalgamated Society of Carpenters and Joiners (1867) allowed ten shillings weekly for twelve weeks and twelve more weeks at six shillings for an unemployed member. Sickness benefit was twelve shillings weekly for 26 weeks; superannuation was eight shillings weekly after 25 years. All these benefits were available for a weekly membership fee of one shilling, and three pence quarterly to the benevolent fund. (Contrast this with the 1908 old-age pension and 1911 sickness and unemployment schemes!) They were fine examples of what Samuel Smiles wrote about in *Self-Help* – God-fearing family men striving to 'better' themselves.

Here is a question that demands a good deal of thought. The extracts show the Victorian belief in individualism. Discuss them with your class and try to understand Victorian attudes, for you are dealing here with ideas of a century ago, not simply a collection of facts. If you can give satisfactory answers to (a), (c) and the second part of (d), then you are well on the way to becoming an historian.

Self-reliance

A. The spirit of self-help is the root of all genuine growth in the individual; and it constitutes the true source of national vigour and strength. Help from without is often enfeebling in its effects,
5 but help from within invariably invigorates Whatever is done *for* men or classes, to a certain extent takes away the stimulus and necessity of doing for themselves.

SAMUEL SMILES, *Self-Help* (1859)

B. If the State is to be summoned not only to
10 provide houses for the labouring classes, but also to supply such dwellings at nominal rents, it will, while doing something on behalf of their physical condition, utterly destroy their moral energies. It will, in fact, be an official proclamation
15 that, without any efforts of their own, certain portions of the people shall enter into the enjoyment of many good things, altogether at the expense of others . . .
The mischief of it would be very serious. It
20 would, besides being a kind of legal pauperization, give a heavy blow and great discouragement to the spirit of healthy thrift now rising among the people . . . It is a melancholy system that tends to debase a large mass of the people to
25 the condition of a nursery, where the children look to the father and mother, and do nothing for themselves.

LORD SHAFTESBURY in a magazine article, 1883

(a) To what extent did the idea of 'self-help' contribute to Britain's economic progress during the period? What undesirable consequences did it have? (6)

(b) How were the working classes able to practise self-help? What evidence was there of a 'spirit of healthy thrift now rising among the people' (lines 22–23)? (4)

(c) Explain 'a kind of legal pauperization' (line 20). (2)

(d) What reforms did Shaftesbury help to introduce to improve the conditions of the poor? Does this interest in reform seem to you to be inconsistent with what he says here? (8)

O & C

Shaftesbury was a complicated person: his attitude to reform was not always straightforward (see page 118)–he was more of a Victorian *individualist* than a *humanitarian*, perhaps.

As the New Model Trade Unions grew in wealth, they hired local – offices some had a central office in London, with a General Secretary who was frequently a man of great personality, capable of talking on equal terms with important employers and so negotiating without a feeling of inferiority. In the 1860s a remarkable group of General Secretaries – Robert Applegarth of the Carpenters, William Allen of the Engineers, Edwin Coulson of the Bricklayers, and Daniel Guile of the Ironfounders – gave the movement a national direction. They were called the *Junta*, and the TUC (1868) owed much to their guidance. It was needed, for a series of disturbances, especially in Sheffield, brought the movement into disrepute. A Royal Commission (1867) reported in favour of the unions, and they gained legal recognition under Gladstone (see page 143). (Glance at the TUC centenary book (1968) – your local library will have a copy.)

Two diaries were published in 1982. One was by John O'Neil, a skilled textile worker, who reveals working conditions and trade unionism in Clitheroe, Lancashire, in the 1860s. The other was by an industrialist, Garnet, from the same area. By looking at both diaries, you can see two sides of particular labour disputes in primary sources that were written without any thought of publication.

New unionism

However, in the 1880s appeared the **new unionism —** a movement of semi-skilled and labouring men who previously had proved too difficult to organise. It was due to technological changes that emphasised the unmechanised parts of industry –gas stokers for city gasworks, for example. Labourers could be vital workers, and this gave them their power once a leader had shepherded them into a union. Such unions were very different from the New Model:

they charged low dues (members could not afford more) and offered few Friendly Society benefits, but they often threatened – and used – the strike weapon to get better wages and conditions. Their leaders were interested in politics, like the Chartists before them, and looked to Parliament for direct intervention to oblige employers to pay fair wages and provide better conditions. This was to lead to the Labour Party.

Middle-class intellectuals helped these trade unionists. The famous London match girls' strike of 1888 was partly organised by Bradlaugh (see page 152) and Annie Bessant (look up Annie Bessant's career; it touched on many things!). In 1889, Karl Marx's daughter helped Will Thorn to lead the London gas workers and to get an eight-hour day simply by threatening a strike. That year Ben Tillett led to the great London Dock Strike. This was a major strike that concentrated attention on the new unionism. The dockers were helped by working-class political leaders such as John Burns and Tom Mann, and the public subscribed £49 000 to save the dockers' families from starvation – dockers in Brisbane, Australia, sent £30 000. Eventually the employers were compelled to grant the 'dockers' tanner'. *The Times* recognised the union's great victory – 'We may look for a large development of future conflicts between capital and labour'. New unionism spread rapidly in other industries – for example, the Miners' Federation of Great Britain (1889) – and total membership of trade unions rose from 750 000 in 1888 to one and a half million in 1892.

The leaders were keen socialists, many of them believing in Karl Marx's ideas of class struggle (ask your teacher to tell you about Marx and his ideas on history, politics, economics and sociology: they have had a great impact on the twentieth century). Marx also influenced some middle-class men, such as Henry Hyndman, a wealthy old Etonian, who formed the Democratic Federation (1881) with a programme that looked forward to the social legislation of the twentieth century. William Morris, a romantic aesthete who dreamed of restoring an 'Olde Englande' in which all men were craftsmen, formed the Socialist League (1884). But neither movement attracted much support or seemed likely to influence governments.

Development of the Labour Party

It was the Fabians, led by Sidney and Beatrice Webb, who really influenced politicians with socialist ideas. Beatrice was wealthy – she had almost married Joseph Chamberlain – and well connected, so that many leading politicians (even cabinet ministers such as Balfour) dined at her house. Writers such as H. G. Wells and George Bernard Shaw joined them. Their slogan was 'the inevitablity of gradualness' and their name came from the Roman general who defeated Hannibal without giving battle. They hoped to get important social reforms by persuading politicians, and they became acknowledged experts on social questions, to whom ministers turned for advice. They played an important part in the development of the Labour Party (Sidney was to become its General Secretary) and helped many young Labour MPs. Some of the claims made for them are exaggerated, but their importance is beyond dispute.

The Labour Party was more than a linking of trade unionism with middle-class intellectuals. It was a movement that drew its strength from ordinary folk, struggling to lead decent lives and to 'improve' themselves (like Samuel Smiles) and to work for greater social justice. Many of its leaders were middle-class, but its organisation in the country depended on working men and women seeking a means to a fuller life for the whole community. There was great idealism – almost a way of life – and religion played its part, for many early Labour men were Methodist lay preachers. There had been working-class MPs since 1874, called 'Lib-Labs' because they depended on Liberal support. But the success of new unionism in the 1880s helped to form a genuine working-class political movement. It held demonstrations and public meetings. Many of these ended in disorder, sometimes provoked by the police. A famous example was 'Bloody Sunday', 1887, when John Burns, a Labour leader, was addressing a meeting in Trafalgar Square and the police charged the crowd.

In 1888 a Scottish Parliamentary Labour Party was formed with Kier Hardie as Secretary. He was elected MP in 1892 and turned up at the House in a cloth cap, preceded by a brass band. In 1893 the Independent Labour Party (ILP) was formed and Kier Hardie became Chairman, with Tom Mann as Secretary. The working-class movement had reached Parliament in style, but it had little impact until the TUC decided to back the Labour Representation Committee (LRC) formed in (1900) with Ramsay Macdonald as Secretary (Macdonald was to become the first Labour Prime Minister in 1924). There was some hostility between the older New Model and the New Unionism over supporting a political party, but the Taff Vale Case (see page 164) forced their hand. Balfour's government showed no wish to reverse the judgement, so the unions entered politics by supporting the LRC and

Bloody Sunday riots, 1887

*The meeting of unemployed people was banned at the
last moment by the Home Secretary. The police intervened
to stop the marching and there was a riot. The police
action was widely interpreted as provocation of the
unemployed and as an attempt to discredit John Burns
who was to have addressed the meeting.*

imposing a 'political levy' on their members to help
pay for the return of Labour MPs, and to maintain
them once elected (MPs were not paid until 1911).

Very soon the LRC showed itself as a significant
force capable of winning by-elections. Herbert
Gladstone, the Liberal Chief Whip, in great secrecy
met Macdonald (1903) and formed an electoral pact
reserving certain constituencies for Labour candidates where no Liberal would stand (so the anti-
Conservative vote was not split). The 'pact' worked
well and in January 1906, 29 LRC members were
returned. They now took the name of Labour Party.
Their influence was immediately felt over the Trade
Disputes Act 1906 (see page 171), but they did not
achieve the other successes for which party workers
hoped, and there was some dissatisfaction felt
among them.

In 1909 the Labour Party suffered a severe blow
when the Osborne Judgement declared it illegal to
use trade union funds for political purposes. As few
Labour MPs could support themselves without the
political levy, the remedy was, once again, legislation. It was achieved in two stages: in 1911 all MPs
received a salary (see page 175), and in 1913 the
Trade Union Act permitted unions to engage in
political activity, provided a majority of members
voted in favour. Union funds could be spent on
political purposes provided the money came from a
special fund, kept separate from other union
moneys, for which members paid a political levy
(every member had the right to 'contract out' of
paying by simply signing a form). The Labour Party
had arrived: John Burns sat in the Liberal cabinet of
1906.

This question draws together a number of strands in the history of Labour.

Lib-Lab relations

A. A determination of the course to be followed by the Liberal Party is urgently needed, for to do nothing is to seem to reject the overtures of the L.R.C. Are the principles and objects of the
5 L.R.C. such as to justify a benevolent attitude? Will the success of the Liberal Party at the polls be too dearly purchased? Ought the Liberal Party to prefer defeat rather than assist in any way to foster the growing power of the Labour party?
A Liberal spokesman in 1903

10 B. This election is to decide whether or not Labour is to be fairly represented in Parliament. The House of Commons is supposed to be the people's House, and yet the people are not there.
The Trade Unions ask the same liberty as
15 capital enjoys. They are refused.
The aged poor are neglected.
Chinese Labour is defended because it enriches the mine owners.
The Labour election manifesto in 1906

C. The House of Commons, and the country,
20 which respected and feared the Labour Party are now approaching a condition of contempt towards its Parliamentary representatives. The lion has no teeth or claws. A great many of the victims to destitution will be in their graves before the
25 Liberal government will have approached the subject of unemployment, which they will sandwich between abolition of the House of Lords and Welsh Disestablishment.
Ben Tillett in 1908

(a) What was the 'L.R.C.' (line 4)? What were its 'principles and objects' (line 5)? In what way did the Liberal Party adopt 'a benevolent attitude' (line 4) to the L.R.C? (4)
(b) What happened to the Liberals in the 1906 election? What success did Labour have in the 'election' (line 10)? (4)
(c) Explain the references to 'The Trade Unions' (line 14) and 'Chinese Labour' (line 17). (4)
(d) Who was Ben Tillet? What did he mean by 'The lion has no teeth or claws' (lines 23–24)? (4)
(e) In what ways were Labour aims fulfilled by the Liberals? (4)

O & C

The great strike movement, 1910–14

There were many influences forming the new unionism. One was **syndicalism**, a movement with considerable following in the USA, France and Italy. The idea was for the important unions to work together to organise a general strike which would paralyse the country and bring the government down so that unions could achieve power and gain their demands. A general strike is a political weapon, not an industrial one: it is really a revolutionary weapon and no Government can tolerate it – the Government must destroy it, if it is to survive. Clearly, it is part of the revolutionary class struggle – Richard Church's *The White Doe* gives a good impression of what the class struggle meant to ordinary folk.

Massive strikes had occurred in the 1890s, but between 1910 and 1914 a wave of strikes began which made people fear for the future of British democracy. They were syndicalist in part, and gained something from the general hysteria of the time: Labour leaders noted how the Conservatives were threatening the future of democracy over Home Rule (see page 177), and followed their example! Disorders were frequent – Churchill sent troops to Tonypandy and shots were fired. Tom Mann was imprisoned for urging soldiers not to shoot on strikers (it was noted that the officers of the 'Curragh Mutiny' (see page 177) were not imprisoned or even reprimanded!).

Attempts to form single unions for each major industry had been made for some time. In 1910, Tom Mann and Ben Tillett formed the National Transport Workers' Federation; in 1913 came the National Union of Railwaymen. These two formed the 'triple alliance' (1914) with the Miners' Federation of Great Britain. Their object was to call a general strike in September 1914. (*Was* the Kaiser so wrong to suppose Britain was in no position to fight a war that summer? You can now put together three important pieces of evidence.) In fact, the outbreak of war prevented the strike – it would have been a very violent affair indeed – instead, patriotism demanded that everyone turn wholeheartedly to the war effort. Those who did not were ostracised and scorned as pacifists. Boldly, Kier Hardie put himself at the head of the pacifists who disapproved of the war. Many respected his deeply religious feelings, but many more turned against him and he lost a great deal of support. He died during the war, some say of a broken heart. The Labour leader of the future was Ramsay Macdonald.

13 The first industrial nation

Changes in industry

Britain was the first nation to experience an Industrial Revolution: it changed society. It meant the country's wealth was now based on industry and expanding trade as well as on agriculture. It meant increasing standards of living and greater opportunities. It meant a social division of rich and poor – and a struggle between the classes. It meant a more open society in which a poor man's son might even become prime minister. It meant a new attitude towards government, for already by the later nineteenth century people were beginning to look towards the state to provide essential services – they called it the **'collectivist state'**. So the Industrial Revolution was much more than some changes in industry – but it is necessary to examine those changes first.

Railways

The railway was a symbol of the changes during the nineteenth century: it meant something more than a means of transport. There was nothing new about pulling loads along a set of rails, but by 1830 railways had come to mean three things – a roadway specially designed to avoid steep inclines; rails secured to 'sleepers' with arrangements for switching and a signalling system, and a locomotive using steam power and capable of drawing huge loads at speeds not imagined before. The achievements of the railway-builders caught the imagination of the Victorians. It was a triumph of British engineering skill – and many of the world's railways began with a British engineer.

There is so much material available on railways that they make an ideal form project. But it needs careful organisation. You need a master plan, and then you should divide up the class to work on separate pieces of it – take, for example, how railways began and how problems were overcome. Now divide into groups, each with a specific task. Group 1 can work on the early attempts to build a satisfactory locomotive, ending with the Rainhill Trials, 1829. Group 2 can study George and Robert Stephenson and Brunel (use L. T. C. Rolt's excellent biographies and try to borrow Samuel Smiles's *Lives of the Great Engineers* from the library). Group 3 can look at the 'Battle of the Gauges' from which a national system emerged. Group 4 can study the navvies (T. Coleman's is the book to use, but don't forget to look for local newspapers of the time!). Group 5 could visit the local Records Office to discover why people were so hostile to railways. It could consult minute books, accounts and timetables to see how the railway companies actually worked. Group 6 might investigate the civil engineering achievements – the great stations, such as Temple Meads, Paddington, St Pancras, York; the huge embankments and tunnels and viaducts that were needed. You might take the opportunity to walk down a local disused railway and note the skill of the engineers in placing bridges and inclines. When each group is ready, gather the reports together and stage an exhibition – in the local library, perhaps even in the foyer of the Town Hall!

Railways quickly destroyed the coaching industry and they tried hard to destroy canals (your local paper might give examples of battles between navvies and canal workers, and an Ordnance Survey map will sometimes show how lines were built deliberately to cut through canals to prevent competition). Remembering this, it is interesting to read the Prospectus of the Liverpool to Manchester Railway Company (1824), the line that properly began the railway age when it was opened in 1830. It complained that the Bridgewater Canal Company charged fifteen shillings a ton for journeys taking 36 hours. This was excessive:

By the projected railroad, the transit of merchandise . . . will be effected in four or five hours and the charge . . . reduced at least one third . . . It is not that the water companies have not been able to carry goods on more reasonable terms, but that, strong in the enjoyment of their monopoly, they have not thought it proper to do so . . . *It is competition that is needed.*

The following question requires specific knowledge as well as a general understanding of the topic (for example, there were *three* classes of railway passengers and only the first class travelled in comfort).

Read the following extract from the Prospectus of the Liverpool and Manchester Railway issued 1824, and then answer the questions which follow:

The Committee of the Liverpool and Manchester Railroad Company think it right to state the grounds on which they rest their claims to public encouragement and support.
5 The importance to a commercial nation of a cheap and safe mode of transit for merchandise will be readily acknowledged. This was the plea upon the first introduction of canals and although that new mode of conveyance interfered
10 with existing and inferior modes and was opposed to the feelings and prejudices of landholders, the great principle of the public good prevailed and experience since has justified the decision.
15 It is upon the same principle that railroads are now proposed to be established: as a means of conveyance superior to existing modes.
The ground has already been surveyed by eminent engineers.
20 The total quantity of merchandise passing between Liverpool and Manchester is estimated at 1,000 tons a day. Goods pass part of the way up the river Mersey, a distance of 16 miles subject to serious delays from contrary winds and even
25 actual loss from tempestuous weather. The present canal establishments are inadequate for the regular and punctual conveyance of goods. Apart from this there is also pilferage, an evil for which there is seldom adequate redress whereas
30 a conveyance by railway, effected in a few hours and where every delay must be accounted for, may be expected to possess much of the publicity and consequent safety of the King's highway.

(a) Name one of the 'eminent engineers' associated with the construction of this railway. (1)
(b) What were the 'existing and inferior modes' of transport before the introduction of canals? (2)
(c) Why did the Committee stress the advantages of a railway between Liverpool and Manchester for the transport of merchandise? (2)

(d) Apart from the River Mersey, how would the 1,000 tons of goods a day have passed between Liverpool and Manchester? (2)
(e) (i) What factors made goods carried by canal especially liable to pilferage? (2)
(ii) What other advantages did railways posses apart from less pilferage? (2)
(f) Why did the Prospectus paint such an attractive picture of railways? Despite this, what dangers, discomforts were encountered by passengers in the early days of rail travel? (4)
(g) Give a brief account of the construction of the Liverpool to Manchester railway. What problems were overcome? (5)
UCLES

Railway building began at incredible speed: there were two 'railway manias', 1835–7, when some £20 million was invested, and the great mania of 1844–7 with £130 million invested. George Hudson of York gained his reputation as 'the Railway King' (he even managed to build his station *within* York city walls – you can still see the old platform). So much money was involved that the government intervened (despite popular *laissez-faire* views). Lord Seymour's Railway Act of 1839 set up a Railway Department at the Board of Trade to supervise railway companies. W. E. Gladstone, as President of the Board of trade, was responsible for the 1844 Railway Act that obliged companies to run at least one stopping train in each direction at one penny a mile, and empowered the Board of Trade to buy up a new railway if it had not complied with regulations – within twenty-one years! Strange to see Gladstone wielding the threat of 'nationalisation'! His concern for the ordinary traveller lead him to take frequent journeys by third class. His Act shows just how bad things could be for such passengers, for the 'parliamentary train' clause reads:

Such train shall travel at an average speed not less than 12 mph for the whole distance . . . including stoppages. The carriages in which passengers shall be conveyed . . . shall be provided with seats, and shall be protected from the weather.

The sheer physical impact of railways on the countryside was overwhelming – 'vaster than the walls of Babylon', complained Ruskin. Social classes might travel separately, but they mixed on the platform (try to see Frith's tremendous picture of Paddington Station), and the sight of working-class housing near the lines must have awakened

The Welland Viaduct
What a change this huge brick viaduct makes to the landscape! Do you think contemporaries would have been impressed?

Railway housing
Railway companies often provided housing for their workers. Much of it was of good quality, spacious and well planned, like this example in Derby. Today, such housing has been renovated and is worth a lot of money, though it may be 100 years old.

many social consciences. The speed of travel altered the whole pace of life, and the number of things that might be done in a day. 'Standard time' was introduced, for one could be in Bristol or even Edinburgh just a few hours after leaving London.

Towns changed, for the city worker could now live in a suburb or village, twenty miles away, but only half an hour by train (the same distance would take almost a day by horse!). Market towns that shunned the railway remained small; Peterborough and Derby swelled suddenly as railway towns. Swindon ceased to be a village; Crewe had 203 people in 1841 but 18 000 in 1871. Poorer people could occasionally travel, and Thomas Cook began a thriving industry as a travel agent. Seaside resorts such as Blackpool and Bournemouth appeared, and Scarborough became the 'Brighton of the North'. Seaside family holidays were now possible even occasionally for artisans and for the annual village choir trip (you might have a photograph of such a trip a hundred years or more ago in an old family album). Public schools found it convenient to be established in remote places. For the first time, travel was an everyday thing – and it was the railway that made possible the mass exodus from

Fig. 22 Railway passenger receipts
Passenger receipts exceed freight receipts up to about 1851. Do not exaggerate the immediate impact of railways on industry , therefore.

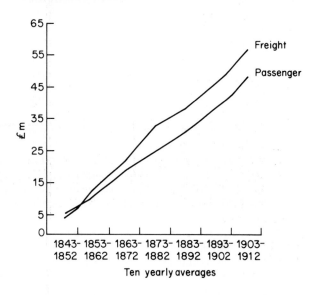

Fig. 23 Imports and exports, 1815–1913
The difference in trade patterns between the first and second half of the century is obvious. By the middle of the century, Britain was emerging as an industrial trading nation, responding to the changing nature of world markets. The effect of easy transport by rail and steamship is clearly demonstrated, as is the considerable trading achievement of the Edwardians.

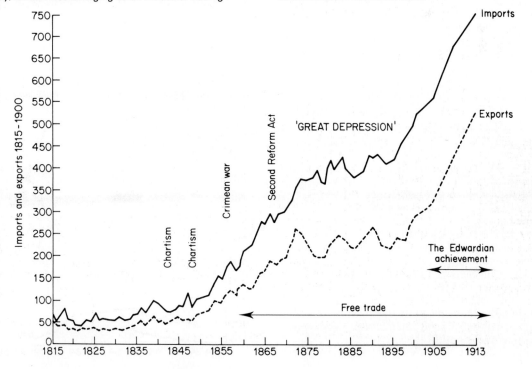

the countryside of unemployed labouring families.

Speed made possible market gardening at some distance from big markets, whether London or county towns. Fishing ports such as Grimsby and Hull became important because of the overnight fish train. Vast quantities of bricks, slate and lime could be transported, and this meant that in towns only the most expensive buildings used local materials. The chance of transporting huge loads in any weather meant big increases in coal and iron (and later steel) production, and for the first time factories could ensure the transport of vast quantities of goods very quickly. Railways helped Britain to become 'the workshop of the world'. They provided many jobs once the lines had been built – building locomotives and rolling stock, supervising the track, and a hierarchy of skilled men, from drivers and signalmen down to porters, as well as a similar multitude of clerks. Both for safety and for the efficient working of the railway, the skilled men had to submit to almost military-style discipline. (Try to find an old railwayman and ask him about his early days – and *his* father's, for there was strong family feeling about the railways. You might even record his recollections.) Business and commerce benefited directly, and the experience of the railway booms helped the Stock Exchange to attract small investors. *Limited liability* (where an investor risks only the money he deposits in *shares* or *debentures*) grew and had to be regulated by Acts of Parliament between 1855 and 1862. Vast sums were earned abroad by railway-building. Ports extended their *hinterland*, and big harbour works were needed for the bigger ships that were being built. Britain's foreign trade grew, ensuring wealth: the railway – and the steamship – played a substantial part.

Among the very many books and novels about railways you might like the unusual touches in Emmeline Garnett's *Hills of Sheep*, and Philip Turner's *Steam on the Line* (about the 1840s), *Devil's Nob* (about the 1890s), Gillian Cross's account of the effect of navvies on a Sussex village in *The Iron Way*, and Frederick Grice's *Young Tom Sawbones*. Elizabeth Gaskell's *Cousin Phillis* is a contemporary novel recording something of the impact of the railway builders. Today there are many local 'revival' lines that run steam trains in summer – you might join a railway preservation society – and there are a surprising number of local museums for the railway enthusiast, quite apart from the national ones at Swindon and York. Steam has a character all its own: but the diesel engines of the 1940s and 1950s are also becoming museum pieces now!

Steamships

During the nineteenth century, traditional wooden sailing ships reached a peak of perfection (visit the *Cutty Sark* at Greenwich to see an example) – but they were overtaken in size and speed by iron steamships. The first effective steamship was the *Charlotte Dundas*, launched on the Forth–Clyde Canal by William Symington in 1802. Many different types appeared in the next twenty years, and in 1819 *Savannah* made the first crossing of the Atlantic. It was a pioneer voyage, but scarcely proved the effectiveness of steam, for the engine was used only 80 hours in the 24 days of the crossing – the *Sirius* made the crossing in 1838 using her engines throughout. Even so, steamships were built with mast and sail – just in case! (It was in 1838 that the *Archimedes* demonstrated the advantages of screw propulsion over paddle.) True to type, Isambard Kingdom Brunel built three monster steamships – he viewed them as extensions to his great railway line from London to Bristol.

You might like to do a project on Brunel's ships, culminating with the *Great Eastern*, which you can see at Bristol, preserved after its long and chequered career. (The jealousy between steam and sailing ships is well portrayed in Frank Knight's *The Partick Steamboat* and his *Clippers to China* about the 1860s.)

Fig. 24 Tonnage capacity of British ships built during the 19th century

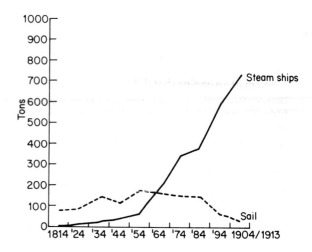

Attempting to launch the 'Great Eastern'

Steam had obvious advantages over sail – it ran to a regular and predictable schedule (the Post Office laid the foundation of several great ocean liner companies, such as Cunard (1839) with the North Atlantic mails contract). In 1828 John Laird of Birkenhead showed that iron hulls were stronger and lighter than wooden ones of the same size (they became lighter still when steel became cheap enough to use after the Bessemer and Siemens processes were adopted in the 1870s). But it was not until the 1850s that iron replaced wood – though iron lasted longer and produced much bigger ships. The initial problem of an engine that did not need nearly all the cargo space for its fuel was overcome by John Elder's compound engine (1854) and the triple expansion marine engine (1881). In 1884, Parsons revolutionised marine engineering with the steam turbine, capable of the unprecedented speed of 34 knots. (Try to obtain *Workshop of the British Empire*, a remarkable book about engineering firms in the west of Scotland, by Michael Moss and John Hume.)

Shipbuilding moved to new sites because iron (and then steel) replaced wood – London shipyards never recovered after 1866, while Clydeside, Tyneside and Merseyside became new centres. As yards grew in size, companies had to grow in order to attract the necessary finance. Bigger docks meant major changes for many ports (a study of a large local port over the last 150 years can reveal some surprising developments). By the 1870s Britain was 'shipbuilder to the world' (Britain held nearly half the world tonnage by 1900) and this brought in considerable *foreign currency earnings.* (It was not only big ships that were iron-built. Visit St Katharine's Dock by the Tower of London and you will see the surprising range of style among the multitude of smaller craft.)

Steamships effectively completed the railway revolution, and Britain grew wealthier from the tremendous increase in trade that followed. Imports of great quantities of raw materials and foodstuffs reduced manufacturers' costs as well as the cost of living. Everyone benefited from the cheaper goods and increased employment – but farmers suffered very badly from foreign competition (see page 197).

Parson's turbine

Machine tools

The Industrial Revolution meant mass production and this meant machines with moving parts that could be replaced immediately by standard parts so that production might not be delayed. The profession of mechanical engineer was born. Standard parts had to be produced to a degree of accuracy possible only by machine – so engineers had to make *machine tools*, machines to make machines. This was a revolution in itself, for traditionally a craftsman made his own tools and developed his own methods: now with machine tools any size of object could be worked to an accuracy unattainable by hand, at great speed, in great quantities and without mistakes or the workers tiring.

James Watt had recognised the importance of machine tools – he got John Wilkinson to bore out the cylinders from his steam engine (see page 31). At the turn of the eighteenth century a group of remarkable engineers developed machine tools independently. Joseph Bramah trained a number of these engineers. His own machines included the basic principle of the self-flushing water closet (1778), a machine for numbering bank notes (enab-

ling the Bank of England to replace 100 clerks) and a famous burglar-proof lock (it remained unpicked from 1784 to 1851!). Henry Maudslay devised the specialised tools necessary to produce naval pulley blocks, making it possible to speed naval construction during the Napoleonic War (by 1808 he had produced 160 000 blocks using ten unskilled men handling his machines – traditional methods would have needed 110 skilled men and very much more time). The domestic water tap was the work of Joseph Clement (the idea of conveniently placed taps in houses had to await such a simple invention, and its effect was a social revolution in itself – mechanical engineers have not received their share of the credit!), and Sir Joseph Whitworth, trained by Bramah and Maudslay, had by 1851 established an international reputation. His micrometer was a star exhibit at the Crystal Palace Exhibition (1851). In 1880 he persuaded the Board of Trade to adopt standard measurements (gauges), especially for screws – ask in the school metal workshop about the Whitworth gauges. His work on interchangeable machine parts helped the advance of mass-production machinery, and his researches into 'work-study' have been taken up in the twentieth century.

Clearly, the Victorian mechanical engineers were far-sighted men. One of them, a gifted amateur, Charles Babbage, developed a mechanical calculator that was effectively a programmed digital computer complete with punched cards carrying data and a 'memory' (1834) – but it proved beyond the technology of the day to complete it. It was the Americans who developed keyboard adding machines (1850) and Herman Hollerith of New York extended the punched card idea so that the 1890 US census data was tabulated electronically – but Babbage had had the original idea. Another remarkable invention was the electric telegraph (1837) which Cooke and Wheatstone installed between Paddington and Slough beside the railway –

in 1845 it was the means that caught the murderer John Tawell. By 1851 the international telegraph network had begun with a submarine cable across the Channel. In 1858 Wheatstone patented a punch-tape system capable of transmitting up to 100 words a minute. Similarly, photography may have been a British invention – look this up in detail for Niépce (1827) and the two rivals Daguerre and Fox-Talbot (1839) were not the first. By the mid-century photography was becoming popular, and Roger Fenton was demonstrating its use in reporting from the Crimean War (1855). By 1900, when the cheap and simple Brownie camera appeared, the *Daily Mail* could announce that there were four million amateur photographers in Britain. The cine-camera gained from Friese-Green's experiments (1885), though motion pictures had to wait until 1895.

Babbage's 'computer'

James Naysmith was the best-known maker of precision tools for heavy engineering; his safety ladle (1838) allowed great quantities of molten metal to be accurately poured at precise timings (if you know an old man who used to work in big forges, ask him about such machines – and the changes since they were replaced!). In 1839, Naysmith produced the famous steam hammer, the only machine capable of forging the paddle shaft of Brunel's *Great Britain*, and yet so accurate as to be capable of just cracking an egg shell.

These were the men whose work made possible the sophisticated engineering industry of the present century. Their machines can be seen in science museums – but it is important to remember that they often worked in small manufactures that we would dismiss as back-yard sheds.

You can catch something of the atmosphere of mid-Victorian engineering and its factories by walking round parts of London, Birmingham, Sheffield and the mill towns. Many of the old buildings have been cleared away, but some remain, and the local Historical Association will be able to put you in touch with enthusiasts for industrial archaeology who will point out the best local places. For those interested in scientific explanations of how the machines worked, the Newcomen Society might be helpful, and so will the Institution of Mechanical Engineers (London) – ask the Library for *Engineering Heritage*, two volumes of articles from their official journal which give much detail about the men and machines of Victorian England. On a different level, you might find interesting *Clean and Decent*, by Lawrence Wright (a history of the water closet and other things).

The Naysmith steamhammer

The Great Exhibition, 1851

Mass production had made Britain the 'workshop of the world', and the confidence of industrialists was marked by their support for free trade. There was considerable enthusiasm for the idea of a huge exhibition to reveal to the world Britain's industrial capacity. It was not an original idea, for there had been large industrial exhibitions in France under the Directory and Napoleon. A powerful committee, headed by Prince Albert, organised a national competition for the design of a hall capable of housing such an exhibition. It would have to be worthy of Britain's industrial strength, but the exhibition would also encourage international trade and promote international peace and harmony – a belief close to the heart of Free Traders such as Richard Cobden (do you see why?).

Victorian art and design has often been condemned, but the choice of Joseph Paxton's design was a tribute to the courage and judgement of the committee. It was novel, daring and incredibly simple – and it patently revealed the skill and capacity of British technology. It was a gigantic glasshouse (enclosing the great elms that then grew in Hyde Park). Built at incredible speed, it combined the principles civil engineers had developed in building iron bridges and big railway stations with techniques of mass production – all its measurements were divisible by twenty-four so that it could be entirely pre-fabricated. A special cradle on runners made it possible to install nearly 300 000 panes of plate glass (itself a tribute to a growing industry, for sheet glass had only been introduced in England in 1832).

The Crystal Palace: Paxton's design, 1850
This design was altered by Barry, the famous architect. Compare it with the familiar photograph of the building that was erected. What did Barry alter? Did it improve the building?

The Exhibition had its enemies – you might like to discover about a certain Colonel Sibthorpe MP, who had some very odd ideas! But the success of the Great Exhibition and its Crystal Palace amazed everyone – over six million visitors came in only 141 days. Railways ran 'exhibition specials' at excursion rates from all over the country, and when the organisers took the daring step of issuing tickets at only one shilling, it was possible for artisans to bring their families in a sort of pilgrimage to Britain's industrial achievement. Remember that the Chartist demonstration of 1848 had seen

The Pound and the Shilling
This famous cartoon has been called 'The meeting of the two nations'. Can you see why? The phrase comes from Disraeli.

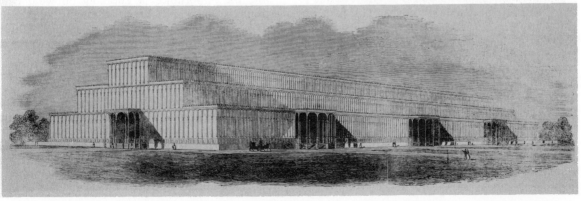

London under martial law – what a change had taken place in three short years!

The rich were genuinely surprised at the good behaviour and suitable dress of the 'respectable' working class – even those from the industrial North! Punch expressed the general feeling:

> Let anyone who wishes to be instructed as to the character of the industrious classes of England and London especially, go to the Exhibition and watch how they behave themselves. He will see them well-dressed, orderly, sedate, earnestly engaged in examining all that interests them, not quarrelsome or obstinate but playing with manifest propriety and good temper the important part assigned to them at this gathering of the nations.

The Great Exhibition was rightly considered a peak of prestige and prosperity: it became a symbol to later generations.

Elizabeth Kyle's novel *The Stiltwalkers* gives some impression of the Exhibition, but try to look at a copy of the *Illustrated London News*, or read the reports in *The Times* or other newspapers – the County Library may let you see copies.

The expansion of steel production

Coal was the great growth industry of the Industrial Revolution, supplying domestic fuel, factories, railways and industrial users – by 1900 some 25 per cent of coal production was exported. Technical advances made deeper mines possible, and coal remained the central indicator of Victorian prosperity. Iron also retained its position as a leading industry, but by the end of the century its place was being challenged by steel (see fig. 9). Steel (an alloy or mixture of iron, carbon and other materials) had numerous advantages over cast or wrought iron. It had been made for centuries; only after the 1850s was it possible to mass-produce it. This was due to three technological breakthroughs. The first was Sir Henry Bessemer's converter (1856) which produced large quantities of molten steel from pig iron by blasting hot air over the molten metal. Robert Mushet added manganese to the molten pig iron to make the steel less brittle. The mass-produced steel could now replace iron – in 1862 steel nails appeared and steel rails were used at Camden Goods Station. In 1863 steel was used in ship-building. But the high phosphorus content of British ores meant that high-quality steel could not easily be produced. Sir William Siemens' open-hearth process (1867) was cheaper than Bessemer's and could produce

better steel, but the problem of phosphorus remained until the Gilchrist-Thomas process (1878), using furnaces lined with dolomite limestone to extract the phosphorous from the pig iron. (The phosphates and other waste products proved useful for fertiliser.) By the 1880s steel began to replace wrought iron as a construction material.

Major shifts in the location of steel-making resulted, first to the ports (South Wales, Middlesbrough and the Scottish Lowlands) to take advantage of cheap foreign ores, and then to the low-quality phosphoric ores fields of Lincolnshire and Northamptonshire. But it was the German producers, utilising the Gilchrist-Thomas process in the Lorraine ore field, and Andrew Carnegie in the USA who applied the new technologies on a vast scale. By 1900 Britain's production had been surpassed: it was an ominous sign of changing times.

The 'Great Depression'

People called the years between 1873 and 1896 the 'Great Depression'. Agriculture apart, they were wrong to do so. But many people felt the prosperous world of mid-Victorian Britain was passing. Competitors, especially in the form of the USA and Germany, had appeared. It seems that there was a crisis of confidence among businessmen. Prices fell in the 1870s, but profits fell with them and by the 1880s unemployment on a fairly extensive scale had appeared: people had already begun leaving the crowded cities of the north in search of better-paid jobs in the London area. Those in work were well placed because *real wages* (what the money actually buys) rose as rapidly as prices fell (see fig. 25).

Fears of foreign competitors rose to hysterical heights in some quarters. Germany was usually cast as the villain (in fact British trade with Germany increased 100 per cent between 1896 and 1914 – note the importance of checking on what contemporaries believed). There were many complaints of Germany 'dumping' goods at *subsidised* prices to undercut British products, and the Board of Trade ordered the country of origin to be stamped on manufactured goods so that people could knowingly 'buy British'. But the policy of Free Trade was not touched: Germany and the USA imposed tariffs against foreign goods, whilst exporting to Britain without a tariff. A Fair Trade League in the 1880s demanded 'retaliatory tariffs' and this idea was later taken up in Joseph Chamberlain's Tariff Reform Campaign of 1903 (see page 162). But there was no change over Free Trade.

Foreign competitors opened factories with the latest machines (sometimes helped by British investments). To compete, the British businessman had to face the expense of re-equipping his factory. British industrial progress seemed slow. Production costs were high and new machinery – where it was installed – was rarely used to full capacity. The old staple industries were beginning to reach the limits of profitability, and the new growth industries, such as chemicals and electricity (both pioneered by Britain), were developed by Germany and the USA. Machine tools suffered a similar fate. This suggests that entrepreneurs were not taking opportunities – and many people blamed the 'Great Depression' on management failure.

British industry was changing at the top: large firms, helped by limited liability, often employed a professional manager by the end of the century. He was a new man, often unconnected with the family that had built up the business – this is called the 'managerial revolution' and was to be of great importance in the twentieth century. Some historians have tried to explain Britain's poorer performance by 1900 in terms of this managerial revolution, arguing that it inhibited adopting new techniques. (Skilled workers certainly resisted technological change when their jobs were affected.) But such explanations are superficial. The 'boss's son' no longer learnt on the shop floor: he went to a new public school –but there he met sons of the wealthy who could well prove useful in raising money for the firm later on. And the very years of the 'Great Depression' saw major achievements: steel largely replaced iron, steam power was increased in industry (look at factories surviving from the last century –when were the big workshops built?), civil en-

---

Fig. 25 *Average real wages and prices, 1850–1913*

If you had a reasonably well paid job, then you would have been far better off in the 1890s than your parents would have been in the 1850s and 1860s – the time of 'Victorian prosperity'. But by 1914 your real wages would have declined and prices would have risen towards the 1850s and 1860s level. You can see why there was so much labour unrest in the years just before the First World War.

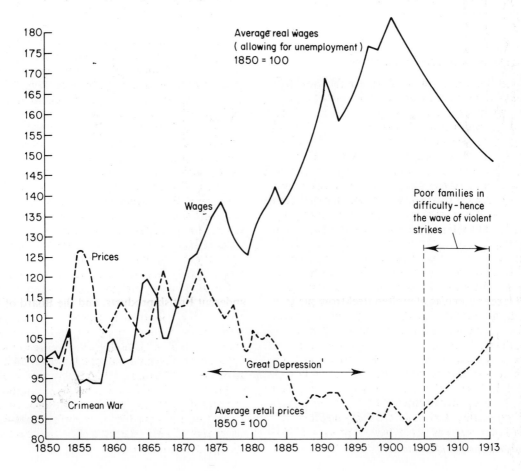

The Forth Bridge under construction

The 'International', as it used to be

gineering saw tremendous achievements (the Forth Bridge, 1882–7, was a wonder of the world), Warwickshire and the Midlands saw the development of light industries, and the boot and shoe industry was 'factoryised' at this time. Firms amalgamated for increased efficiency – Cammell-Laird shipping, and the Armstrong and Whitworth armaments and machine-tool factories, for example. In the retail trade, specialised multiple grocery stores, such as Lipton's and Home and Colonial, and chain stores such as Hepworth the Tailor and Boots the Chemist began. Does this show inadequate management failing to take opportunities?

Whatever some contemporaries said, late Victorian management was not complacent, and the Edwardians went on to achieve a record in exports and foreign earnings. Certainly there was competition – but perhaps the 'Great Depression' was not severe enough to oblige wholesale reconstruction! Foreign competition and hostile tariffs proved a greater threat in Britain's traditional markets. Consequently, Britain looked increasingly to her Empire and the tropics as an increasing market for manufactured goods and a source of raw material and foodstuffs. The Empire absorbed what Europe did not take. Here was an important reason for the popularity of Imperialism.

Farming after 1846

In 1846 the agricultural interest was convinced that repealing the Corn Laws would ruin British agriculture (see page 122). These people were quite wrong, for the mid-Victorian years proved the 'golden age' of British agriculture – 'high farming', as Sir James Caird called it. There was no sudden collapse of corn prices; instead, growing prosperity among urban workers meant an increasing demand for foodstuffs, a demand railways helped to supply. Farmers invested heavily in improvements. Peruvian guano, Chilean nitrates, German potash (after 1860) and bone fertilisers were among the new fertilisers widely used. Scientific principles were applied extensively (though not on all farms!) and the draining of heavy soils was greatly increased by Fowler's 'mole' plough and machines capable of producing 20 000 feet (6100 metres) of clay piping in a day. New machines, including large steam ploughs, became common, and these involved grubbing up hedgerows to make bigger fields. In many areas, farming became very prosperous.

Then came the 'Great Depression'. It was very real in agriculture because of the railways and the steamships. After the United States Civil War, a rapid building of railways opened up the Mid-West

Ploughing by steam engine

plains, and the increasing size of steamships meant that huge cargoes of wheat could now reach Europe. In Liverpool, Chicago wheat fell from sixty-five shillings a ton (1868) to twenty-four shillings (1882), which meant much cheaper bread, and this benefited the artisan class in particular. They had been enfranchised in 1867, thus no British government dared impose a tariff on foreign corn to save the British producer, lest they lose the working-class vote.

However, this was not all. In the 1870s bad harvests, together with crop diseases and epidemics among livestock, dealt severe blows to farmers. Disraeli, who had made his name defending the agricultural interest against Peel in 1845–6, showed no disposition to return to Protection. Imports increased, prices fell and British grain production suffered. Then came another blow: in 1880 the first refrigerated meat and butter from Australia arrived

and in 1882 the *Dunedin* brought refrigerated butter and meat from New Zealand.

Refrigerated meat and dairy produce (travelling by rail as well as by sea) brought a new threat to farmers' prosperity – you can see why! In 1882, however, *The Times* only confirmed the technological breakthrough:

> Today we have to record such a triumph over physical difficulties as would have been incredible, and even unimaginable, a very few years ago. Had anyone suggested New Zealand would send into our London Market 5000 dead sheep at a time, and in good condition as if they had been slaughtered in some suburban abattoir, he should have brought on himself a storm of derision.

The New Zealand cargoes came in freezers made by the Glasgow firm of Bell Brothers – no hint here of failing to take advantage of new opportunities!

High-quality meat remained profitable for British farmers, but this *speciality market* was not available to many of them, and livestock farmers faced bankruptcy. Between 1871 and 1914 the number of agricultural workers fell from 1 250 000 to about a million, although the total population rose by some 40 per cent. Young men and girls left the countryside for the towns, or emigrated – here was the real exodus from the countryside, and a new atmosphere appeared in rural England (you can read of this in Flora Thompson's book, *Lark Rise to Candleford* and in Alison Uttley's *The Country Child*). Throughout the century, agriculture had been declining as a proportion of national wealth (for Britain was becoming an industrial nation). Now the process speeded up–see fig. 27).

Two Royal Commissions investigated the 'agricultural depression' and in 1889 the Ministry of Agriculture was established – but there was little direct help to farmers. British agriculture was left to fight its way out of the depression: Chamberlain's Tariff Reform Campaign (see page 162), which might have helped the farmer, was firmly rejected at the 1906 election. Britain retained free trade and cheap food – a new balance had been established in the British economy. The urban voters produced manufactured goods and enjoyed the benefit of getting over half their food imported from abroad at prices cheaper than it could be produced at home. It was hard on some farmers and most farm labourers, but town dwellers experienced a rising prosperity, especially in Edwardian times, so much so that people looked back to those days at the beginning of the century as an 'Indian summer' before the shattering experience of the First World War.

*Fig. 26 (a) Wheat and barley imports, 1860s–1913
(b) Wheat and bread prices, 1840–1913*

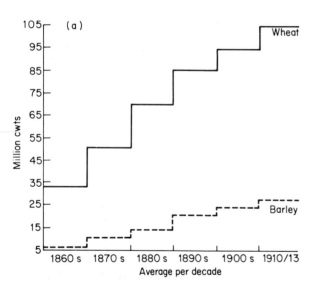

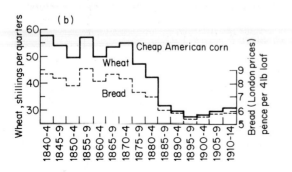

Fig. 27 (a) Distribution of national income, 1801–1901
(b) Distribution of employment, 1801–1911

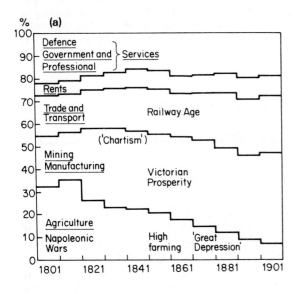

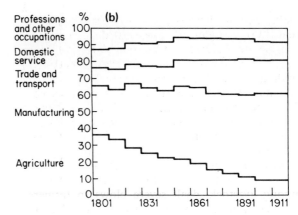

(a) Note the rapid decline of agriculture from the largest sector of the economy (1820), and the growing importance of mining, manufacturing and service industries.
(b) The share of agriculture declines throughout the period; the share of manufacturing industry increases. Domestic service remains fairly constant until 1914 – the great decline in this, and the growth in the professions, happens after the First World War. (A good impression of domestic service and the changes about the time of the war is given in Gordon Cooper's An Hour in the Morning)

This question helps to indicate the differences between town and country, and gives an indication of living standards.

Although the level of question is not very high, good use is made of the simple sources and an effort made at empathy and the use of imagination.

SOURCE A *Weekly budget of a farm labourer from Lavenham, Suffolk, in 1843*

Name	Age	Earnings		Expenditure		
		s	d		s	d
Robert Crick	42	9	0	Bread	1	0
Wife	40		9	Potatoes	1	0
Boy	12	2	0	Rent	1	2
Boy	11	1	0	Tea		2
Boy	8	1	0	Sugar		3½
Girl	6		–	Soap		3
Boy	4		–	Blue		½
				Thread etc.		2
		——		Candles		3
Total Earnings		13	9	Salt		½
		——		Coal and		
				wood		9
				Butter		4½
				Cheese		3
				——		
				Total	13	9

SOURCE B *Weekly expenditure of a semi-skilled town worker with three children in 1841*

Bread	3	6½
Meat	2	1
Beer	1	2
Coals		9½
Potatoes	1	4
Tea and sugar	1	6
Butter		9
Soap and candles		6½
Rent	2	6
Schooling		4
Sundries		5½
Total	15	0

(N.B. 1s 0d = 5 new pence; 15s 0d = £0.75)

1. How might the children of Robert Crick have earned their money?
2. Why was it likely that children of agricultural labourers would have to work in the mid-nineteenth century?
3. What evidence is there in the two sources to suggest that one family is better off than the other?
4. What further evidence would you need to establish this suggestion?
5. What do the sources reveal as to standard of living and diet of the two families?

SREB

The Warwickshire union organises a strike of agricultural labourers
 Joseph Arch organised several trade unions among farm labourers. This activity was much disapproved of by landowners, but Arch was successful in raising wage levels. However, his movement was destroyed largely by the impact of the 'Great Depression' on agriculture.

The greater awareness of poverty

Undoubtedly, for those in employment, the thirty years before 1914 were prosperous days. But they were days that also saw an increasing awareness and understanding of the grinding poverty in which many workers lived, made the more obvious by the evident prosperity of the artisans. For the moderately wealthy, Edwardian England was a time of indulgence in fairly expensive clothes for many different social occasions, in eating huge meals and in drinking a good deal – usually not beer!

What Disraeli had once called the 'two nations' is clearly shown by the contrast. 'The Condition of England Question' (what to do about the huge number of very poor people in this land of plenty) became a matter of intense interest.

Visit your local museum and examine the costumes of the period and a reconstructed room. Look at the lavish decorations in theatres that survive from Edwardian times, or at the facades of Edwardian commercial buildings in town centres: this will give you an idea of the prosperity of the period. Then look at photographs of the 'Edwardian crowd' – working men and women who clearly owned few clothes, their children, many without boots or in boots handed down from others, many with faces misshapen from dietary diseases.

Towards the end of the nineteenth century, a number of writers and investigators published reports on the poor that had considerable influence on public opinion and which revealed the extent and nature of poverty. Mearns' *The Bitter Cry of Outcast London* (1883) caused a stir because it showed things had not improved much since Chadwick's day (see page 177). Mearns did not exaggerate: General Booth of the Salvation Army showed this in his book, *In Darkest England – And the Way Out* (1890), but the most influential of all was Charles Booth's *The Life and Labour of the People in London* (1886–1903), a thorough survey in several volumes. Beatrice Webb was one of his assistants. He found that some 30 per cent of Londoners lived in hardship, with less than enough income to secure a proper livelihood. Booth's clear sociological and statistical survey made it impossible any longer to dismiss poverty as the just reward of idleness and self-indulgence, or to believe that poverty was confined to a small group at the very bottom of the social pyramid. In 1899 Seebohm Rowntree showed that what was true of the metropolis was also true of medium-sized cities such as York. In *Poverty: A Study of Town Life*, he showed that 27.8 per cent of York's population fell below what he defined as a 'poverty line'. He distinguished between 'primary poverty' – those 'whose total earnings were insufficient to obtain the minimum necessaries for the maintenance of merely physical efficiency' and 'secondary poverty' where families were not able to climb above his poverty line because of some extra expenditure forced on the family. Like Booth, he revealed that drunkenness and improvidence were real causes of poverty, but more serious causes were temporary unemployment, sickness and low wages (Chadwick had already hinted at this in his Poor Law Report of 1834). A great radical historian, R. H. Tawney, made the point:

> The problem of poverty is not primarily to assist individuals who are exceptionally unfortunate. It is to make the normal conditions under which masses

Peter Robinson's London store

The Edwardian crowd
The contrast between fashionable society and the poor was very real: the group in this photograph have not been specially gathered, they were a common enough slight.

Note the children without boots, and those wearing boots that were 'handed down'. The police often distributed old clothing to the poor. Note also the faces showing signs of dietary diseases. Here was the proof of real poverty.

of men work and live such that they may lead a healthy, independent and self-respecting life when they are not exceptionally unfortunate.

There was an increasing realisation that poverty was not necessarily the fault of the poor, and a growing body of opinion favoured the state seeking to underpin the life of the poor so that they might evade poverty. Already by the 1880s the idea of what was called the collectivist state was gaining acceptance, by which the state's powers should be used to achieve a more acceptable society. Sidney Webb was able to show how far collectivism had grown by the end of the century:

> The individualist town councillor will walk along the municipal pavement, lit by municipal light and cleansed by municipal brooms with municipal water, and – seeing by the municipal clock in the municipal market, that he is too early to meet his children coming from the municipal school, hard by the county lunatic asylum and the municipal hospital, will use the national telegraph system to tell them not to walk through the municipal park, but to come by the municipal museum, art-gallery and library, where he intends . . . to prepare his next speech in the municipal town hall in favour of the nationalisation of canals and the increase of government control over the railway system.
>
> 'Socialism, Sir,' he will say, 'don't waste the time of a practical man by your fantastic absurdities. Self-help, Sir, individual self-help, that's what has made our city what it is.'

Different people had different ideas as to what 'socialism' meant. Webb meant 'municipal socialism', or the practice of town councils providing a range of services, paid for by the local rates (see page 207). Such services (where they existed) used to be provided by private companies or individuals. The growth of municipal services was one of the minor social and political revolutions of late Victorian and Edwardian Britain. What was being achieved at local level could be applied in some form to the country as a whole.

A developing industrial society was a complex entity that could not merely be left to run itself under *laissez-faire* principles. This, indeed, was one of the issues that divided Joseph Chamberlain from Gladstone: in the 1885 election, Chamberlain's manifesto was called the 'Unauthorised Programme' (see page 154). Twenty years later the Balfour government appointed a Royal Commission on the Poor Law (1905) – it reported in 1909, agreeing that the 1834 Poor Law was no longer adequate for the changing circumstances, and the Minority Report (1909), compiled by the Webbs, was to have considerable influence on social legislation during the twentieth century. The Liberal government that was returned in 1906 (no doubt aware of the large number of Labour members) contained men who were anxious to develop the powers of the state to relieve the worst poverty. Winston Churchill spoke of 'drawing a line below which we will not allow persons to live and labour'. Between 1906 and 1914 the broad lines of what was to develop into the Welfare State of the future were laid down (see chapter 12). Theirs was a new form of liberalism, one that Gladstone would have resisted, but one appropriate to the twentieth century.

In this chapter we have been concerned with what historians call economic factors. No explanation of events in history can be complete without considering such factors: can you see how closely they relate to political events?

Organise a class debate on the motion 'that this house believes economic factors are more important in history than political events'.

14 Social conditions

Population growth

One of the most important changes of the nineteenth century was in the size of the population (see page 3). Around the 1770s the population had suddenly leapt forward at a rate never before experienced; conditions would never be the same again. Within a very few years the tremendous increase – in the country areas quite as much as in towns – was creating a whole range of new problems and conditions. The increase continued throughout the nineteenth century (see Fig. 1), but the *rate of growth* declined, particularly after the 1870s, when the birth rate began to drop quite

steeply. (Try to explain why the population should continue to increase markedly, although the birth rate was dropping.) The death rate continued to decline after the 1840s. (Can you suggest reasons for this, and can you see what effects this might have on the population as a whole?)

The population increase affected the whole country, but it was most noticeable in the big towns, simply because of the huge numbers – and remember that before 1800 there were very few big towns at all. Traditionally, the well-off and the poor had lived side by side in towns (you can still see today in some villages the large rectory and the imposing doctor's house beside quite small

Fig. 28 Growth of certain towns, 1801–1911
Remember that it was 1851 before more people lived in towns than in the countryside. There were not many huge towns before 1851: even so the rate of growth of towns was very rapid. By the end of the century a number of towns had reached 100,000 people. Bath was exceptional. York and Derby reflected the importance of railways and

their associated industries. Blackpool shows the impact of the 'holiday industry' arising out of increased spending power as much as railway transport. But Coventry shows how new light engineering industries could bring a new lease of life from the 1880s – the time of the 'Great Depression', remember!

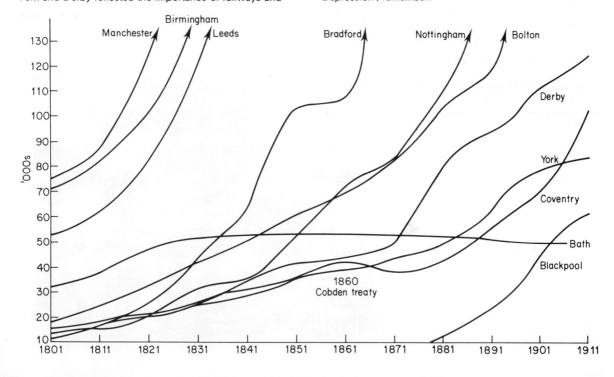

cottages – the smaller ones that once existed have disappeared). This helped *social cohesion*, so that even the small town felt a genuine sense of community. By the nineteenth century, however, the wealthy were beginning to live in different parts of town from the poor; their districts would have paved streets and cobbled roads, with squares, and would on the whole be spacious. The streets would be lit by gas light (Albert Winsor in 1807 had shown how the individual domestic gas plants that William Murdoch had developed could be adapted to light a whole area from a central gas plant), and there would be crossing sweepers to clear the road for pedestrians – remember that traffic was horse-drawn. The poorer areas were already noted for their slums, with overcrowding and noisome conditions. This was already true of London during the later eighteenth century, and became true of other large towns. This division into 'better' areas and slums, compounded class consciousness and the appearance of 'two nations'.

Public health

What distinguished the nineteenth century, however, was not the development of slums (there was nothing new about bad and overcrowded housing) but a determined effort to improve the conditions under which people lived, even for the very poor who could contribute little to the huge expense involved. The first problem was one of size. In villages, there was little need to make serious provision for good drainage and pure water; when

villages grew into big towns, this became essential. Edwin Chadwick had made the point quite simply and starkly by contrasting the average life expectancy of men from different classes in rural Rutland (38 years for labourers) with those in Manchester – 17 years only for labourers! The incredible thing was that the urban population continued to increase in such conditions, and not necessarily because families came in from elsewhere (remember that the 'exodus' from the countryside was in the later part of the nineteenth century, *after* the huge towns had developed – you can check this from the enumerator's book, see page 5).

In the 1830s several committees of enquiry were appointed and their reports made worrying reading. The Victorians were prepared to tackle directly problems that previous generations had left alone, and this was not merely because the problems were more obvious and pressing. There was widepread interest in social conditions – you might dip into Peter Quennell's selection of pieces by that indefatigable investigator, Henry Mayhew – it is called *Mayhew's London*, taken from *London Labour and London Poor* (1851). Engels, the man who helped Marx, made full use of the official reports in his *Condition of the Working Class in England in 1844* (see page 109). Look at this book: you will see why historians use it as a source!

> Immediately under the railway bridge there stands a court, the filth and horrors of which surpass all the others by far . . . Everywhere before the doors refuse and offal. . . privies are so rare here that they are either filled up every day or are too remote for most of the inhabitants to use them.

Father Thames offering his offspring to the Fair City of London
Why would you be able to date this drawing easily?

The absence of mains drainage meant that excrement lay in unpaved streets and oozed down the walls of cellars, each of which might be 'home' for several families. Death was a constant companion: sometimes the coffin could lie for several days, the family living about it, until burial arrangements had been made. Rats might gnaw the corpse in its open coffin. Urban graveyards were full, often so full that the ground level was artificially high and the 'peculiar, indescribable smell' of putrefying bodies pervaded them. Water supply was a major problem. If water was drawn from the local river it was likely to be contaminated – Henry Mayhew reported what he saw on a visit to Bethnal Green:

> As we gazed in horror at the pool, we saw drains and sewers emptying their filthy contents into it, we saw a whole tier of doorless privies in the open road built over it . . . And yet, as we stood gazing in horror at the fluvial sewer, we saw a child from one of the galleries opposite lower a tin can with a rope, to fill a bucket that stood beside her.
>
> In each of the rude and rotten balconies, indeed, that hung over the stream, the self-same bucket was to be seen in which the inhabitants were wont to put mucky liquid to stand, so that they might . . . skim

the fluid from the solid particles of filth and pollution which constituted the sediment.

The Thames was tidal, so that filthy waste (made worse when early water closets flushed directly into the rivers) was washed back up-stream several times before it could get away or sink to the muddy bottom. The situation became so bad that in 1858 there was the 'great stink' when members of Parliament found conditions unbearable – no wonder the Embankment was built on the north side of the river! If drinking water were drawn from local wells or if it had been piped to a stand-pipe, there was danger of seepage from cesspools, graveyards, slaughter-houses or industrial waste.

Doctors were only just beginning to understand about infection (how diseases spread). (The development of nineteenth-century medicine makes a fascinating special study – read up about Lister, Pasteur and Koch and their scientific work). Many doctors supposed disease was caused by 'bad air' (the atmospheric theory). They confused, however understandably, the effect with the cause, for the bad smells came from chemical action by microbes and other organisms which were the real agents of

The Bazzelgate's scheme for the Thames Embankment The area between the houses and the river was reclaimed land. What uses was it put to? Can you recognise the Railway Station and the bridge? Are they still there?

infection. It was only later in the century that this was properly understood. Chadwick, for example, got the causes of disease quite wrong. Epidemics were common. The most dramatic was cholera – new to England, it struck first in 1831 and returned several times until the 1860s, on each occasion striking with frightening suddenness, especially in the summer months, and killing rich people as well as poor. Each new epidemic was greeted with wild panic. Study a large-scale map of any large nineteenth-century town and you will find a cholera cemetery, often just outside what then were the boundaries of the town. (Christopher Hibbert's book, *King Cholera,* will tell you a great deal about the disease and its effects.) In 1854, Dr John Snow showed that cholera was water-borne – he simply plotted the deaths and the wells in Golden Square, London, and this showed clearly which well was contaminated! But for all the panic that cholera caused, little was done. *The Times* frankly declared that the true Britisher would 'not be bullied into health'. But the 1866 cholera epidemic killed over 6000 people in London alone, and it was his work among the dying poor that persuaded Dr Barnardo to begin his great work for the care of destitute children. However, more than private charity was needed: the resources of the state had to be called into action.

In 1836, compulsory registration of births and the causes of deaths was required, and by analysing the resulting figures William Farr was able to pin-point public health 'black spots' – he called it 'statistical noseology' (can you see why?). Already, Edwin Chadwick had been drawn to the problem of public health by his work on the Poor Laws (see page 112). His investigations led him to publish his epoch-making *Report on the Sanitary Condition of the Labouring Population* (1842) revealing the nature of the problem and suggesting a whole programme of reforms – such as the wholesale removal of waste. (He had a scheme for carrying it off in solution in sewage pipes, and the Doulton pottery made its fortune producing the salt-glazed piping for the job, as well as for lavatory pans. Joseph Bazalgatte was to adapt Chadwick's model to his great scheme for the mains drainage of London in 1858.) Chadwick's suggestions also included street cleansing, supplying pure running water – and he argued ingeniously that the cost of the measures would be less burdensome than the cost of extra poor relief arising from disease and death of family breadwinners.

Chadwick had joined Dr Southwood Smith, Lord Shaftesbury and the young Disraeli to found the Health of Towns Association (1839), but their efforts to promote reform were blocked by councils anxious to keep rates low, by the prevalent *laissez-faire* views and by the host of private companies, such as private water companies and contractors for waste removal. However, the Public Health Act 1848 set up the General Board of Health in London with the power to create local boards where 10 per cent of the population demanded it or where the death rate was over 23 per 1000. Chadwick was appointed Secretary of the Board. But slackness and indifference, as well as powerful opposition from vested interests, obstructed the Board's work. Chadwick complained 'self-satisfied bumbledum, in town and parish, incapable of grasping the implication of the crisis, cried out against centralisation'. But 'bumbledum' won: the Central Board was dissolved and Chadwick withdrew into private life (1854).

This was a great blow to the reformers, and it was not until 1866 that the Sanitary Act compelled local authorities to take action to supply adequate water and provide sewage and waste disposal services. Even so, the public was apathetic – although this was the time of Victorian prosperity! There was no lack of money. In 1871 the Local Government Board was created to supervise the working of local councils and to take over general responsibility for public health, but it was not until 1875 that Richard Cross's Public Health Act (see page 146) codified the many regulations into a single body of law and obliged the appointment of a Medical Officer of Health (Leicester and Liverpool had appointed theirs in the 1840s). But it was well into the twentieth century before adequate water supplies or the provision of water closets became normal for working class housing.

The story of public health is worth following in detail–it was very slow-moving, considering the dreadful epidemics, but remember that it was also very new and the Victorians were not accustomed to such rapid changes as we are today. It has been popular at times to pour scorn on the Victorians, but this is perhaps unfair when you consider how great was their achievement and how they strove to solve the problems with which they were faced. You might trace the development of public health in your own town – make a series of plans showing what was built of your town at different times and which streets had piped water to the houses and proper mains drainage (the local Planning Office may help with early maps). Find out when your town first appointed a Medical Officer of Health, and consult his annual Reports (in the Record Office) to see what problems he faced.

Housing in towns

The Victorians were **pragmatists**; they did what they thought practical in the circumstances, whatever their political ideas. This is well illustrated in their attitude to housing. As the size of towns increased, it was soon necessary to impose some by-laws to establish a basic standard at least for the poor. As early as the 1860s, some progressive councils gained powers of *compulsory purchase* so that the very worst slums might be cleared (Liverpool and Glasgow provide examples), and the Torrens Act 1868 granted this power to any council seeking to clear away insanitary dwellings. The Artisans' Dwellings Act 1875 permitted larger areas of slums to be purchased and cleared. Even so, rebuilding was generally in the hands of private builders and landlords: there was very little council housing before 1919. Even Joseph Chamberlain, the Radical mayor of Birmingham, who had in the 1870s 'parked, paved, assized, marketed, gas-and-watered and *improved*' the city, had to admit in 1884 that the cost was too great: 'we have done all this generation at any rate will be able to do', he declared. A hundred years later there were still slums. Remember, however, that people's idea of what constitutes a slum can differ both in different parts of the country and at different times – it is a matter of the standards one expects. Have a look at the 1885 Ordnance Survey map (large-scale) of your town to see if there was 'back-to-back' housing and note where it was sited: does this lead you to any conclusions? To get a good idea of what much working-class housing was like in about 1900, have a glance at *The Classic Slum* by Robert Roberts.

Private charity, always very important to the Victorians, did much to help particular areas. Examples are the blocks of flats built by the Peabody Trust in London after 1869 or Octavia Hill's work in the 1870s. However, this was necessarily on a limited scale and did not touch the very poor whose need was greatest, but who could not

Peabody Square, model dwellings, Blackfriars Road, London

afford to pay anything like an economic rent. Industrialists, of course, would occasionally build 'estate villages' (rather as the landed aristocracy had done) – like the grid-plan for old Middlesbrough the Quakers began in the 1830s, before it was swamped by housing for the workers in the Cleveland iron trade. Barrow-in-Furness was another example. Sir Titus Salt built Saltaire (1860s) with its park, public library and social club – but no pub! Port Sunlight, built by W. H. Lever, was also a 'dry' town, so was George Cadbury's Bournville (1879) and Rowntree's New Earswick (in York) – the Temperance Movement was very important in Victorian England. But these towns were on a small scale; it in was the big towns that the problems lay.

There was no lack of ideas for urban development. Municipal parks began to appear towards the

end of the century – try to discover if your town has an example. If it has, examine its site and decide whether it was intended for the very poor, the ordinary poor, the artisans or the well-to-do. Perhaps the most formative influence was the idea of the garden city, bringing together the benefits of town and country for the nineteenth-century town destroyed the green of the countryside. Ebenezer Howard's *Tomorrow, a Peaceful Path in Reform* appeared in 1898. His 'garden city' involved planning the whole area of a town as a single unit. The land would be owned in common and the town area divided into zones for specialised land-use: factory areas would be separated from housing areas and a 'green belt' would preserve agricultural land around the town from any unplanned urban expansion. Letchworth (1903) and Welwyn Garden City (1919) were planned along Howard's principles. In 1909,

Ebenezer Howard's plan for a section of a Garden City

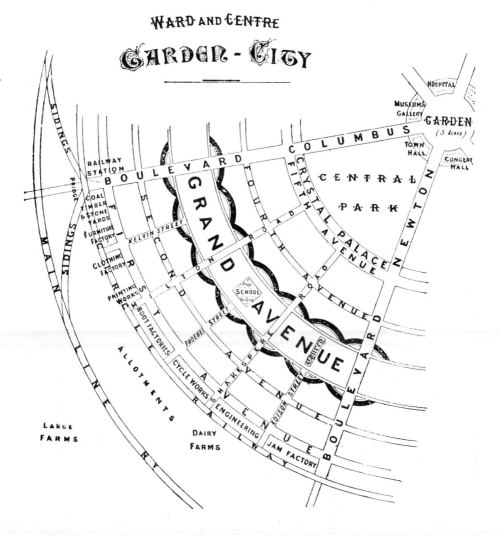

the government passed a Housing and Town Planning Act in the hope of encouraging better planning in towns. The Act lacked effective powers, but it was a big step away from the traditional *laissez-faire* attitudes to property.

It is easy to forget that the housing problem was not simply something to do with the poor. Even the well-to-do had to come to terms with the problems arising from the size, the costs and the smells of the large industrial town. Broadly, you would find four types of housing in late-Victorian English towns: large villas or substantial terraces with big gardens, for the well-off with their large families and perhaps several servants; terraces of well-built small houses with a small garden for the clerks and artisans (you can recognise this type in every Midlands town, often brick-built to a very similar plan – and now often thought 'poor' areas); terraces of crowded housing with little greenery or trees for the ordinary poor; and the real slum areas for the very poor. Few examples of the last type remain, though a good deal of the first and second can be seen in most towns.

If your town provides good examples, it would be worth arranging with the geography department to do a 'transect' of the town or a part of the town. You could discover the date of construction of villas and terraces (there could be a date on the wall, or the street name could give a clue – Alma Terrace would be the 1850s or 1860s, Kimberly Street or Mafeking Terrace could be the 1900s) and colour a sketch map to show when the streets were built and for which type of person (remember the census returns might give you the job of the head of the house, which would help you). You could show how the nineteenth century street pattern has changed (if at all) and suggest why; you could see whether there has been much change in land-use over a hundred years (is it still housing, or have small factories appeared, or old factories been cleared away?). As you conduct your survey, note the detail of the buildings – how the brickwork changes, how some terraces and villas might use different-coloured bricks, or specially moulded or designed bricks. Little details can often tell you a great deal about the type of person for whom the terraces were originally built, for if you use your eyes you can often see a great deal more history about you than you might get from books. If you can identify terraces intended for office workers, try to decide how they got into the town centre each day for their long day's work. You might read George Grossmith's *The Diary of a Nobody* for an amusing insight into the kind of life

such people led – does it differ essentially from what happens today? If you find this book entertaining, you might try Gillian Avery's *Victorian People*, which shows how ordinary men and women lived (using novels as evidence), or the same author's *The Echoing Green* which used extracts from diaries of young people at the time to show what life was like for Regency and Victorian youth.

It is important to try to get as broad a picture of the social life of the past as you can, for otherwise one's ideas could be too coloured by the reports of social investigators who were demonstrating how the poor and very poor lived, in the hope of encouraging politicians to bring in reforms – such evidence may be entirely correct and true, but it could exaggerate the general picture that it gives, even if there was no intention of so doing in the author's mind. Without intending it, they may have produced a *biased* account. (But be careful: it is very easy indeed to see bias in everything.)

Municipal and other developments

Water, gas and electricity

Since the 1850s, urban living standards had been rising. Public health measures were bringing purer water and clearing away waste, and there were fewer of the worst type of slums built – although progress was never as rapid as it might have been. The Baths and Wash-houses Act 1846 permitted local authorities to provide these amenities, for running water piped to individual housing was often a rarity even at the end of the century. Public lavatories became more common also towards the end of the century. Town gas made a big difference to street lighting, domestic cooking and industrial heating – though there was tremendous variation in the quality and supply of gas and in the gas fittings, because the gas works were locally owned. By the 1880s electrical power, easier to install than gas and more convenient for domestic use, began a new chapter in social history. Dartford was the first large power station to be built (1889), though local companies were normally responsible for producing electrical power and this meant a mass of different currents and fixtures all over the country.

Water, gas and electricity are examples of *utilities:* if they were not supplied by the local authority, then they came under special by-laws. Such utilities made a substantial contribution to improving conditions in towns (country villages were less fortunate). Developments in local transport also helped.

Transport

By the 1880s horse-drawn trams had appeared, and in the 1890s steam trams were introduced, shortly to be replaced by electric trams (Leeds was the first major city to electrify its trams – in 1891). Trams worked a minor social revolution, for this form of transport made travel from town centre to the terminus near the countryside quick and convenient. Many workers were now able to live at a little distance from their workplaces because of the tram service – but many families below the income level of artisans could simply not afford even the cheap fares!

> Try to trace the old tram tracks in your town from old maps – see if the routes were intended to serve the poor or the better-paid sections of the community. You might find a report, complete with photography or drawings, of the opening of a new route or tram works in an old local paper. There is a national tram museum at Crich in Derbyshire with actual working nineteenth-century trams, and several industrial museums have examples of trams.

By 1905, the petrol-driven omnibus was appearing. It was cheaper to run than trams, it could travel anywhere in town and go on into the countryside. (The London Transport Museum at Covent Garden is the place to visit and see how these vehicles have changed.) The improvement of local transport facilities must have contributed greatly to enlarging the experience of people and to making their lives easier – and think of the difference a regular cheap bus service would make to a little village too far away from town for easy walking! The London 'tubes' were electrified by 1901 and they did much to create 'suburbia'.

When the motor-car appeared, it was the plaything of the rich: at first it was restricted by the 'Red Flag Act' requiring a man to walk in front carrying a flag – its repeal in 1896 is commemorated each year by the London-to-Brighton annual run of vintage cars. For those who could afford it, the motor-car gave almost unlimited travel, and the clouds of dust thrown up from the roads soon encouraged the new County Councils to put down a new hard surface (tar macadam) which made English main roads, and many minor roads, among the best in the world by 1914. Commercial vehicles, also, by 1914 had encroached on local waggoners' preserves increasing the speed and quantities of deliveries over short distances. Far less dramatic, but perhaps more important for the less wealthy, was the development of the bicycle. Throughout the nineteenth century there had been various designs, including the picturesque 'penny-farthing', but the modern design was perfected in 1885 by J. K. Starkley (the three-speed gear invented by Sturney – Archer, came in 1902). Dunlop's development of the pneumatic tyre (1888) made

An electric tram in Liverpool

cycling – and motoring – more comfortable. Cycling became a popular past-time in Edwardian England, and brought new fashions in clothing. It also helped women to have a wider social life – ask your grandparents about Edwardian cycling clubs (you can still see the signs for them outside some country cafés). Even so, it was a past-time for the comfortably off, as the machines were quite expensive.

These new methods of transport created new industries and skills: the old Midlands textile towns began to turn to metal trades and light engineering, and even in the villages many a local garage began as a cycle shop. Here was a quiet social revolution with important consequences for the economy. (And have you noticed that these developments in transport were coming in during the time that manufacturers were complaining of a 'Great Depression' (see page 194)? Does this suggest that the businessman had lost his inventiveness and his touch?)

London to Brighton veteran car rally

Suitable clothes for cycling

Bicycles of about 1874
The lady's is a Starkley bicycle

Education and the emancipation of women

There were other quiet social revolutions in the later nineteenth century. Two important and obvious ones are the growing emancipation of women and the gradual development of a state education system. Both make ideal topics for project work, since there are ample secondary sources for both, and primary sources are not difficult to find. (Some city schools dating from the 1870s still have their original buildings, and many village school buildings remain – so do many log books kept by the schoolmaster with great care and attention to detail.) You can also ask old people about their recollections of the early years of the century and about what *their* grandparents told them – but remember that 'oral evidence' presents many problems for the historian: how to check on the stories that you hear, for example.

If you do a project on either of these topics – or on any other, for that matter – remember how important it is to organise it well. Try to prevent the situation arising where you have so many pieces of information that the project becomes no more than a story or a sketch-book which ends by asking and answering no particular question. Always have a clear purpose in mind, a definite question to which an answer may be found, and use this question as the basis for searching out your primary and secondary sources. Try to bring in as much local material as you can, in order to illustrate your general theme, and don't be afraid to use advanced textbooks – they usually have good indexes to help you find relevant material. As you gather material and learn more about your topic, try to give it a definite shape by dividing it into convenient sections.

On the 'emancipation' of women, make sure that you understand what your real purpose is – do you intend to do a study of the suffragettes or a wider issue? If it is the latter, then decide what social class you are especially concerned with – who controls a wife's property is of little relevance to working-class life. Make a list of the disadvantages that women suffered and find out when they were removed – entry to professions, to universities, to local councils, to the House of Commons. Do you see how all these are concerned with well-to-do middle class women? You might like to consider how difficult life could be for such people.

Jane Austen's novels portray the life of well-to-do people at the beginning of the nineteenth century; there are also many novels about life at the beginning of the twentieth century. H. G. Wells wrote a book about the problems of a young lady hoping to break free from convention, *Anne Veronica*. You might also enjoy E. M. Forster's *Howard's End,* which gives a detailed picture of how comfortably-off people lived at this time. At a less adult level, you could read Barbara Willard's *Hetty* or Brian Fairfax-Lucy and Philippa Pearce's *The Children of the House* in order to catch a glimpse of Edwardian England. K. M. Peyton has written three novels in *Flambards* about prosperous life in the countryside that also introduce flying machines, the invention of the future.

With a project on education, be sure that you have decided which type of school and what age group is the object of your enquiry. If you are showing the development of the state system, then public schools (although they have some relevance) should scarcely appear in your work. If it is elementary schools (up to age ten or so), then secondary and grammar schools should appear only as the next stage to which some of the children might go. If you are tracing the growth of state education, you would be largely concerned with elementary schooling: make a list of items of importance.

Types of school available to children of working men/artisans in 1830s
First government grants – 1830s
Training of teachers, and the types of subject taught
Payment by results
Disputes between Church of England and Nonconformist schools
Education Act 1870 and its problems
Enforcement of attendance (you will find there are different problems in town schools from country schools)
Providing free education at elementary level
Half-time system
Balfour's Education Act 1902 and the changes it introduced

To make your list you need first to read the section on education in a good social and economic history book. Then make the list that will be appropriate and helpful to you. Then show the list to your teacher and discuss your primary and secondary and oral sources. In this way you can organise your work well and save a lot of time – but try to use as many primary sources as you can, and if your teacher knows of an important incident about a local school, remember that local newspapers can prove very helpful if they have preserved their back copies. Again, photography has been available for well over a hundred years: you might well find some interesting old photographs that could set you examining a new line of thought.

Here is an exercise that might help you to decide how to tackle a project on education, and what line to argue.

War on Ignorance

The great mass of the people want education for their children; they are sick to death of the obstacles you throw in their way. I believe that when our extended franchise throws more
5 power into the hand of the multitude, you will see that what I say is true—that there's a feeling of national education which will sweep away all those cobwebs with which you attempt to blind the mass of the people . . .
10 I don't think it is safe for us as a nation to be the most ignorant Protestant people on the face of the earth. This is a period in the world's history when the very security, the trade and the progress of a nation depend not so much on the
15 contest of arms as on the rivalry in the science and the arts which must spring from education . . . I don't think we can wait. And this is why I am tired to death of the sectarian quarrel which is preventing people from being educated.
20 Why, it has been stated in our public records that the poor people don't send their children to school, upon an average, more than two or three years, and in some cases not more than ten months.

RICHARD COBDEN in a speech in 1851

(a) What education was available at the time this speech was made? How had its further development been hindered by 'the sectarian quarrel' (line 18) and by financial problems?
(5)
(b) Why did the poor fail to send their children to school (lines 21–23)? (2)
(c) Describe the development of a national system of education after 1870, showing how education was made compulsory and free, and how it was financed. (12)
(d) Explain 'our extended franchise' (line 4) (1)

O & C

Questions (a) and (c) are asking you to repeat what you have memorised for the examination: they do not require the passage and can be answered by a well-prepared list. Much, much more could have been made of (d) – what was at stake in extending the franchise and how this should affect the provision of schooling, for example. Question (b) asks you to go beyond the passage to explain the pressures on the poor – the need for money that drove parents to send their children out to work as soon as possible (do you see how this could be used to ask about the importance of compulsory attendance – does it suggest people are better paid, or that there are fewer jobs, for example?). Do you think the questions asked actually use the passage? Make sure that when you quote in your projects, you make good use of your material. There is no purpose in quoting, unless the quotation contributes to the point you want to make as forcibly as possible.

Town and country houses

In the period covered by this volume, Britain was well served by generations of outstanding architects and interior decorators. Tastes change, and what is popular at one time is often out of fashion a generation later. This was true throughout the hundred and fifty years or so covered by this volume. But, whatever their tastes, the British aristocracy and their friends throughout these years were prepared to spend lavishly on their houses and gardens, not necessarily to produce convenient and cosy dwellings, but to build in a way that later generations would respect. Their judgement, and the skill of their architects, is justified each year as large numbers visit both the major country houses and the smaller, less well-known places.

The architecture of the eighteenth century was very distinctive. The designs were formal, simple and strongly classical. As it was a prosperous age, vast sums were spent on parks, country houses and town houses and developments. Many of the latter were in the form of large terraces, sometimes covering considerable distances, or large and elegant squares – a feature of central London today. Several cities were partly built in the later eighteenth century – Edinburgh and Bath are good examples, the latter showing how great terraces can be made to appear even more impressive by sweeping round a steep hillside. The Bath terraces were built by the Woods, fashionable architects of high quality. They were following an example set by men such as Chambers and the Adam brothers, whose studies in Italy had given them a secure foundation for devising their own style of town architecture. Their interiors were carefully designed, with contrasting colours and highly ornate plaster work. Robert Adam (1728–92) employed a plasterer from Bristol, called Rose, whose work helped to make Adam's houses outstanding examples of Georgian taste.

Town houses

The town house was compact, often built as part of a terrace or square, with a garden behind, leading to a coach house and stables. A mews would often divide one terrace from another to enable the servants to get the coach and horses under cover – today the stables have often been converted into very expensive mews flats! The houses frequently had as many as three storeys, as well as a basement and cellars below that. The big houses might be of stone or of brick faced with plaster, and were generally set back from the pavement to allow an 'area' for access to the basement, and sometimes to storerooms actually beneath the pavement itself. Railings made the 'area' safe, and sometimes a winch allowed the raising and lowering of heavy provision baskets. The ironwork was usually of high-quality wrought iron, often with finely-worked designs. In front of the grander houses the iron railings extended into an archway to hold a lantern, with a 'snuffer' to extinguish the lantern wick. Above the main door there was usually a fanlight to give extra light to the hall.

A typical Adam interior—The Etruscan Room at Osterley Park

Bath, the Royal Crescent and other terraces

Houses of this period had sash windows. The ground floor and first floor of the big houses had very tall windows, for on these floors were reception rooms. The family would sleep on the second floor, and servants probably in the attics, well concealed from the street by a balustrade. Their rooms were small and crowded, but then they had little time to spend in them! Originally, even in the big windows, panes were small, for it was not until the 1830s that glass could be made in large enough sections to allow one pane per sash window. You can often see where Victorian single-paned windows have replaced the original six-paned ones.

The furniture in the best rooms was of high quality, perhaps actually made by Chippendale or Hepplewhite, though more probably by a local craftsman working from published designs (a new feature of the Georgian age). The kitchen was in the basement, and there the cook–housekeeper ruled. Occasionally a hand lift might be installed; otherwise the servants had to carry food, linen, cases, and coal (for the many fires) up countless stairs. Some architects, such as the Adam brothers, designed a whole house including the interior decoration and specific furniture to stand at exact points. Some of these houses have managed to keep most of their original furniture, and you can see how fine the whole design was if you visit them. Even where the furniture is certainly not original, it is rare to find an eighteenth-century design that looks out of place in a Georgian town house. This is a tribute to the designs of popular furniture-makers, and to the skill of local craftsmen, none of whom, remember, had machines, even for cutting delicate veneers!

Country houses

The country house was a very grand affair indeed. The great ones were the centre of large estates that may well have been 'improved' by landscape gardeners of the quality of 'Capability' Brown, or Repton – men who used to construct a hill, or remove a small rise, in order to give the house a better view, or add avenues of trees and plantations so that the house might suddenly be seen across the grass to best effect. Often, a 'ha-ha' (dry ditch) was constructed so that one could have an uninterrupted view of fields without the danger of livestock coming right up to the house. Eighteenth-century landscape gardeners in England achieved incredible results, as their parks still testify. Their skill was carried on in Victorian days, when more and more foreign plants and trees were introduced from all over the world, some to be grown in the popular conservatories and ornamental greenhouses, others to be left to mature as trees in the open. An excellent example of the genius of such men is provided by Cragside, Philip Webbs' great late-Victorian house in Northumberland. If you go there, you will see photographs of the house and grounds as they appeared when the house was finished a hundred years ago. They show bleak valley sides with tiny

Hepplewhite chairs, 1789

Cragside, one of Philip Webb's major buildings, in the 1880s

Philip Webb was one of a group of imaginative architects at the end of the nineteenth century who had considerable influence on later architects such as Lutyens, for example

trees, where now stand majestic trees filling the view. Those Victorian gardeners, like their predecessors were able to visualise the grand effect the tiny trees they were planting would have a hundred years later!

The Georgian country house was generally based on Palladian principles: a central block, grander but not so high as a town house, with two independent wings linked by a curved corridor. In very grand mansions there were four wings or pavilions, housing stables, kitchens, utility rooms and extra rooms for guests. The Palladian style came from Andeas Palladio in Italy and was introduced by Lord Burlington, whose villa at Chiswick is one of the best examples of a Palladian villa in Britain. It is a square block with a central hall, and pillars supporting a pediment at the main entrance. An imposing stairway adds to the height and dignity of the building. The style became very popular, and the Adam brothers did much to make it typical of the Georgian period. The principal rooms were magni-

ficently decorated with plaster work and pilasters, and the great hall might be surmounted by a dome. There would normally be an imposing staircase with outstandingly delicate ironwork, leading to the ornate bedrooms. (Servants would use concealed stairways for their many tasks, not the main stairs.)

Such houses were never built to the same plan. Each was unique, although using the same basic ideas. For this reason it is best to visit several great Georgian houses and so get the full impression of how the wealthy lived then. That there remain so many great Georgian houses of this type is indicative of the enormous wealth of the country in the eighteenth century. And they were not the only fine country houses, for the local squire and the prosperous farmer rebuilt their houses on similar lines, if on a much smaller scale. In the village, the doctor's house might be something of a compromise between a town and country house.

The Georgian style, with its accent on classical motifs and the 'orders of architecture' (the Circus at

Bath uses the three Greek ones on different storeys), was not the only style by the end of the century. During George III's reign the 'Gothick' style became increasingly popular. Horace Walpole was one of its principal advocates, and he went back to medieval designs to produce smaller, more intimate buildings with typical Gothic windows, impressive chimney stacks and gabled roofs – almost the opposite of Palladian ideas. Some of the 'Gothic revival' buildings were of gigantic scale – like cathedrals. (You might like to find out about the buildings of William Beckford, one of the richest men of the time.) Often the Gothic style produced some strange buildings – the Brighton Pavilion is a good example, where all sorts of styles are mixed. But in a pure form it produced some magnificent buildings, for example Eaton Hall. The Gothic buildings often used new types of building material, especially iron. For some thirty years the Georgian and the Gothic rivalled each other, but by the 1830s it was the Gothic that was in fashion.

The consequence of Gothic revival you can see in many Victorian churches and the villas of prosperous manufacturers and mill owners. The best exam-

Fonthill Abbey: 'gothick' style taken to extremes
The abbey cost a fortune to build in the 1780s and was recognised as a leading example of the 'gothick' style. The central tower lacked foundations and collapsed within 40 years.

Eaton Hall, Cheshire
Despite the 'gothick' exterior, much of the building is constructed with iron girder supports

ples are outstanding, but too often local architects lacked the skill to carry off the intricacies of the design (for these were very much more complex than Palladian designs). Cost was another factor, and a preference for red brick (and sometimes various colours of tile or slate for the roofs) too frequently gave an impression of cheapness and carelessness in design.

By the middle of the century there was a well-developed revolt against poor design, poor workmanship and poor planning. William Morris was one of the leaders of this revolt, calling for a return to a lost tradition of old English craftsmanship, and he sought to master as many different crafts as he could. His designs have influenced a long line of artists and are still popular today. Among his students and followers was a group of young men who became remarkable architects – Philip Webb, Norman Shaw and perhaps the greatest of English architects since Wren, Lutyens. These architects moved away from the Gothic and produced build-

ings of an individual style, but heavily influenced by traditional local designs. They did much to encourage the architects who were to produce the remarkable buildings of Edwardian Britain.

Gothic revival buildings in Victorian hands could achieve great success – Gilbert Scott's work has some fine examples, and St Pancras Station remains one of the more noteworthy achievements of a remarkable age. Another outstanding architect, capable of using Gothic with originality, was Alfred Waterhouse. It is worth visiting the Natural History Museum (1881) in South Kensington simply to note the intricate detail of the design of each part of the building, and how delicately Waterhouse used iron to give height and lightness to the structure.

But perhaps the most remarkably forward-looking of the late Victorian architects was Mackintosh. whose use of iron prefigured developments in the twentieth century. Try to see photographs of the Glasgow School of Art, for example. Mackintosh was also an influence upon the Art Nouveau

St Pancras Station

movement at the end of the century, a remarkable style that seemed to sweep aside most Victorian ideas and bring in the very different world of the twentieth century. Liberty's of London did much to popularise the movement. But the best way of studying artists and architects is not to list names and styles, but to choose two contrasted men and study their work in order to produce a project.

Mackintosh: design for chairs
Note the change of fashion and the simple, functional shapes compared with the illustration on page 215

Aubrey Beardsley produced many illustrations in dramatic black and white
Beardsley was a remarkable artist working in the 1890s. His drawings did much to popularise Art Nouveau and have influenced designers ever since. Try to find out about his life and work.

Art Nouveau: Textile design [over]
At the end of the century artists and designers were exploring new and exciting art forms and materials. There were many artists who drew their inspiration from the Pre-Raphaelites of the previous generation, or from William Morris, or from Japanese art which became very fashionable in the 1890s. Their designs were of a definite character and influenced artists all over the world, and became known as the Art Nouveau movement. Liberty & Co. of London specialised in these designs: you can still see them in the old building of the London store. British artists and designers earned a high reputation at this time. It is worth visiting the Victoria and Albert Museum, or asking in your local museum and art gallery, to see examples of Art Nouveau.

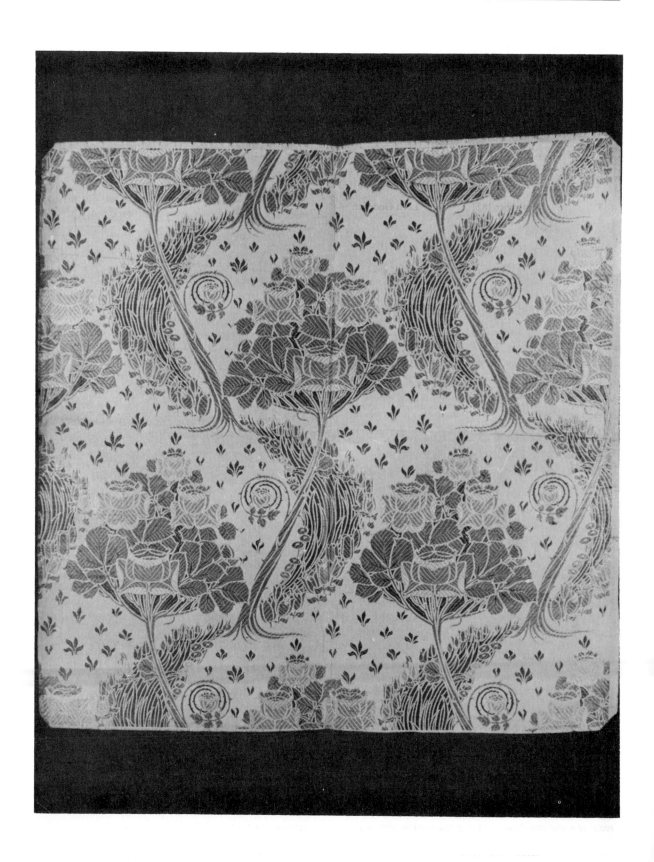

Appendix

Ministries, 1812–1914

Party	Date formed	Prime Minister	Chancellor of Exchequer	Foreign Secretary
T	June 1812	Lord Liverpool	(From January, 1823, F. J. Robinson)	Lord Castlereagh (From September 1822, George Canning)
T	April 1827	George Canning	George Canning	Lord Dudley
T	September 1827	Lord Goderich		
T	January 1828	Duke of Wellington		(From June 1828, Lord Aberdeen)
W	November 1830	Lord Grey	Lord Althorp	Lord Palmerston
W	July 1834	Lord Melbourne	Lord Althorp	Lord Palmerston
C	December 1834	Sir Robert Peel	Sir Robert Peel	Duke of Wellington
W	April 1835	Lord Melbourne		Lord Palmerston
C	September 1841	Sir Robert Peel		Lord Aberdeen
W	July 1846	Lord J. Russell		Lord Palmerston
C	February 1852	Lord Derby	B. Disraeli	Lord Malmesbury
Coalition	December 1852	Lord Aberdeen	W. E. Gladstone	Lord J. Russell
W	February 1855	Lord Palmerston	W. E. Gladstone	Lord Clarendon
C	February 1858	Lord Derby	B. Disraeli	Lord Malmesbury
W–L	June 1859	Lord Palmerston	W. E. Gladstone	Lord J. Russell
W–L	October 1865	Lord Russell	W. E. Gladstone	Lord Clarendon
C	June 1866	Lord Derby	B. Disraeli	Lord Stanley
C	February 1868	B. Disraeli		Lord Stanley
L	December 1868	W. E. Gladstone	R. Lowe	Lord Clarendon (From June 1870, Lord Granville)
C	February 1874	B. Disraeli (became Lord Beaconsfield, August 1876)		Lord Derby (From April 1878, Lord Salisbury)
L	April 1880	W. E. Gladstone	W. E. Gladstone	Lord Granville
C	June 1885	Lord Salisbury	Sir M. Hicks Beach	Lord Salisbury
L	February 1886	W. E. Gladstone	Sir W. V. Harcourt	Lord Rosebery
C	August 1886	Lord Salisbury	Lord Randolph Churchill (From January, 1887, G. J. Goschen)	Lord Salisbury
L	August 1892	W. E. Gladstone	Sir W. V. Harcourt	Lord Rosebery
L	March 1894	Lord Rosebery	Sir W. V. Harcourt	Lord Kimberley
C	June 1895	Lord Salisbury	Sir M. Hicks Beach	Lord Salisbury (From October 1900, Lord Landsdowne)
C	July 1902	A. J. Balfour	C. T. Ritchie (From May 1903, Austen Chamberlain)	Lord Lansdowne
L	December 1905	Sir H. Campbell-Bannerman	H. H. Asquith	Sir Edward Grey
L	April 1908	H. H. Asquith	D. Lloyd George	Sir Edward Grey

T = Tory; W = Whig; C = Conservative; L = Liberal

Fig. 29
   *The list shows a pattern of Whig/Tory, Liberal/
Conservative alternating during the century. This has
led historians to talk of the 'two party system'. But party
lines were not clearly fixed until the time of Gladstone and
Disraeli. Can you work out a list of leading ministers
between 1760 and 1812?*

Glossary

History is more than a portrait of an age: it is also a technical form of study. It uses technical terms in a particular sense, and makes use of a range of vocabulary that is not always commonly heard. Some of the words in this book are Hanoverian or Victorian and they give a sense of period. It helps to avoid *anachronism* and to achieve *empathy* if we get to know them. The following words are only a few of the historical and technical expressions used in the text. They are listed to help you understand better. For the other words, not listed here, you will need to ask your teacher, or use a dictionary, or (like a true historian) seek out your own references.

absentee landlords: landowners who did not live on their estates but left them in the charge of a bailiff or steward, and lived off the rents they received. Many English landlords in Ireland were absentee landlords.

agents-provocateurs: a French term for spies used by governments and others to trap opponents into committing serious offences, e.g. encouraging workers to plot the overthrow of a government by force and then to lead them into a prepared trap so that they are captured. The government had recourse to such methods in their efforts to destroy the movement for Reform during and after the French Revolution and the Napoleonic Wars.

capitalist: a system in which private property and wealth lies entirely in the hands of particular individuals who might do as they wished with it. This idea became the basis of nineteenth century attitudes and is one of the big dividing points between 'the West' and communist countries today.

Chartist: the name given to the working-class movement for Parliamentary Reform in the 1830s and 1840s

coalition: a group of leading politicians agreeing to act together in a common cause. Used also of the league of countries joined in fighting against France, for example.

collectivist state: the name given to the idea of using the powers of central and local government to provide a whole range of services for individuals and certain groups in society. It was an idea that gradually became popular and involved a turning away from the mid-Victorian idea of individualism. Eventually, the Welfare State of the mid-twentieth century was to develop out of collectivist ideas.

constitutional convention: a clear understanding as to what should happen in a particular case, although there is no actual statute (Act of Parliament) which lays down the rule. For example, the Lords, by a constitutional convention, did not amend money bills—though they could reject outright a budget until 1911.

counter-revolution: the name given to a political movement, the object of which is the destruction of a revolution. Used to describe royalist attempts to overthrow the French Revolution.

coup d'état: a French term for a forcible seizure of power to gain control of a country.

despotism: a king having absolute power without any constitutional check. The Stuart kings in the seventeenth century were accused of this.

Domestic System: the name given to the way skilled work was organised before the changes of the Industrial Revolution. Generally, goods were produced by skilled craftsmen in their own homes; only a few goods could be produced by each person and they tended to be expensive.

enclosure: the name given to the practice of changing the pattern of ownership of land so that strips from the open field might be consolidated together and enclosed to form individual fields.

factory system: the name given to the new methods of production that came as a result of the Industrial Revolution. Goods were produced by machinery powered by water or steam-power, in large buildings. This allowed for *mass production* (huge quantities of identical goods). Great wealth was made by the factory owners, but the workers often earned a very low wage and suffered bad working conditions. As a result, there were a number of Factory Acts passed to improve things.

franchise: the right and qualification to vote (as opposed to suffrage—the legal right to vote, hence *suffragette*, see page 177).

Free Trade: a system of trade between nations whereby as few barriers as possible were permitted (e.g. tariffs, or customs duties). If there were no artificial barriers to trade, then the trade of the world would increase, to everyone's benefit.

humanitarianism: the word used to describe the attitude of people who showed considerable concern for those in distress. Usually, they were bothered about the poor, especially in towns, and the conditions in which people and especially children lived and worked. They were also opposed to slavery because of the bad conditions the slaves had to suffer.

impeachment: a legal process by which an important person is charged with a serious crime by the House of Commons and tried by the House of Lords. After the Hastings impeachment, the practice soon fell out of use.

imperialism: the idea of an expanding empire, if possible greater than that of one's rivals. This became an important part of late nineteenth century politics and led, in part, to the First World War. Generally, Disraeli and the Conservatives were for Empire, whilst the Liberals were not; but it was not so simple a division—many prominent Liberals were also imperialists (like Asquith).

indemnity: the technical term for the payment of a fine imposed on a defeated country by the victors, presumably to pay towards the cost of the war.

individualism: a popular idea in the nineteenth century, namely that it was morally good for a person to work hard and achieve independence and maintain his family by his own efforts. If governments interfered and provided services for people who did not really need them, then, people believed, working-class people especially would become lazy and indolent, expecting the government to provide things for them. Both Liberals and Conservatives firmly believed in this idea, but as the century progressed people began to realise that many working-class families could not make ends meet however hard they tried, and the idea of individualism came to be modified.

Industrial Revolution: the name given to the great changes in the way industry worked, that were introduced during the eighteenth and nineteenth centuries. As a result society was completely altered, great towns developed and many people had to work in factories tending machines all day.

Jacobites: the followers of James Stuart and his son 'Bonnie Prince Charlie' who each claimed to be rightful king of England. There were two serious rebellions (1715 and 1745) but after these had been ruthlessly suppressed, there was no further serious trouble from the Jacobites.

journeyman: a skilled worker who had finished his basic apprenticeship and who continued to work for a master craftsman until he could save enough to start on his own as a craftsman.

laissez-faire: a French term meaning the removal of as many restrictions on the freedom of an individual as possible, so that the field of government action might be reduced to an absolute minimum. Very popular in the nineteenth century and closely linked with individualism and also the theory and practice of Free Trade.

Luddite movement: a movement of protest against bad conditions that usually took the form of breaking particular pieces of machinery. In 1811 there were widespread disturbances that caused the government a great deal of worry; the disturbances were carried out by skilled workers who made a closely guarded secret of their activities. The popular idea that they were resisting new methods of machinery is not quite true; they were resisting bad conditions, not new ideas.

Mercantile System: the system of controlling an important country's trade. Its colonies were only allowed to trade with the home country and could not compete with it. There were also many government regulations about conditions of trading, quality of goods and the employment of craftsmen and their trainees.

mercenary: a soldier who is paid to fight, having joined an army simply for the money.

militia: the part-time, non-regular force on which magistrates often had to rely, because there was no police force before 1829 and the army was too small to carry out duties of public control. The militia had a reputation for being unreliable.

municipal socialism: the idea that local authorities should provide those necessary services which individuals living in the area could not provide easily for themselves, even if they were rich. Such things as public health requirements, street-lighting and pavements were obvious, but there were also utilities like water, gas and local public transport, and such social services as better housing and local welfare schemes. Joseph Chamberlain was a great exponent of municipal socialism, as were the Fabians.

National Debt: the sum of money owed by the government to bankers and individuals who had loaned the money. Until the twentieth century it was the ambition of every Chancellor of the Exchequer to pay off the National Debt—none succeeded.

nationalism: during the nineteenth century, people became more and more conscious of their historical roots and of close links of language and race. There were many political movements to unite all those speaking a particular language or occupying a particular area into what they called a nation (although they were never very clear what they meant exactly by the word). These nationalist movements resulted in several major wars and many minor ones and they helped to create the new kingdom of Italy and the new German Empire. Nationalist disturbances were one of the causes of the First World War, and nationalism continues to be an active force today.

New Unionism: in the 1880s there was a movement to form trade unions among unskilled and semi-skilled men who had not generally joined trade unions formerly. These new unions were usually much bigger than the skilled workers' unions and they were much more inclined to strike and to play a part in national and local politics.

pacifists: people who are opposed to war. Some people are so opposed to war that they will refuse to take part in one when war is declared. Such people tend to be unpopular and suffer insults or even worse, despite the sincerity of their views. Many of them were imprisoned and harshly treated during the First World War.

patronage: the habit of wealthy lords providing for servants or supporters by granting them jobs or land. Important for controlling a great lord's supporters in the House of Commons.

progressive and regressive taxation: the name given to forms of taxation which have the effect of drawing money from different groups in the country. Progressive taxation tends to be paid by the better-off and so is to the advantage of the poor (it also has a tendency towards redistributing wealth). Regressive taxation is paid by all citizens, regardless of their own means; a tax on essential foodstuffs is a serious case of regressive taxation, for the poor suffer.

Protectionism: the policy of governments intervening to prevent competition from other countries, usually by imposing a very high tariff on goods that compete with those produced at home.

Radicals; Whigs; Tories: these were names used to describe people's political beliefs. The names go back to the political struggles of the seventeenth century, but by the end of the eighteenth century the names had lost their original meaning and came to be associated with general attitudes to reform. Radicals believed in very important and big measures of reform to change things fundamentally; Whigs were often in favour of one or two big reforms (like Parliamentary Reform), but

they were anxious that no change should affect the political power of the wealthy landed classes. Tories tended to support the king's government and to be in favour of moderate reform if there was a genuine need for it.

reversionary interest: the patronage which the heir to the throne has, on the understanding that he will become king and exercise full powers of royal patronage. In the eighteenth century, as the old king aged, politicians gathered round the Prince of Wales, hoping to become a Minister when he became king.

socialists: a word frequently used towards the end of the nineteenth century, but rarely clearly defined. Generally, it meant people who believed the government should actively intervene in the daily life of the community to provide acceptable conditions of work and living; the money to pay for this would come from the wealthy through heavy taxes. Some socialists had more extreme views, hoping to change the nature of society; their opponents tended to use the term as an insult.

syndicalism: the idea of using strike action for political ends. If trade unionists in vital industries were to get together and agree to strike on a certain day, then the whole country would be paralysed by what would be, in effect, a General Strike. The government would either have to offer immediate reforms or would fall. Syndicalism was a revolutionary idea, popular in France; it was certainly much discussed during the labour troubles between 1910 and 1914.

tithes: a form of *tax in kind* (produce) paid to the clergy. Tithes were much resented and one reason for enclosure was that it provided a simple method of *commuting* the tithes (converting the tax to a money payment).

toll: a payment for passing through a barrier, along a roadway or over a bridge. One of the ways in which the Turnpike Trusts paid for their road improvements.

transportation: a criminal was 'transported' to a penal colony to serve his sentence. To escape and return often meant hanging if you were caught, for transportation was frequently given instead of the death sentence. The system fell into disuse by the middle of the nineteenth century.

vested interest: the name given to the situation where a person, institution or government has an advantage in a particular situation. It is usually a selfish advantage; for example, an employer might well support a law that banned trade unions because this might prevent strikes which reduce his profits.

Index